BORDERLANDS

TABLE OF CONTENTS

Planet Pandora is a sparsely populated wasteland where the rule of law gets rewritten daily in the smoke of the last gun battle. Civilization consists of small outposts on the fringe of human influence, in an area called the Borderlands. Pandora's one tourist attraction is a mythical Vault packed with fantastic riches, supposedly stashed eons ago somewhere on the planet by an advanced alien culture.

ABOUT THIS GUIDE

In your hands is one of the biggest and best strategy guides we at BradyGames have ever created. Our team of authors, editors, and designers has worked tirelessly—and in direct cooperation with Gearbox Software—to pack this book with every possible gem of information you need to survive the journey to the Vault...

Welcome TO PANDORA

Think you can find the Vault? Maybe go it alone? If you're tough enough, you can keep all that loot for yourself… Or perhaps you should bring in a few allies to watch your back. Cooperation could be vastly profitable, and it's wise not to be the only item on the menu when a pack of starving skags breaks loose.

You are ready to risk it all. But whether you're a Soldier, Hunter, Siren, or Berserker, the real quest is freeing the formidable powers within yourself. Every firefight makes you stronger. Every successful mission pushes your deadly skills toward the next level. The conquest of the Vault is about to unfold, and with it… your story.

Missions: A massive, detailed walkthrough with step-by-step tactics and maps for all of the game's 120+ quests, featuring special coverage of the bosses and exclusive tips from the development team at Gearbox Software!

Vault Hunters: This chapter not only gives you some background on each of the four playable character classes, but also reveals their entire skill trees, class mods, and provides strategies for customizing your character for solo and team-based play.

Wasteland Wanderers: The bestiary portion of this book divulges all stats and tactics for understanding and destroying every critter, bandit, and guardian in Pandora— including individually calibrated Threat Level meters and Critical Hit Region diagrams.

Weapons: And then there's the section we lovingly call "The Arsenal." Not only do we break down the game's momentous weapon-generation system in painstaking detail not found anywhere else, but we've also put together an extensive Gun Catalog. This section features hundreds of exemplary custom-built tools of destruction—covering every weapon category from all nine gun manufacturers.

And the content doesn't end there. We've also prepared an exhaustive **Mission & Challenge Checklist**, a complete inventory of **Achievements & Trophies**, and a thorough primer on **Survival Basics**. This is the ultimate guide to a fantastic game. Bring it along for the journey.

Survival BASICS

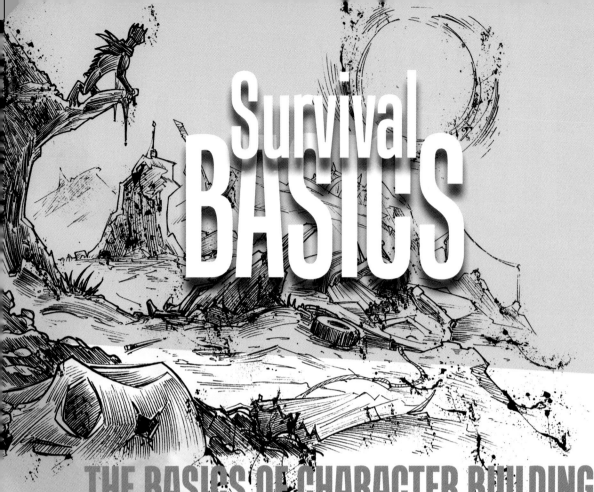

THE BASICS OF CHARACTER BUILDING
CHOOSING YOUR CHARACTERS

When you begin a new game of *Borderlands*, you can choose between one of four characters: Roland the Soldier, Moredecai the Hunter, Lilith the Siren, and Brick the Berserker. All four characters have the same stats and can use any weapon in the game, however, they differ in the following three ways:

HUNTER

Master of long range combat
PREFERRED WEAPONS:
Sniper Rifles and Revolvers
ACTION SKILL:
Bloodwing

Ⓐ SELECT THIS CHARACTER

KING OF CLAP

ACTION SKILLS: AT LEVEL FIVE, EACH CHARACTER WILL EARN THEIR FIRST SKILL POINT, WHICH CAN ONLY BE USED TO UNLOCK THEIR ACTION SKILL. AN ACTION SKILL IS A SPECIAL ABILITY THAT ONLY THAT CHARACTER CAN USE. IT IS ACTIVATED BY PRESSING ⚅ (XBOX 360) OR ⚅ (PS3). AFTER ITS USE, IT ENTERS A COOLDOWN STATE IN WHICH IT SLOWLY RECHARGES. LATER, YOU'LL ACQUIRE ARTIFACTS THAT CAN ADD ELEMENTAL PROPERTIES TO THE DAMAGE DEALT BY YOUR CHARACTER'S ACTION SKILL. ONCE SELECTED AND USED FROM THE INVENTORY MENU, YOU CAN EQUIP THESE ARTIFACTS IN THE SKILLS MENU.

SKILL TREES: AFTER LEVEL FIVE, CHARACTERS WILL EARN AN ADDITIONAL SKILL POINT EACH TIME THEY LEVEL UP. ONCE THEIR ACTION SKILL IS UNLOCKED, ADDITIONAL SKILL POINTS CAN BE SPENT TO PURCHASE SKILLS FROM THREE SKILL TREES. EACH SKILL TREE ENHANCES A CERTAIN STYLE OF PLAY EXCLUSIVE TO THAT CHARACTER. FOR EXAMPLE, SIRENS CAN PURSUE AN ASSASSIN SKILL TREE, WHICH IS DESIGNED FOR PLAYERS WHO ENJOY USING THE PHASEWALK ACTION SKILL TO CREATE DEADLY MELEE STRIKES. SOLDIERS CAN PURSUE A MEDIC SKILL TREE THAT IMBUES THEM WITH THE ABILITY TO HEAL ALLIES WITH GUNFIRE OR BEING WITHIN CLOSE PROXIMITY TO THEIR TURRET. SEE THE "VAULT HUNTERS" CHAPTER OF THIS BOOK FOR FULL COVERAGE OF EACH CHARACTER'S SKILLS.

CHARACTER-SPECIFIC CHESTS: EACH CHARACTER HAS A FAVORED WEAPON TYPE THAT WILL APPEAR MORE OFTEN DURING THEIR QUEST. WHEN A RED CHEST IS OPENED, IT WILL OCCASIONALLY CONTAIN CHARACTER-SPECIFIC CONTENTS THAT CONSIST OF A RANDOM GUN OF THE CHARACTER'S PREFERRED TYPE AND A CLASS MOD FOR THAT CHARACTER. THE LONE EXCEPTION HERE IS FOR BERSERKERS; THE OVERSIZED ROCKET LAUNCHERS IN THEIR CHARACTER-SPECIFIC CHESTS LEAVE NO ROOM FOR CLASS MODS. THERE ARE OTHER CHARACTER-SPECIFIC, RED-CHEST CONTENTS FOR THE CHARACTERS WHO YOU OR YOUR TEAMMATES USE MORE FREQUENTLY.

CHARACTER	FAVORED GUN
SOLDIER (ROLAND)	Combat Rifle
HUNTER (MORDECAI)	Sniper Rifle
SIREN (LILITH)	Submachine Gun
BERSERKER (BRICK)	Rocket Launcher

PURCHASING SKILLS

As noted previously, your character will earn one skill point after leveling up after level five. After unlocking the action skill, you can spend the remaining skill points on the 21 skills that are exclusively available to each character. By spending a second skill point on a skill that is already unlocked, you'll raise its level and the strength of its effect. Note that you can purchase up to five levels in each skill.

The skills are arranged into three skill trees, each of which is arranged into four rows. At first, you can only buy the two skills on the top row of each tree. After spending a total of five points in a skill tree, you can acquire the skills in the second row of that tree. Spend another five points (on any row of skills within the tree) and you'll unlock the third row. You must spend 15 skill points in a single skill tree before the ultimate skill at the bottom is unlocked.

The maximum level a character can reach is 50. So at most, it's possible to reach the ultimate skill of two different skill trees. Putting a few points into every skill provides a taste of each ability, allowing you to enjoy the effects of a wider variety of Class Mods. After selecting your favorites, though, it's wise to focus on getting all five points into your chosen skills. When combined with Class Mods, it's feasible to boost these skills above level five, potentially creating devastating combos!

RESPEC-ING YOUR CHARACTER

Your skill purchases are not set in stone. If you want to explore a different skill tree or re-build your character with online teamwork in mind, just visit the terminal of any New-U station and select "Reset Skill Points." For a nominal fee, this refunds all of your used skill points, so that you can reassign them.

There is no limit to the number of times you can purchase a respec.

EQUIPPING CLASS MODS

You receive your first Class Mod after completing the final plot mission in Fyrestone. Class Mods are specific to each character and offer a special stat boost (oftentimes for a single type of gun) and free levels in multiple skills. High-level Class Mods are among the game's most valuable items. These mods are found in red chests, the occasional pile of skag vomit, or purchased from medical vending machines.

It's not possible to fully utilize your Class Mods if you don't already know the skills they boost. For example, if a Class Mod offers a +2 bonus to the Siren's Quicksilver skill, but you haven't spent any skill points to acquire that skill, the bonus will not take effect. Note that there is no max level for skills; if you already have the Quicksilver skill at level 5 (the maximum you can buy), the Class Mod will raise it to level 7 and the +25% Fire Rate bonus offered by level 5 Quicksilver will increase to a +35% bonus.

EARNING WEAPON PROFICIENCIES

Regardless of the preferred weapons listed on the Character Select screen, any character can become proficient with any weapon simply by using it on a regular basis. There is a list of seven major gun types on the Character page of the menu screen (Revolvers and Repeaters are combined into a single "Handgun" type). Whenever an enemy is hit with a shot from a gun, a point is added to that gun type's weapon proficiency bar. A level in that weapon's proficiency is gained when the bar fills, providing a small bonus whenever a gun of that type is used (+3% to damage, +6% to reload speed, and so on). The effect is particularly noticeable on sniper rifles, as you can repeatedly earn "stability" bonuses to reduce the wavering of the gun's sights when lining up a shot.

KING
OF CLAP

UPGRADING YOUR STORAGE DECK

Everything your character carries goes into your Storage Deck, which is some sort of inter-dimensional pocket in space-time that, uh…well, who cares how it works? The point is, there's a limit to how much stuff your character can carry. Knowing that, you should upgrade the Storage Deck as soon—and as often—as possible.

☐ **AMMO UPGRADES:** THE MAXIMUM AMOUNT OF AMMUNITION AND GRENADES YOUR CHARACTER CAN CARRY APPEARS IN BLUE TEXT AT THE BOTTOM OF THE INVENTORY MENU UNDER THE ICON OF EACH AMMUNITION TYPE. TO UPGRADE MAXIMUM AMMO CAPACITY, YOU MUST PURCHASE A STORAGE DECK UPGRADE FOR EACH TYPE OF AMMUNITION.
THESE UPGRADES, WHICH ARE ONLY AVAILABLE FROM AMMO VENDING MACHINES, APPEAR IN MULTIPLE COLOR-CODED LEVELS. EACH ONE INCREASES YOUR CHARACTER'S CAPACITY OF THAT AMMO BY ROUGHLY 25%. YOU DON'T NEED TO OWN A LEVEL 2 UPGRADE TO PURCHASE A LEVEL 3 UPGRADE; YOU CAN SKIP DIRECTLY TO ANY LEVEL YOU WISH.

☐ **EQUIP-SLOT UPGRADES:** A CHARACTER BEGINS WITH TWO WEAPON EQUIP SLOTS. AFTER COMPLETING THE "RETURN TO ZED" PLOT MISSION, A THIRD SLOT IS UNLOCKED (IT IS QUICK-KEYED TO THE LEFT DIRECTION OF THE D-PAD). THE FINAL SLOT IS UNLOCKED UPON THE COMPLETION OF THE "ROAD WARRIORS: BANDIT APOCALYPSE" PLOT MISSION.

☐ **INVENTORY UPGRADES:** AT THE START OF THE GAME, YOUR CHARACTER HAS 12 GENERAL INVENTORY SLOTS THAT ARE USED TO HOLD EXTRA GUNS, SHIELDS, GRENADE MODS, MED KITS, AND SO ON. IT SOUNDS LIKE A LOT, BUT WITH ALL THE LOOT IN THIS GAME, THESE SLOTS WILL QUICKLY FILL UP.

TO PERMANENTLY INCREASE YOUR CHARACTER'S INVENTORY CAPACITY, SIMPLY COMPLETE THE "CLAPTRAP RESCUE" QUESTS. THERE ARE DAMAGED CLAPTRAPS IN 10 DIFFERENT GAME AREAS, USUALLY PLACES THAT ARE ONLY VISITED DURING OPTIONAL MISSIONS. ACCEPT THE QUEST BY SPEAKING TO THE CLAPTRAP, THEN FIND A REPAIR KIT AND RETURN IT TO THE CLAPTRAP TO COMPLETE THE MISSION. FOR COMPLETING THIS TASK, YOU RECEIVE AN "SDU UPGRADE" ITEM THAT ADDS THREE PERMANENT INVENTORY SLOTS! PLAYERS WHO SAVE ALL 10 CLAPTRAPS TO REACH THE MAXIMUM OF 42 INVENTORY SLOTS UNLOCK THE "FULLY LOADED" ACHIEVEMENT/TROPHY.

THE BASICS OF LIFE & DEATH

SHIELDS & HP

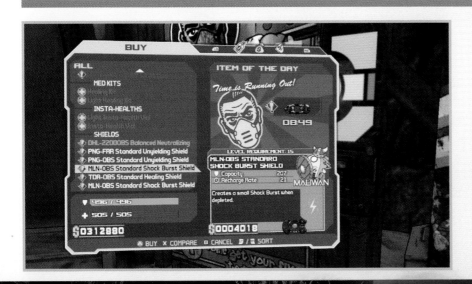

Your character's HP bar expands in size with each new level that is gained and it also grows by using certain shield properties and abilities. A character's HP is completely refilled whenever a level is gained. To restore lost HP, just purchase some red med kits from Dr. Zed's vending machine, or pick them up after defeating certain enemies.

You acquire your character's first energy shield, which has its own HP, early in the game. When your character absorbs damage, that damage is subtracted from your energy shield. Only after the HP from the energy shield is depleted will your character take actual damage. The shield has the ability to recharge and starts to do so roughly five seconds after the last time your character took damage, completely regenerating its own lost HP. Effectively, this allows you to take sporadic attacks without your character losing his own HP. When enemies surround your character or if he is under heavy fire, your foes can quickly punch through your character's shield.

Shields also take extra damage from elemental shock attacks, so it's possible to drain an enemy's entire shield with one shot from a shock-type weapon. When facing enemies with shock-type weapons, the same could easily happen to your character.

There are literally thousands of shields in the game, all differing in capacity (amount of HP), recharge rate, and special abilities. Some shields can slowly regenerate lost HP or offer protection against special types of damage (like corrosive, fire, or shock). Other shields have offensive abilities, like firing off their own explosive burst of corrosive damage when they're depleted.

CALL IT THE WINDMAKER

CONSIDER EQUIPPING ONE WEAPON SPECIFICALLY FOR DEALING WITH "FIGHT FOR YOUR LIFE" SITUATIONS. THIS MAY SEEM LIKE YOU'RE WASTING A WEAPON SLOT, BUT A HIGHLY ACCURATE REVOLVER WITH A FAST RELOAD CAN SAVE THE DAY WHEN THINGS GO SOUTH.

—ROB HEIRONIMUS, TECHNICAL DESIGNER

HEALING IN MULTIPLAYER GAMES

In co-op games, any player can save a fallen comrade while they're in a crippled state. To do so, simply approach the downed ally and hold the Use/Reload button to begin the revival process. It takes a short while to revive another character and during that time the character who is doing the reviving cannot take another action. The character who is being revived can continue to aim and shoot, so it is up to that person to protect the other player. When revived, a character receives a full shield recharge and 25% of his max HP.

CATCHING A SECOND WIND

Your character enters a "crippled" state when his HP hits zero, but he won't immediately die. While in this state, you can't move and the screen starts to slowly darken. On the plus side, your character retains the ability to aim and shoot, meaning it's possible to kill an enemy before your character bleeds out (represented by the red bar on the lower-left corner of the screen). When this occurs, your character catches a "second wind."

The second wind completely refills your character's shields and 25% of his life bar. If there are no enemies around, just press the Use/Reload button to say goodbye to this cruel world. After doing so, your character appears at the last New-U pole you triggered. Note, however, that the timer for achieving a second wind exponentially quickens each time a second wind is attained. Eventually, the timer will run out too quickly to get a second wind. After your character dies and re-spawns, the timer is reset to the original speed.

MEET THE NEW-U

When it all goes wrong and your character fails to achieve a second wind (or a restoration from your playing partner), your character rematerializes at the last New-U pole that was triggered. To fund this valuable service, the New-U Corporation helps themselves to 10% of your cash.

Whatever game progress you've made to that point is preserved, plus any items or XP that has been acquired since your last visit to the New-U pole remains. If the death occurs while fighting a boss, the boss will remain on the battlefield. In addition, the boss will likely have regenerated any lost HP that occurred during the fight.

THE BASICS OF MISSIONS & QUESTS

PLOT MISSIONS & SIDE QUESTS

While you're always free to wander around and explore the world of *Borderlands*, the only way to advance the story and unlock new areas and game mechanics is to complete missions. There are 126 different missions in the game. Of that total, roughly 47 revolve around the game's central story of the search for the legendary Vault. When each plot mission ends, the next plot mission begins.

The remaining 79 missions are optional side quests. Once offered, you can accept and pursue them at your leisure. Many of these missions take place in areas that you normally wouldn't visit during the course of the plot missions. The missions routinely have unique enemies and bosses and the rewards for completing them are oftentimes rare and powerful items. Pursuing side quests is also a great way to earn XP; only extremely skilled players can complete certain plot missions without first leveling up by pursuing side quests.

You receive missions by talking to other characters in the game, or by checking the bounty boards in many of Pandora's cities. Typically, new side quests become available after a plot mission is completed, but some side quests are arranged into quest trees in which completing one quest unlocks the next one. (These quests typically have a colon in their name. For example, completing "Altar Ego: Burning Heresy" unlocks "Altar Ego: The New Religion".)

There is no need to explore Pandora in search of new missions after completing a mission. Whenever there's a new quest available from a character or bounty board, a Claptrap radios in to provide the news. (There are a few exceptions, though, which are covered in the walkthrough.)

DON'T BE A HERO
FIGHTING A BOSS THAT IS A HIGHER LEVEL THAN YOUR CHARACTER CAN BE VERY DIFFICULT, BECAUSE YOUR BASE DAMAGE IS REDUCED. IF YOU EVER FEEL OVERMATCHED, IT'S TIME TO FINISH SOME SIDE QUESTS TO LEVEL UP UNTIL YOUR CHARACTER IS AT LEAST AT AN EQUAL LEVEL COMPARED TO THE BOSS.
—PAUL HELLQUIST, SENIOR GAME DESIGNER

CLAPTRAP DANCE OFF

PURSUING MULTIPLE MISSIONS

After accepting a mission, it goes into your Mission Log where it is ordered by the game area in which it takes place. Missions never expire and cannot be failed, plus there is no limit to the number of mission you can pursue at once. It's a good idea to accept every mission that is offered, regardless of whether or not you intend to pursue it.

In your Mission Log, you can set one mission as your active mission. This puts a waypoint on the map pointing to the next destination in that mission. However, you don't need to make a mission your active mission in order to pursue it. For example, in the "Relight the Beacons" side quest, the goal is to activate two beacons. If you set "Relight the Beacons" as your active mission, the waypoint points toward the first beacon. But if another mission is the active mission, you can still locate and activate both beacons without making "Relight the Beacons" your active mission. (All mission-related objects that you can interact with appear in a green color, whether or not they're related to the active mission.) If you haven't accepted the mission, you can't interact with the beacon at all.

THE WAYPOINT WILL BETRAY YOU
WAYPOINTS DON'T ALWAYS LEAD YOU DIRECTLY TO THE OBJECTIVE. SOMETIMES YOU NEED TO SEARCH AROUND IN THE VICINITY OF THE WAYPOINT TO FIND THE OBJECTIVE.

—MARK FORSYTH, 3D/FX ARTIST

MISSIONS IN MULTIPLAYER

After completing missions in multiplayer games, each player who accepted the mission, or could accept the mission, gets credit for completing it (unless, of course, they've already completed it). Players who are not at a point where they would be offered that mission are unable to earn the rewards for completion. That player can participate in the mission, finding and lighting all the beacons (mentioned in the previous example), but when the mission results are turned in that player will not receive any experience, money, or bonus prizes, nor will the mission be filed as "completed" in his Mission Log. In

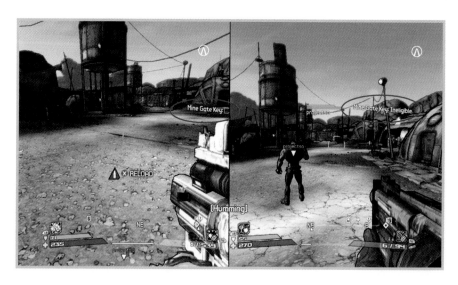

multiplayer games, more advanced players should allow less advanced players to host the game and help them complete their current plot missions until everyone is near the same point in the game.

In addition to the multitude of missions, *Borderlands* offers over 100 "challenges." To view them, press ⓨ (Xbox 360) or △ (PS3) on your Mission Log page.

Players are rewarded for achieving a certain number of something during challenges: slain skags, sold guns, acid-weapon kills, and so on. Most challenges have four tiers and rewards are given for completing each tier. For example, the "Punchy" challenge rewards a player for 50 melee kills, "Brawler" pays off at 250 melee kills, "Boxer" at 1,000 melee kills, and "Heavyweight Champion" at 2,500 melee kills. Highlight any challenge in your Mission Log to see how close you are to completing it. You receive XP for completing challenges, with greater rewards for the higher tiers of the challenge.

You don't need to do anything to pursue Challenges; just play the game and aim for a wide a variety of experiences—you'll complete Challenges without even trying. Many Challenges are also linked to Achievements (Xbox 360) and Trophies (PS3). For example, earning $1,000,000 in the game both completes the "The Rich Get Richer" Challenge and earns you the "Pandora-dog Millionaire" Achievement/Trophy. But while Achievements are linked to your account, challenges are linked to your characters. So if you create a new character, that character starts at zero for each challenges category.

CHALLENGE YOURSELF
PAY ATTENTION TO YOUR CHALLENGE LOG. THE EXPERIENCE YOU GET FROM COMPLETING CHALLENGES CAN MAKE A BIG DIFFERENCE, PARTICULARLY EARLY IN THE GAME.

—CHRIS BROCK, DEVELOPER

THE BASICS OF GETTING AROUND

GENERATING VEHICLES AT THE CATCH-A-RIDE

The world of Pandora is absolutely huge. It would take an extremely long time to walk from one end of the world to the other. Thankfully, Pandora is studded with Catch-A-Ride stations. These stations allow you to generate armed dune buggies, known as "Runners", and use them to quickly travel from one place to another. There are usually several Catch-A-Rides in each area, marked by steering-wheel icons on the auto-map.

Here's the small print: You can only generate Runners after unlocking the ability in the "Catch-A-Ride" quest. Runners are absolutely free, but you can only generate one Runner at a time. When a new one is generated, an older Runner will cease to exist. (In multiplayer games, only the player who generates the current runner can create a new one.)

In addition to generating Runners, the terminal at Catch-A-Rides allows players to warp directly to either the driver's seat or the turret of the current Runner. This is particularly helpful during multiplayer games, where a player who's been left behind can catch up by warping directly into his party's vehicle.

Runner Capabilities

The Main Turret: There are eight colors and two weapon systems to choose from when creating a Runner. The colors are purely cosmetic, but the weapons play a significant role. The rocket launcher has a slow rate of fire, but the rockets create large explosions on impact. The machine gun is less powerful, but has a quicker rate of fire.

In single-player games, pressing the Left Trigger causes the mounted weapon to fire toward the center of the screen. Alternatively, you can press the Ⓐ (Xbox 360) or ✕ (PS3) button to lock the turret into auto-targeting the nearest foe; simply press it again to jump to the next closest foe. You can also press Ⓨ (Xbox 360) or ⬢ (PS3) to jump into the turret seat and pull up a set of crosshairs for direct firing control. This allows you to use your Runner as a stationary turret.

Roles in Co-op Play: During multiplayer games, one player sits in the turret seat, while the other player drives the vehicle. Additional players can hold onto the side of the Runner and fire their currently held weapons as normal.

If players attempt to switch positions (by pressing Ⓨ (Xbox 360) or ▲ PS3), a request is given to the player who is currently in the desired position. That player can press the same button to agree to a switch, or simply ignore the request altogether.

Other Offensive Capabilities: The Runner also comes equipped with a front-mounted machine gun that the driver can fire by pressing the Right Trigger. This gun, which fires straight ahead, is not a particularly effective weapon. The preferred way of killing foes that

are straight ahead is simply to run them down; making contact with a foe while driving a Runner causes a ton of damage to that foe, but it also inflicts a small amount of damage (based on the target's HP) to the Runner.

Runner XP Penalties: Eliminating enemies while using a Runner, whether via the turrets or by running them over, results in less XP earned per kill. When you're trying to level up, it's best to do your fighting on foot instead of from behind the wheel of a Runner.

Defensive Capabilities: The Runner comes equipped with an energy shield that functions like your character's energy shield. The only difference is that the Runner has no HP of its own and will explode when its shield hits zero. If a character is inside a Runner when it explodes, your character's shield gets wiped out and he gets ejected with only 1 HP.

Needless to say, it's important to keep an eye on your Runner's shields and bail out (press the ✕ [Xbox 360] or ● [PS3]) button when it begins to run low. Enemies will not typically target an abandoned Runner, so fighting while outside of it usually gives its shields time to recharge. However, the damaged Runner can still be hit with stray bullets or grenades. If this occurs, it can explode with deadly force, so don't stand too close to a heavily damaged Runner.

Runner Advancement: All of the Runner's parameters, including its shield strength and weapon damage, are based on the level of the player who generated it.

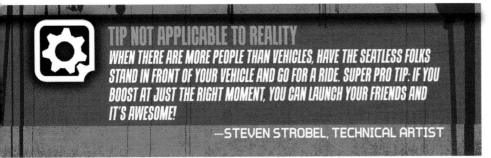

USING THE FAST TRAVEL NETWORK

In the game's second chapter, you repair the Fast-Travel Network and gain the ability to teleport from one area to another.

Fast Travel uses the network of New-U stations, allowing you to teleport to or from any New-U station that has a computer terminal. Some New-U stations only have the pole, which means it serves to save your game progress and acts as a re-spawn point, but it does not allow you to Fast Travel. In a single-player game, you can travel to any New-U stations that you have previously discovered. In a multi-player game, you can only travel to New-U stations that every player has previously visited.

THE BASICS OF LOOT

SCAVENGING FOR MONEY & AMMO

Your expedition to the Vault won't be cheap. You'll need an arsenal of guns, shields, and Grenade Mods, a tanker trunk full of ammunition and plenty of cold, hard cash. Fortunately, Pandora is a world awash in treasure. Well, that may be overstating things a bit. You won't find chests filled with gold dubloons or anything like that, but you can always swipe $20 out of someone's mailbox, dig a rusty gun out of a pile of skag dung, or find a grenade in a toilet bowl. It ain't glamorous, but it gets you by.

You can search any object that has a glowing green light on it or gassy green aura around it. The items contained within these glowing objects are randomly generated, although there are a few ground rules. Most everyday objects only contain money, ammunition, and possibly healing items, but never guns or shields. The exceptions to this rule are the following: dumpsters, which may contain low-quality equipment; skag droppings, a few may hold high-quality items; and the large, upright lockers that occasionally contain shields, Class Mods, and pistols.

THE SWEET, SWEET LOOT OF STORAGE BOXES

The best loot comes from storage boxes, of which there are three types. Gray chests always contain ammo, typically in large amounts. Long silver chests contain guns and other equipment. However, these items are typically a few levels below the level of the mission in which you would typically first encounter them. Red chests always hold ammo and new equipment, plus the items tend to be at or even above the level of the quests in which you'd first encounter them.

Each time you exit the game and reload it, storage boxes (like every other type of container) are refilled. This allows you to raid the same chests repeatedly and earn different randomly generated loot. However, the chests will always contain items of a level appropriate to that area, so high-level characters won't find anything interesting when they revisit chests in areas that are visited early in the game.

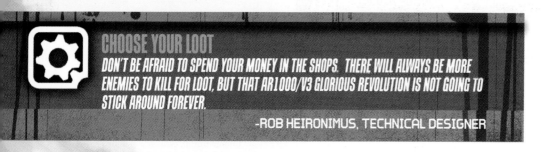
LOOT FROM ENEMY DROPS

When defeated, enemies also drop items, which may include guns and other equipment. Bosses drop a larger number of items, and typically higher quality ones. Many bosses even drop their own personal weapons, which have slight random differences in stats, but are typically strong.

In a single-player game, equipment dropped by standard enemies is almost always lower quality than the stuff found in red chests, but the more players there are in your game, the more the quality of enemy loot improves. The quantity of items dropped by enemies also increases, but only by about 25% per additional player. You'll all be fighting over a limited amount of equipment, but at least it will be pretty good stuff!

In addition to the usual cash, ammo, and med kits, some enemies have super-rare drops that include Elemental Artifacts, "Skag Pearls," and Marcus Bobbleheads—the latter two are treated as cash items and are usually worth twice the value of standard cash drops.

RANDOMIZATION OF ITEMS

Guns, shields, Grenade Mods, and Class Mods are created based on a basic template (a specific model from a specific manufacturer), and then customized with random parts and abilities. This is covered in greater detail in the Arsenal chapter of this guide, but basically, this means that any two guns with similar names could have different stats, abilities, and even external appearances. Even preset items, such as the weapons used by bosses or earned as missions rewards, may have slightly different stats for each player—the stats listed in the walkthrough are just a rough average, at best.

Equipment also comes in six different levels of rarity; the more rare the item, the higher the quality of its parts and the more enhancements it has. Rarer items are not necessarily better than common items; a super-rare gun with a level requirement of 10 could be inferior to a common gun with a level requirement of 16, for example. And since the added abilities of weapons are random, the combinations won't always make sense. A shotgun could have a higher rarity level and resale value because it has a high-quality scope—which is next to useless on a low-accuracy shotgun. Instead of relying on the resale value and rarity levels of weapons when trying to determine which is better, use the Compare feature in your inventory menu to check their stats line by line. When you look at a weapon on your field, the stats of your currently held weapon are displayed for comparison.

KING OF CLAP

RARITY BY COLOR

The color of an item's on-field glow and inventory text reveals its rarity. Rarer items are not necessarily better than common ones, but are composed of more and higher-quality components.

COLOR	EQUIPMENT QUALITY/ RARITY
White	Common
Green	Good
Blue	Very Good
Purple	Rare
Orange	Rarest

ERIDIAN WEAPONS

The rarest guns in *Borderlands* are Eridian Weapons, mysterious relics that can discharge energy in the form of lasers or heat-seeking bolts of lightning, or have other strange properties. Eridian Weapons don't require ammo, but can only be fired a few times in rapid succession before they must recharge, which can take several seconds.

Eridian Weapons are so uncommon that you could play through the entire game without ever seeing one. They are found very rarely in red chests, and sometimes as rare item drops from defeated high-level enemies. If you finish the game and begin a second playthrough from your old saved file, the odds of finding Eridian Weapons increase significantly during the subsequent playthrough.

Note that the color-coded rarity of Eridian Weapons reflects the weapon's quality in comparison to other Eridian Weapons; even a white- or green-colored Eridian Weapon is a treasure to cherish, so think carefully before you sell it or trade it away.

BUYING AND SELLING AT VENDING MACHINES

You can purchase a wide range of items from vending machines, although none of them is very good compared to the sorts of items you could find on the field. Vending machine guns tend to be at either white or green levels of rarity, and are typically at a lower level than most characters would be when they reach the area where they're sold. They're also very expensive; they sell for seven times the cost of their resale value, so a weapon from a chest with a listed value of $2,000 would cost $14,000 from a vending machine.

But vending machines do have several useful functions. Ammo vending machines sell ammunition, which is particularly essential in multiplayer games where there won't be enough of that stuff to go around. They also sell Storage Deck Upgrades that permanently increase the maximum amount of ammunition you can hold for each weapon.

Dr. Zed's medical vending machines sell shields (again, only at white or green rarities), med kits, and insta-healths—the closest you'll get to resting at an inn in Borderlands. Later in the game, his vending machines begin selling Class Mods, and his machines do stock high-rarity versions.

Even the gun vending machines can be useful when random drops just won't give you a decent sniper rifle, shotgun, or some other essential weapon. Vending machines also have a special "item of the day" that is only available for 15 minutes. These items are generally much higher quality than the machine's normal stock. Once the 15 minutes are up, the inventory resets and a new item of the day becomes available.

You can resell your extra loot at any vending machines. This is a great way to make money, and re-selling guns earns you XP from challenges and even an achievement/trophy. If you sell something you regret, the vending machines will sell it back to you for the exact same price you sold it for—but only during the same game session.

THE BASICS OF MULTIPLAYER

PLAYING WITH FRIENDS

While you can have a completely satisfying experience playing *Borderlands* solo, you can also share that experience with up to three friends. Check your game manual to see the particulars on setting up a multiplayer session in your version of the game. Players can use the same character in their multiplayer games that they do in single-player.

In a multiplayer game, one player acts as the host. That player sets up the game and can invite in the other players. The host's plot mission becomes the party's plot mission, and their world state becomes the party world state. For example, if the host hasn't unlocked the Catch-A-Ride stations, then no player can use Catch-A-Ride stations, even if they've unlocked them in their own games. Players get no credit for completing plot missions that they themselves are not far enough into the game to pursue, and cannot pursue their own plot missions if the game's host is further along than they are. As a general rule, the player who is the least far along in the game should act as host, and the advanced players should help them run through their plot missions until everyone is at roughly the same point. If a mission is completed in a multiplayer game, every player who is capable of accepting that mission gets credit for completing it.

WHAT CHANGES IN MULTIPLAYER

When you're playing a multiplayer game, several things change. Enemies become stronger and more numerous and you're more likely to encounter the powerful versions of each enemy; Badass Psychos instead of normal Psychos, for example. The rewards scale in a similar fashion. Enemies

HOW ENEMIES STATS SCALE IN MULTIPLAYER GAMES

1 player	Health 1.0x, Damage 0.9x
2 players	Health 1.5x, Damage 1.3x
3 players	Health 2.0x, Damage 1.5x
4 players	Health 2.5x, Damage 1.7x

drop larger amounts of loot, and its quality improves slightly with each additional player. In other words, the more players you have, the more likely you are to see high-rarity items.

SHARING THE WEALTH

In a multiplayer game, whenever any player kills an enemy, everyone gets XP for it, whether they contributed to the kill or not. The XP values are determined by each player's individual level, with low-lever players getting more XP than higher-level players. Again, they don't even need to contribute; you can quickly level up a character by joining a higher-level friend's game and having that friend go on a killing spree while you do nothing at all.

Money is also shared automatically; whenever anyone picks up a pile of cash, everyone in the party receives that amount of cash. However, everything else in the game is first-come, first-served. You'll have to work it out with your party how to share the guns, ammo, and healing items for party finds.

PLAYER VS. PLAYER COMBAT

If you have a dispute—perhaps over who gets a particularly desirable piece of loot—you can always settle it with a duel. In standard combat, players cannot hurt each other, but one player can request a one-on-one duel by melee attacking his partner—a virtual glove slap that does no damage. The duel will not be accepted unless the target responds with a melee strike at the attacker. Then it's game on; a barrier appears to lock in the dueling players until one of them takes his or her rival down. The fallen player automatically receives a second wind, and the duel ends. Players do not get healed at the end of duels, so they shouldn't be attempted lightly. But you'll need to try a duel at some point if you hope to win the "Duelinator" and "Duel-icious" trophies.

If you're looking for something a little meatier than an impromptu duel, an arena is the place for you. There are three arenas in all: Fyrestone Coliseum, The Cesspool, and the Devil's Footstool. If you enter these areas with a party of two or more, you can to approach what looks like a bounty board and arrange your party into color-coded teams of any combination of players. Select the bottom option to start the game, and everyone warps into an arena that has been specially designed for player-vs.-player combat. Players respawn until one team scores three wins, and then everyone is returned to the entrance, with all the health and ammo they had when they started the arena match. The only prizes for victory are bragging rights and the "Can't We Get BEYOND Thunderdome?" achievement/trophy.

COOPERATIVE STRATEGIES

While you'll be playing the same basic game in co-op that you play solo, you quickly learn to play it far differently. There are many effective tactics that can only be used in co-op play, and since the walkthrough in this guide focuses primarily on solo play, we'll outline a few co-op tactics here:

RESPEC YOURSELF: EVERY CHARACTER CLASS HAS ABILITIES THAT CAN BUFF OR HEAL THEIR TEAMMATES, EXCEPT FOR BERSERKERS (AND EVEN THEY CAN CONTRIBUTE TO THEIR TEAM BY FOCUSING ON THE TANK SKILL TREE AND DISTRACTING THE PARTY'S FOES WITH RELENTLESS FRONTAL ASSAULTS). SINCE PLAYERS ARE FREE TO PURCHASE A RESPEC AT ANY NEW-U STATION, YOU CAN AND SHOULD SWITCH TO MORE MULTIPLAYER-FOCUSED SKILLS BEFORE A LONG GAMING SESSION WITH FRIENDS. DON'T FORGET TO ADJUST YOUR CLASS MODS FOR MULTIPLAYER, AS WELL.

SNIPE AND PROTECT: THIS ONE'S A LITTLE OBVIOUS, BUT IT'S A GREAT STRATEGY WHEN GOING UP AGAINST ANY BANDIT COMPOUND. MOST BANDIT TEAMS ARE COMPOSED OF BANDIT SOLDIERS THAT HANG BACK AND SHOOT FROM AFAR, MIXED WITH PSYCHOS THAT RUSH IN TO MELEE RANGE. THE BEST COUNTER-TACTIC IS TO POSITION YOURSELF BEHIND COVER AT A DISTANCE THAT'S TOO FAR AWAY FOR THE BANDITS' SMG AND COMBAT RIFLE FIRE TO BE FULLY ACCURATE, AND HAVE YOUR MOST EFFECTIVE SNIPER PICK OFF THE SHOOTERS. MEANWHILE, EVERYONE ELSE CAN GRAB A SHOTGUN AND PROTECT THE SNIPER BY GREETING ONRUSHING PSYCHOS WITH A FLURRY OF SHOTGUN HEADSHOTS.

FIGHTING AT DEATH'S DOORSTEP: WHEN FIGHTING IN TIGHT PLACES, YOU CAN RUTHLESSLY EXPLOIT *BORDERLANDS'* GENEROUS SECOND WIND AND RECOVERY SYSTEMS. HAVE ONE CHARACTER CROUCH BEHIND COVER WHILE ANOTHER CHARACTER STANDS NEXT TO HIM, OUT IN THE OPEN AND FIRING UPON FOES. WHEN THE CHARACTER IN THE OPEN FALLS, THE CHARACTER BEHIND COVER CAN CONTINUOUSLY REVIVE HIM. SINCE THE FALLEN CHARACTER IS STILL ABLE TO FIRE AS HE'S BEING REVIVED, YOU CAN MAINTAIN YOUR SAME RUTHLESS OFFENSE, AND THE ENEMIES WILL IGNORE THE HEALER AND CONTINUE TO FRUITLESSLY TARGET THE ALREADY FALLEN SOLDIER. THIS FEELS SO WRONG, BUT... STRATEGICALLY, IT'S OH-SO RIGHT.

BAIT AND RUNNER GUNNER: WHEN OBSTACLES PREVENT YOU FROM DRIVING YOUR RUNNER INTO AN ENEMY COMPOUND, PARK IT AT THE DOOR AND HAVE ONE CHARACTER STAY IN THE TURRET, WHILE THE OTHER GOES IN ALONE. THE INFILTRATING CHARACTER WILL CATCH THE ATTENTION OF YOUR ENEMIES AND THEN FLEE BACK TO THE RUNNER OR ANY OTHER COVER, WHERE THE PURSUING FOES ARE CHOPPED TO PIECES BY THE RUNNER TURRET. (IF THE BAIT FLEES BACK TO THE RUNNER'S DRIVER SEAT FOR SAFETY, HE OR SHE CAN PUT THE FRONT-MOUNTED GUN TO GOOD USE, TOO.) BERSERKERS WITH SPECIALIZED IN TANK SKILLS NATURALLY MAKE THE BEST BAIT.

AND MOST IMPORTANTLY. . .
PLAYING BORDERLANDS WITH A GUITAR CONTROLLER IS INEFFECTIVE.
—CHRIS BROCK, DEVELOPER

ROLAND as "The Soldier"

■ MILITARY TRAINED KILLER

■ PREFERS COMBAT RIFLES AND SHOTGUNS

Atlas records state that Roland was honorably discharged from the Crimson Lance. Unfortunately, Crimson Lance doctrine states that the only type of discharge is dishonorable, which generally involves a bullet through the skull. When questioned about either his involvement in or departure from the Crimson Lance, Roland quickly changes the subject to loot, of which he firmly believes there is always room for more.

ROLAND'S CLASS MODS

CLASS	BENEFITS	FOCUS	MANUFACTURERS
Commando	Personal	Shotguns	S&S MUNITIONS JAKOBS
Heavy Gunner	Personal	Magazine Size	DAHL TORGUE
Rifleman	Personal	Combat Rifles	VLADOF TORGUE
Shock Trooper	Personal	Shock Damage	MALIWAN ANSHIN
Leader	Team	Experience	DAHL JAKOBS
Support Gunner	Team	Ammo Regeneration	VLADOF S&S MUNITIONS
Tactician	Team	Shield Regen	MALIWAN ANSHIN

ACTION SKILL

SCORPIO TURRET

COOLDOWN:
100 seconds

The Scorpio Turret was designed by Atlas Manufacturers SE. Originally, it was developed as a turret that would be deployed to cover Hyperion elite soldiers as they escaped from hot combat zones. Once it was discovered that the majority of Scorpios were being used offensively instead of as escape tools, the designers then added protective shields and increased the bullet caliber.

KING OF CLAP

"IT'S LIKE HAVING ANOTHER SOLDIER ON THE FIELD! ROLAND

CLAPTRAP DANCE OFF

VAULT HUNTERS: ROLAND

Whenever the rigors of roaming the wastelands of Pandora have Roland feeling down and lonely, all he needs to do is deploy his Scorpio Turret to perk right up. This specialty machinegun turret stays active for 20 seconds and automatically targets nearby enemies, effectively serving as a temporary partner. The Scorpio Turret comes equipped with a pair of energy shields that provide cover for Roland, so long as he crouches down behind them. The Scorpio Turret is a magnet for enemies, particularly Skags and other lower lifeforms— use it to distract enemies and quickly flank them for a clear shot at their blindside! Though the Scorpio Turret is of limited use against Rakk or other enemy types in elevated positions, and can be out-maneuvered in open spaces, the Scorpio Turret is positively lethal in tight corridors. Use it to clog up choke-points and doorways, then fall back and watch the bodies pile up.

CUSTOMIZATION STRATEGIES

SOLO PLAY

Roland is the ideal character to select for first-time players and for those who prefer medium-range combat, given the option to upgrade his shotgun and combat rifle capabilities through Infantry skills. He's also a great choice for those looking to develop a character for long-term solo play thanks to his deployable Scorpio Turret, which effectively serves as a partner on the battlefield. Roland's three skill branches are Infantry, Support, and Medic. And though he won't have much need for several of the Support and Medic skills in solo play, there are benefits to be had from all three categories.

When beginning play as Roland, it's a good idea to focus early upgrades on Impact, Defense, and Fitness until better shields and higher levels of HP are attained. Focus mid-level upgrades on Impact and Sentry in the Infantry branch, while targeting Defense and the Quick Charge skill in the Support branch. Continue to allocate Skill Points to the Infantry branch to unlock the Refire skill and, eventually, the Guided Missile skill. When playing alone, it's important to maximize the effectiveness of the Scorpio Turret; reducing its cooldown and increasing its firepower are the keys to achieving this goal. Similarly, additional Skill Points should be used to upgrade the Barrage and Deploy skills in the Support branch. As far as the Medic branch of Roland's skill tree is concerned, we recommend maximizing the Fitness ability and allocating one or two Skill Points to Aid Station and Overload, but the bulk of your Skill Points should be spent in the other categories before using them to unlock the valuable Grit skill.

TEAM PLAY

Roland can be re-spec'd a number of ways for co-op, depending on your personal style of play, as well as the number and skill of the people you're playing with. Although there may be times when an aggressive Infantry build-up is helpful (especially if you're a newer player being escorted through early missions by higher-level player), most of the time you'll want to expand on Roland's Medic and Support skills. Boosting Roland's these areas is a sure-fire way to increase your chances of being welcomed into other people's parties.

AN OPEN INVITATION TO JOIN
A SOLDIER WITH MEDIC SKILLS (SUCH AS "CAUTERIZE" OR "STAT")
IS ALWAYS A WELCOME ADDITION TO ANY PARTY.

— JONATHAN HEMINGWAY, GAME DESIGNER

Allocate several points to Impact and Sentry just to give yourself a little extra firepower, then turn your attention to the Support branch. Maximize the Defense, Stockpile, and Barrage skills to unlock the Supply Drop skill—the additional ammo is vital during intense firefights with a full team. Next, turn your attention to the Medic branch. Max out the Aid Station skill to heal all nearby players when the Scorpio Turret is active, then divide remaining points between Fitness and Cauterize to unlock the Revive skill.

MEDIC!!!

Looking to become the best battlefield medic you can be? You won't be able to inflict much damage, but you'll have no trouble keeping your party alive. Set your Skill Points in the following manner: Fitness = 5, Aid Station = 5, Cauterize = 5, Revive = 5, and Stat = 5. Use the remaining points to upgrade Support and Infantry skills as available to decrease the cooldown time for the Scorpio Turret. The more frequently you can deploy the Scorpio Turret, the better your team's odds of survival will be.

JUST LIKE TWINKIES AND COCKROACHES
A TEAM OF FOUR ROLANDS IN THE MEDIC TREE WOULD PROBABLY
SURVIVE THE APOCALYPSE.

— STEVEN STROBEL, TECHNICAL ARTIST

CLAPTRAP
DANCE OFF

SKILLS

INFANTRY SKILLS

IMPACT

Increases Bullet Damage with all weapon types.

LEVEL 1	LEVEL 2	LEVEL 3
+3% Bullet Damage	+6% Bullet Damage	+9% Bullet Damage

LEVEL 4	LEVEL 5	
+12% Bullet Damage	+15% Bullet Damage	

SENTRY

Increases Scorpio Turret damage.

LEVEL 1	LEVEL 2	LEVEL 3
+7% Scorpio Turret Damage	+14% Scorpio Turret Damage	+21% Scorpio Turret Damage

LEVEL 4	LEVEL 5	
+28% Scorpio Turret Damage	+35% Scorpio Turret Damage	

SCATTERSHOT

Increases shotgun damage and spread.

LEVEL 1	LEVEL 2	LEVEL 3
+3% Shotgun Damage +5% Shotgun Spread	+6% Shotgun Damage +10% Shotgun Spread	+9% Shotgun Damage +15% Shotgun Spread

LEVEL 4	LEVEL 5	
+12% Shotgun Damage +20% Shotgun Spread	+15% Shotgun Damage +25% Shotgun Spread	

METAL STORM

Killing an enemy increases your Fire Rate for a few seconds.

LEVEL 1	LEVEL 2	LEVEL 3
+6% Weapon Fire Rate +15% Recoil Reduction	+12% Weapon Fire Rate +30% Recoil Reduction	+18% Weapon Fire Rate +45% Recoil Reduction

LEVEL 4	LEVEL 5	
+24% Weapon Fire Rate +60% Recoil Reduction	+30% Weapon Fire Rate +75% Recoil Reduction	

REFIRE

Shooting an enemy reduces the cooldown of your Scorpio Turret. This effect can only occur every 2 seconds.

LEVEL 1	LEVEL 2	LEVEL 3
Cooldown reduction per hit: 1 (in seconds)	Cooldown reduction per hit: 2 (in seconds)	Cooldown reduction per hit: 3 (in seconds)

LEVEL 4	LEVEL 5	
Cooldown reduction per hit: 4 (in seconds)	Cooldown reduction per hit: 5 (in seconds)	

ASSAULT

Increases Magazine Size and reduces Recoil with Combat Rifles.

LEVEL 1	LEVEL 2	LEVEL 3
+9% Magazine Size and Recoil Reduction	+18% Magazine Size and Recoil Reduction	+27% Magazine Size and Recoil Reduction

LEVEL 4	LEVEL 5	
+36% Magazine Size and Recoil Reduction	+45% Magazine Size and Recoil Reduction	

GUIDED MISSILE

Your Scorpio Turret launches guided missiles in addition to using its regular gun.

LEVEL 1	LEVEL 2	LEVEL 3	LEVEL 4	LEVEL 5
Fire a missile every 8 seconds.	Fire a missile every 7 seconds.	Fire a missile every 6 seconds.	Fire a missile every 5 seconds.	Fire a missile every 4 seconds.

SUPPORT SKILLS

MEDIC SKILLS

DEFENSE

Increases how quickly your shields recharge.

LEVEL 1	LEVEL 2	LEVEL 3
+4% Shield Recharge Speed	+8% Shield Recharge Speed	+12% Shield Recharge Speed

LEVEL 4	LEVEL 5
+16% Shield Recharge Speed	+20% Shield Recharge Speed

STOCKPILE

Players near the Scorpio Turret regenerate ammo for the weapon that is currently in their hands.

LEVEL 1	LEVEL 2	LEVEL 3
+1 Ammo Regeneration Rate	+2 Ammo Regeneration Rate	+3 Ammo Regeneration Rate

LEVEL 4	LEVEL 5
+4 Ammo Regeneration Rate	+5 Ammo Regeneration Rate

QUICK CHARGE

Killing an enemy causes your shields to quickly regenerate for a few seconds.

LEVEL 1	LEVEL 2	LEVEL 3
+2% Shields per seconds	+3% Shields per seconds	+4% Shields per seconds

LEVEL 4	LEVEL 5
+6% Shields per seconds	+7% Shields per seconds

BARRAGE

Increases the number of shots your Scorpio Turret fires in each burst.

LEVEL 1	LEVEL 2	LEVEL 3
+1 Shots fired per burst	+2 Shots fired per burst	+3 Shots fired per burst

LEVEL 4	LEVEL 5
+4 Shots fired per burst	+5 Shots fired per burst

GRENADIER

Killing an enemy increases your grenade damage and causes you to regenerate grenades for a few seconds.

LEVEL 1	LEVEL 2	LEVEL 3
+2 Grenades per minute +3% Grenade Damage	+3 Grenades per minute +6% Grenade Damage	+5 Grenades per minute +9% Grenade Damage

LEVEL 4	LEVEL 5
+6 Grenades per minute +12% Grenade Damage	+8 Grenades per minute +15% Grenade Damage

DEPLOY

Reduces cooldown for your Scorpio Turret.

LEVEL 1	LEVEL 2	LEVEL 3
Cooldown reduction +20%	Cooldown reduction +40%	Cooldown reduction +60%

LEVEL 4	LEVEL 5
Cooldown reduction +80%	Cooldown reduction +100%

SUPPLY DROP

The Scorpio Turret periodically fires out supply pickups to resupply players.

LEVEL 1	LEVEL 2	LEVEL 3	LEVEL 4	LEVEL 5
Supply drop every 7 seconds	Supply drop every 6 seconds	Supply drop every 5 seconds	Supply drop every 4 seconds	Supply drop every 3 seconds

FITNESS

Increases your Maximum Health.

LEVEL 1	LEVEL 2	LEVEL 3
+5% Maximum Health	+10% Maximum Health	+15% Maximum Health

LEVEL 4	LEVEL 5
+20% Maximum Health	+25% Maximum Health

AID STATION

Allies near the Scorpio Turret regenerate health.

LEVEL 1	LEVEL 2	LEVEL 3
Regenerates +1% health per second	Regenerates +2% health per second	Regenerates +3% health per second

LEVEL 4	LEVEL 5
Regenerates +4% health per second	Regenerates +5% health per second

OVERLOAD

Increases magazine capacity with all weapon types.

LEVEL 1	LEVEL 2	LEVEL 3
+12% Magazine size	+24% Magazine size	+36% Magazine size

LEVEL 4	LEVEL 5
+48% Magazine size	+60% Magazine size

CAUTERIZE

Shooting team members heals them. This effect also works with grenades and rockets.

LEVEL 1	LEVEL 2	LEVEL 3
Converts +6% damage to health	Converts +12% damage to health	Converts +18% damage to health

LEVEL 4	LEVEL 5
Converts +24% damage to health	Converts +30% damage to health

REVIVE

The Scorpio Turret has a chance to instantly revive nearby crippled friends when deployed.

LEVEL 1	LEVEL 2	LEVEL 3
+14% Revival Chance	+28% Revival Chance	+42% Revival Chance

LEVEL 4	LEVEL 5
+56% Revival Chance	+70% Revival Chance

GRIT

Increases your resistance to Bullet Damage.

LEVEL 1	LEVEL 2	LEVEL 3
+3% Bullet Resistance	+6% Bullet Resistance	+9% Bullet Resistance

LEVEL 4	LEVEL 5
+12% Bullet Resistance	+15% Bullet Resistance

STAT

Killing an enemy increases health regeneration for you and nearby friends for a few seconds.

LEVEL 1	LEVEL 2	LEVEL 3	LEVEL 4	LEVEL 5
Regenerates +1% health per second	Regenerates +2% health per second	Regenerates +3% health per second	Regenerates +4% health per second	Regenerates +5% health per second

CLAPTRAP DANCE OFF

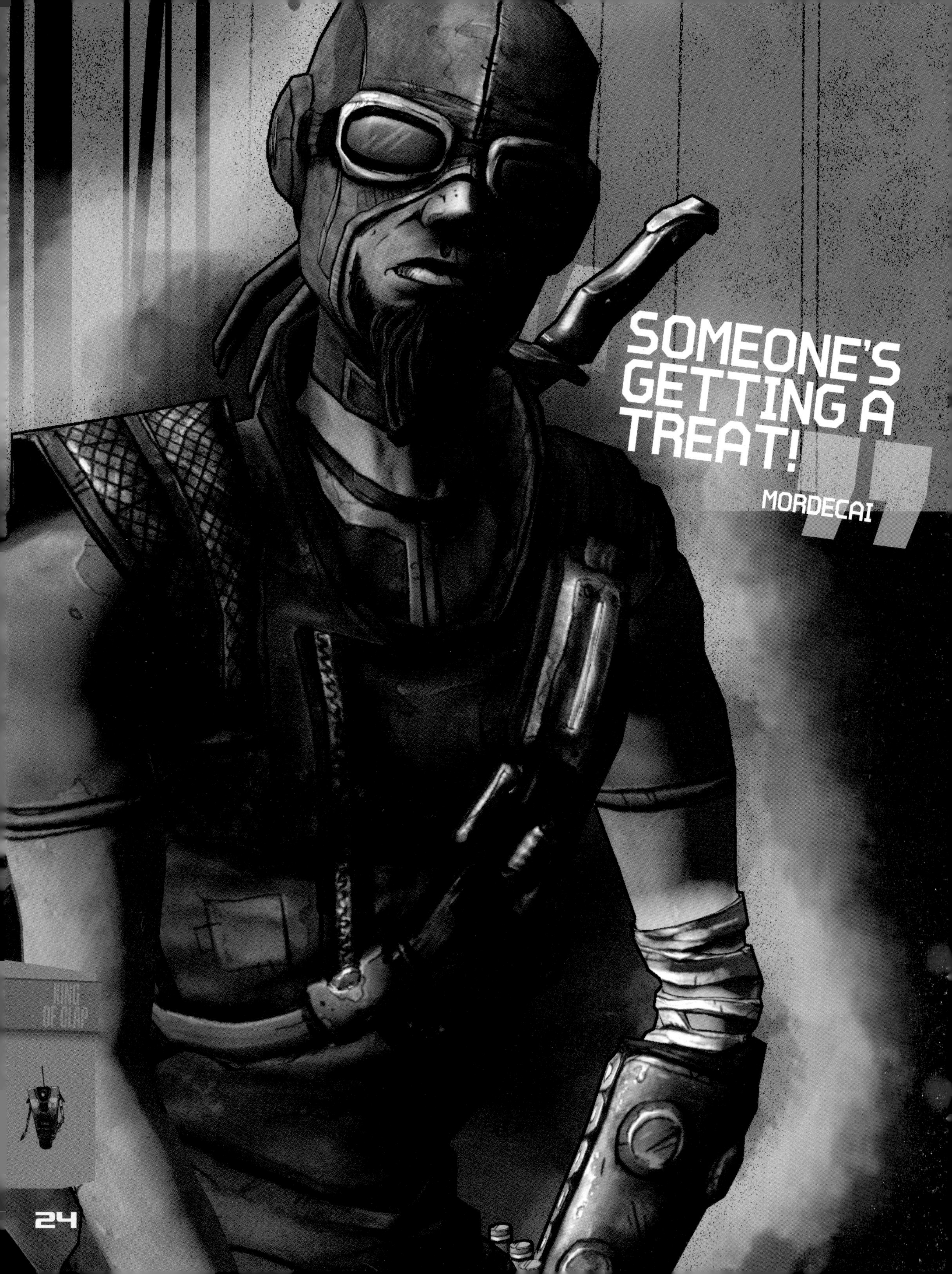

"SOMEONE'S GETTING A TREAT!"

MORDECAI

MORDECAI as "The Hunter"

▌ MASTER OF LONG RANGE COMBAT
▌ PREFERS SNIPER RIFLES AND REVOLVERS

At the age of 17, Mordecai won an Interplanetary Sharpshooting competition with a pistol. The other competitors, who were using Sniper Rifles, accused him of cheating and eventually got him banned from the competition for "unsportsmanlike conduct," although many witnesses noted that he didn't display any unsportsmanlike behaviors until after the accusations began. He now travels from planet to planet searching for "everything this freaking universe owes me," which Mordecai has defined as a better gun and unlimited dollars.

MORDECAI'S CLASS MODS

CLASS	BENEFITS	FOCUS	MANUFACTURERS
Assassin	Personal	Corrosive Damage	MALIWAN HYPERION
Gunslinger	Personal	Pistols	VLADOF S&S MUNITIONS
Hunter	Personal	Bloodwing	VLADOF JAKOBS
Sniper	Personal	Sniper Rifles	JAKOBS HYPERION
Ranger	Team	Accuracy	TEDIORE S&S MUNITIONS
Scavenger	Team	Item Find	TEDIORE PANGOLIN
Survivor	Team	Health Regen	MALIWAN PANGOLIN

ACTION SKILL

BLOODWING

Bloodwings are highly sought after as exotic pets by animal trainers. Unfortunately, very few ever take a liking to humans and end up killing them, making the number of trained Bloodwings extremely rare.

CLAPTRAP DANCE OFF

The life of a Hunter can be a lonely one, but that's not the case for Mordecai. He turned to the age-old tradition of falconry for companionship and dedicated years to training the most lethal Bloodwing that's ever flapped its wings across Pandora. On Mordecai's command, his pet Bloodwing vaults from its perch on Mordecai's arm and targets the nearest enemy. It uses the strength of its beak and the ripping power of its talons to inflict significant, if not fatal, damage to its prey.

Mordecai can increase the number of enemies Bloodwing targets during each flight via the Bird of Prey skill, but under normal conditions the Bloodwing returns to him after one assault. If no enemies are present, the Bloodwing will fly around Mordecai's vicinity for 18 seconds in search of a target before returning to its perch.

The Bloodwing's rapid cooldown makes it a versatile action skill. Use it to eliminate nearby low-level enemies while Mordecai hangs back and snipes distant foes. Adding an Elemental Artifact engulfs the Bloodwing in an elemental aura that can prove even more useful under the right circumstances.

CUSTOMIZATION STRATEGIES

SOLO PLAY

Mordecai is the perfect character for those seeking to embrace the life of a loner, as well as those who enjoy using firearms but prefer precision marksmanship over the spray-and-pray approach. Although Mordecai lacks Roland's valuable Medic abilities and his action skill is not immediately as potent against a wave of enemies as the Scorpio Turret, experienced crack-shots can certainly wreak havoc—and collect a wealth of loot—when playing as Mordecai.

MASTER OF ALL
MORDECAI'S FOCUS SKILL IMPROVES YOUR ACCURACY WITH ALL WEAPON TYPES, MAKING IT INVALUABLE NO MATTER WHAT TYPE OF GUN YOU PREFER TO USE.

- JONATHAN HEMINGWAY, GAME DESIGNER

Mordecai's skills fall into three branches: Sniper, Rogue, and Gunslinger. There are skills in all three branches that any solo player should learn. Since a player wouldn't choose Mordecai if he wasn't fond of sniping, it's recommended that you place your early Skill Points in the Caliber and Deadly skills. Many shots will no doubt be Critical Hits and Deadly will amplify the damage they inflict.

Upgrade Swift Strike to begin boosting the abilities of the Bloodwing. Continue to upgrade these skills until the second tier skill become available. Consider upgrading Out for Blood or Riotous Remedy if health has been difficult to maintain. Otherwise, focus on strengthening Mordecai through the Smirk and Lethal Strike skills.

Several of the skills in the third tier can really aid your pistol-wielding abilities and are worthy of Skill Points if you enjoy using that weapon type. Otherwise, focus on reducing the Bloodwing's cooldown time by upgrading the Carrion Call and Predator skills. It should be the goal of every person playing as Mordecai to eventually upgrade the Bird of Prey skill within the Rogue branch to increase the number of targets the Bloodwing can attack.

TYPE O POSITIVE
IF YOU FIND YOURSELF RUNNING LOW ON HEALTH, TRY PUTTING SOME POINTS IN THE OUT FOR BLOOD SKILL AND EQUIPPING A TRANSFUSION GRENADE MOD.
— J. KYLE PITTMAN, PROGRAMMER

PROFESSIONAL PISTOLERO

We know you're out there. You're the person who tries to survive the entire game with only a pistol, aren't you? Well, if so, Mordecai is your man. It should be noted that this approach won't be easy and there is no secret Achievement or Trophy available, but the following build-out should aid in the quest to be the ultimate gunslinger. Allocate your Skill Points this way: Focus = 5, Gun Crazy = 5, Deadly = 5, Lethal Strike = 5, Hair Trigger = 5, and Relentless = 5. And don't forget to equip an Assassin or Gunslinger Class Deck!

TEAM PLAY

Mordecai doesn't have the obvious team-benefitting support and healing abilities of Roland, but it's possible to re-spec him for team play in a way that will guarantee you an invite to any party. For starters, assign multiple Skill Points to the Swipe skill to increase the amount of loot that gets dropped during each Bloodwing attack. Next, spread some Skill Points across Focus and Caliber to unlock the Smirk skill, then max out Smirk—your teammates will love the 15% XP bonus! Now it's time to focus on increasing Mordecai's survivability via the Out for Blood and Riotous Remedy skills. Allocate several Skill Points to each skill to ensure that Mordecai doesn't become a drain on the party's healing items. Finally, maximize the Ransack skill to boost the amount of loot dropped. One of the biggest challenges teams face when playing cooperatively is the relative lack of ammo drops compared to when they are alone. It's imperative that you boost Swipe and Ransack in the Rogue branch to keep your team armed and loaded!

SNIPER SKILLS

FOCUS

Increases accuracy with all weapon types.

LEVEL 1	LEVEL 2	LEVEL 3
+5% Accuracy -10% Sniper Rifle Sway	+10% Accuracy -20% Sniper Rifle Sway	+15% Accuracy -30% Sniper Rifle Sway

LEVEL 4	LEVEL 5
+20% Accuracy -40% Sniper Rifle Sway	+25% Accuracy -50% Sniper Rifle Sway

CALIBER

Increases damage with Sniper Rifles.

LEVEL 1	LEVEL 2	LEVEL 3
+4% Sniper Rifle Damage	+8% Sniper Rifle Damage	+12% Sniper Rifle Damage

LEVEL 4	LEVEL 5
+16% Sniper Rifle Damage	+20% Sniper Rifle Damage

SMIRK

All players on your team (including you) gain additional experience when you kill an enemy with a Critical Hit.

LEVEL 1	LEVEL 2	LEVEL 3
+3% Experience Bonus	+6% Experience Bonus	+9% Experience Bonus

LEVEL 4	LEVEL 5
+12% Experience Bonus	+15% Experience Bonus

KILLER

Killing an enemy increases your Damage and Reload Speed with all guns for a few seconds.

LEVEL 1	LEVEL 2	LEVEL 3
+8% Damage +6% Reload Speed	+16% Damage +12% Reload Speed	+24% Damage +18% Reload Speed

LEVEL 4	LEVEL 5
+32% Damage +24% Reload Speed	+40% Damage +30% Reload Speed

LOADED

Increases Magazine Capacity with Sniper Rifles.

LEVEL 1	LEVEL 2	LEVEL 3
+14% Magazine Capacity	+28% Magazine Capacity	+42% Magazine Capacity

LEVEL 4	LEVEL 5
+56% Magazine Capacity	+70% Magazine Capacity

CARRION CALL

Shooting an enemy with a Sniper Rifle reduces the cooldown time of your Bloodwing.

LEVEL 1	LEVEL 2	LEVEL 3
0.8 seconds Cooldown Reduction per hit	1.6 seconds Cooldown Reduction per hit	2.4 seconds Cooldown Reduction per hit

LEVEL 4	LEVEL 5
3.2 seconds Cooldown Reduction per hit	4.0 seconds Cooldown Reduction per hit

TRESPASS

Your bullets have a chance to ignore shields. Also, slightly increases Bullet Damage.

LEVEL 1	LEVEL 2	LEVEL 3	LEVEL 4	LEVEL 5
20% chance to Penetrate Shields +1% Bullet Damage	40% chance to Penetrate Shields +2% Bullet Damage	60% chance to Penetrate Shields +3% Bullet Damage	80% chance to Penetrate Shields +4% Bullet Damage	100% chance to Penetrate Shields +5% Bullet Damage

SKILLS

ROGUE SKILLS

SWIFT STRIKE

Increases the Bloodwing Damage and movement speed.

LEVEL 1	LEVEL 2	LEVEL 3
+20% Bloodwing Damage +8% Bloodwing Speed	+40% Bloodwing Damage +16% Bloodwing Speed	+60% Bloodwing Damage +24% Bloodwing Speed

LEVEL 4	LEVEL 5
+80% Bloodwing Damage +32% Bloodwing Speed	+100% Bloodwing Damage +40% Bloodwing Speed

SWIPE

The Bloodwing causes enemies to drop additional money, ammo, and healing items when it attacks.

LEVEL 1	LEVEL 2	LEVEL 3
Maximum number of additional items dropped is 1	Maximum number of additional items dropped is 2	Maximum number of additional items dropped is 3

LEVEL 4	LEVEL 5
Maximum number of additional items dropped is 4	Maximum number of additional items dropped is 5

FAST HANDS

Increases Reload Speed with all weapon types.

LEVEL 1	LEVEL 2	LEVEL 3
+8% Reload Speed	+16% Reload Speed	+24% Reload Speed

LEVEL 4	LEVEL 5
+32% Reload Speed	+40% Reload Speed

OUT FOR BLOOD

When your Bloodwing strikes an enemy, you gain health based on the amount of damage inflicted.

LEVEL 1	LEVEL 2	LEVEL 3
+7% of Damage converted to Heatlh	+14% of Damage converted to Heatlh	+21% of Damage converted to Heatlh

LEVEL 4	LEVEL 5
+28% of Damage converted to Heatlh	+35% of Damage converted to Heatlh

AERIAL IMPACT

Attacks from your Bloodwing can Daze enemies, reducing their movement speed and accuracy.

LEVEL 1	LEVEL 2	LEVEL 3
20% chance to Daze (vs an equal level enemy)	40% chance to Daze (vs an equal level enemy)	60% chance to Daze (vs an equal level enemy)

LEVEL 4	LEVEL 5
80% chance to Daze (vs an equal level enemy)	100% chance to Daze (vs an equal level enemy)

RANSACK

the amount of loot you receive from other enemies killed for a few seconds.

LEVEL 1	LEVEL 2	LEVEL 3
20% chance to drop an additional item	40% chance to drop an additional item	60% chance to drop an additional item

LEVEL 4	LEVEL 5
80% chance to drop an additional item	100% chance to drop an additional item

BIRD OF PREY

Increase the number of targets the Bloodwing can attack before returning.

LEVEL 1	LEVEL 2	LEVEL 3	LEVEL 4	LEVEL 5
Bloodwing attacks up to 2 targets	Bloodwing attacks up to 3 targets	Bloodwing attacks up to 4 targets	Bloodwing attacks up to 5 targets	Bloodwing attacks up to 6 targets

GUNSLINGER SKILLS

DEADLY

Increases Critical Hit damage.

LEVEL 1	LEVEL 2	LEVEL 3
+6% Critical Hit Damage	+12% Critical Hit Damage	+18% Critical Hit Damage

LEVEL 4	LEVEL 5
+24% Critical Hit Damage	+30% Critical Hit Damage

GUN CRAZY

When using pistols, you have a chance to fire two shots with each pull of the trigger instead of just one.

LEVEL 1	LEVEL 2	LEVEL 3
8% chance to fire two shots	16% chance to fire two shots	24% chance to fire two shots

LEVEL 4	LEVEL 5
32% chance to fire two shots	40% chance to fire two shots

LETHAL STRIKE

Increases melee damage. Also, every melee attack has a 35% chance to be a Lethal Strike and deal extremely high damage.

LEVEL 1	LEVEL 2	LEVEL 3
+10% Melee Damage Lethal Strikes deal +100% damage	+20% Melee Damage Lethal Strikes deal +200% damage	+30% Melee Damage Lethal Strikes deal +300% damage

LEVEL 4	LEVEL 5
+40% Melee Damage Lethal Strikes deal +400% damage	+50% Melee Damage Lethal Strikes deal +500% damage

RIOTOUS REMEDY

Killing an enemy provides a chaotic health regeneration for a few seconds.

LEVEL 1	LEVEL 2	LEVEL 3
Healed up to 3% of your maximum Health over seven seconds	Healed up to 6% of your maximum Health over seven seconds	Healed up to 9% of your maximum Health over seven seconds

LEVEL 4	LEVEL 5
Healed up to 12% of your maximum Health over seven seconds	Healed up to 15% of your maximum Health over seven seconds

PREDATOR

Decreases the cooldown time of your pet Bloodwing.

LEVEL 1	LEVEL 2	LEVEL 3
Bloodwing Cooldown reduced by three seconds	Bloodwing Cooldown reduced by six seconds	Bloodwing Cooldown reduced by nine seconds

LEVEL 4	LEVEL 5
Bloodwing Cooldown reduced by 12 seconds	Bloodwing Cooldown reduced by 15 seconds

HAIR TRIGGER

Increases Fire Rate and Magazine Size with pistols.

LEVEL 1	LEVEL 2	LEVEL 3
+4% Fire Rate +6% Magazine Size	+8% Fire Rate +12% Magazine Size	+12% Fire Rate +18% Magazine Size

LEVEL 4	LEVEL 5
+16% Fire Rate +24% Magazine Size	+20% Fire Rate +30% Magazine Size

RELENTLESS

Killing an enemy increases your fire rate and gives every bullet fired a 25% chance to be a Killer Shot and deal additional damage. This effect only lasts a few seconds.

LEVEL 1	LEVEL 2	LEVEL 3	LEVEL 4	LEVEL 5
+8% Fire Rate +20% Killer Shot damage	+16% Fire Rate +40% Killer Shot damage	+24% Fire Rate +60% Killer Shot damage	+32% Fire Rate +80% Killer Shot damage	+40% Fire Rate +100% Killer Shot damage

CLAPTRAP DANCE OFF

"IS THAT ALL YOU'VE GOT?"

LILITH

4# with LILITH as "The Siren"

- USES DECEPTION AND TRICKERY
- PREFERS INCENDIARY, SHOCK, AND CORROSIVE GUNS

So far only 13 people have publicly demonstrated so called "magical" abilities, all of whom are women. Due to the gender bias, these gifted individuals are often called "Witches" or "Sirens," although no official term exists. Studying the cause of these women's powers has proven difficult, as they are always prone to wanderlust and have little patience for extending scientific probing. Lilith claims her powers come from her crossing the "Hotness Threshold." "Any woman as good looking as me can do what I do," is her official statement for such inquiry. The other gifted women offer equally useful explanations for their powers.

LILITH'S CLASS MODS

CLASS	BENEFITS	FOCUS	MANUFACTURERS
Firefly	Personal	Incendiary Damage	DAHL MALIWAN
Mercenary	Personal	SMG	DAHL [ATLAS]
Plague Bearer	Personal	Corrosive Damage	S&S MUNITIONS HYPERION
Tempest	Personal	Shock Damage	S&S MUNITIONS PANGOLIN
Catalyst	Team	Skill Booster	MALIWAN ANSHIN
Defender	Team	Max Shield	ANSHIN PANGOLIN
Tormentor	Team	Elemental Bonuses	[ATLAS] HYPERION

ACTION SKILL

PHASEWALK

COOLDOWN:
36 seconds

Gain the ability to turn invisible and move incredibly fast. Upon entering and leaving Phasewalk, you create a Phase Blast that damages nearby enemies. Note that you can perform a Melee attack to end Phasewalk early.

CLAPTRAP DANCE OFF

VAULT HUNTERS: LILITH

It's normal for women of Lilith's caliber to tire of having every Bandit, Psycho, and Bruiser staring at them all the time—especially through the scope of their rifles—but only Lilith has the option to go invisible. Lilith's magical Phasewalk ability grants her seven seconds in cloaking heaven, during which time she can pass by any enemy without detection. This is absolutely perfect for getting the drop on foes in turret guns and for escaping a sticky situation when health and ammo run low. Enemies won't fire or attack what they can't see!

Lilith enters and exits Phasewalk with a powerful Phase Blast that damages all nearby enemies. It's also possible to end Phasewalk early by performing a melee attack that combines the power of Phase Blast with Lilith's normal melee strike.

Lilith has a number of skills at her disposal to magnify the effects of Phasewalk, thus making it possible to weaken enemies by simply Phasewalking past them. This action skill comes in handy during team play (team players can see Lilith's ghostly shadow) and, provided someone is watching Lilith's back, it allows her to Phasewalk into multiple enemies and live to tell about it.

CUSTOMIZATION STRATEGIES

SOLO PLAY

Playing as Lilith demands a different approach to *Borderlands* from that of Roland and Mordecai. Firearms are still her primary means of attack, but Lilith relies more on cunning and deception than brute force. Lilith is not unlike a mage character in other role-playing games: to best utilize her abilities, you must exploit elemental attacks and take advantage of the elemental vulnerabilities of many enemy types.

It also requires employing guerilla hit-and-run tactics. Lilith must dash behind enemy lines, unleash her Phase Blast, then quickly retreat while her Phasewalk action skill cools down and becomes active again.

How you spec Lilith as the game progresses should be a reflection of how you enjoy playing the game. Lilith's skills are divided across the following three focuses: Controller, Elemental, and Assassin. Always spend a number of Skill Points in the Controller category, then let your play style dictate whether to invest heavily in the Elemental or Assassin branches.

Try starting her customization by focusing on her Diva and Silent Resolve skills to increase her Shield capacity and keep her safe after exiting Phasewalk. Allocate some Skill Points to Hit & Run and Quicksilver early on. If you start to rely heavily on guns and less on melee attacks or Phasewalking, then continue to upgrade skills in the Assassin branch, particularly Enforcer and High Velocity. On the other hand, if you make frequent use of Phasewalk and are making the most of elemental effects, then focus Skill Points on Spark, Hard to Get, Radiance, and Phase Strike.

CAT FIGHT!

Just because Brick has all those muscles doesn't mean he's the only one who can lay the hurt on the opposition with melee attacks. It's possible to spec Lilith in such a way as to make her a devastating close-quarters combatant. Give the following build a try: Striking = 5, Spark = 5, Radiance = 5, Venom = 5, Silent Resolve = 5, Hit & Run = 5, Blackout = 5, and Phase Strike = 5. Naturally, this is only possible very late in the game, but it's worth it for those who like to forego weapons.

TEAM PLAY

When playing cooperatively as Lilith, you must commit to using Phasewalk frequently and making the most of her elemental abilities. Your teammates will expect nothing else. Re-spec Lilith to boost her Shield powers and overall resistance to damage by assigning Skill Points to Diva and Silent Resolve just as you would for solo play, then assign points to Spark, Radiance, Hit & Run, Hard to Get, and Blackout. It's important to reduce the cooldown time of Phasewalk as much as possible so you can reuse it quickly after exiting it. This allows you to strike several enemies with Phase Blast without being too exposed in the process.

Lilith only has one skill that directly benefits the entire team (Intuition boosts the amount of experience the team earns with each kill), but there are others that can make the battles easier for everyone. You can't upgrade them all due to the limited number of Skill Points, but Mind Games has a chance to Daze each enemy hit with a bullet and Phoenix deals Fire Damage to any nearby enemies after you make a kill. Phoenix also provides a chance to save ammo, which everyone on your team will appreciate.

CLAPTRAP DANCE OFF

SKILLS

CONTROLLER SKILLS

DIVA

Increases the capacity of your shield.

LEVEL 1	LEVEL 2	LEVEL 3
+5% Shield capacity	+10% Shield capacity	+15% Shield capacity

LEVEL 4	LEVEL 5
+20% Shield capacity	+25% Shield capacity

STRIKING

Your melee attacks can Daze enemies, reducing their movement speed and accuracy.

LEVEL 1	LEVEL 2	LEVEL 3
+20% Chance to Daze (vs an equal level enemy)	+40% Chance to Daze (vs an equal level enemy)	+60% Chance to Daze (vs an equal level enemy)

LEVEL 4	LEVEL 5
+80% Chance to Daze (vs an equal level enemy)	+100% Chance to Daze (vs an equal level enemy)

INNER GLOW

You regenerate Health while Phasewalking.

LEVEL 1	LEVEL 2	LEVEL 3
Regenerate 1% of your Health per second while Phasewalking	Regenerate 3% of your Health per second while Phasewalking	Regenerate 4% of your Health per second while Phasewalking

LEVEL 4	LEVEL 5
Regenerate 6% of your Health per second while Phasewalking	Regenerate 7% of your Health per second while Phasewalking

DRAMATIC ENTRANCE

Your Phase Blast can Daze enemies, reducing their movement speed and accuracy.

LEVEL 1	LEVEL 2	LEVEL 3
+20% Chance to Daze (vs an equal level enemy)	+40% Chance to Daze (vs an equal level enemy)	+60% Chance to Daze (vs an equal level enemy)

LEVEL 4	LEVEL 5
+80% Chance to Daze (vs an equal level enemy)	+100% Chance to Daze (vs an equal level enemy)

HARD TO GET

Decreases the Cooldown time of Phasewalk.

LEVEL 1	LEVEL 2	LEVEL 3
Phasewalk cooldown reduced by three seconds	Phasewalk cooldown reduced by six seconds	Phasewalk cooldown reduced by 10 seconds

LEVEL 4	LEVEL 5
Phasewalk cooldown reduced by 13 seconds	Phasewalk cooldown reduced by 16 seconds

GIRL POWER

Killing an enemy causes your Shield to quickly regenerate for a few seconds.

LEVEL 1	LEVEL 2	LEVEL 3
Regenerates 2% of your Shield per second	Regenerates 3% of your Shield per second	Regenerates 4% of your Shield per second

LEVEL 4	LEVEL 5
Regenerates 6% of your Shield per second	Regenerates 7% of your Shield per second

MIND GAMES

Each bullet has a chance to Daze enemies, reducing their movement speed and accuracy.

LEVEL 1	LEVEL 2	LEVEL 3	LEVEL 4	LEVEL 5
+5% Chance to Daze (vs an equal level enemy)	+10% Chance to Daze (vs an equal level enemy)	+15% Chance to Daze (vs an equal level enemy)	+20% Chance to Daze (vs an equal level enemy)	+25% Chance to Daze (vs an equal level enemy)

ELEMENTAL SKILLS

QUICKSILVER

Increases your Fire Rate with all weapons.

LEVEL 1	LEVEL 2	LEVEL 3
+5% Fire Rate	+10% Fire Rate	+15% Fire Rate

LEVEL 4	LEVEL 5
+20% Fire Rate	+25% Fire Rate

SPARK

Causing Elemental Effects with Elemental Weapons.

LEVEL 1	LEVEL 2	LEVEL 3
+4% Elemental Chance	+8% Elemental Chance	+12% Elemental Chance

LEVEL 4	LEVEL 5
+16% Elemental Chance	+20% Elemental Chance

RESILIENCE

Increases your resistance to Fire, Shock, Corrosive, and Explosive damage.

LEVEL 1	LEVEL 2	LEVEL 3
+6% Elemental Resistance	+12% Elemental Resistance	+18% Elemental Resistance

LEVEL 4	LEVEL 5
+24% Elemental Resistance	+30% Elemental Resistance

RADIANCE

You deal Shock Damage to nearby enemies while Phasewalking. Damage is based on your Level and the Skill's Level.

LEVEL 1	LEVEL 2	LEVEL 3
+1 Shock Damage	+2 Shock Damage	+3 Shock Damage

LEVEL 4	LEVEL 5
+4 Shock Damage	+5 Shock Damage

VENOM

Adds Corrosive Damage to your melee attacks. Also, your melee attacks have a chance to Corrode enemies, causing additional damage over time.

LEVEL 1	LEVEL 2	LEVEL 3
+5% Melee Damage	+10% Melee Damage	+15% Melee Damage

LEVEL 4	LEVEL 5
+20% Melee Damage	+25% Melee Damage

INTUITION

Killing an enemy increases your movement speed and the experience you and your team earn for a few seconds.

LEVEL 1	LEVEL 2	LEVEL 3
+10% Movement Speed +4% Team Experience	+20% Movement Speed +8% Team Experience	+30% Movement Speed +12% Team Experience

LEVEL 4	LEVEL 5
+40% Movement Speed +16% Team Experience	+50% Movement Speed +20% Team Experience

PHOENIX

Killing an enemy causes you to deal Fire Damage to nearby enemies, making your shots not always cost ammo for a few seconds. The Fire Damage increases with your Level.

LEVEL 1	LEVEL 2	LEVEL 3	LEVEL 4	LEVEL 5
+5% Chance to save ammo +1 Fire Damage	+10% Chance to save ammo +2 Fire Damage	+15% Chance to save ammo +3 Fire Damage	+20% Chance to save ammo +4 Fire Damage	+25% Chance to save ammo +5 Fire Damage

ASSASSIN SKILLS

SLAYER

Increases your Critical Hit Damage.

LEVEL 1	LEVEL 2	LEVEL 3
+5% Critical Hit Damage	+10% Critical Hit Damage	+15% Critical Hit Damage

LEVEL 4	LEVEL 5
+20% Critical Hit Damage	+25% Critical Hit Damage

SILENT RESOLVE

Increases your resistance to damage for a few seconds after Phasewalking.

LEVEL 1	LEVEL 2	LEVEL 3
+14% Damage Reduction	+28% Damage Reduction	+42% Damage Reduction

LEVEL 4	LEVEL 5
+56% Damage Reduction	+70% Damage Reduction

ENFORCER

Killing an enemy increases your accuracy and Bullet Damage for a few seconds.

LEVEL 1	LEVEL 2	LEVEL 3
+7% Accuracy +2% Bullet Damage	+14% Accuracy +4% Bullet Damage	+21% Accuracy +8% Bullet Damage

LEVEL 4	LEVEL 5
+28% Accuracy +8% Bullet Damage	+35% Accuracy +10% Bullet Damage

HIT & RUN

Gain increases Melee Damage and Phasewalk duration.

LEVEL 1	LEVEL 2	LEVEL 3
+7% Melee Damage +0.8 Phasewalk duration (in seconds)	+14% Melee Damage +1.6 Phasewalk duration (in seconds)	+21% Melee Damage +2.4 Phasewalk duration (in seconds)

LEVEL 4	LEVEL 5
+28% Melee Damage +3.2 Phasewalk duration (in seconds)	+35% Melee Damage +4.0 Phasewalk duration (in seconds)

HIGH VELOCITY

Increases Bullet Damage and Velocity.

LEVEL 1	LEVEL 2	LEVEL 3
+20% Bullet Velocity +4% Bullet Damage	+40% Bullet Velocity +8% Bullet Damage	+60% Bullet Velocity +12% Bullet Damage

LEVEL 4	LEVEL 5
+80% Bullet Velocity +16% Bullet Damage	+100% Bullet Velocity +20% Bullet Damage

BLACKOUT

Killing an enemy reduces the cooldown time of Phasewalk.

LEVEL 1	LEVEL 2	LEVEL 3
1.2 seconds of cooldown reduction per kill	2.4 seconds of cooldown reduction per kill	3.6 seconds of cooldown reduction per kill

LEVEL 4	LEVEL 5
4.8 seconds of cooldown reduction per kill	6.0 seconds of cooldown reduction per kill

PHASE STRIKE

Using a melee attack while Phasewalking deals additional damage.

LEVEL 1	LEVEL 2	LEVEL 3	LEVEL 4	LEVEL 5
+160% Melee Damage	+320% Melee Damage	+480% Melee Damage	+640% Melee Damage	+800% Melee Damage

CLAPTRAP DANCE OFF

and BRICK as HIMSELF

▮ IGNORES PAIN AND HITS HARD
▮ PREFERS EXPLOSIVE WEAPONS AND HIS FISTS

The source of Brick's size and strength is baffling considering his mother and father are both slightly under five feet tall. Depending on the day, he attributes his physique to either his daily vitamin consumption or the lucky paw of his beloved dog Priscilla that he wears around his neck. Regardless of the cause of his strength, he continues to bring his fists to a gun fight and still manages to come out on top.

BRICK'S CLASS MODS

CLASS	BENEFITS	FOCUS	MANUFACTURERS	
Berserker	Personal	Melee Combat	TEDIORE	VLADOF
Blast Master	Personal	Explosives	DAHL	TORGUE
Bombardier	Personal	Rocket Launchers	TEDIORE	DAHL
Titan	Personal	Max Health	[ATLAS]	PANGOLIN
Centurion	Team	Max Health	[ATLAS]	PANGOLIN
Skirmisher	Team	Melee Combat	VLADOF	PANGOLIN
Warmonger	Team	Weapon Damage	TORGUE	HYPERION

ACTION SKILL

BERSERK

COOLDOWN:
60 seconds

Try to gain the ability to go Berserk. While in this state, use the Aim and Fire Buttons to throw punches. Also, you gain resistance to all damage and you regenerate health while Berserking.

BRING IT ON!

BRICK

CLAPTRAP
DANCE OFF

LT HUNTERS: BRICK

Brick is unlike any other character in that he is more than happy to toss aside the guns and throw down in a bare-knuckles fight to the death. His Berserk skill sends him into a seething fit of rage, giving the player direct control over his left and right fists. Rush toward the nearest enemies and throw a vicious combo of left and right punches to knock them out for good. Berserk lasts for 18 seconds (without skill upgrades) and regenerates health while active.

Of course, Brick's shields will likely take considerable damage as he rushes toward his target—and he'll be dangerously close to surviving enemies when Berserk runs out—so hold off on using Berserk against tougher enemies until his strengthening skills have been upgraded.

Berserk is a tremendously fun skill that requires a completely different approach to playing *Borderlands*, but it should not be taken lightly. As strong as Brick is, Berserk can land him in a heavily compromising position, potentially surrounded by enemies.

CUSTOMIZATION STRATEGIES

SOLO PLAY

Choosing Brick for solo play is not recommended for first-time players. Although he's plenty capable with all of the same weapons the other characters use, he lacks the skills that give them their helpful bursts of power and ability. Instead, Brick's skills are primarily geared toward melee combat, health regeneration, and explosives. His skills and action skill are designed to enhance his ability as a pugilist. Although he doesn't have any weapons deficiencies, he doesn't have many weapons skills either. Brick's many skills are divided into the following three branches: Brawler, Tank, and Blaster.

KING OF CLAP

NOT THE BOSS OF ME
BRICK'S BRAWLER TREE IS BRILLIANT UNTIL YOU START GOING UP AGAINST SOME OF THE BOSSES. YOU MIGHT RESPEC YOUR SKILLS TEMPORARILY, KILL THE BOSS, THEN GET BACK TO PUNCHING THE LIGHTS OUT OF PANDORA'S CRITTERS.

- STEVEN STROBEL, TECHNICAL ARTIST

Assign early Skill Points to Safeguard and Hardened, regardless of how much you plan to utilize Berserk. Then, if you're plan to use Berserk quite often, start upgrading Endless Rage and Iron Fist to extend the duration and melee strength while in Berserk.

Sting Like a Bee is an excellent skill that makes it easier to dash from one enemy to the next during Berserk. Note that this reduces the amount of time that gets wasted simply moving about. Toward the middle stages of the game, spend some Skill Points upgrading the Tank abilities such as Juggernaut and then focus on those skills conducive to your play style. If you are constantly reaching for a gun, then upgrade Rapid Reload and Revenge. Then once you have a Rocket Launcher, invest in the devastating power of Wide Load and Master Blaster. On the other hand, if you want to strictly be a brawler, then spend your Skill Points on Heavy Handed and Short Fuse.

HE'S GOT A BIG HEART

THE HIGHER BRICK'S MAXIMUM HEALTH, THE MORE HEALING HE WILL RECEIVE FROM HIS "BLOOD SPORT" SKILL SO USE ITEMS TO INCREASE HIS MAXIMUM HEALTH AND GET THE HARDENED SKILL.

— JONATHAN HEMINGWAY, GAME DESIGNER

DEMOLITIONS EXPERT

Brick may be known for his willingness to holster his weapons and settle disputes with his fists, but his skill with Explosive effects cannot be overstated. Not only can he dish out extreme Explosive damage, but he can be spec'd in such a way as to be virtually immune to Explosive damage. Give the following build-out a try: Hardened = 5, Safeguard = 5, Endowed = 5, Wide Load = 5, Liquidate = 5, Cast Iron = 5, and Master Blaster = 5. With a reliable rocket launcher at the ready and this set of skills upgraded, you can alternate lengthy bursts of rocket fire with short bouts of Berserk.

TEAM PLAY

There's no question that Brick is much easier to play as in a cooperative setting than he is on his own. As tough as he is, even Brick needs someone to provide some cover fire or revive him after he gets downed. Of course, your teammates won't always come to your aid—they'll have their own battles to focus on—so max out the Hardened and Safe Guard skills just in case.

You can also upgrade the Diehard skill in the Tank class, then focus on the Brawler or Blaster skills. If going the Brawler route, work your way through the skill tree and max out the Prize Fighter skill to shower your teammates in cash prizes! If you'd rather hang close to your teammates and focus on heavy artillery, grab a Rocket Launcher and spend your Skill Points in the Blaster section.

Upgrade the Endowed skill, then upgrade Wide Load, Liquidate, and finally Master Blaster. The latter skill, when fully upgraded, provides a never-ending supply of ammo for the Rocket Launcher. And if that doesn't earn you some friends (or help you win duels), then nothing will!

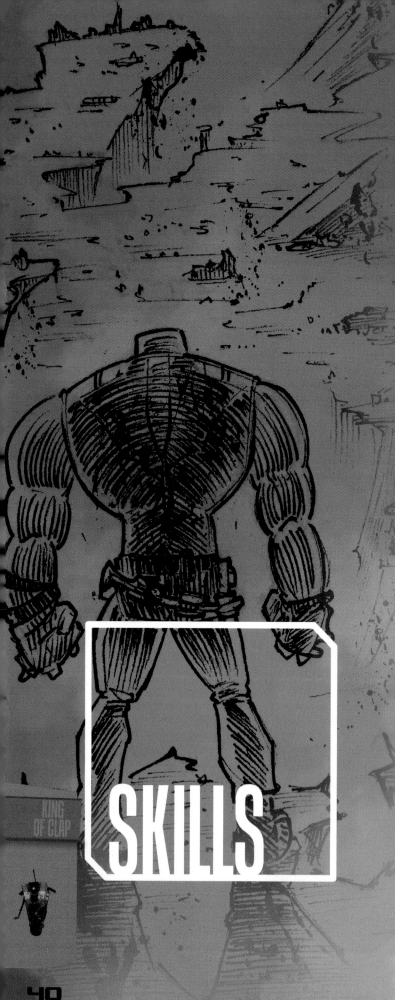

SKILLS

BRAWLER SKILLS

IRON FIST

Increases the melee damage you deal.

LEVEL 1	LEVEL 2	LEVEL 3
+6% Melee Damage	+12% Melee Damage	+18% Melee Damage

LEVEL 4	LEVEL 5
+24% Melee Damage	+30% Melee Damage

ENDLESS RAGE

Increases the duration of Berserk.

LEVEL 1	LEVEL 2	LEVEL 3
+10% Berserk Duration	+20% Berserk Duration	+30% Berserk Duration

LEVEL 4	LEVEL 5
+40% Berserk Duration	+50% Berserk Duration

STING LIKE A BEE

Punching while Berserk causes you to dash forward and slug your enemies.

LEVEL 1	LEVEL 2	LEVEL 3
Dash Distance: 4 feet	Dash Distance: 8 feet	Dash Distance: 12 feet

LEVEL 4	LEVEL 5
Dash Distance: 16 feet	Dash Distance: 20 feet

HEAVY HANDED

Killing an enemy greatly increases your melee damage for a few seconds.

LEVEL 1	LEVEL 2	LEVEL 3
+12% Melee Damage	+24% Melee Damage	+36% Melee Damage

LEVEL 4	LEVEL 5
+48% Melee Damage	+60% Melee Damage

PRIZE FIGHTER

While Berserk is active, your melee attacks have a chance to spawn cash prizes.

LEVEL 1	LEVEL 2	LEVEL 3
6% chance to spawn a cash prize	12% chance to spawn a cash prize	18% chance to spawn a cash prize

LEVEL 4	LEVEL 5
24% chance to spawn a cash prize	30% chance to spawn a cash prize

SHORT FUSE

Decreases the Cooldown time of Berserk.

LEVEL 1	LEVEL 2	LEVEL 3
Berserk Cooldown reduced by six seconds	Berserk Cooldown reduced by 12 seconds	Berserk Cooldown reduced by 18 seconds

LEVEL 4	LEVEL 5
Berserk Cooldown reduced by 24 seconds	Berserk Cooldown reduced by 30 seconds

BLOOD SPORT

Killing an enemy while Berserk is active regenerates some health.

LEVEL 1	LEVEL 2	LEVEL 3	LEVEL 4	LEVEL 5
+2% Health Regenerated	+4% Health Regenerated	+6% Health Regenerated	+8% Health Regenerated	+10% Health Regenerated

KING OF CLAP

TANK SKILLS

HARDENED

Increases your maximum health.

LEVEL 1	LEVEL 2	LEVEL 3
+12% Maximum Health	+24% Maximum Health	+36% Maximum Health

LEVEL 4	LEVEL 5
+48% Maximum Health	+60% Maximum Health

SAFEGUARD

Increases the strength of your shield.

LEVEL 1	LEVEL 2	LEVEL 3
+8% Shield Strength	+16% Shield Strength	+24% Shield Strength

LEVEL 4	LEVEL 5
+32% Shield Strength	+40% Shield Strength

BASH

Gives your melee attacks a chance to Daze enemies, slowing them and reducing their accuracy.

LEVEL 1	LEVEL 2	LEVEL 3
10% Chance to Daze	20% Chance to Daze	30% Chance to Daze

LEVEL 4	LEVEL 5
40% Chance to Daze	50% Chance to Daze

JUGGERNAUT

Killing an enemy creates resistance to all damage for a few seconds.

LEVEL 1	LEVEL 2	LEVEL 3
+10% Damage Resistance	+20% Damage Resistance	+30% Damage Resistance

LEVEL 4	LEVEL 5
+40% Damage Resistance	+50% Damage Resistance

PAY BACK

After your shields become depleted, you gain a damage bonus for 10 seconds.

LEVEL 1	LEVEL 2	LEVEL 3
+8% Damage Bonus	+16% Damage Bonus	+24% Damage Bonus

LEVEL 4	LEVEL 5
+32% Damage Bonus	+40% Damage Bonus

DIEHARD

Increases the amount of health you regain when revived by a friend or by Second Wind. Also, increases the amount of time you have before you die when you are Crippled.

LEVEL 1	LEVEL 2	LEVEL 3
+30% Revived Health Bonus +20% Time to be Revived	+60% Revived Health Bonus +40% Time to be Revived	+90% Revived Health Bonus +60% Time to be Revived

LEVEL 4	LEVEL 5
+120% Revived Health Bonus +80% Time to be Revived	+150% Revived Health Bonus +100% Time to be Revived

UNBREAKABLE

When your shield is depleted, you gain five seconds of powerful shield regeneration.

LEVEL 1	LEVEL 2	LEVEL 3	LEVEL 4	LEVEL 5
+3% Shield Strength regenerated per second	+6% Shield Strength regenerated per second	+9% Shield Strength regenerated per second	+12% Shield Strength regenerated per second	+15% Shield Strength regenerated per second

BLASTER SKILLS

ENDOWED

Increases the Explosive Damage you deal.

LEVEL 1	LEVEL 2	LEVEL 3
+3% Explosive Damage	+6% Explosive Damage	+9% Explosive Damage

LEVEL 4	LEVEL 5
+12% Explosive Damage	+15% Explosive Damage

RAPID RELOAD

Increases your Reload Speed and reduces Recoil with all weapons.

LEVEL 1	LEVEL 2	LEVEL 3
+4% Reload Speed +6% Recoil Reduction	+8% Reload Speed +12% Recoil Reduction	+12% Reload Speed +18% Recoil Reduction

LEVEL 4	LEVEL 5
+16% Reload Speed +24% Recoil Reduction	+20% Reload Speed +30% Recoil Reduction

REVENGE

Killing an enemy increases your damage with all weapons for a few seconds.

LEVEL 1	LEVEL 2	LEVEL 3
+10% Damage	+20% Damage	+30% Damage

LEVEL 4	LEVEL 5
+40% Damage	+50% Damage

WIDE LOAD

Increases the number of Rockets your Rocket Launcher can hold in its magazine.

LEVEL 1	LEVEL 2	LEVEL 3
+1 Launcher Magazine Size	+2 Launcher Magazine Size	+3 Launcher Magazine Size

LEVEL 4	LEVEL 5
+4 Launcher Magazine Size	+5 Launcher Magazine Size

LIQUIDATE

Dealing Explosive Damage to an enemy reduces the Cooldown time of Berserk.

LEVEL 1	LEVEL 2	LEVEL 3
Cooldown reduction per hit: 1 second	Cooldown reduction per hit: 2 seconds	Cooldown reduction per hit: 3 seconds

LEVEL 4	LEVEL 5
Cooldown reduction per hit: 4 seconds	Cooldown reduction per hit: 5 seconds

CAST IRON

Increases your resistance to Explosive Damage.

LEVEL 1	LEVEL 2	LEVEL 3
+8% Explosive Damage Resistance	+16% Explosive Damage Resistance	+24% Explosive Damage Resistance

LEVEL 4	LEVEL 5
+32% Explosive Damage Resistance	+40% Explosive Damage Resistance

MASTER BLASTER

Killing an enemy increases your Fire Rate with all weapons and causes you to regenerate rockets for a few seconds.

LEVEL 1	LEVEL 2	LEVEL 3	LEVEL 4	LEVEL 5
+12% Fire Rate 2 Rockets generated per minute	+24% Fire Rate 4 Rockets generated per minute	+36% Fire Rate 6 Rockets generated per minute	+48% Fire Rate 8 Rockets generated per minute	+60% Fire Rate 10 Rockets generated per minute

CLAPTRAP DANCE OFF

VAULT HUNTERS: BRICK

1-1 LAST BUS TO FYRESTONE

CLAPTRAP

REPAIR KIT

GENERATOR

BANDIT CAMP
(NORTH ENTRANCE)

DR. ZED

POWER COUPLING

FYRESTONE
COLISEUM

KING
OF CLAP

FIRST SKAG HOLE

ARID BADLANDS

LEGEND	TREASURE CHEST	NEW-U POLE/STATION	MEDICAL VENDING MACHINE	AMMO VENDING MACHINE	GUN VENDING MACHINE
	▬	●	▢	▢	▢

The Arid BADLANDS

Next stop: Fyrestone. There are no signs of the Vault in this miserable dump of a city, but the mysterious voice in your head is convinced that you belong here, and your driver is just as eager to have you off his bus. Thus begins the first six missions of Borderlands, which act as a quick tutorial to the game's basic controls and structure. If you already know what you're doing, they'll fly by in a flash.

QUESTS:

1. Fresh Off The Bus
2. The Doctor Is In
3. Skags at the Gate
4. Claptrap Rescue
5. Fix'er Upper
6. Blinding Nine Toes

LET THE CLAPTRAP LEAD THE WAY

You'll step off the bus to find yourself at the east entrance to Fyrestone, with nothing in your possession but a single low-quality gun. Speak to the Claptrap to get your HUD online, then follow it to the New-U station, where you'll automatically save your progress. If you use the console at the New-U station, you can open up a menu that allows you to change your character's name and color scheme (to distinguish yourself in multiplayer sessions). Later in the game, the New-U stations will also offer an option to redistribute your skill points.

GEAR UP IN THE HOTEL RUINS

After demonstrating the New-U, the Claptrap rolls toward the north gate of Fyrestone. Rather than following him, give the area a thorough search for money, ammo, and guns. You can search any object with a flashing green light (even discarded toilets), but around here, only the dumpsters have a chance of holding new guns.

Red chests, on the other hand, always hold weapons (or at least Grenade Mods). The game's first **red chest** is on the roof of the hotel, and there are several ways to reach it. The easiest way is to jump from the generator on the hotel's south porch directly to the roof. The chest typically offers two new guns, both of which are probably more powerful than your default weapon.

CHARACTER CLASS	STARTING GUN
HUNTER	Sniper Rifle
SOLDIER	Combat Rifle
SIREN	SMG
BERSERKER	Shotgun

CRASH THE RAIDING PARTY

Now that you have a gun in each slot and a pocket full of ammo and cash, it's time to catch up with your Claptrap. Meet him at the Fyrestone gates, where he opens the door just as a bandit raiding party bursts into town.

Instead of rushing at the bandits, use the ruins of the city to your left as cover. This allows you to fire at the nearest bandit while keeping a wall between yourself and his friends. If you have a reasonably accurate weapon, like a combat rifle or repeater, aim for headshots to score deadly critical hits. With shotguns or submachine guns, you should instead aim to score as many hits as possible with dead-center body shots.

After you take out the first wave of five or six bandits, Claptrap stops at another **red chest** containing a fixed set of Repeaters. These basic handguns provide a good opportunity to see each manufacturer's specialty: The Torgue deals extra damage, the Hyperion has superior accuracy, the Vladof has a faster fire rate, and the S&S offers an extended magazine. Grab them even if they aren't better than your current guns—you can always sell them later for cash at any vending machine.

Duck under some rubble to follow the Claptrap to a second New-U pole, then leap over a small iron wall toward a second group of bandits. As you blast your way through town, keep an eye out for piles of green-glowing skag vomit that may hold ammo and recovery items. You'll also find a dark **grey chest**, which contains a large supply of ammunition, at the westernmost point in town.

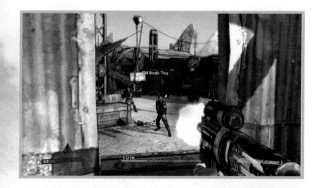

GET A CHECK-UP FROM DR. ZED

With the raiding party slain, the residents of Fyrestone can safely open their doors to the world. Or at least, they could if they weren't stuck shut. Accept the "The Doctor Is In" quest, and follow the green waypoint finder to the door switch just to the left of the Claptrap. Talk to the newly liberated Dr. Zed to complete the quest, collect your reward, and unlock a new quest: "Skags At The Gate." When you're done looting Dr. Zed's lockers, cashboxes, and mailbox, catch up with your Claptrap and follow it to the gate.

1 FRESH OFF THE BUS

LEVEL 2

Client: Guardian Angel
Follow Claptrap into Fyrestone

A mysterious, disembodied woman spoke to you and told you to follow this little robot into town. That seems like the best course of action, for now.

REWARDS: NONE

2 THE DOCTOR IS IN

LEVEL 2

- ■ *Building 03 open (1)*
- ■ *Dr. Zed talked to (1)*

Client: Dr. Zed
Open Building 03 in Fyrestone, and meet Dr. Zed.

I thought I was a goner that time! Damn bandits won't leave us alone. Had to lock the place up tight, and now the damn door won't open. Blasted circuits are on the fritz again. Give it a go from the switch out there, would you?

REWARDS: 48 XP

TAKE THE HIGH GROUND
IF YOU FEEL OVERWHELMED WITH BAD GUYS, QUICKLY FIND A HIGH, OUT OF REACH SPOT (LIKE THE ROOF OF A BUILDING OR A TALL BOULDER) AND SNIPE.
—NATHAN OVERMAN, LEVEL DESIGNER

3 SKAGS AT THE GATE

LEVEL 2

- ☐ *Skags killed (5)*

Client: Dr. Zed

Kill skags and return to Dr. Zed.

Outside of Fyrestone, just past the gate and across the road, you'll find several skag dens. A skag is a vicious four-legged creature, and they'll eat anything, including you. I wanna know if you can handle yourself in a fight against some of these beasts, so head on out there and kill some of 'em for me. If you're still in one piece, then c'mon back.

REWARDS: 144 XP + $313

4 CLAPTRAP RESCUE

LEVEL 2
- ☐ *Diagnostic performed (1)*
- ☐ *Repair Kit (1)*

Client: Claptrap

Perform a diagnostic on Claptrap, then find the Repair Kit and repair him.

Claptrap has been shot by the bandits, but the damage looks minor. Perform a quick diagnostic, then see if you can find a Repair Kit somewhere in Fyrestone. You might be able to revive him.

REWARDS: 72 XP

BRACE FOR AN AMBUSH AT THE GATE

When your Claptrap goes to open Fyrestone's southern gate, he takes a hit from a sudden bandit strike. Try to rush in and peg the bandits with headshots as they land from leaping over the walls. If you're too late, then take cover and pick the bandits off as they attempt to maneuver around it.

Once the coast is clear, examine your whimpering friend to unlock "Claptrap Rescue" and make that your active quest. After diagnosing the wound, follow the waypoint finder to a Repair Kit outside the building across from Dr. Zed's. Bring it back to complete that quest and resume the skag hunt.

You won't have to venture far into the Arid Badlands to find the skag hole—it's right across from town. If you have a weapon with a good scope, try to snipe out a skag or two before they see you, then switch to a heavier weapon like a shotgun or SMG to blast them as they close the distance. A skag's weak point is its mouth, which it exposes right before it charges or when it's in mid-lunge toward you. If they catch up to you while you're reloading, use a melee attack to knock the skag back without interrupting your reloading process.

Visit Dr. Zed after downing your fifth skag to collect your reward and unlock the next quest, "Fix'er Upper."

AN EYE TO THE SECOND WIND
IF YOU FEEL LIKE YOU'RE ABOUT TO BE DOWNED, KEEP A WEAKER ENEMY ALIVE SO THAT YOU CAN QUICKLY TARGET AND KILL THEM TO RECOVER.

—CHRIS BROCK, DEVELOPER

GET THE MED VENDOR HUMMING

Barred from practicing medicine, Dr. Zed has been reduced to a mere vending-machine supplier—and even his vending machines don't work right! Help him get the one in his home up and running by scavenging a Power Coupling that's just south of town and down the road to the east. Stick close to the road to avoid provoking another attack from the first skag hole, but prepare to face a new pack of skags as you approach the Power Coupling. Blast them as they emerge from their hole across the road from the fallen vending machine, and don't claim your prize until you're sure the coast is clear.

Snap the coupling into place on the side of Dr. Zed's vending machine, and then fire it up to do some shopping. In addition to the machine's normal stock of TDR-085 Standard Shields, which typically offers a capacity of around 60 and a sluggish recharge rate, you can find another option in the "Item of the Day" box. The "Item of the Day" shield typically has superior stats, but a much higher price, and it may have a minimum level requirement that leaves you unable to use it right away. If you can't quite afford it, remember that you can make money selling off your extra guns. If you don't like the Item of the Day that you're offered, you can wait until the counter ticks down to zero and a new one goes on display. If you have money left over, pick up a few Minor Healing Kits, which you can use from your inventory menu to regenerate 60 HP.

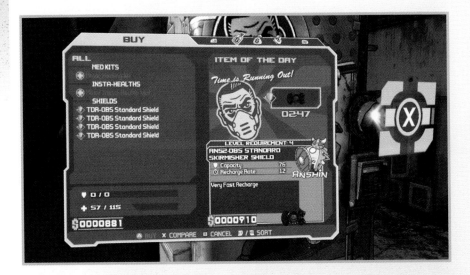

SILENCE NINE-TOES' SPIES

After reporting the completion of the "Fix'er Upper" quest to Dr. Zed, he offers up a much more challenging mission: Blinding Nine-Toes by slaying the bandit spies in the camp southwest of town.

There are three entrances to the bandit outpost. The closest entrance is from the north, and that's probably your best bet. The east and southwest entrances (the latter of which is really just a thin gap you can squeeze through) offer good cover, but are both close to skag holes, and you don't want to deal with skags attacking from behind while you're battling the bandits.

As you approach the camp from the north, you'll see a flashy sign for the arena that's attached to a corrugated wall and a circular shack. Sneak around to the right side of the structure to put yourself in a good position to snipe at bandits, who seem to be expecting an attack from another direction. Don't miss the bright red barrel near their position—a few bullets will turn that into a Bandit-scorching fireball.

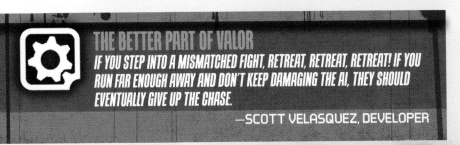

THE BETTER PART OF VALOR
IF YOU STEP INTO A MISMATCHED FIGHT, RETREAT, RETREAT, RETREAT! IF YOU RUN FAR ENOUGH AWAY AND DON'T KEEP DAMAGING THE AI, THEY SHOULD EVENTUALLY GIVE UP THE CHASE.
—SCOTT VELASQUEZ, DEVELOPER

MISSION TAGS

5 FIX'ER UPPER

LEVEL 2

- ■ *Power Coupling (1)*
- ■ *Med Vendor repaired (1)*
- ■ *Shield purchased (1)*

Client: Dr. Zed

Obtain a Power Coupling, repair the med vendor, and buy a shield.

If you're gonna head out of town, you need a shield. A shield forms an invisible barrier around you that absorbs damage. Normally, you'd buy one from the med vendor here, but this one took a bullet during the bandit raid. Fortunately, it just needs a new Power Coupling, and it so happens there's an old vendor we can use for parts. It's right outside of town, down the road east. Go grab the part, install it into the med vendor, and buy yourself a shield.

REWARDS: 192 XP + $188

6 BLINDING NINE-TOES

LEVEL 2

- ■ *Bandits killed (8)*

Client: Dr. Zed

Kill bandits and return to Dr. Zed.

Nine-Toes placed a few men at a small outpost outside of town, across the road and west. Those men report every move we make, so our next move should be to make them dead.

REWARDS: 480 XP + $313

If you're playing in a multiplayer game, attack from opposite sides of the wall to keep the bandits off guard, while still staying close enough to come to each other's aid when necessary. If you're playing solo, you can switch back and forth between the left and right sides of the wall to catch the bandits from different directions, and to quickly eliminate new recruits emerging from the tent itself. If you're lucky, a timely skag attack from the south will force the bandits to fight on two fronts.

You only need to kill eight bandits to complete this quest, but you may find more than a dozen in the outpost. Don't leave without finishing them all off; clear the outpost and you can raid the bandits' **red chest** for a new pair of weapons! You'll also find the entrance to the Fyrestone Coliseum, where groups of players can engage in team-building exercises by shooting each other in the face. (Outside of a New-U save point, you won't find anything in the coliseum if you're playing solo).

Once you've looted the bandits' treasures, return to Dr. Zed, who sends you to visit Fyrestone's only other surviving resident.

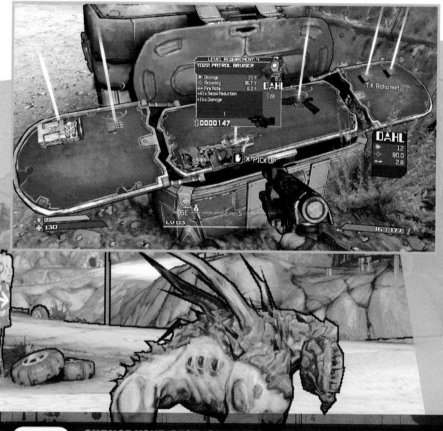

CHANGE YOUR DECK, CHANGE THE WORLD
STORAGE DECK UPGRADES INCREASE THE AMOUNT OF AMMO YOU CAN CARRY FOR A WEAPON TYPE, BUT THEY ALSO SECRETLY INCREASE HOW MUCH OF THAT AMMO TYPE DROPS IN THE WORLD.
—JONATHAN HEMINGWAY, GAME DESIGNER

HASHING IT OUT IN THE FYRESTONE COLISEUM

The Fyrestone Coliseum allows players in multiplayer games to take a break from bandits and skags to compete against each other in free-for-all or team battles. To begin, have the game's host approach the bulletin board and divide the

players into teams by selecting their names and assigning them colors (every player who shares a color ends up on the same team). When you're satisfied, choose "Ready" to begin a game. You warp to an arena that features unique terrain that has been specially designed for competitive play. The first player or team to score three kills wins the match and end the game.

1-2 NINE-TOES TOO MANY

Nine-Toes's relentless attacks on Fyrestone provide a good opportunity to show off your keen conflict-resolution skills. With the help of a Mr. T.K. Baha, you travel to Skag Gully to put a bullet (or several) in Nine-Toes' head, and win the trust of Fyrestone's few surviving citizens.

QUESTS:

1. Nine-Toes: Meet T.K. Baha
2. Nine-Toes: T.K.'s Food
3. Got Grenades?
4. Nine-Toes: Take Him Down
5. Nine-Toes: Time To Collect
6. Job Hunting

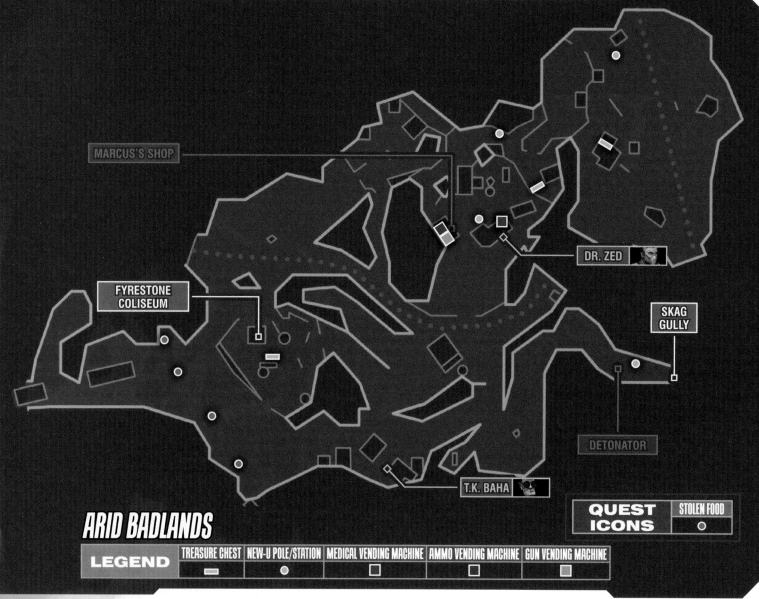

MARCUS'S SHOP

DR. ZED

FYRESTONE
COLISEUM

SKAG
GULLY

DETONATOR

T.K. BAHA

QUEST ICONS	STOLEN FOOD
	◉

ARID BADLANDS

LEGEND	TREASURE CHEST	NEW-U POLE/STATION	MEDICAL VENDING MACHINE	AMMO VENDING MACHINE	GUN VENDING MACHINE
	▬	◉	☐	☐	▭

MEET MR. T.K. BAHA

Walk south past that first skag hole, then hang a right to find the shotgun shack where T.K. Baha resides. Report to him directly to earn the modest reward for completing "Nine-Toes: Meet T.K. Baha," and to unlock the "Nine-Toes: T.K.'s Food" quest. Before you go charging off after his missing foodstuffs, make sure to give his property a thorough once over. You can't get into his house (yet), but you can find some minor loot on the roof by leaping from his cashbox or the tire-headed scarecrow, and there's plenty more in the outhouse to the south.

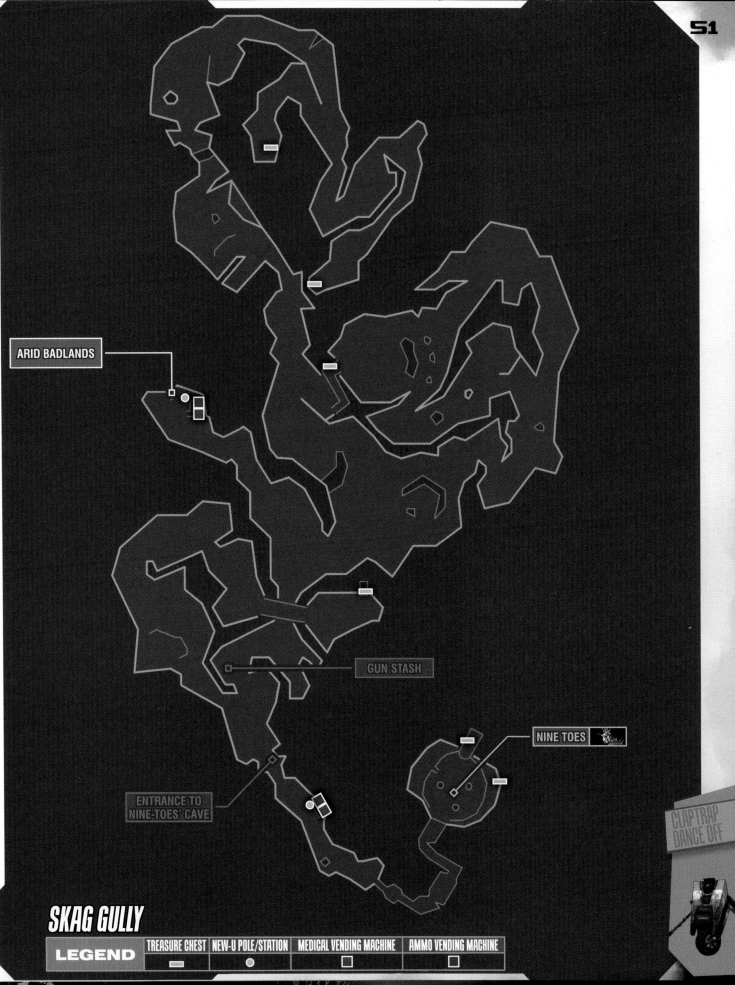

ARID BADLANDS

GUN STASH

NINE TOES

ENTRANCE TO
NINE-TOES' CAVE

CLAPTRAP
DANCE OFF

SKAG GULLY

LEGEND	TREASURE CHEST	NEW-U POLE/STATION	MEDICAL VENDING MACHINE	AMMO VENDING MACHINE

NINE TOES: MEET T.K. BAHA

LEVEL 3

- ■ *T.K. Baha met (1)*

Client: Dr. Zed

Talk to T.K. Baha at T.K.'s Claim

There's a reward for the death of Nine-Toes, but he's elusive. We don't really know where his hideout is. Talk to T.K. Baha at his farm south of Fyrestone. He's blind as a bat, but no one knows the area better than he does. Maybe he can help.

REWARDS: 90 XP

NINE TOES: T.K.'S FOOD

LEVEL 2

- ■ *Stolen Food (4)*

Client: T.K. Baha

Recover the stolen food items and return to T.K. Baha

I did hear it! Damned skags gettin' into my food! Damn them all to hell! You! Whoever you are, I want you to go kill those rat-bastards. They just stole half my food stores! Go get my food back, then we'll talk after I ain't so pissed off.

REWARDS: 480 XP + $313

RUN TWO ERRANDS FOR T.K.

You'll find all four pieces of stolen food in the open desert to the west. Proceed with caution; in addition to the usual low-level Skag Pups, you'll find a few level 4 Skag Whelps guarding the goods that take several hits to bring down. Snipe them from afar, then aim for headshots as they run toward you. That should cause them to roar, allowing you to blast them with a pentuple-damage shot in the mouth. If they catch up to you while you're reloading, remember that you can dish out melee attacks during your reloading animation while still refreshing your clip.

When you return the food to T.K., he sends you back to Fyrestone to buy grenades. Marcus Kincaid will contact you shortly after you accept the quest. He reports that his shop (just west of Dr. Zed's) is now open for business. Marcus isn't inside, but you will find a pair of vending machines. One sells guns; they're typically worse than the ones you can find in the wild, but the Item of the Day may be good. The other sells ammunition, including the three-pack of grenades that's necessary to complete the quest. (If playing in a multiplayer game has allowed you to fill up on grenades already, you'll need to toss at least one to complete the quest by buying more.) The Item of the Day in that machine is a grenade mod that boosts the power of grenades and gives them special properties. They don't come cheap, though, and you'll get a good one for free soon enough. After looting Marcus's many chests and lockers, return to T.K. and report your vending-machine shopping triumph.

BLAST A PATH TO SKAG GULLY

When you return to T.K., he gives you the quest you've been waiting for: "Nine-Toes: Take Him Down." To find Nine-Toes, you must travel east to the entrance to Skag Gully, then activate T.K.'s detonator to blow open a path. As the name implies, you can expect plenty of skags in the new area. They're tough, but you'll level up quickly, almost certainly hitting level 5 at some point on this quest. When you do, promptly spend that skill point to unlock your class's action skill, then get some practice in with it before facing the boss.

There are two vending machines at the entrance to Skag Gully. The ammo vending machine sells the usual stuff, plus level-1 Storage Deck Upgrades for $616 apiece. You can buy these for each type of ammo to increase the maximum amount of that ammo you can carry by 30-50%. If you can afford them, pick one up for your primary weapons and grenades. The medical supplies machine may have a few upgraded shields in stock, including "Healing Shields," which gradually recover lost HP in addition to shield energy.

HUNT FOR NINE-TOES' HIDEOUT

After blowing away a small army of skags southeast of the entrance, head south under the stone arch to pursue Nine-Toes. The skags in the valley basin to the north are about level 7, so you'll be quickly overwhelmed if you attempt to make a sport of them.

Follow your waypoint south to the gun stash behind T.K.'s wife's grave. You'll find two guns here: One is random and the other is a unique weapon named "Lady Finger"—a highly accurate, low-recoil repeater with a critical-hit bonus and the inscription "Omnia vincit amor"—Latin for "love conquers all". (Note that the exact stats of even preset weapons like these contain random factors. The stats presented below represent a rough average; yours may vary slightly.) T.K. Baha will never know one way or the other, so don't feel obligated to use this gun against Nine-Toes if you already have something better.

The entrance to Nine-Toes' hideout is just past the graveyard. When the gate opens, a pair of Mutant Midget Psychos come charging out to join the skags already on the battlefield. If you're lucky, they'll fight each other. If you're not, act fast to headshot the Psychos before they can get within melee range. If they manage to kill you, don't panic; they have very little health and are easy to eliminate with your dying breath, granting you an HP-restoring second wind.

LADY FINGER

DAMAGE	11
ACCURACY	91.2
FIRE RATE	4.6
MAGAZINE	2
ELEMENT	None

Omnia vincit amor

+100% Critical Hit Damage

-48% Recoil Reduction

+47% Accuracy

DON'T STICKY THE PSYCHOS
STICKY GRENADES ARE GREAT, JUST DON'T USE THEM ON THE PSYCHOS; YOU WOULDN'T WANT A PSYCHO CHARGING AT YOU, LET ALONE ONE WITH EXPLOSIVES ATTACHED TO HIM.

—JASON REISS, LEVEL DESIGNER

3 GOT GRENADES?

LEVEL 2

- ☐ *Grenade Purchased (1)*

Client: T.K. Baha

Buy at least one grenade, then return to T.K. Baha

Good news! I just heard Marcus reopened his weapon vendor in Fyrestone! Before you go after Nine-Toes, you gotta get yourself some grenades. I'm so happy you killed them skags that I'd just hand you some, but I don't have any left after my last fishin' trip. So head over to Fyrestone and buy some grenades. Then come on back.

REWARDS: 48 XP

4 NINE-TOES: TAKE HIM DOWN

LEVEL 4

- ☐ *Barricade destroyed (1)*
- ☐ *Gun stash found (1)*
- ☐ *Nine-Toes killed (1)*

Client: T.K. Baha

Destroy the barricade, enter Skag Gully, and kill Nine-Toes

Nine-Toes is in Skag Gully, but I barricaded the nearest entrance when the skags started actin' up. I rigged it with explosives, just in case I ever wanted to get back in. "Always plan ahead," I say. Once you're in, look for my wife's grave. It so happens that I stashed one of her favorite guns behind the grave marker. Use it to kill Nine-Toes. She would've wanted it that way.

REWARDS: 2,880 XP

PREPARE TO BATTLE NINE-TOES

Nine-Toes's lair is guarded by strong Bandit Thugs with shields that you must blast through, so this might be a good time to dig into your grenade supply. You can always replenish them at a nearby pair of vending machines and save your progress at a New-U pole. Whether or not you then go on to face Nine-Toes is up to you; a level 5 or 6 character should have a decent shot of bringing him down, but it won't be easy. If you feel under-leveled, travel up the hills to the northwest to battle higher-level skags and maybe even earn some useful loot in the process.

There are only a few guards in Nine-Toes' hideout, but they can be tough to get past with so little useable cover. Use your special abilities to pound them (Berserker), sneak past them (Siren), hit them from above (Hunter), or create some cover and an auto-firing companion (Soldier). Make sure to hang out afterward until your ability's cooldown phase ends—you'll want it fully charged for Nine Toes.

⚙ **BE PREPARED**
MAKE SURE THAT YOU'RE LEVEL 5 BEFORE FIGHTING NINE TOES. YOUR ACTION SKILL MAKES ALL THE DIFFERENCE IN THE WORLD DURING THAT FIGHT.
—CHRIS BROCK, DEVELOPER

5 NINE-TOES: TIME TO COLLECT

LEVEL 7

☐ *Return to Zed (1)*

Client: T.K. Baha
Go to Dr. Zed in Fyrestone and collect your reward

Good job killin' Nine-Toes, but I sure as hell ain't gonna pay you for it. You'll want to go back to Zed in Fyrestone. He oughta have a big ol' payday for you, seein' as you did his dirty work and saved his ass.

REWARDS: 108 XP + $2,210 + GRENADE MOD

6 JOB HUNTING

LEVEL 7

☐ *Return to Zed (1)*

Client: Dr. Zed
Check the bounty board in Fyrestone for your next job.

I think you're gonna make a real stir here on Pandora. If you're lookin' for more work, go check the bounty board and see what's available.

REWARDS: 108 XP

LEVELING UP IN THE SKAG HILLS

The hills northwest of Nine-Toes' lair are populated primarily by level 4 Skag Whelps and Rakks. Hit the winged rakks in the air to get their attention, then prepare to nail them with a shotgun blast when they swoop down to retaliate. Don't advance until the coast is clear, or you'll provoke even more skag attacks while the rakks are still striking from above.

Cross the stone bridge carefully—there are loads of skags on the other side—and make sure you don't fall off while you're backing up! Expect to find great gear in the **red chest** at the end, but you may not be leveled up high enough to use it yet. When you're done looting, drop off the south side of the stone bridge and continue in that direction to get back to Nine-Toes.

KILL NINE-TOES AND HIS LITTLE PETS, TOO

Bring a good mid- to long-range weapon with you before dropping into Nine-Toes' lair, and be ready to use it—you can get a few solid shots off while Nine-Toes casually saunters onto the battlefield. When he starts returning fire, you'll need to step things up, because his mighty pet skags Digit and Pinky soon emerge from the pipes to either side of Nine-Toes.

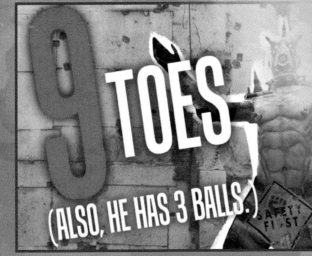

9 TOES

(ALSO, HE HAS 3 BALLS.)

It's a good idea to finish off Nine-Toes before you turn to his pets, since it's tough to fight them effectively while he's still shooting at you. Use your special abilities to hammer Nine-Toes with everything you've got from the very start of the fight.

Soldiers should throw down a turret and Hunters should make heavy use of their Bloodwings. Berserkers can charge in, enter Berserker Mode, and pound the tar out of Nine-Toes. Things are a bit tougher for Sirens, who just have to trade shots and grenades with Nine Toes until Pinky and Digit are upon them. At that point, Phasewalk to get behind Nine Toes and resume the battle at close range by emptying a gun into the back of his head. Since you'll be firing with wild abandon, a low-recoil weapon with a high fire-rate is ideal here. If you don't have a combat rifle or SMG with these properties, a repeater like the Lady Finger will do the job nicely.

When Nine-Toes is down, turn your attention to his pets. Pinky has more hit points, but shooting her in the head elicits a roar, providing you with a good shot at a critical. That won't work as well against the heavily-armored Digit, so just take whatever shots you can get. If you have any grenades left, save 'em for Digit.

KING
OF CLAP

LEVEL	HEALTH	XP	WEAK POINT	RESISTANCES	SHIELDS
5	5	10	Head	None	Yes

Nine-Toes is completely insane, and loves his two pet skags just a little too much. He stages frequent raids on Fyrestone, hoping to curry favor with Sledge. He acquired the name one morning when he woke up missing a toe, with no idea how or why it was cut off. He suspects that Bone Head took it to use in his voodoo ceremonies.

THE CLIPPER

DAMAGE	8
ACCURACY	71.7
FIRE RATE	9.0
MAGAZINE	20
ELEMENT	Fire x1

Highly effective vs. Flesh

Chance to light enemies on fire

Don't drop it...might lose a toe.

+7% Fire Rate

DIGIT

LEVEL	HEALTH	XP	WEAK POINT	RESISTANCES	SHIELDS
4	4	7.5	Mouth	None	None

PINKY

LEVEL	HEALTH	XP	WEAK POINT	RESISTANCES	SHIELDS
4	5	7.5	Mouth	None	None

CLAPTRAP DANCE OFF

MOP UP AND GET PAID

Once defeated, Nine-Toes always drops his personal weapon, a flame-type repeater known as "The Clipper (see weapon details on previous page)." The "Don't drop it… might lose a toe" notation refers to an unlisted, but significant, melee damage bonus. You may find other weapons near the remains of all three bosses, and you'll always find a silver weapons locker and a **red chest** in the area surrounding the boss battlefield.

When you're done looting, return to T.K. for a bunch of XP and the "Nine-Toes: Time To Collect" quest, which is really just an invitation to shake Dr. Zed down for another reward. The good doctor will give you a little over $2,000 and the Explosive MIRV Grenade Mod, which makes your grenades scatter other grenades that cause a second, wider explosion. It's good to equip this when fighting large groups of foes, but it tends to have weaker Grenade Damage than other mods, making it less effective against bosses.

Dr. Zed also offers the Job Hunting quest, which you can complete by walking a few steps to the south and taking a quick peek at the Fyrestone bounty board.

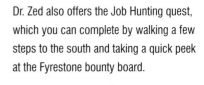

1-3 (OPTIONAL): SECRETS OF SCAG GULLY

Now that the Fyrestone bounty board is open, you can pursue three different quests. But "Catch-A-Ride" is going to lead you straight to a tough level 10 quest, and the even-harder "Hidden Journal: Arid Badlands" quest can't be completed without first finishing the Catch-A-Ride quest tree. That leaves "T.K. Has More Work" as your best option, since it leads to three optional Skag Gully quests that are both the easiest and most lucrative options at this point in the game.

QUESTS:

1 T.K. Has More Work (optional)
2 T.K.'s Life And Limb (optional)
3 Why Are They Here? (optional)
4 By The Seeds Of Your Pants (optional)

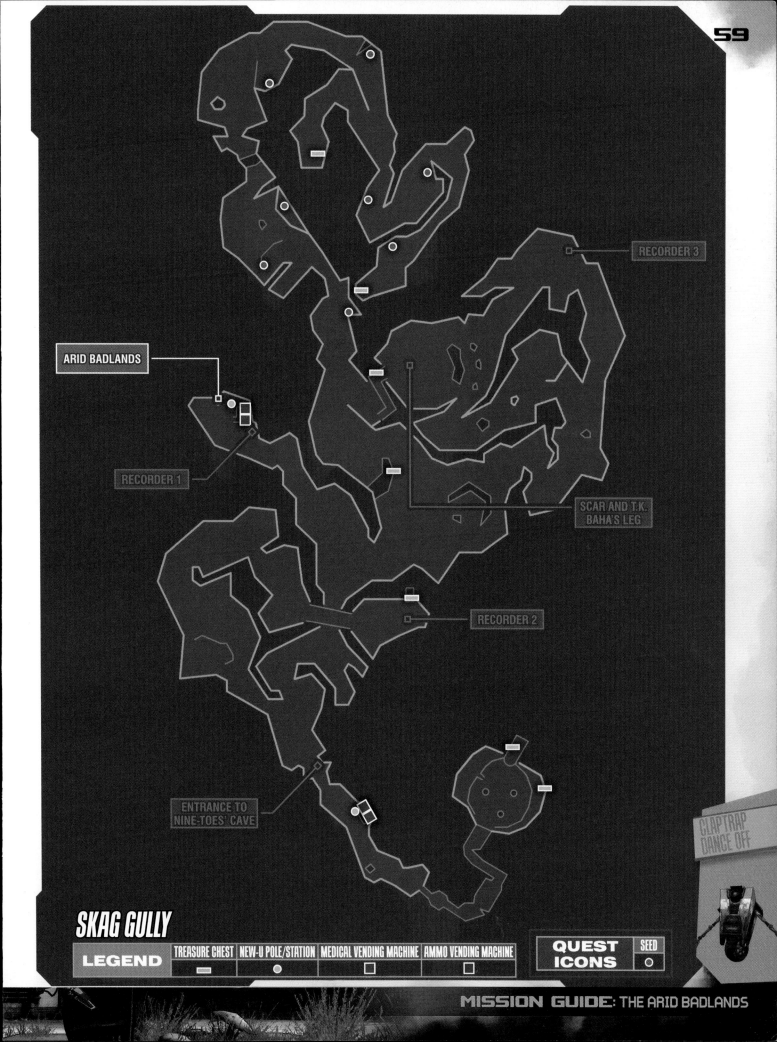

RECORDER 3

ARID BADLANDS

RECORDER 1

SCAR AND T.K.
BAHA'S LEG

RECORDER 2

ENTRANCE TO
NINE-TOES' CAVE

SKAG GULLY

LEGEND	TREASURE CHEST	NEW-U POLE/STATION	MEDICAL VENDING MACHINE	AMMO VENDING MACHINE	QUEST ICONS	SEED
	▬	●	☐	☐		○

CLAPTRAP
DANCE OFF

HEAR T.K.'S LATEST GRIEVANCES

To open this quest thread, accept the "T.K. Has More Work" quest from the Fyrestone Bounty Board, and then visit T.K. to complete it and unlock two new quest options. "T.K.'s Life And Limb" is the easier of the two, and the only normal-difficulty quest for level 6-7 characters. But since "By the Seeds of Your Pants" takes place in the same area, you might as well accept that, too, and accomplish as much of it as you can.

As soon as you arrive at Skag Gully, you'll find a **Bandit Data Recorder** just past the vending machines. This device triggers the "Why Are They Here?" quest, which you can pursue concurrent to the other two.

GRAB RECORDER #2 AND SOME NEW GUNS

Let's begin by tracking down Recorder #2, which you may have already noticed (but been unable to collect) near the red chest on the cliffs north of Nine-Toes's hideout. To reach it, head right (south) at the first fork, traveling under the stone archway. Pass T.K.'s wife's grave, and make a hard right where you see the sign promising "trouble" to the left. You can proceed slowly, taking out each skag and rakk in turn so that they can't later strike you from behind, or you can make a mad dash to the **recorder**, loot the **red chest**, and dive off the mountain to avoid further pursuit.

While you're in the neighborhood, swing by Nine-Toes' lightly defended lair to raid all of his weapon chests a second time. If you've exited the game and restarted since the last time you were here, the chests should all be full of new loot. Nine-Toes will also be back, but he's a cinch to beat without his pets.

HEAD NORTH TO FIND RECORDER #3

After dropping back down to the Skag Gully's central crossroads, follow the waypoint north. Stick as close to the east wall as you can to avoid provoking unnecessary encounters.

Keep an eye out for new Spitter Skags, which can vomit up blobs of corrosive goo. Strafe from side to side as you fire at them to easily sidestep their projectiles. Spitter Skags are also especially weak to melee attacks, so a good smack in the face with your melee damage-boosting Clipper will make a serious impact. At levels 6 and 7, the enemies you'll face here are much tougher than the ones in the southern part of the map, so you must proceed slowly. Look to the sky and reach for your shotgun as soon as you hear the telltale screech of the rakks.

Keep following the east wall until you reach a small tent with two corpses and the third **recorder**. This concludes the "Why Are They Here?" quest, but unless you're on death's doorstep, you shouldn't run back to the Fyrestone Bounty Board to report it. You're only a few steps away from a great sniping spot for the "T.K.'s Life And Limb" quest.

1 T.K. HAS MORE WORK

LEVEL 10

- ☐ *T.K. Baha visited (1)*

Client: T.K. Baha
Go see T.K. Baha

Hey stranger! If you're still alive, I've got some more work for you! Come see me and I'll fill you in.

REWARDS: 360 XP + $776

2 T.K.'S LIFE AND LIMB

LEVEL 7

- ☐ *Scar killed (1)*
- ☐ *T.K. Baha's Leg (1)*

Client: T.K. Baha
Kill Scar in Skag Gully and return T.K. Baha's Prosthetic Leg.

I used to be a go-getter like you… till a skag named Scar bit my leg off. I stabbed him through the eye, but it didn't kill him! I had another go after Dr. Zed whipped up a replacement leg, but Scar got that one, too! Pulled the thing clean off, and I was barely able to drag myself home. Say, you mind getting my leg back from Scar? If you kill him while you're at it, I got a special gift for you!

REWARDS: 4,320 XP + $2,210 + UNIQUE GUN

SNIPE SCAR FROM THE RIDGE

Continue west along your mountain path. Stay close to the north wall to end up at the tip of the jagged ledge. From this perch, look down on the wide basin where Scar makes his home and snipe at him with long-range weapons. A weapon with elemental properties is ideal—the fire, acid, or electricity will eat away at Scar while you're lining up your next shots. If you're lucky, you can snipe Scar out of the game without him ever realizing where your shots are coming from! However, if things go horribly wrong and you end up having to battle Scar at close range, back away from him while he runs at you (to stay outside the range of his area attack), and circle around him when he stops (so he can't hit you with his breath attack). Keep a steady offense going, as Scar will regenerate its lost health if you wait too long between shots.

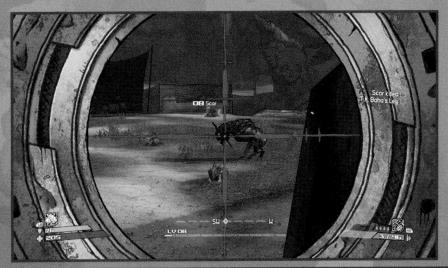

SCAR

LEVEL	HEALTH	XP	WEAK POINT	RESISTANCES	SHIELDS
8	8	16	Mouth	None	None

Scar is T.K. Baha's arch nemesis. In their first encounter, the skag bit T.K.'s leg off. T.K. later went back for revenge, and then Scar ate his new prosthetic leg.

When Scar falls, it drops T.K.'s leg, along with a nice spread of cash and random items. Snipe out any other skags and prepare to face several additional waves when you go to recover the loot. You'll also find a **red chest** at the west end of Scar's basin. From here, you can either dash down the ramp and run south to get back on the trail to the Arid Badlands, or continue north in search of T.K.'s Bladeflower Seeds.

COLLECT BLADEFLOWER SEEDS #1-3

The skags that guard the gully's northern loop are much tougher than the ones you've faced elsewhere, and range from level 8 to 10. Equip a sniper rifle and shotgun to your D-pad slots. This allows you to snipe skags when you have the high ground and quickly switch to your shotgun when they catch up to you. Make sure to set "By The Seeds Of Your Pants" as your active quest so the waypoints will lead you straight to each seed. Note that you'll need to take a long leap from the northern ledge to grab the third seed.

The steep ledge northwest of the third seed is an ideal sniping spot, and you'll need the advantage to deal with the level 10 Badass Skag that emerges after the first few skag fatalities. The Badass Skag has a ton of hit points, so blast it in the head, then hold your fire for around five seconds. It should then open its mouth and roar at you, leaving itself vulnerable to a pentuple-damage critical hit.

MISSION TAGS

3 BY THE SEEDS OF YOUR PANTS
LEVEL 9

☐ *Bloodflower Seed (8)*

Client: T.K. Baha
Gather Bladeflower Seeds and return to T.K. Baha

I'll only survive the winter if I can plant my crop soon enough, but I'm out of Bladeflower Seeds. I haven't been able to restock since I closed up Skag Gully. I used to get my seeds from the caves in there while I was hunting skag. Their vomit must make for amazing fertilizer. Blasted smelly piss mongers apparently are good for something. If you're willing to risk your life and personal hygiene to give a blind man a hand, I'll reward you.

REWARDS: 1,980 XP + $1,386

COLLECT BLADEFLOWER SEEDS #4-8

The fifth Bladeflower Seed offers a good position from which to snipe at the skags to the south, but it's nowhere near as safe as your previous perch. The high-level skags will quickly find you and attack from the west. A Soldier can lay down a turret to guard that flank, while a Siren can easily Phasewalk past them and take a new sniping position further west. Well-timed berserker rages and Bloodwing strikes should come in handy for the other character classes.

4 WHY ARE THEY HERE?

LEVEL 7

- ☐ *1st Data Recorder (1)*
- ☐ *2nd Data Recorder (1)*

Client: Fyrestone Bounty Board
Find two more data recorders in Skag Gully

You've discovered a beat-up data recorder dropped by the bandits. The data is too garbled to be of any use, but there may be other recorders like this in Skag Gully. Search for additional evidence, and take any you find back to the bounty board in Fyrestone.

REWARDS: 1,944 XP + $1,658 + SHIELD

Inflict as much damage as possible with your sniper rifle, then wade into the caves with a shotgun or another close-range weapon to collect two **red chests** and the final three seeds. Once you have the final chest, snipe at the enemies below, then leap off the ledge. It's an easy dash back to the Arid Badlands, where you can report your victories to T.K. Baha and the bounty board.

COLLECT YOUR SPECIAL QUEST REWARDS

In addition to the usual rewards of XP and cash, T.K. hands over the unique weapon "T.K.'s Wave" for completing "T.K.'s Life And Limb." This shotgun fires pellets in a wave pattern that spread out and ricochet off nearby objects. Its stats are a bit weaker than the shotguns found in red chests at level 9 or 10, but creative players can exploit its special properties in enclosed areas by bouncing pellets around corners. The wide spread is also great for blasting rakks. You'll also receive a solid shield with a superfast recharge rate as a reward for the "Why Are They Here?" quest.

T.K.'S WAVE	
DAMAGE	~16 x 9
ACCURACY	26.9
FIRE RATE	~1.0
MAGAZINE	6
ELEMENT	None

Ride the Wave, Dude!
Variable Recoil Reduction
+50% Critical Hit Damage

1-4 A TICKET TO RIDE

You've done all that you can in the Fyrestone area, and now it's time to see what else the Arid Badlands have to offer. There's no getting past Piss Wash gully on foot, though. Before you can rent a vehicle from the local Catch-A-Ride, you must first go after a bandit sub-commander named Bone Head to retrieve the crucial Digistruct Module.

QUESTS:

1. Catch-A-Ride
2. Bone Head's Theft
3. The Piss Wash Hurdle
4. Get A Little Blood On The Tires (optional)
5. Return to Zed
6. Sledge: Meet Shep

FOLLOW THE TRAIL OF THE DIGISTRUCT MODULE

To complete the "Catch-A-Ride" quest, just head to the Catch-A-Ride Station south of Fyrestone and use the terminal at its central pole. This completes the quest, but it won't get the station up and running, since an ungentlemanly fellow by the name of Bone Head has swiped its valuable Digistruct Module. Thus begins your next quest: "Bone Head's Theft." Most of the enemies on this quest are around level 10, so if you're attempting this immediately after beating Nine-Toes, you're in for an excruciatingly tough fight. You may want to complete some or all of the quests in Section 1-3 first.

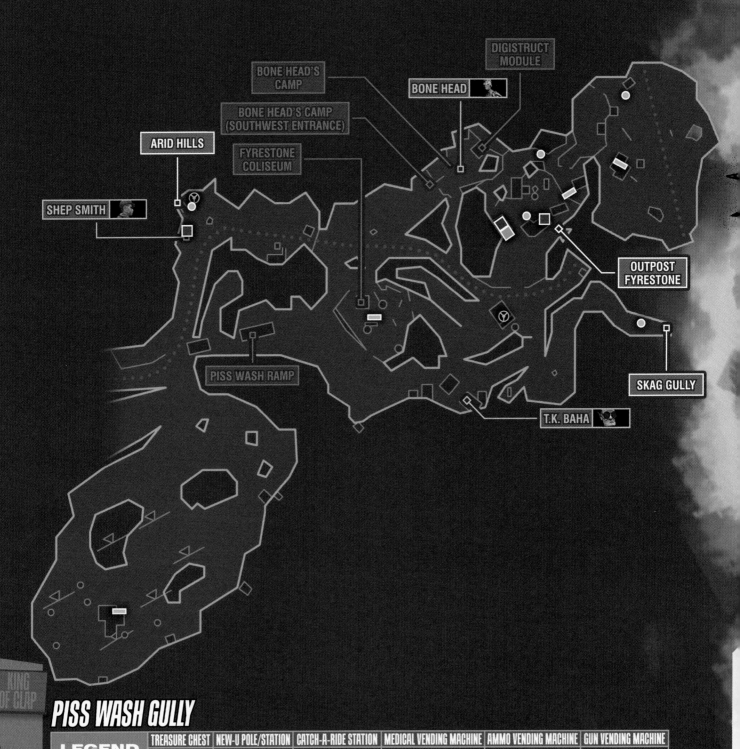

PISS WASH GULLY

LEGEND	TREASURE CHEST	NEW-U POLE/STATION	CATCH-A-RIDE STATION	MEDICAL VENDING MACHINE	AMMO VENDING MACHINE	GUN VENDING MACHINE

ASSASSINATE BONE HEAD

There are two approaches to Bone Head's camp, and it would be worth your while to take the long way around by continuing northwest past the thin canyon to approach the lair from the southwest instead.

Before you approach the corrugated-metal walls to Bone Head's camp, pick off any nearby skags so they can't come at you from behind.

Grab some cover at the entrance to the compound (kneeling behind one of those tires works great) to get some crystal-clear shots at Bone Head and his men as they circle their camp. If you have a good sniper rifle and a steady hand, you can punch through Bone Head's shields and bring him down with a few critical headshots. If you can't quite finish the job from your sniping position, turn to your special ability—an automated turret or bloodthirsty falcon can dish out the final points of damage, and a Siren can always Phasewalk up to him for a long spray of headshots from a fast-firing weapon.

BONE HEAD

LEVEL	HEALTH	XP	WEAK POINT	RESISTANCES	SHIELDS
11	6	12	Head	None	Yes

Bone Head is one of Sledge's lieutenants, and has had a long-standing rivalry with Nine-Toes. Sledge eventually grew tired of their bickering, and issued a challenge to *them*: Whoever took over Fyrestone and killed the other would prove themselves worthy to become Sledge's right-hand man. Bone Head is also rumored to practice voodoo.

When defeated, Bone Head drops his personal weapon, the highly-accurate Bone Shredder SMG. It's great at shredding foes, but be careful—it will shred your SMG ammo supply just as quickly. A further search of the area reveals the Digistruct Module in a **silver chest**, and one of the recorders from the "Hidden Journal: The Arid Badlands" quest. (We'll get to that quest later.)

BONE SHREDDER

DAMAGE	10 x 2
ACCURACY	80.6
FIRE RATE	8.3
MAGAZINE	60
ELEMENT	None

The lead wind blows

2.4x Weapon Zoom

CLAPTRAP DANCE OFF

1 CATCH-A-RIDE

LEVEL 7

☐ *Catch-A-Ride used (1)*

Client: Scooter
Find and use the Catch-A-Ride Station outside of Fyrestone

Hey, this here's Scooter. If there's anyone out around Fyrestone, I'd sure appreciate you givin' the Catch-A-Ride a try. It's just south of town and it ain't seen activity for months. I doubt it even works anymore, what with Nine-Toes and Sledge and all the other bandits on the rise.

REWARDS: 108 XP

2 BONE HEAD'S THEFT

LEVEL 10

☐ *Bone Head killed (1)*
☐ *Digistruct Module (1)*

Client: Scooter
Get the Digistruct Module from Bone Head

Damned if the Catch-A-Ride station ain't totally busted. Diagnostics report the primary Digistruct Module is missing. Without it, that station won't do diddly. I'd hit up Bone Head and his gang. They got a camp just down the road a bit, tucked away next to Fyrestone. I bet those sons of bitches took it. Get the Digistruct Module back from them and reinstall it into this station.

REWARDS: 4,320 XP + $1,552

CATCH A RIDE AT THE CATCH-A-RIDE

Bring your Digistruct Module back to Scooter's Catch-A-Ride station, and the console will update with the new "The Piss Wash Hurdle" quest. Examine the Catch-A-Ride console again to bring up the vehicle-generation menu. This enables you to create a Runner in one of eight colors (each has a slightly different design) and with either a mounted machine gun or rocket launcher. You can also teleport straight to the driver's seat or, to handle the shooting in a multiplayer game, to the gunner's seat.

Before you head out to the Piss Wash Hurdle, exit your Runner to check the bounty board at Fyrestone and accept the "Get A Little Blood On The Tires" quest. All you have to do to complete this one is run down 10 or more enemies of any type. Vehicular manslaughter causes a tiny hit to your Runner's shields, but it's easier and more fun than trying to line up a shot with your mounted weapons. Sadly, this fun does come at a slight cost; you earn less XP when you kill enemies with vehicles than you do for gunning them down on foot.

LEAP PISS WASH AND OPEN THE GATE

Drive west down the clearly marked road until you reach a locked gate. Take a detour south, where you'll spot a long ramp that stretches above Piss Wash Gully. Straighten out your Runner and hit the ramp straight down the middle, giving yourself a turbo boost before you fly off the lip. You should land safely on the other side, in a part of the map you could never reach on foot.

The entirety of the Arid Badlands is now open to you. Before you go exploring, though, head northeast up the road to reach the other side of that locked gate. The ramp is a one-way affair, and you'll need the gate open if you want to return to Fyrestone to report the completion of your quests.

BETTER THAN ROCKETS
SOMETIMES, IN A VEHICLE, A MOUNTED MACHINE GUN IS A BETTER OPTION THAN A ROCKET LAUNCHER. CONSTANT, SMALL DAMAGE IS OFTEN BETTER THAN PERIODIC, LARGE DAMAGE.

- CHRIS BROCK, DEVELOPER

Run down the guards at the gate and use your mounted turret to hit any survivors who have found a place to hide. Then get out and flip the glowing switch on the right side of the gate. This concludes "The Piss Wash Hurdle," and commences a new mission, "Return to Zed." Completing that is as easy as driving through the gate back to Fyrestone.

MEET YOUR NEWEST CLIENT

Your reward for the "Return to Zed" quest includes an upgrade to your Storage Deck that allows you to equip a third weapon, this time to the left direction of your control pad. Speak to Dr. Zed again for your next mission, "Sledge: Meet Shep," the first step on a quest tree that will end in a battle with the true bandit boss of the Arid Badlands. While you're in town, swing by the bounty board to report the completion of "Get A Little Blood On The Tires" and pick up a new quest, "Shock Crystal Harvest."

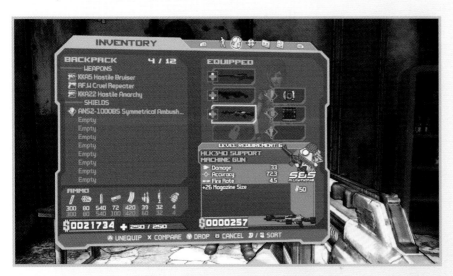

MISSION TAGS

3 THE PISS WASH HURDLE

LEVEL 10

- Runner driven (1)
- Piss Wash jumped (1)
- Gate switch found (1)

Client: Scooter
Jump over Piss Wash gully and open the bandits' gate

Y'all got one last hurdle to escape Fyrestone. Sledge's bandits put up a gate across the main road. The controls are on the far side. To reach them controls, ya need to get yourself a Runner from that there Catch-A-Ride, then drive up the ramp and jump the gully we call "Piss Wash." once you're over, attack 'em from behind and open that gate!

REWARDS: 720 XP

4 GET A LITTLE BLOOD ON THE TIRES

LEVEL 10

- Roadkill (10)

Client: Fyrestone Bounty Board
Roadkill enemies with the Runner vehicle

Scooter's lettin' you drive his Runners, huh? You know what's fun? Roadkillin'. Runnin' over every living thing that's stupid enough to wander in front of your grille. I bet you're squeamish, though. I bet good money you haven't got the guts to go roadkillin' yourself.

REWARDS: 1,152 XP + $2,329

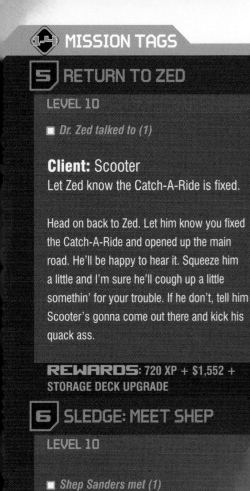

5 RETURN TO ZED

LEVEL 10

■ *Dr. Zed talked to (1)*

Client: Scooter
Let Zed know the Catch-A-Ride is fixed.

Head on back to Zed. Let him know you fixed the Catch-A-Ride and opened up the main road. He'll be happy to hear it. Squeeze him a little and I'm sure he'll cough up a little somethin' for your trouble. If he don't, tell him Scooter's gonna come out there and kick his quack ass.

REWARDS: 720 XP + $1,552 + STORAGE DECK UPGRADE

6 SLEDGE: MEET SHEP

LEVEL 10

■ *Shep Sanders met (1)*

Client: Dr. Zed
Talk to Shep Sanders near the crossroads.
I think you're ready to go after Sledge now. You'll probably find him in the old Headstone Mine, but you can't just waltz in there. The place is locked down tight. If there's any way to get inside, Shep Sanders knows it. He was a foreman for Dahl until they pulled out and left him here. You'll find him near the crossroads, keeping an eye on the bandits.

REWARDS: 144 XP

Drive back to the west through the newly opened gate. You'll come to a small shack with a vending machine and a Mr. Shep Smith leaning against the wall. In addition to the next main quest, "Sledge: The Mine Key," Shep offers you two optional quests: "Get The Flock Outta Here," and "Braking Wind."

1-5 RECLAIMING THE ZEPHYR SUBSTATION

In addition to the first part of the next major storyline quest ("Sledge: The Mine Key"), Shep offers you another pair of quests that take place in the same small area: The Zephyr Substation, south of his current position. You'll also find the third Hidden Journal there, allowing you to kill several birds with one stone by pursuing all four quests at once.

QUESTS:

1. Hidden Journal: The Arid Badlands (optional)
2. Sledge: The Mine Key
3. Get the Flock Outta Here (optional)
4. Braking Wind (optional)

PICK UP THREE JOURNALS ON THE WAY OUT OF TOWN

If you haven't picked up the first three **Hidden Journals** yet, now is a good time to do so. The first one is along the north wall of Bone Head's bandit camp, and the second is near the **red chest** in the smaller bandit camp southwest of Fyrestone. The fourth (in chronological order) is atop the watchtower on the west side of Sledge's gate (the one you opened during "The Piss Wash Hurdle" quest). What happened to the third? It's in the Zephyr Substation, along with all of the targets in the "Sledge: The Mine Key," "Get the Flock Out of Here," and "Braking Wind" quests.

RUN DOWN THE ZEPHYR SUBSTATION RAKKS

To find the Zephyr Substation, drive due south from Shep Smith's shack; when the road turns west, follow the mountains to the southeast instead. You eventually encounter the hive that's generating the rakks Shep wants killed. You don't even need to get out of your Runner; just drive back and forth alongside the hive and all the Rakks will dive bomb you in a futile attempt to protect their home. Your Runner may take a few hits, but it will hold strong while the rakks end up splattered all over your grille. That's one quest down!

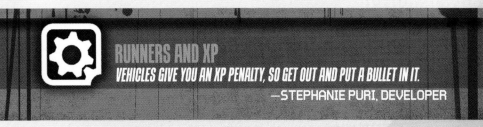

RUNNERS AND XP
VEHICLES GIVE YOU AN XP PENALTY, SO GET OUT AND PUT A BULLET IN IT.
—STEPHANIE PURI, DEVELOPER

THE DAHL HEADLAND

LOST CAVE

JOURNAL
DAY 172

HEADSTONE MINE

PISS WASH GULLY

LEGEND	TREASURE CHEST	NEW-U POLE/STATION	CATCH-A-RIDE STATION	MEDICAL VENDING MACHINE	AMMO VENDING MACHINE	GUN VENDING MACHINE
	▬	●	Ⓨ	☐	☐	◼

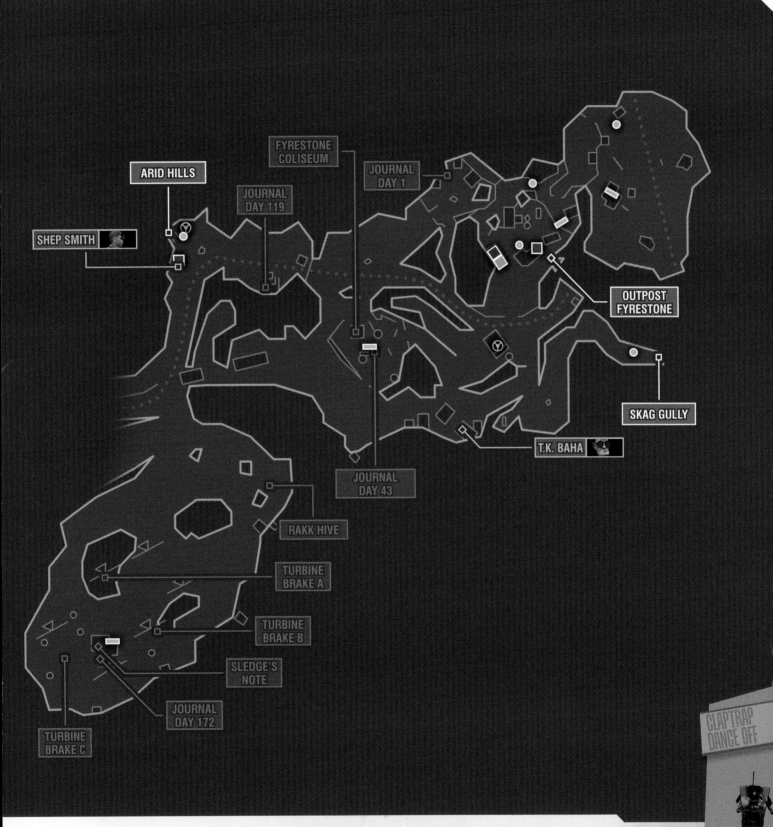

ARID HILLS

FYRESTONE COLISEUM

JOURNAL DAY 119

JOURNAL DAY 1

SHEP SMITH

OUTPOST FYRESTONE

SKAG GULLY

T.K. BAHA

JOURNAL DAY 43

RAKK HIVE

TURBINE BRAKE A

TURBINE BRAKE B

SLEDGE'S NOTE

JOURNAL DAY 172

TURBINE BRAKE C

CLAPTRAP DANCE OFF

LEVEL 13
- ☐ *Journal Day 1 (1)*
- ☐ *Journal Day 43 (1)*
- ☐ *Journal Day 76 (1)*
- ☐ *Journal Day 119 (1)*
- ☐ *Journal Day 172 (1)*

Client: Fyrestone Bounty Board
Download 5 Log Entries from Data Recorders in the Arid Badlands

This is Patricia Tannis, calling for anyone with two brain cells to run together. I hid five of my Data Recorders in the Arid Badlands, but now I've decided I want them back. Listen to each one, and your ECHO device will record them. Once you have all five recordings, upload them to the bounty board.

REWARDS: 2,699 XP + $5,454

2 SLEDGE: THE MINE KEY

LEVEL 10
- ☐ *Mine Gate Key (1)*

Client: Shep Sanders
Go to Zephyr Substation and get the Mine Key

You want to kick Sledge out of Headstone Mine, huh? Good for you. I think you're crazy, but I'll give you a hand. You need the key. Last I checked, there was one down in the Zephyr Substation office. Of course, the bandits aren't going to make it easy for you.

REWARDS: 1,440 XP

RETAKE THE ZEPHYR SUBSTATION

Set your active quest to "Sledge: The Mine Key" and follow the waypoint southwest to the Zephyr Substation's main office. The compound is heavily guarded, but that's what your mounted weapons are for. Greet the soldiers that come pouring out of the front door with a rocket or stream of machinegun fire, then use your auto-target button to ferret out the rest of the nearby soldiers. Blow 'em away or run 'em down—it's a good time either way.

When you step out of the Runner to explore the area on foot, new enemies appear from the surrounding tents, but it's difficult for them to surround you if you've already slaughtered the first batch. Before entering the building, circle it to ensure there aren't any bandits alive on the roof; if you go inside before clearing the roof, they'll shoot you through a hole in the ceiling. If you can't get a clear shot, detonate the giant propane tanks from a safe distance—that should flush them out.

After opening the door to the substation, quickly sweep the room for soldiers, then pick up the note that Sledge left for you on the desk. That will conclude the "Sledge: The Mine Key" quest and trigger "Sledge: To The Safe House." You'll also get a message from your Claptrap, informing you that several new optional quests are available at the Fyrestone Bounty Board.

REACTIVATE THE ZEPHYR WINDMILLS

Step back outside and jump from the dumpster to the overhang to the substation roof. There's a **red chest** in one corner and the missing third **Journal** in a garbage incinerator.

Next, make "Braking Wind" your active quest and follow the waypoints to the three windmills. Pull a switch on each to complete the quest. That should leave you with a green checkmark by every quest except for "Hidden Journal: The Arid Badlands."

RECOVER THE LAST HIDDEN JOURNAL

Find your Runner and drive it back the way you came, but make a hard left just before you would rejoin the main road. Make "Hidden Journal: The Arid Badlands" your active quest and drive southwest toward the waypoint that marks the final journal entry. You'll find the area defended by tough level 12 bandits and a swarm of rakks—these beasts are perfectly capable of destroying your Runner when working in concert. If its shields get low, bail out so you don't get caught in the explosion, then take a position behind the giant boulder to the south, where you can refill your shields and pick off the remaining foes.

When the coast is clear, approach the three metal barrels located between the boulders—the **journal** is in their midst. Grab the **recorder** and flee south to find another Catch-A-Ride and a New-U pole outside of the nearby Headstone Mine. "Get you one," as Scooter suggests, and drive it back to Shep and the Fyrestone bounty board to report your various triumphs.

 **MISSION TAGS**

3 GET THE FLOCK OUTTA HERE

LEVEL 10

■ *Rakk killed (10)*

Client: Shep Sanders
Kill rakk, then return to Shep Sanders

There's a flock of rakk that keep flying around the wind turbines at Zephyr Substation. The bandits may have control of the turbines for now, but I plan to take them back, and in the meantime, I don't need rakk flying into the blades and damaging the equipment. So, I'm willing to pay you to eliminate the entire flock of rakk.

REWARDS: 2,880 XP + $2,329

4 BRAKING WIND

LEVEL 10

■ *Turbine Brake A released (1)*
■ *Turbine Brake B released (1)*
■ *Turbine Brake C released (1)*

Client: Shep Sanders
Release the emergency Turbine Brakes at Zephyr Substation

During one of their first raids, the bandits took over Zephyr Substation and set the emergency brakes on all the wind turbines. They tried to ransom the region's power supply, but Helena Pierce refused to negotiate. We've been running off generator power ever since. Since you're on some sort of anti-bandit crusade anyway, why not release those brakes and turn the power back on? There'll be a reward for your trouble.

REWARDS: 3,023 XP + $2,329 + SHIELD

CLAPTRAP DANCE OFF

THE SEARCH FOR SLEDGE

Upon completion of the "Sledge: The Mine Key" quest, you automatically commence "Sledge: To The Safe House." This challenging mission sends you north through the new Arid Hills area and into a large, heavily-guarded compound. It's a long way to travel, so you might as well visit the Fyrestone bounty board and pick up the optional "Scavenger: Sniper Rifle" quest to do on the way there, as well as the far tougher "The Legend Of Moe And Marley" quest to do on the way back. If you'd like to earn a bit of XP first, try some of the quests in the "Circle Of Death" tree, which we'll cover in the next section.

QUESTS:

1 Scavenger: Sniper Rifle (optional)

2 Sledge: To The Safe House

3 Claptrap Rescue: Safe House (optional)

4 The Legend of Moe and Marley (optional)

HOOF IT THROUGH THE ARID HILLS

Drive a Runner to Shep's shack, and ditch it—you'll have to do this area on foot. The entrance to the Arid Hills is just to the north.

Upon entering the hills, you discover a New-U station and a pair of vending machines. The ammo machine here sells level 2 Storage Deck Upgrades for $6,104 a piece, allowing you to further increase the amount of each type of ammunition you can hold. (Purchasing the level 1 versions is not even required; you can skip straight to level 2!) You'll also find some interesting items in Dr. Zed's vending machine, including Light Healing Kits and Light Insta-Health Vials, as well as higher-level healing shields and shields that fire off a burst of elemental damage when their energy is depleted.

OUTFIGHT THE BANDITS ON THE TRAIL

It's a long walk to the compound with the sniper rifle parts, and there isn't much loot along the way. Stronger characters can dash straight past the enemies in the southern part of the map, but weaker characters should proceed slowly, earning valuable XP from the relentless waves of enemy skags and bandits.

After passing through the pipes north of the vending machines and eliminating a few waves of skags, leap up a row of metal platforms along the west wall to avoid a second wave of skags to the east. Don't worry—you won't miss any good loot.

SNIPER RIFLE BARREL

SNIPER RIFLE STOCK

SNIPER RIFLE SIGHT

SLEDGE'S SAFEHOUSE

MOE AND MARLEY

SNIPER RIFLE BODY

ARID BADLANDS

ARID HILLS

LEGEND	TREASURE CHEST	NEW-U POLE/STATION	MEDICAL VENDING MACHINE	AMMO VENDING MACHINE
	▬	●	☐	☐

As you near the house, sneak behind it and take a running jump off of the dumpster to get onto the roof. Snipe the two enemies on the bridge far to the north, then rain bullets and grenades upon the troops surrounding the house, none of whom is capable of jumping up to challenge you directly. This new class of bandits can be a powerful bunch, but you can always just crouch on the opposite eave to let your shields regenerate when battling from a rooftop. If you're playing co-op, this position also makes it easy to safely rescue fallen partners.

CLAPTRAP DANCE OFF

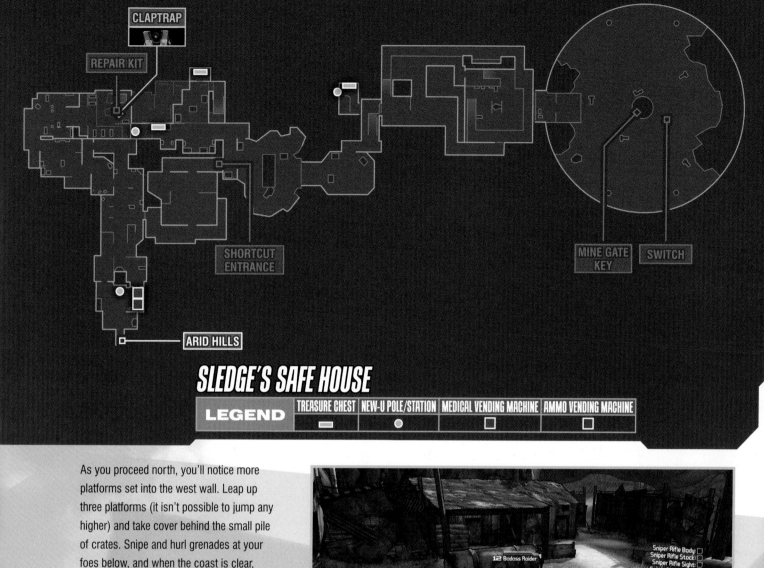

CLAPTRAP

REPAIR KIT

SHORTCUT
ENTRANCE

MINE GATE
KEY

SWITCH

ARID HILLS

SLEDGE'S SAFE HOUSE

LEGEND	TREASURE CHEST	NEW-U POLE/STATION	MEDICAL VENDING MACHINE	AMMO VENDING MACHINE
	▬	●	☐	☐

As you proceed north, you'll notice more platforms set into the west wall. Leap up three platforms (it isn't possible to jump any higher) and take cover behind the small pile of crates. Snipe and hurl grenades at your foes below, and when the coast is clear, head north, making sure to pass the New-U pole on your way out.

KING
OF CLAP

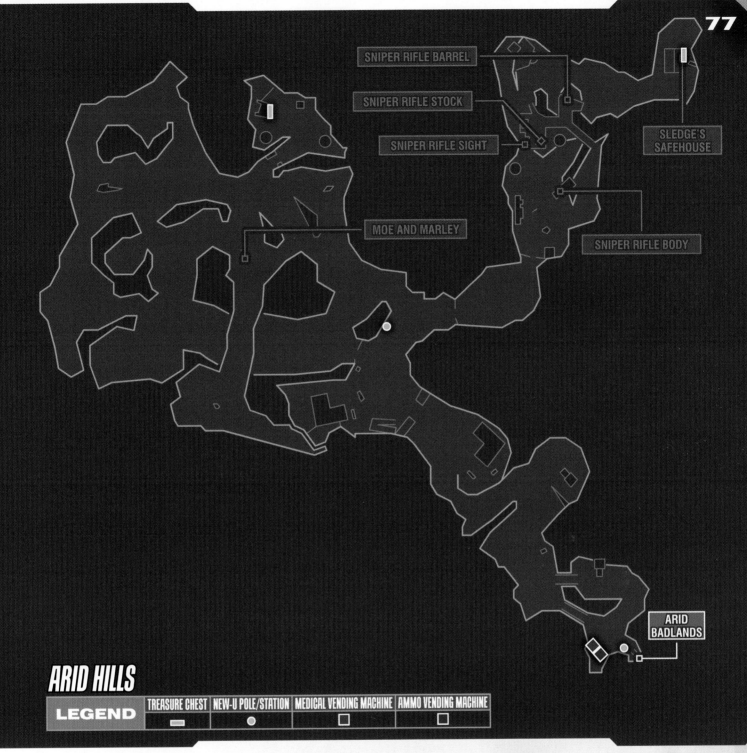

ARID HILLS

SNIPER RIFLE BARREL

SNIPER RIFLE STOCK

SNIPER RIFLE SIGHT

SLEDGE'S SAFEHOUSE

MOE AND MARLEY

SNIPER RIFLE BODY

ARID BADLANDS

LEGEND	TREASURE CHEST	NEW-U POLE/STATION	MEDICAL VENDING MACHINE	AMMO VENDING MACHINE
	▬	●	□	□

As you near the house, sneak behind it and take a running jump off of the dumpster to get onto the roof. Snipe the two enemies on the bridge far to the north, then rain bullets and grenades upon the troops surrounding the house, none of whom is capable of jumping up to challenge you directly. This new class of bandits can be a powerful bunch, but you can always just crouch on the opposite eave to let your shields regenerate when battling from a rooftop. If you're playing co-op, this position also makes it easy to safely rescue fallen partners.

CLAPTRAP DANCE OFF

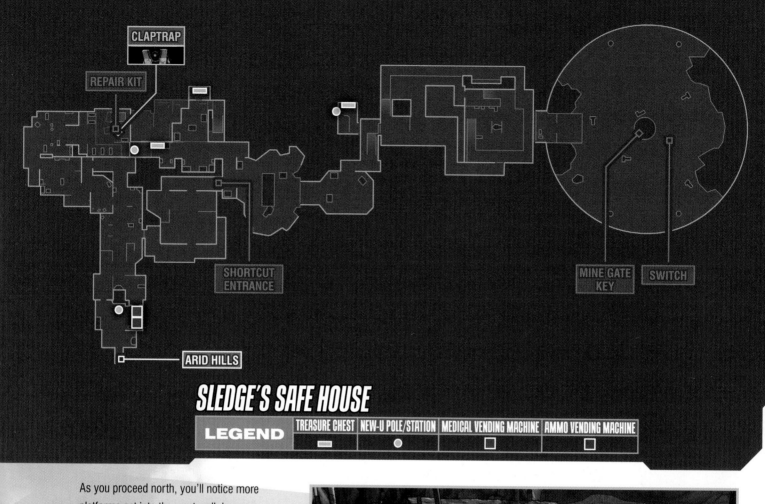

CLAPTRAP

REPAIR KIT

SHORTCUT ENTRANCE

MINE GATE KEY   SWITCH

ARID HILLS

SLEDGE'S SAFE HOUSE

LEGEND	TREASURE CHEST	NEW-U POLE/STATION	MEDICAL VENDING MACHINE	AMMO VENDING MACHINE
		●	☐	☐

As you proceed north, you'll notice more platforms set into the west wall. Leap up three platforms (it isn't possible to jump any higher) and take cover behind the small pile of crates. Snipe and hurl grenades at your foes below, and when the coast is clear, head north, making sure to pass the New-U pole on your way out.

BATTLE BANDITS FOR YOUR SNIPER RIFLE PARTS

The compound that dominates the northeast portion of the map has a scattered, confusing layout that leaves your foes plenty of positions from which to snipe at you. Rather than proceeding slowly, hunting down each individual bandit and killing all the swarms of circling rakks, make a mad dash along the western wall and into the empty shack at the end of the road. That provides you with good cover and forces your foes to approach from a single direction. When the enemy's charge is exhausted, there will still be a few foes lurking in the maze of tents and crates to the south, but you'll be able to take them one at a time as you hunt down the four sniper rifle parts.

Your waypoint won't be much use when tracking down the parts, since it points to a general location between the four, not to each part in turn.

YOU'LL FIND THE BODY ON THE BALCONY OF THE SOUTHERNMOST SHACK ON THE UPPER LEVEL.

THE STOCK IS ON A ROOFTOP ON THE WEST SIDE OF THE UPPER PLATFORM. YOU MUST LEAP FROM THE PROPANE TANK TO REACH IT.

THE SIGHT IS IN A GARBAGE PILE ON THE GROUND FLOOR. YOU'LL LAND RIGHT ON IT IF YOU FALL WEST FROM THE ROOFTOP WHERE YOU FOUND THE STOCK.

THE BARREL IS EASY TO SPOT; IT'S ON A BENCH AT THE NORTH END OF THE UPPER PLATFORM.

CLAPTRAP DANCE OFF

1 SCAVENGER: SNIPER RIFLE

LEVEL 11

- Sniper Rifle Body (1)
- Sniper Rifle Stock (1)
- Sniper Rifle Sight (1)
- Sniper Rifle Barrel (1)

Client: Fyrestone Bounty Board
Find all of the sniper rifle parts.

I used to hunt skags from the east ridge near the mine. I was working on a new sniper rifle so I could really take 'em down. I never quite finished and had to stash the parts around so the bandits wouldn't find 'em. If you retrieve the pieces, it's all yours. I need the Stock, Body, Sight, and Barrel.

REWARDS: 1,794 XP + UNIQUE WEAPON

2 SLEDGE: TO THE SAFE HOUSE

LEVEL 14

- Mine Gate Key (1)

Client: Shep Sanders
Obtain the Mine Gate Key and take it to Headstone Mine

The note you found suggests that the Mine Gate Key can be found at Sledge's Safe House to the north.

REWARDS: 5,760 XP

Bring the parts back to Fyrestone and you get an above-average Maliwan-made Fearsome Sniper Rifle as a reward. Its exact stats are random, but it typically offers a +150% Critical Hit Damage bonus and fire element x3. However, it's a long hike back to town, so you should continue on to Sledge's Safe House in the northeast if you'd rather not make an extra trip. Before entering the safe house, loop around the entrance to find a **red chest** on the roof.

INFILTRATE SLEDGE'S SAFE HOUSE

Sledge's Safehouse is an indoor maze of furniture and corridors, quite unlike the open battlefields of previous missions. The enemies are tough and well armed, so you must learn how to use the terrain to your advantage. Throw grenades through doorways and duck back behind walls so that your foes have no choice but to pursue you (and blunder straight into your SMG fire). Use sniper rifles to scan ahead—your enemies are well camouflaged, but it's possible to score a critical headshot before they even notice you if you're vigilant. While scanning for foes, keep an eye out for barrels painted with skulls. Blast them from a distance to rain corrosive goo on any nearby enemies. Most of your foes have strong shields, so you may want to have one player focus primarily on discharging shields with a shock weapon in a co-op game.

MIGHT AS WELL JUMP
JUMP ON EVERYTHING. THERE ARE CHESTS HIDDEN IN ALL KINDS OF PLACES.
— STEPHANIE PURI, DEVELOPER

There are several chain-link fences in the safe house, and experienced gamers may be tempted to use them as cover. But that won't fly in Borderlands—if light can pass through it, so can bullets.

DO A GOOD DEED FOR A GREAT REWARD

When a barricade of furniture impedes your progress on the ground floor, you must climb up a rubble ramp to an upper floor to get around it. There you'll find a New-U pole, several enemy soldiers, and a stairway back down. Once you've returned to the ground floor and cleared the area around the

stairwell, turn right (west) to discover a **red chest** and a wounded Claptrap. Speak to the Claptrap to begin the "Claptrap Rescue: Safe House" quest.

To find the Repair Kit, go back upstairs and head toward the rubble ramp. There's a room just south of the ramp with a hole in the floor and a network of ventilation shafts; you'll see the **Repair Kit** atop one of those shafts. Jump onto a nearby crate to get high enough to grab it, then bring the kit back to

the Claptrap to obtain a "Backpack SDU" Storage Deck Upgrade. This is a normal item that goes into your inventory. Once you select and use it, you'll permanently gain three inventory slots! And that's not the only the prize for this quest; follow the newly repaired Claptrap to a code-locked door, which the Claptrap opens to reveal another **red chest**!

THE CYCLE OF DEATH
ALWAYS MAKE IT A PRIORITY TO REPAIR BROKEN CLAPTRAPS. MORE BAG SPACE = MORE SOLD ITEMS = MORE MONEY = BETTER GUN.

—CHRIS BROCK, DEVELOPER

CLAPTRAP DANCE OFF

BATTLE A PSYCHO HORDE FOR THE MINE GATE KEY

After triggering the third New-U pole and looting a red chest and two grey ammo chests, proceed east. There are several routes you can take; the best is through the stairway to your left. It leads to two more **ammo chests** and a nice high catwalk where you can snipe at the handful of foes in this area. When your weapons are loaded and your shields are full, step into the massive arena at the east end of the compound— a level 15 Roid Rage Psycho awaits.

The Roid Rage Psycho can hurl grenades, throw deadly lunging punches, and pound the ground for a powerful area attack. However, all of these attacks can be avoided if you continuously circle around him from a safe distance. His weak spot is his head, but criticals only do double damage, so don't waste time lining up headshots when you could just as easily unload a shotgun blast

or burst of SMG fire at his chest. Weapons and abilities with elemental properties are particularly effective against him.

The Roid Rage Psycho enters the battlefield with a small army of Mutant Midget Psychos. Cull the herd a bit with an immediate Bloodwing strike, turret attack, or Phasewalk blast (Berserkers should probably save their special attack for the leader), but avoid the temptation to wipe them all out before you turn to the Roid Rage Psycho. It's nice to have a few Mutant Midget Psychos wandering around when you need an easy kill for a Second Wind.

When the battle is over, flip the hanging switch to raise the central pillar with the Mine Gate Key. Grab it and prepare for a long slog back to the Arid Hills; by now, most of the Safe House soldiers have respawned. On the bright side, a pair of previously locked doors have now opened, allowing you to avoid the entire northern region and cut straight from the circular room at the center of the map to the entrance. If you want an even quicker shortcut, select Exit from the Pause menu, and then reload your game. You'll resume at the New-U station at the entrance to Sledge's Safe House. As an added bonus, the **red chest** just outside will be refilled with loot!

KING OF CLAP

SLAY MOE AND MARLEY ON THE WAY BACK TO FYRESTONE

Moe and Marley roam the wilds on the western half of the Arid Hills, and are typically far enough away from each other to battle them one at a time. If you still have acceptable levels of health, ammo, and derring-do after completing the Safe House, you'll likely be able to take Moe and Marley down.

All Alpha Skags, including Moe and Marley, are heavily armored in the front, which reduces the damage dealt by conventional weapons. Their hindquarters lack this armor, so you can do significantly more damage by surrounding Alpha Skags in co-op games. Solo players can set up attacks from behind with the Soldier's turret or sneak behind the skags with the Siren's Phasewalk, but will generally have to fight face to face.

Despite his superior stats, Marley's cautious nature makes him the easier of the two. Clear away any other skags in the area, then fight him as you would a Spitter Skag, by going for a critical hit, then sidestepping when Marley opens his mouth to spit out a blob of electrified plasma. (If you're a really good shot, you can shoot the blob away in mid-air!) Marley has a ton of hit points, so attack with flaming or corrosive weapons that inflict additional damage between hits. Shock weapons are completely ineffective against him.

Moe is a more in-your-face fighter, capable of both a ring-of-flames area attack and a heavily-damaging blazing charge. Run backward while firing constantly, scoring a quick critical when Moe rears up to do his area attack, and then leaping back to avoid the damage. Flame weapons are not effective, but corrosive and shock weapons can be. However, Moe will stay close to you, so a reasonably accurate shotgun is probably the quickest way to finish him off. After reporting their deaths to the Fyrestone Bounty Board, you receive an Incendiary Artifact that, when equipped, adds fire-type properties to your character's action skill!

 **MISSION TAGS**

3 CLAPTRAP RESCUE: SAFE HOUSE

LEVEL 14

- Repair Kit (1)

Client: Claptrap
Find the Repair Kit and repair this Claptrap

You've discovered a defunct Claptrap. It looks like the bandits were pretty rough on him. Perhaps there's a Repair Kit nearby?

REWARDS: 960 XP + STORAGE DECK UPGRADE

4 THE LEGEND OF MOE AND MARLEY

LEVEL 15

- Moe killed (1)
- Marley killed (1)

Client: Fyrestone Bounty Board
Kill Moe and Marley

Rumors speak of Moe and Marley, two of the toughest skags to ever walk Pandora. I want their skulls mounted on my wall, but I'm too busy to go track them down myself. Instead, I'm offering to pay anyone to find them and take them down.

REWARDS: 6,120 XP + $4,105 + INCENDIARY ARTIFACT

Moe and Marley are both alpha skags, ruling over the same pack of skags. This dynamic isn't fully understood, but it is generally believed that Moe is "the bitch."

MARLEY	LEVEL	HEALTH	XP	WEAK POINT	RESISTANCES	SHIELDS
	16	16	48	Mouth	Shock	None

MOE	LEVEL	HEALTH	XP	WEAK POINT	RESISTANCES	SHIELDS
	16	10	30	Mouth	Fire	None

To finally complete the "Sledge: To The Safe House" quest, hold your Mine Gate Key to the lock at the Headstone Mine. In addition to triggering the mandatory "Sledge: Battle For The Badlands" quest, this also causes the Fyrestone Bounty Board to update with the "Scavenger: Combat Rifle" quest and Shep to offer the new "What Hit The Fan" mission. With the as-yet-incomplete "Shock Crystal Harvest" and "Circle of Death: Meat and Greet" already in your Mission Log, you have plenty of quest options available. Attempting some or all of these optional quests is a great way to level up and acquire new gear before entering the Headstone Mine to battle the mighty Sledge.

QUESTS:

1. What Hit The Fan (optional)
2. Scavenger: Combat Rifle (optional)
3. Circle of Death: Meat And Greet
4. Circle of Death: Round 1
5. Circle of Death: Round 2
6. Circle of Death: Final Round
7. Shock Crystal Harvest (optional)
8. Claptrap Rescue: Lost Cave (optional)

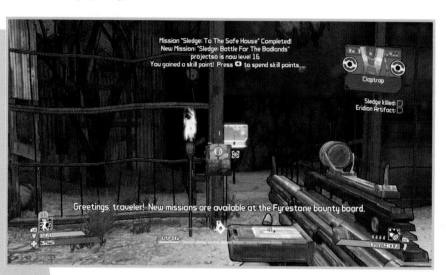

BLAST SHEP'S WINDMILL CLEAN

As you drive west down the main road of the Arid Badlands, a green windmill shimmers in the distance. Keep driving, hanging a right in the northwest part of the map to drive up a steep path just past the windmill. The ledge at the end of this path provides a perfect shot at the blades. You don't even need to get out of your Runner; just move to the turret seat, aim your machine gun or rocket launcher at the glowing green chunks of rakk poop, and fire away.

KING OF CLAP

RECOVER THE COMBAT RIFLE PARTS

To find the combat rifle parts, head back the way you came, and stop at the heavily fortified bridge that's marked by scaffolding on either side of the road. If you're playing as a Hunter (or any other character with a good sniper rifle and a steady hand), you can jump up the stairway of metal platforms that have been built into the large boulder near the entrance to the bridge, then snipe at foes from above. Even if your wavering sights make it hard to hit the distant bandits, you'll at least make your presence known, and tempt many of the bridge guardians into giving up their cover to rush your position. Wipe them out as they approach you, then pick off the remaining soldiers as you search the bridge for combat rifle parts. When you have all four, you can turn them into the Fyrestone bounty board for a randomly-generated combat rifle.

☐ AFTER CROSSING THE BRIDGE, FOLLOW THE PLATFORM THAT LEADS UP AND TO THE RIGHT, THEN FOLLOW ANOTHER THAT LEADS UP AND TO THE LEFT. YOU'LL FIND THE BODY ATOP A CRATE IN THE TENTED PAVILION.

☐ THE STOCK IS EASY TO SPOT, ATOP A CRATE ON THE BRIDGE ITSELF.

☐ AFTER CROSSING THE BRIDGE, FOLLOW THE PLATFORM UP AND TO THE RIGHT, PASS THROUGH THE SHACK, THEN FOLLOW ANOTHER PLATFORM UP TO A SHACK WITH A RED CHEST. AFTER HELPING YOURSELF TO THE HIGH-LEVEL LOOT, LOOK FOR THE SIGHT BEHIND THE SHACK.

☐ AFTER CROSSING THE BRIDGE, FOLLOW THE PLATFORM BELOW AND TO THE RIGHT, WHICH TAKES YOU STRAIGHT TO THE BARREL.

1.7 MISSION TAGS

1 WHAT HIT THE FAN

LEVEL 13

■ *Droppings removed (6)*

Client: Shep Sanders

Shoot the rakk droppings off of the wind turbine in Howling Defile

All of the wind turbines are functioning, except for the one in Howling Defile. For some reason, the rakk always flock over that one, so the whole thing is covered in rakk droppings. The turbine blades won't even turn! I'm offering a cash reward to anyone who goes out and shoots all that crap off.

REWARDS: 2,699 XP + $4,363

2 SCAVENGER: COMBAT RIFLE

LEVEL 15

■ *Combat Rifle Body (1)*
■ *Combat Rifle Stock (1)*
■ *Combat Rifle Sight (1)*
■ *Combat Rifle Barrel (1)*

Client: Fyrestone Bounty Board

Find all of the combat rifle parts

I was working on a custom rifle. I didn't want the bandits to get a hold of my design so I dismantled it and scattered the components around. If you find all of these components, I can reassemble the weapon for you. Bring me the Body, Stock, Sight, and Barrel.

REWARDS: 2,346 XP + COMBAT RIFLE

CLAPTRAP DANCE OFF

THE DAHL HEADLAND

RAKK-POOP WINDMILL

WINDMILL FIRING POINT

CIRCLE OF DEATH

RADE ZAYBEN

COMBAT RIFLE SIGHT

COMBAT RIFLE STOCK

LOST CAVE

COMBAT RIFLE BARREL

COMBAT RIFLE BODY

HEADSTONE MINE

MINE GATE

KING OF CLAP

PISS WASH GULLY

LEGEND	TREASURE CHEST	NEW-U POLE/STATION	CATCH-A-RIDE STATION	MEDICAL VENDING MACHINE	AMMO VENDING MACHINE	GUN VENDING MACHINE
	▭	●	Ⓨ	☐	☐	▣

BANDIT CAMP
REPAIR KIT
ARID BADLANDS
BANDIT CAMP
CLAPTRAP

LOST CAVE

QUEST ICONS	CRYSTAL ◇

LEGEND	TREASURE CHEST ▭	NEW-U POLE/STATION ●	MEDICAL VENDING MACHINE ▢	AMMO VENDING MACHINE ▢

SURVIVE THE CIRCLE OF DEATH

Just across from the bridge, a large beast skull and a sign with two arrows mark the entrance to a deep cavern. Inside you'll find a New-U pole, three vending machines, and Rade Zayben, your target for the "Circle of Death: Meat And Greet" quest. Rade offers you the "Circle of Death: Round 1" quest, which pits you against a swarm of level 10 and 11 skags, typically led by a level-13 Alpha Skag. That should be an easy win at this point in the game.

Emerge victorious and Rade offers the "Circle of Death: Round 2" quest. This one's a little tougher, typically featuring level 13 skags, as well as a few high-level elemental skags and Alpha Skags. Circle the room so no one can get a bead on you. Use your action skill often to pick off the weenies and hopefully inflict some nasty status conditions on the tougher foes. In co-op games, surround Alpha Skags so that someone always has a clear shot from behind.

CLAPTRAP DANCE OFF

3 CIRCLE OF DEATH: MEAT AND GREET

LEVEL 11

■ *Rade Zayben met (1)*

Client: Fyrestone Bounty Board
Talk to Rade Zayben

Think you've got what it takes to be a gladiator? Enter the arena and put your life on the line for the amusement of our spectators and gamblers! Direct all enquiries to Rade Zayben, director of events.

REWARDS: 468 XP

4 CIRCLE OF DEATH: ROUND 1

LEVEL 11

■ *Round survived (1)*

Client: Rade Zayben
It's kill or be killed!

Get in there. You live, you get paid. You die, I get paid a lot more. Either way, I win. Oh, and if you're gonna die, at least try to put on a good show. Scream and spurt blood a lot, the crowd loves that.

REWARDS: 1,560 XP + $1,739

This quest tree ends with "Circle of Death: Final Round." It's listed as a level 18 quest, but is perfectly doable for level 15 or 16 characters. You'll face several rounds of level 13 to 16 skags, possibly including high-level "badass" elemental skags that are best dealt with quickly. The final enemies are typically at level 18. If you've used your action skill to clear the room of the weaker skags, you should be able to beat them easily with status conditions and critical-hit shotgun blasts.

The quest description didn't promise a bonus reward, but the oh-so-generous Rade will throw victors a high-quality Repeater (with variable stats)!

HUNT FOR SHOCK CRYSTALS IN THE LOST CAVE

Turn off the road as you would to reach the Zephyr Substation, but head west along the north wall until you spot the New-U pole that marks the entrance to the Lost Cave. Here you'll find small Electric Crystal formations that can be shot (or melee attacked, if you're being stingy with ammo) until they break into five crystal pieces. The crystals shatter after a set number of hits, not a set amount of damage, so they're most easily broken with shotguns that fire multiple pellets or a long stream of fire from a weak weapon. Don't worry if you can't recover all the pieces; there are many more crystals in the cave than you need, so you'll be able to collect 50 pieces without much difficulty.

Dealing with the monsters and bandits that guard the crystals won't be so easy, however. Lightning-spitting Larva Crab Worms make their debut near the entrance. These vile creatures respawn regularly in the eastern part of the cave. They can tunnel underground, so back away when they begin to burrow to avoid having them pop up behind you. Their weak point is their giant eye, and there's no better way to exploit it than a pointblank shotgun blast. Crab Worms are a great source of XP, so if you're feeling under-leveled, wiping them out is a good way to boost your strength before the greater challenges ahead.

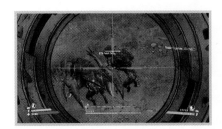

The cave is also full of skags and bandits, and if you're running low on ammo (or just want to be creative), you can play the various factions off each other. All you need to do is get the attention of a group of worms and lead them toward an active skag hole, or get a pack of skags on your tail and charge into a bandit camp. While all these beasts are fighting each other, you can find a nice sniper perch and pick off the victors. Needless to say, the Siren's action skill makes it a cinch to pick fights and get out of the crossfire alive. (Of course, you won't gain XP from enemies that are killed by other enemies.)

FIND THE CLAPTRAP IN THE BANDIT CAMP

The bandits have made a heavily fortified camp at the cave's central choke point, and it won't be easy to get past it. Skilled snipers should take a position at the nearby New-U pole to pick off any soldiers that foolishly expose their heads. Sirens can Phasewalk through the camp and take a position in the southwest trail (near another red chest) to hit the bandits from behind. (Then Phasewalk back to the New-U pole area, do some sniping, and repeat.) Berserkers and Soldiers may prefer to use their abilities to finish the battle at closer range.

Once you've cleared the camp, turn your attention to the poor Claptrap that lies wounded at its entrance. He'll give you the "Claptrap Rescue: The Lost Cave" quest, which can earn you another Storage Deck Upgrade (the kind that opens up three inventory slots).

CLAPTRAP DANCE OFF

5 CIRCLE OF DEATH: ROUND 2

LEVEL 15

- ■ *Round survived (1)*

Client: Rade Zayben
It's kill or be killed!

Back for more, eh? It's gonna be tougher this time. I don't expect a punk like you to last very long, but you understand the sequel has to up the ante.

REWARDS: 2,652 XP + $4,105

6 CIRCLE OF DEATH: FINAL ROUND

LEVEL 18

- ■ *Round survived (1)*

Client: Rade Zayben
It's kill or be killed!

No one has gone three rounds in the circle that ain't skag food right now. You got the smell of skag food.

REWARDS: 4,800 XP + $9,612

FIGHT ANOTHER BANDIT TROOP FOR THE REPAIR KIT

Continue north, where you'll find a second bandit encampment after battling another wave of skags. Take cover behind one of the large sheets of corrugated metal, allowing you to snipe at enemy bandits, then duck behind the metal to safely regenerate your shields. Although this cover protects you from the bullets of the bandit soldiers, it won't stop the bandit psychos from circling around the metal to flush you out. Soldiers can set up a turret to protect their flanks, while everyone else will need a shotgun quick-keyed and fully loaded to quickly headshot the psychos.

The Repair Kit is in a pipe atop the metal bridge at the end of the second bandit camp, and you'll likely have found 50 Shock Crystals by the time you reach it. That's everything you need from this cave, so it isn't necessary to enter the large open cavern at the east end of the bridge. Those who wish to tempt fate will find the cavern guarded by several level 15 Alpha Skags, but patient and skillful players should be able to kill most of them by sniping from the safety of the steep cavern lip. The cavern holds the last two **red chests** of this highly lucrative area.

KING OF CLAP

Leap from the bridge to return to the bandit camp where your Claptrap is waiting, but expect a fight—the bandits will have likely respawned. At least you'll be hitting them from behind this time, and can catch them with grenades while they're all bunched up near the hut. Fight your way to the Claptrap and give him the Repair Kit. He won't lead you to any extra treasures like the Claptrap in Sledge's Safe House did, so there's no need to stick around. You can fight your way out for some more rich Crab Worm XP, or break into a run and hightail it past all the respawned foes between the Claptrap and the exit. Report your victory to the Fyrestone bounty board to earn a Shock Artifact that you can equip (in place of the Incendiary Artifact) to give your action skill electrical properties!

⚡1-7 **MISSION TAGS**

7 SHOCK CRYSTAL HARVEST

LEVEL 15

☐ *Shock Crystals (50)*

Client: Fyrestone Bounty Board
Harvest Shock Crystals in the Lost Cave
Shock Elemental Artifacts allow you to customize your skills with the power of lightning. The key component for such an artifact is the Shock Crystal. I can fashion an artifact for you, but you'll need to provide the crystals. Go to the Lost Cave and shoot the Crystal Clusters to break them apart. Watch out for the bandits that have taken over the cave.

REWARDS: 3,672 XP + SHOCK ARTIFACT

8 CLAPTRAP RESCUE: THE LOST CAVE

LEVEL 15

☐ *Repair Kit (1)*

Client: Claptrap
Find the Repair Kit and repair this Claptrap
You've discovered yet another defunct Claptrap here. Doubtless, he wandered in here and was destroyed by the inhabitants of the cave. Perhaps there is a Repair Kit nearby?

REWARDS: 1,020 XP + STORAGE DECK UPGRADE

CLAPTRAP DANCE OFF

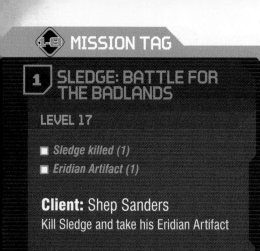

1 SLEDGE: BATTLE FOR THE BADLANDS

LEVEL 17

- ■ *Sledge killed (1)*
- ■ *Eridian Artifact (1)*

Client: Shep Sanders
Kill Sledge and take his Eridian Artifact

It's time to push the attack! Infiltrate Headstone Mine and kill Sledge. If you get the chance, grab that Eridian Artifact of his. As Dr. Zed put it, nobody wants another bandit to find it and start another blood-fueled crusade for the Vault. If you manage to come out of this fight alive, head on back to Zed and let him know what happened.

REWARDS: 9,804 XP + $6,866 + CLASS MOD

QUEST:

1 Sledge: Battle For The Badlands

1-8 SLEDGE'S FINAL RECKONING

SLEDGE
PS. YOU GUYS AREN'T FRIENDS.

Now that our mission log is clear, the time is right to infiltrate the Headstone Mine and put an end to Sledge's reign as the bandit king. The battle for the Badlands ends here!

INFILTRATE THE HEADSTONE MINE

You encounter Sledge's guards after leaving the safety of the building with the New-U pole and vending machines. Proceed slowly with a sniper rifle in hand, claiming territory, building by building, with long-range shots from behind safe cover. Your bandit foes are quite capable of sniping back with their accurate combat rifles, so scan for them carefully. Don't miss the enemies perched atop the elevated railway to the west.

GATE SWITCH

ARID BADLANDS

TURRET

SLEDGE

ERIDIAN ARTIFACT

HEADSTONE MINE

LEGEND	TREASURE CHEST	NEW-U POLE/STATION	MEDICAL VENDING MACHINE	AMMO VENDING MACHINE
	▬	●	◻	◻

CLAPTRAP DANCE OFF

BOLT FROM THE BLUE
HUNTERS CAN PAIR AN ELECTRIC BLOODWING (SHOCK WING) WITH A FIRE OR CORROSIVE WEAPON FOR A DEADLY ONE-TWO PUNCH AGAINST SHIELDED FOES.

—J. KYLE PITTMAN, PROGRAMMER

The mine's main gate is closed, but the switch that opens it is atop a set of stairs to the northwest of the entrance. Hit it for your backtracking convenience, but continue to proceed along the upper level. You're safe from the enemy turret up here and can loot a pair of gun-filled **chests** (one **red** and the other **silver**).

The room with the red chest has an open balcony to the south with a stairway that leads down to the mine's central yard. This is the ideal place to make a stand; snipe at foes from above, then kneel behind the railing and gun down anyone foolish enough to rush up the stairs after you.

TAKE THE CENTRAL TURRET

From your perch atop the stairs, scan to the south with your scope. There's a level 17 Mounted Turret on a platform on the opposite side of the yard. Destroying a turret is possible, but not easy; the better tactic is to destroy the bandit at the helm, although you can only target the very top of his head from here. If you can't make the shot with a sniper rifle, and you're lucky enough to have a rocket launcher, you can fire that at the turret until the splash damage kills the bandit at the helm. If you're unable to take out the bandit from afar, or a new bandit moves in to take the turret, then run downstairs and follow the west wall of the yard, moving carefully between cover and pausing at each safe spot to kill any newly spawned foes. Don't miss the hut with the **silver chest** along the way!

When you approach the turret platform, run up the ramp toward the turret, and pause at a height where the platform railing blocks any turret shots directed at you. From this location, you can zoom in and pick off the turret operator at your leisure. With the operator dead and the turret intact, you can hop right in and mow down any remaining foes in the yard below.

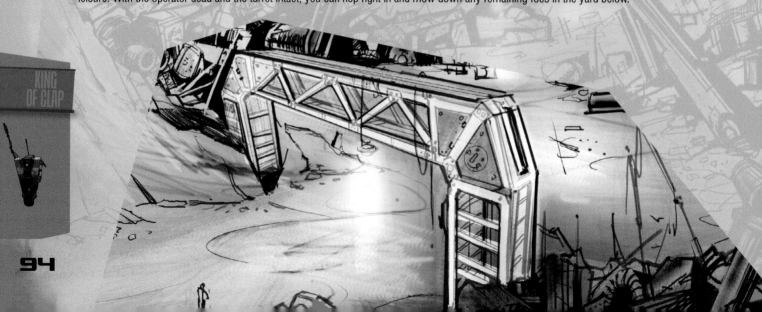

PROCEED THROUGH THE MINE RAILYARD

Continue south past the turret until you reach a fork in the road. The path that leads to Sledge is to the right, through the tunnel. However, it's worth taking a quick detour to the left, where you'll find a handful of bandits guarding an open area with two small buildings. One holds a **red chest**, and the other connects to the set of elevated train tracks before ending at a **silver chest**!

The tunnel and the processing area beyond feature more of Sledge's favorite combo: Bandits that snipe from afar and Psychos that rush in for melee strikes. Keep your best sniper rifle and shotgun at your fingertips—you'll be switching between them often. As you proceed to the wider areas in the southeastern part of the map, you face larger squads of foes. Keep a lookout for natural sniping points from which you can even the odds, like the ledge beneath the stone archway along the west wall and the three-story building that's just north of the elevated train tracks. With your foes as bunched up as they are in the railyard below, the windowed building offers a particularly fun position for sniping with a rocket launcher (if you've been lucky enough to find one).

Stay on the ground (and not the elevated rails) as you move east through the railyard. You face one last group of bandits outside of a building with a **red chest**, which also contains an elevator activated by a green switch. Pull that switch to rise to an upper level with a New-U pole, vending machines, and, past a corridor to the north… Sledge.

CLAIM SLEDGE'S LIFE AND ARTIFACT

Sledge wields two weapons—a shotgun that is absurdly powerful, but wildly inaccurate, and a hammer that can pound the floor to deliver damaging shockwaves. Always fight him from as far away as possible to stay out of hammer range and safe from all but a small percentage of his shotgun's payload. If Sledge does corner you and reaches for his hammer, leap as soon as he swings it so that you're in mid-air when the shockwaves hit.

Use an electrified weapon to chip away at Sledge's shields, which shouldn't refill again. Then holster your weapon and reach for something without elemental properties, since Sledge is highly resistant to fire, shock, and corrosive damage. Weapons that are powerful and accurate at long range, such as combat rifles and revolvers, are probably your best bet. But keep a shotgun handy for when you turn a corner and stumble into a psycho or some other foe; Sledge's minions appear from time to time, and you won't have time to kill them with finesse. Even if you have to absorb a few hits, it's best to just charge these enemies and blow them away at pointblank range.

Such tactics will take a toll on your health, so switch to Transmutation Grenades if you have them. No grenade is going to do much damage to Sledge, but stealing health from Sledge can certainly help keep *you* alive.

SLEDGE	LEVEL	HEALTH	XP	WEAK POINT	RESISTANCES	SHIELDS
	18	12	24	Head		Yes

Leader of a bandit tribe, Sledge is blunt and uncreative, to the extent that when he named his iconic weapon, he simply called it "Hammer." What he lacks in brainpower, however, he makes up for with brute strength and a high pain tolerance.

KING OF CLAP

96

SLEDGE'S SHOTGUN

DAMAGE	57 x 11
ACCURACY	0.0
FIRE RATE	4.2
MAGAZINE	2
ELEMENT	None

The Legend Lives

+150% Melee Damage

+106% Damage

+200% Burst Fire Count

REAP THE REWARDS OF VICTORY

When Sledge finally falls, he drops his shotgun. It's a brutally powerful weapon, but has an accuracy rating of zero and can hold only two rounds, both of which fire with one pull of the trigger. It's only worth using at pointblank range, but it can be useful to have it quick-keyed for when an enemy is suddenly on top of you. Note the added melee damage bonus, which allows you to continue to pound incoming foes even as you're reloading. The reloading process will be interrupted, but the melee strike should give you a bit of breathing room to reload and fire again.

You'll also find the Eridian Artifact in a **silver chest** near Sledge's throne. A side door opens when you do, allowing you to exit through a balcony. From there, you can run northeast, drop down a cliff that parallels the main gate, and dash back to the Arid Badlands. Summon a vehicle at the nearby Catch-A-Ride, then return to Fyrestone and report your triumph. Dr. Zed throws in an additional reward of an equippable Class Mod, which gives your character class-specific stat boosts and free levels at certain skills!

GETTING BOSS-READY

FIGHTING A BOSS THAT'S AT A HIGHER LEVEL THAN YOUR CHARACTER CAN BE VERY DIFFICULT BECAUSE YOUR BASE DAMAGE IS REDUCED DUE TO THE BOSS'S GREATER EXPERIENCE LEVEL. IF YOU EVER FEEL OVERMATCHED, IT'S TIME TO FINISH SOME SIDE MISSIONS TO LEVEL UP UNTIL YOU'RE AT LEAST AT AN EQUAL LEVEL TO THE BOSS.

-PAUL HELLQUIST, SENIOR GAME DESIGNER

1-9 A LITTLE UNFINISHED BUSINESS (OPTIONAL)

The road out of Fyrestone takes you far to the west, past a final chunk of the Arid Badlands the locals call "Titan's End." The Fyrestone bounty board has a pair of quests to accomplish in Titan's End. In terms of difficulty balance, this is the time to do them. There's also the "Schemin' That Sabotage" quest, which allows you to destroy Sledge's base in a massive, cathartic explosion. If you're eager to move on to the Dahl Headland, you can always come back to do these later, but don't expect much of a challenge if you do.

QUESTS:

1. Find Bruce McClone (optional)
2. Product Recall (optional)
3. Insult to Injury (optional)
4. Schemin' That Sabotage (optional)

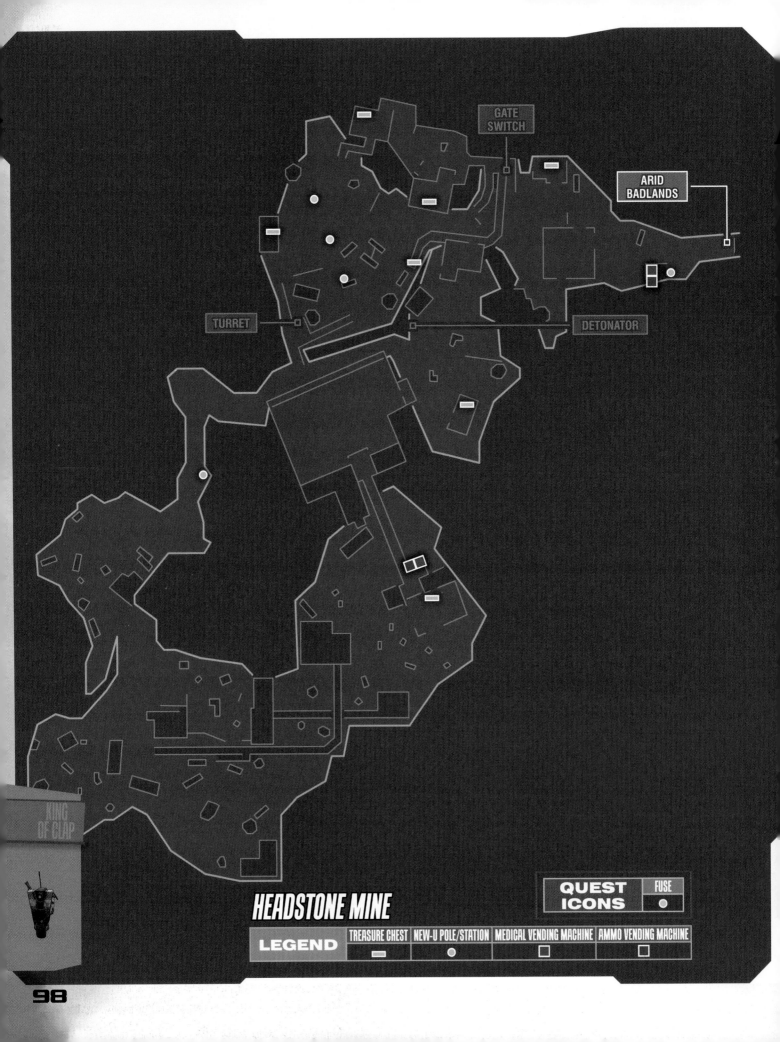

GATE
SWITCH

ARID
BADLANDS

TURRET

DETONATOR

KING
OF CLAP

HEADSTONE MINE

QUEST
ICONS

FUSE

LEGEND	TREASURE CHEST	NEW-U POLE/STATION	MEDICAL VENDING MACHINE	AMMO VENDING MACHINE

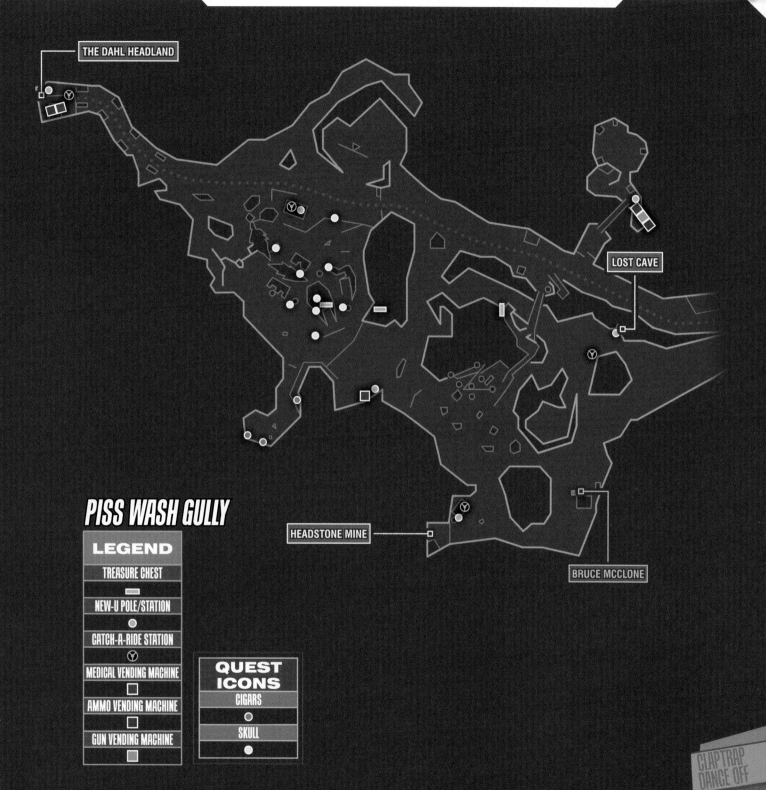

THE DAHL HEADLAND

LOST CAVE

PISS WASH GULLY

HEADSTONE MINE

BRUCE MCCLONE

LEGEND

TREASURE CHEST	
NEW-U POLE/STATION	
CATCH-A-RIDE STATION	
MEDICAL VENDING MACHINE	
AMMO VENDING MACHINE	
GUN VENDING MACHINE	

QUEST ICONS

CIGARS	
SKULL	

CLAPTRAP DANCE OFF

1 | FIND BRUCE MCCLONE

LEVEL 15

☐ *Bruce McClone found (1)*

Client: Fyrestone Bounty Board

Find Bruce McClone

Can anyone help me? I haven't heard from my fiancé in weeks. His name is Bruce McClone, and he lives in a shack out near Zephyr Substation. Last I saw him, he was bragging about how rich he was about to become and how he was gonna buy us a flight off this planet. Whatever he was up to, I bet it got him into trouble. Please, someone, find my fiancé.

REWARDS: 3,060 XP

FIND BRUCE MCCLONE'S SECRET HIDEOUT

In the first Bruce McClone quest, the waypoint guides you to a small cabin west of the Zephyr Substation. Enter through the back door to find a secret tunnel dug into the floor. Blow away the pair of Mutant Midget Psychos who have made it their home, then examine Bruce's journal to complete "Find Bruce McClone" and unlock its follow-up, "Product Recall." Don't miss the chance to raid Bruce's **red chest** and weapon vending machine!

SABOTAGE THE HEADSTONE MINE

While we're in the neighborhood, jog a short distance west to return to the Headstone Mine for the "Schemin' That Sabotage" quest. If you haven't exited the game since beating Sledge, you may want to do so after you get inside and activate the New-U pole. Exiting and reloading refills the half-dozen red and silver gun chests that you can easily revisit during this quest.

Inside the mine, you'll face pretty much the same enemies you fought the first time. Being a bit stronger now, you can probably survive a mad dash to the turret—it's

slightly riskier, but a lot more fun than taking cover and playing peek-a-boo with the bandit army. Run right through the first batch of foes, up the ledge past the gate switch, and then down along the west wall to reach the turret. Use your action skill to eliminate the turret operator and claim the turret for yourself. No one can touch you when you sit down in the turret and start blowing away the remaining enemies in the lower yard.

All three of the fuses are in the lower yard, each set on a support pillar of the elevated railway. Activate them in any order, then head back toward the turret and up the stairs behind it. Hang a left and follow the cliff ledge to the detonator. Make a wish, push the lever, and turn toward Sledge's home to watch the fireworks. (As wrecked as it may seem, you can still return to Sledge's room for a rematch at any time.)

KING OF CLAP

TAKE THE BACK DOOR TO TITAN'S END

The main entrance to Titan's End is just off of the road that heads west from Fyrestone. But to pick up one of Bruce's cigar boxes, you must find a different point of entry. Get a Runner from the Catch-A-Ride outside of the Headstone Mine and drive it along the south wall until you spot the tent with one of Dr. Zed's vending machines. Jump up onto a boulder and take a running leap from there to a thin trail that runs along the southern mountains. At the end of the trail, you'll find a tent with a few desks, a **red chest**, and a box of Bruce's finest.

The other two boxes of cigars are right below you, so equip a sniper rifle (or better yet, a rocket launcher) and gun down the bandit guards. When you drop down to claim your prizes, you'll find yourself deep inside Titan's End.

RECOVER THE ARCHAEOLOGISTS' SKULLS

If you set "Insult To Injury" as your active quest, several glowing green quest markers appear atop spear-mounted skulls. Don't try to recover these skulls, though, until you've first flushed out the army of bandits living here. They're scattered throughout the camp, and the numerous buildings and natural rock formations make it hard for them to gang up on you. Hit them hard and fast before they can regroup, using the red dots on your compass to hunt them down one at a time.

2 PRODUCT RECALL

LEVEL 15

⬛ *Box of Cigars (3)*

Client: Fyrestone Bounty Board
Find Bruce's Boxes of Cigars near Titan's End

In the journal, Bruce described a scam where he gathered local plant leaves, rolled them into cigars, then sold them to bandits while claiming they were prized off-world tobacco. With the money he'd hoped to marry his fiancée and take her away from Pandora. Apparently his first customer immediately died of massive internal bleeding, and the bandits forced Bruce to use his own product as payback. You'd better round up these cigars before some kid gets hold of one and smokes it in a back alley. The journal mentions that Bruce's customers were primarily the bandits around Titan's End.

REWARDS: 3,468 XP + $4,105

MISSION TAG

3 INSULT TO INJURY

LEVEL 15

■ *Skulls removed (10)*

Client: Fyrestone Bounty Board
Remove the human skulls from the pikes at Titan's End

The bandits took over my dig site in the Arid Badlands. Members of my team attempted to defend themselves, but they were failures and now the bandits have hung up their skulls like trophies. This is unsanitary and inappropriate for an archaeological dig site. I will pay someone to go to Titan's End and remove their skulls from the pikes.

REWARDS: 4,080 XP + $2,736 + GUN

When the camp is clear, start collecting the skulls. They're on spears set outside of huts, at the entrance to Titan's End, and even atop raised platforms. Your waypoint can lead you to each one, but don't follow it so single-mindedly that you miss the pair of **red chests** in the camp's southernmost structure: There's one chest in the suspended shack on the top level, and another in the hut in the pit below!

SAY FAREWELL TO THE FYRESTONE BOUNTY BOARD

Once you have all 10 skulls, leave Titan's End through the northern entrance, where a New-U Station and Catch-A-Ride await. Take one last trip east to report to the Fyrestone bounty board; you receive a random gun as a reward for "Insult To Injury" and a random Grenade Mod as a reward for "Schemin' That Sabotage." You should also unlock the "Made in Fyrestone" achievement/trophy, a final reward for completing every last quest in the Arid Badlands.

That concludes our business here, at least for now. Drive all the way west, past even Titan's End, to find the Claptrap waiting at the gates to the Dahl Highland.

CHAPTER 1 COMPLETE!
YOU KNOW WHAT YOU NEED? COOKIES! GO TO THE KITCHEN AND MAKE YOURSELF SOME COOKIES!
- MATTHEW ARMSTRONG, GAME DIRECTOR

MISSION TAG

4 SCHEMIN' THAT SABOTAGE

LEVEL 18

- ☐ *Fuses placed (1)*
- ☐ *Fuse B placed (1)*
- ☐ *Fuse C placed (1)*
- ☐ *Pipeline Destroyed (1)*

Client: Fyrestone Bounty Board
Infiltrate the Headstone Mine, place the fuses, and use the detonator.

This here's a job for anyone who thinks they got a pair that clank. Everyone knows how the bandits overran the Headstone Mine. They've been sellin' irridium on the black market. I don't know who's buyin' it, but screw 'em. Anything fundin' bandits needs to stop. I tried blowing the emergency valves on the main line, but they chased me out before the job was done. I need someone to get in there, finish connecting the fuses, then blow them up. Any takers?

REWARDS: 4,800 XP + $7,689 + GRENADE MOD

2-1 GETTING LUCKY AT THE LAST CHANCE WATERIN' HOLE

QUESTS:

SQUASH YOUR WAY TO THE TOP
FIGHTING SCYTHIDS IS A GREAT WAY TO LEVEL UP. THEY HAVE RELATIVELY LOW HEALTH FOR THE EXPERIENCE THAT THEY ARE WORTH.

—CHRIS BROCK, DEVELOPER

dahl HEADLAND

You've earned the trust of the few decent people in the Arid Badlands, and they want you to speak to their leader, Helena Pierce, in New Haven. But between the badlands and New Haven lies the sun-scorched Dahl Highland, where a bandit named Mad Mel controls the roads with his fleet of stolen Runners. If you can free Lucky Zaford from Mel's grasp, he'll help you find a way to New Haven.

MEET ERNEST IN THE DAHL HEADLAND

You enter the Dahl Headland through a thin ridge in the northeast corner of the map. At the end of the road you'll find Ernest, who greets you with the "Getting Lucky" mission, as well as the optional "Big Game Hunter" side quest (which we'll cover in the next section). Once you accept his missions, he lifts the gates to the Headland's vast central mesa.

Before hitting the Catch-A-Ride, check the vending machines, which sell quite a few new items of interest. The ammo machines now offer level 3 Storage Deck Mods at $16,427 apiece, for your ammo hoarding convenience. Even more exciting are the Grenade Mods that are now sold from Dr. Zed's vending machines. These mods can be quite a bit more powerful than the freebie you got from Zed, but they don't come cheap, typically falling in the $15,000 to $50,000 range. If you can't find a good one for your class, keep checking; the Class Mod stock changes every time the Item-of-the-Day timer hits zero.

UNDERGROUND

ARID
BADLANDS

ERNEST WHITTING

ENTRANCE TO
LUCKY'S

LUCKY'S LAST CHANCE
WATERING HOLE

LUCKY ZAFORD

BOUNTY BOARD

BREAKER

BREAKER

MASTER
SWITCH

KING
OF CLAP

NEW
HAVEN

DAHL HEADLANDS

LEGEND	TREASURE CHEST	NEW-U POLE/STATION	CATCH-A-RIDE STATION	MEDICAL VENDING MACHINE	AMMO VENDING MACHINE	GUN VENDING MACHINE

There are two ways out of Ernest's ridge, but no self-respecting Vault-hunter would pass up the chance to rent a ride, hit the nitro, and soar off of Ernest's ramp. A good jump should put you in the air for over two seconds—sufficient for completing the "Hang Time" challenge, but not quite long enough to accomplish the other hang-time challenges. (We'll take care of that in the next section.)

When you build your ride, consider your weapon carefully, as Mad Mel's men are piloting Runners of their own. In a multiplayer game, a human at the turret can do great things with a rocket launcher, but if you're playing solo and using the lock-on targeting, you'll find that the fast-moving Runners can often stay ahead of your rockets. Even Mad Mel's men can't outrun the bullets from the mounted Machine Gun, making that the weapon of choice for solo play.

BREAK THE SIEGE ON LUCKY'S TAVERN

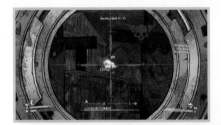

The doors to Lucky's are locked up tight, and the only way in is through a gap in the fence to the north. Rather than barging in, loiter outside the gap and snipe at any bandit you can get a clear shot at. This gets the Burning Psychos, Badass Psychos, and Mutant Midget Psychos in the compound running in your direction, but since they must pass through the same small gap to reach you, you'll know exactly where to point's Sledge's Shotgun to give them an enthusiastic welcome.

Once you've sniped out the bandits on the opposite balcony and blown away all the psychos, ease into the compound and pick off the remaining bandits. There are exactly 15 of them, and the gate to Lucky's backyard opens when the last one dies. Stay sharp as you loot the **red** and **silver chests** in this area, though, because there's a swarm of Badass Psychos and Mutant Midget Psychos in the yard that will rush you as you approach the gate. Recharge your shields and reload once you've dealt with them to prepare for one last guard coming your way—a hearty Badass Bruiser that emerges from the tavern itself. Try to nail him with a status condition like fire or corrosion to help chew through his considerable life bar.

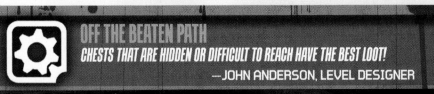

CLAPTRAP DANCE OFF

1 LEAVING FYRESTONE

LEVEL 18

- ■ *Claptrap talked to (1)*
- ■ *Ernest found (1)*

Client: Dr. Zed

Travel to the Dahl Headland and speak with Ernest Whitting

Pierce agreed to bump up your clearance level. She wants you to go to New Haven and meet with her. So, drive west to the Dahl Headland gate, and speak with the Claptrap robot there. He'll let you through. When you get past the gate, talk with Ernest Whitting on the other side. He knows the Headland better than anyone, and can bring you up to speed.

REWARDS: 1200 XP

2 GETTING LUCKY

LEVEL 18

- ■ *Bandits killed (15)*
- ■ *Lucky rescued (1)*

Client: Ernest Whitting

Rescue Lucky Zaford at the Last Chance Waterin' Hole.

You showed up at just the right time! Bandits decided to lay siege to the Last Chance Waterin' Hole to the south, and my friend Lucky is trapped inside! He called me for help just before you showed up. I wasn't sure what to do, but you're here now. Please, go help my friend!

REWARDS: 2,400 XP + $1,922 + GRENADE MOD

When the coast is finally clear, look for a pile of tires leaning against the side of Lucky's bar, and use them to jump onto the roof. From there, you can reach another gun-filled **silver chest**. Drop back into the yard, head through the back door, and break Lucky out of his cell to complete the quest and unlock your next mission.

FLIP THE BREAKERS ON THE FAST TRAVEL NETWORK

The two breakers Lucky wants you to throw may be only a few steps to the southeast, but you should bring your Runner anyway. Hop from one corrugated plank to the next to reach the breaker atop the first electric tower, then give it a flip. That gets the power humming and also spawns an attack from a new family of fast-moving insect monsters known as the Scythid. Fighting them on foot might be tough, so why bother? Jump back to your Runner and splatter them beneath your tires! Scooter never needs to know.

The second breaker is a little trickier to reach. You must to duck under a steel bar on the third platform, and then leap from there to another steel bar to reach it. You may trigger a bandit outrider attack when you flip the switch, so keep your own Runner close.

THROW THE FAST TRAVEL-NETWORK MASTER SWITCH

The electric station with the master switch is just down the road from the breakers, but Mad Mel's men won't let you reach it without a fight. There are a good dozen guards waiting to jump you when you step through the door, but there's really no need to step through it at all. Instead, drive up to the entrance and use your mounted weapon to hit anyone within auto-target range. When you run out of targets, get out of your Runner, walk to the doorway, and then run right back to your turret. That should provoke your foes to chase you down, and charge right into your machine-gun spray. You won't get as much XP as you would for fighting on foot, but Runner shenanigans like these allow you to clear the entire compound before you ever set foot inside.

The master switch is at the top of the stairs, but don't flip it until you've prepared yourself for a second round of combat. A new wave of enemies emerges from the shipping crates below, so switch to your sniper rifle and pick off as many as you can. Keep Sledge's Shotgun handy—any creeps that make it up the stairs can get blasted right back down. If you don't feel like fighting, leap over the railing, dash to your Runner, and hightail it out of there.

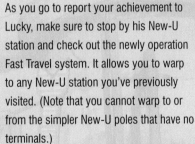

As you go to report your achievement to Lucky, make sure to stop by his New-U station and check out the newly operation Fast Travel system. It allows you to warp to any New-U station you've previously visited. (Note that you cannot warp to or from the simpler New-U poles that have no terminals.)

3 — POWERING THE FAST TRAVEL NETWORK

LEVEL 20

- ☐ *Breakers thrown (2)*
- ☐ *Master switch flipped (1)*

Client: Lucky Zaford
Throw the Fast Travel breakers and flip the master switch.

I wanna get back to Ernest, but I can't face another bandit. Fast Travel would be okay, but it's been offline around here for ages. Mad Mel blocks Scooter from coming to fix it. If Fast Travel were working, we could instantly teleport to any New-U stations we've ever visited, even the one to Ernest's Emporium. Will you fix it, please? You just gotta climb the poles and throw the breakers, then hit the master switch over at the station. Easy, right?

REWARDS: 2,376 XP + $2,411

4 — ROAD WARRIORS: HOT SHOTS

LEVEL 18

- ☐ *Runner Patrols destroyed (8)*

Client: Lucky Zaford
Eliminate Bandit Runner Patrols.

Mad Mel has blocked the road to New Haven, and he spends most of his time terrorizing the southern part of the Headland. He hardly ever comes up here. If you want him to face you, you'll need to get his attention first. What says "I'm going to kick your ass" better than killing a bunch of his men and destroying a lot of his hardware?

REWARDS: 2,400 XP + $1,922

JACK OF ALL TRADES
KEEP A VARIETY OF CLASS MODS IN YOUR BACKPACK.
THEY'RE GREAT TO HAVE WHEN YOU WANT TO RE-ROLL YOUR SKILLS.
—GRAEME TIMMINS, LEVEL DESIGNER

CLAPTRAP DANCE OFF

SEND A MESSAGE TO MAD MEL

Mad Mel has the road to New Haven blocked, so you must lure him into a fight to get past. To do that, Lucky wants you to blow away eight of his Runner Patrols. Solo players should have a machine-gun mounted Runner for this job, while co-op parties can put either weapons to good use. (Parties with more than three players should have the third and fourth players find a safe spot, such as the roof of the bandit garage marked by the waypoint, and use Rocket Launchers to join in the fun.) You need to kill eight Mad Mel Patrols to complete the quest; normal outriders won't count. You can almost always find targets by driving around the lake across from Lucky's.

When the deed is done, Lucky gives you the "Road Warriors: Bandit Apocalypse" mission. This allows you to finally battle Mad Mel for the right of free passage to New Haven.

2.2 (OPTIONAL): SIDE QUESTS IN THE DAHL HEADLAND

Upon reactivating the Fast Travel Network, you also got power flowing through the bounty board behind Lucky's New-U station. There are no less than five optional Dahl Headland missions there. Along with the "Big Game Hunter" quest from Ernest, they offer a compelling reason to enjoy the scenic beauty of the Dahl Highland for just a little bit longer.

QUESTS:

1 Scavenger: Revolver

2 Well There's Your Problem Right There

3 Fuel Feud

4 Death Race Pandora

5 Big Game Hunter

6 Ghosts Of The Vault

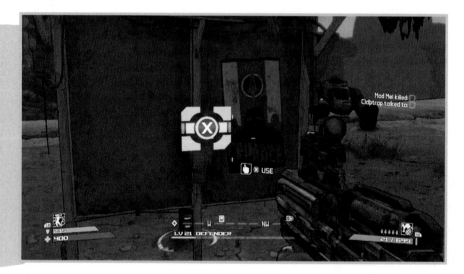

TURN A VALVE AND COLLECT THE BAIT

The key locations for the "Big Game Hunter," "Survivor: Revolver," "Fuel Feud," and "Well There's Your Problem Right There" quests overlap, so you can save yourself a few trips by pursuing them all at once.

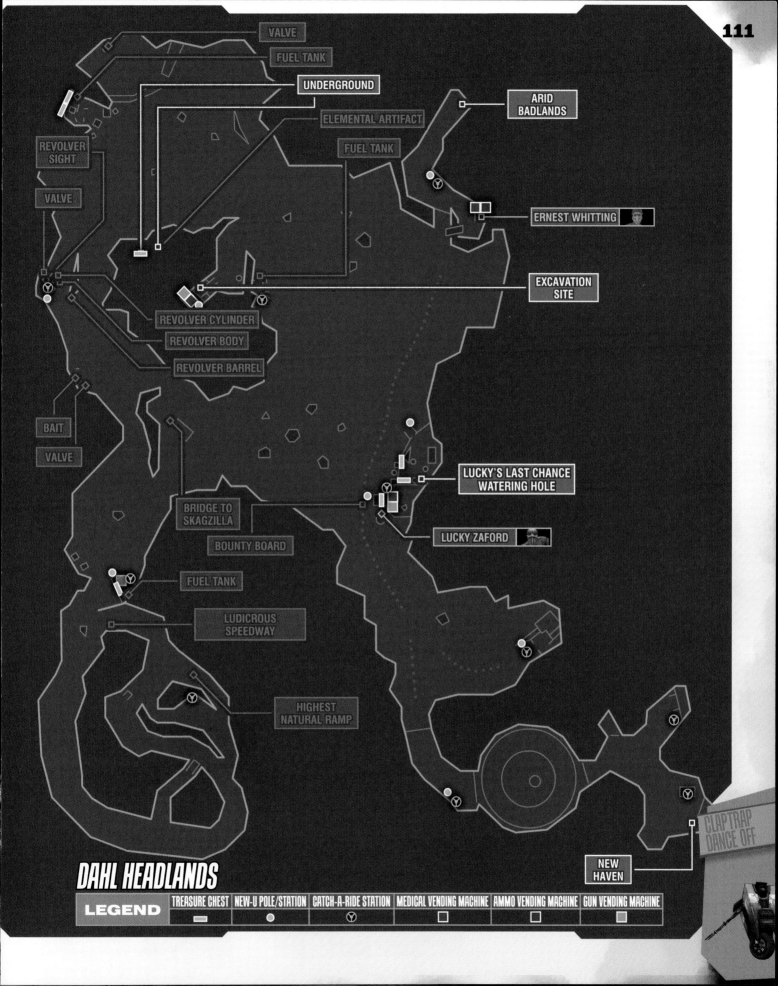

VALVE

FUEL TANK

UNDERGROUND

ARID
BADLANDS

ELEMENTAL ARTIFACT

FUEL TANK

REVOLVER
SIGHT

VALVE

ERNEST WHITTING

EXCAVATION
SITE

REVOLVER CYLINDER

REVOLVER BODY

REVOLVER BARREL

BAIT

VALVE

LUCKY'S LAST CHANCE
WATERING HOLE

BRIDGE TO
SKAGZILLA

BOUNTY BOARD

LUCKY ZAFORD

FUEL TANK

LUDICROUS
SPEEDWAY

HIGHEST
NATURAL RAMP

CLAPTRAP
DANCE OFF

NEW
HAVEN

DAHL HEADLANDS

LEGEND	TREASURE CHEST	NEW-U POLE/STATION	CATCH-A-RIDE STATION	MEDICAL VENDING MACHINE	AMMO VENDING MACHINE	GUN VENDING MACHINE
	▬	●	Ⓨ	▢	▢	▢

1 SCAVENGER: REVOLVER

LEVEL 20

- *Revolver Body (1)*
- *Revolver Cylinder (1)*
- *Revolver Sight (1)*
- *Revolver Barrel (1)*

Client: Lucky's Bounty Board
Find all of the revolver parts

There are components to a revolver scattered around. If you find all of these components, I can reassemble the weapon for you. Bring me the Body, Cylinder, Sight, and Barrel.

REWARDS: 3,036 XP + REVOLVER

2 WELL THERE'S YOUR PROBLEM RIGHT THERE

LEVEL 18

- *Valves closed (3)*

Client: Lucky's Bounty Board
Close all Fuel Pipe Valves around the Lucky's Last Chance

What with all the gunfights going on around here, my fuel pipes have got more holes than Swiss cheese. I think the system is salvageable. I just need somebody to close a few valves for me. I'd do it myself, but I'm afraid there'd soon be holes in me, too!

REWARDS: 6,000 XP + $7,689

Start by driving due west from Lucky's, then turning north to pass under the patchwork bridge. Follow the west wall to a bandit camp where a handful of bandits are congregating around a boar on a spit. Blow them away with your vehicle's armaments, then dismount and take that pig for yourself—it's the bait in the "Big Game Hunter" quest. Look to your left after you grab your porky prize, and you'll notice the first Valve in the "Well There's Your Problem Right There" quest. Give it a crank and return to your Runner.

COLLECT THE REVOLVER PARTS AND TURN VALVE #2

Continue to drive north, following the west wall. You eventually come across a mostly abandoned compound that's glowing green with its high concentration of quest objects, including all four revolver parts and another valve.

☐ THE REVOLVER BODY IS UNDER THE ELEVATED RUNNER IN THE BUILDING NEXT TO THE CATCH-A-RIDE.

☐ TURN TO THE NORTH AND YOU'LL SEE THE CYLINDER ON A CORRUGATED-METAL PLATFORM. TO REACH IT, CLIMB UP THE LEDGE TOWARD THE WATER TOWER AND JUMP FROM THE LEDGE ONTO THE ROOF OF THE BUILDING WHERE YOU FOUND THE BODY. FROM THERE, MAKE A RUNNING LEAP TO THE PLATFORM WITH THE CYLINDER.

☐ JUMP FROM THAT SAME ROOFTOP TO THE ROOFTOP OF THE CATCH-A-RIDE—YOU'LL BE ABLE TO SEE A LEDGE CUT INTO THE ROCKS TO THE WEST. TAKE A RUNNING LEAP TO THE LEDGE, THEN JUMP UP THE SERIES OF BOULDERS TO YOUR RIGHT. FROM THE TOP, LEAP TO A METAL PLATFORM WITH THE SIGHT. FROM THERE, DROP INTO THE GATED AREA BENEATH THE WATER TOWER AND TURN THE SECOND VALVE.

☐ FROM THE CATCH-A-RIDE, LOOK EAST TO SEE THE CHARRED SHELL OF AN OLD RUNNER ON THE ROCKY RIDGE ACROSS THE ROAD. THE BARREL IS IN ITS COCKPIT.

BLAST A FUEL TANK AND TURN THE LAST VALVE

There are two more outposts along the west wall, and you have business in both of them. Drive north to a bandit compound that has been dug deep into the mountain. You must leave your Runner to get inside, but you can always enter the compound to lure out the bandits, then run back to it. When the compound is clear, help yourself to the bandits' two **red chests** and pump a few bullets into their fuel tank.

A short distance to the east is a thin gap in a rocky ridge that allows you to approach the final valve on foot. Turn the valve and hurry out of there—there's no point in staying to fight the Scythids. Return to Lucky's to receive the rewards for the work you've completed so far; that XP will come in pretty handy for the more challenging quests ahead.

DESTROY THE REMAINING FUEL TANKS

Head west from Lucky's, then follow the south wall to a concrete building with a Catch-A-Ride, a gun-vending machine, and a New-U pole. Enter through the unlocked side door to find the building overrun with Scythids. Make your way to the back yard, pausing to kill only the Scythids that are blocking your way. The fuel tank is out back, along with a pile of tires in a corner that you can use to climb to the roof, where a **red chest** awaits. The entrance to the Dahl Racetrack is right behind the building, so you may want to attempt the "Death Race Pandora" quest while you're in the neighborhood.

3 FUEL FEUD

LEVEL 18

- *Fuel Tanks destroyed (3)*

Client: Lucky's Bounty Board
Destroy the Bandit Fuel Tanks

The worst part about living out here isn't the frequent skag attacks. It's the traffic. And by traffic, I mean those bandit bastards that think they have a right to shoot anything that moves. Hit 'em where it hurts. Destroy their fuel tanks so we can ride free!

REWARDS: 4,800 XP + $3,844 + GRENADE MOD

4 DEATH RACE PANDORA

LEVEL 20

- *Scythid killed (50)*

Client: Lucky's Bounty Board
Kill the Scythid Crawlers at the racetrack

There's an old racetrack in the Dahl Headland, called the Ludicrous Speedway. It was great in its day, but it's been abandoned since the corporations pulled out. I'm thinking of reopening the place, but there's a catch. It's been overrun with vermin. I need someone to go out there and kill all the bugs.

REWARDS: 5,280 XP + $4,099 + ROCKET LAUNCHER

CLAPTRAP DANCE OFF

5 BIG GAME HUNTER

LEVEL 20

- ☐ *Skagzilla Bait (1)*
- ☐ *Bait placed (1)*
- ☐ *Skagzilla killed (1)*

Client: Ernest Whitting
Get some bait, place it outside the cave, then kill Skagzilla.

See all the giant bones? Dug them up myself. I thought these creatures were extinct until, down at Wellspring Bluff, I came across a skag bigger than any I had ever seen! Its diet of cesium cactus, Runner fuel, and of course, human flesh, seems to have endowed it with incredible mutations. Truly, Skagzilla is a marvel of adaptation and survival. So I want you to acquire some bait, lure it out, and kill it!

REWARDS: 4,823 XP + $5,280 + SNIPER RIFLE

The final fuel tank is northwest of Lucky's, just south of the excavation site. This is the most heavily guarded one of the bunch, with a small army of bandits led by a level 21 Badass Bruiser. It's also the only one that isn't near any red chests, so there's no point hanging around any longer than necessary. After clearing a path with your Runner, you may want to ignore the surviving foes, empty a clip into the fuel tank, and get the hell out of there. In addition to your reward for completing the quest, destroying the fuel tanks keeps the roads free of Bandit Outriders for good.

CLEAR OUT THE RACETRACK AND GIVE IT A SPIN

Killing 50 Scythids sounds like a lot, but when they're happy to throw themselves in front of a moving vehicle, it doesn't take long. However, those who are willing to take the time to fight on foot can earn quite a bit of XP from the easily destroyed Scythids, and will have a much easier time collecting the loot. Badass Sycthids often drop elemental artifacts, so keep an eye out for those.

Drive slowly during the quest, but when your mission has been completed, kick the nitro on and try to do a lap in under 31 seconds to earn the "Speedy McSpeederton" achievement/trophy. (The timer won't be displayed on the screen, but the game does keep track of your time.) If you can avoid crashing into anything and use a couple of nitro blasts on the relatively straight stretches, you can beat 30 seconds with ease.

The Ludicrous Speedway provides an opportunity to complete the "Airborne," "This is not a flight simulator," and "Orbit Achieved" challenges (worth a total of 8,000 XP) by getting five full seconds of hang time. The trick is to go to the very end of the course, but stop before you would drive off the natural ledge that stops you from doing the course backwards. At the lip of the ledge, turn around to face a steep hill (we've labeled this "Highest Natural Ramp" on our map). Gun the nitro as you speed up the center of the ramp, and then turn so that you launch off of the right lip of the ramp and soar over the Catch-A-Ride.

MISSION TAG

6 GHOSTS OF THE VAULT

LEVEL 20

■ Scythid killed (50)

Client: Lucky's Bounty Board
Visit the Haunted Excavation and recover the Elemental Artifact

This is Tannis. I was digging in the Dahl Headland, and came very close to uncovering an Elemental Artifact, most likely from the Vault. I was forced to abandon the dig when my brain-dead team quit. They said they saw ghosts, or Bigfoot, or something. If you're someone who isn't a superstitious dolt, I invite you to recover the artifact for yourself. Here's the freight lift code so you can access the site.

REWARDS: 5,280 XP + $2,893 + EXPLOSIVE ARTIFACT

LUDICROUS SPEEDS
FOR THOSE WHO WANT TO GET THE BEST POSSIBLE TIME AROUND THE LUDICROUS SPEEDWAY, I SAY "SEEK THE SHORTCUT IN THE CAVE."

—KEITH SCHULER, MISSION GURU

HUNT DOWN SKAGZILLA

After claiming the bait in the "Big Game Hunter" quest, the waypoint moves west to an off-the-map area. To get there, drive to the ridge marked "Bridge to Skagzilla" and exit your vehicle at the entrance to the ramshackle bridge. Drop into the pit at the end o the bridge, and you'll find yourself in Skagzilla's off-map lair.

Set your bait at the row of metal spikes to the left of the cave, and you'll lure out a small pack of skags. As soon as you blow them away, the main attraction begins. Skagzilla always gives a good long roar when it enters the battlefield, so be ready to take advantage of the critical-hit opportunity presented by its wide-open mouth.

Skagzilla's attacks are powerful, but they're easy to avoid when you get the hang of the pattern. Strafe from side to side to avoid charges and projectile attacks, and when it jumps, leap right before it lands to avoid the damage from the tremors. That's a great time to blast the beast in the face with

Sledge's Shotgun, which works surprisingly well here. (Skagzilla is resistant to most forms of elemental damage, so there's no point in trying anything fancy.)

When Skagzilla opens its mouth to fire off a white energy beam, you'll have a great opportunity to nail it with multiple critical hits. Move to Skagzilla's side so you'll be out of range of the beam (which can only hit an area of roughly 60 degrees in front of the creature) and start fanning that hammer. Even if you can't see the red of its gums, you can still land criticals.

WHITTING'S ELEPHANT GUN	
DAMAGE	263
ACCURACY	98.3
FIRE RATE	0.6
MAGAZINE	6
ELEMENT	None

Why don't you go shoot yourself an elephant?

+113% Damage

+150% Critical Hit Damage

SKAGZILLA

LEVEL	HEALTH	XP	WEAK POINT	RESISTANCES	SHIELDS
21	30	72	Mouth	⚡ ☣ 🔥	None

It is unknown how large a skag can grow. The relatively recent human incursion on Pandora may have disrupted the natural life cycle of these creatures. If Skagzilla is any indication, though, a skag will continue to grow larger and larger until something kills it, or it starves to death.

When you report to Ernest Whitting, he'll throw in Whitting's Elephant Gun, a powerful sniper rifle that lacks a scope. But unlike the Rider, its Damage stat is probably much higher than any of the scoped sniper rifles available to you at this point in the game. Its low Fire Rate will be tough to work around, but it may be worth experimenting with.

LIBERATE TANNIS'S EXCAVATION SITE

"Ghosts of the Vault" is the most rewarding of the Dahl Highland quests, but also potentially the toughest. The entrance to the excavation site is heavily guarded by Badass Bruisers and other high-level bandits, so deal as much damage as you can from your Runner, and don't be afraid to flee back to it when a Bruiser is on your tail. Your goal is to reach the elevator at the center of the compound, which takes you to the underground excavation site.

After facing a brief onslaught of psychos and saving your game at the New-U pole, make your way through the wide cavern into the room with the Explosive Artifact. As you do, the two eerie statues burst into flame, heralding the arrival of a new type of foe: Guardian Spectres and Guardian Wraiths. These mysterious apparitions use bladed weapons, move rapidly, and fight primarily at close range. They have very high-capacity shields, so shock weapons provide a significant advantage against them. If you don't have a good one handy, you should at least have the Shocking Artifact from the Lost Cave, which should get the job done for Soldiers, Berserkers, and Hunters. Once you've zapped a Guardian's shield, switch to something powerful and accurate and start putting bullets in its head for a nice critical damage bonus—Whitting's Elephant Gun isn't half bad here.

As promised, you'll find the Explosive Artifact at the end of the cavern, which adds a moderately powerful secondary explosion to your action skill. It's a higher-level item than your Incendiary or Shocking Artifacts, so it should be your default choice when you don't have any particular need for status conditions. You'll also find a **red chest** that usually contains conventional weapon— if you're lucky, it may hold a rare Eridian energy weapon!

118

2-3 DRIVING MAD MEL TO THE GATES OF HELL

There's no escaping the Dahl Headland while Mad Mel continues to draw breath. Now that you've got his attention by wiping out his patrols, you're free to enter his compound (south of Lucky's) and challenge his dominance of the Headland.

QUEST:

1 Road Warriors:
Bandit Apocalypse

2-3 MISSION TAG

1 ROAD WARRIORS:
BANDIT APOCALYPSE

LEVEL 20

- ■ *Mad Mel killed (1)*
- ■ *Claptrap talked to (1)*

Client: Lucky Zaford
Kill Mad Mel, then talk to Claptrap to be allowed into New Haven.

Finally, payback against that Mad Mel! It's great to see someone with a brave heart willing to go out there and live dangerously. Well done! With Mad Mel no longer a concern, I will happily open the gate to New Haven for you.

REWARDS: 10,560 XP + $9,646
+ SDU UPGRADE

LUCKY'S LAST CHANCE WATERING HOLE

BOUNTY BOARD

LUCKY ZAFORD

CLAPTRAP

CLAPTRAP DANCE OFF

MAD MEL'S RACETRACK

NEW HAVEN

DAHL HEADLANDS

LEGEND	TREASURE CHEST	NEW-U POLE/STATION	CATCH-A-RIDE STATION	MEDICAL VENDING MACHINE	GUN VENDING MACHINE
	▬	●	Ⓨ	☐	☐

SURVIVE MAD MEL'S DEADLY THUNDERDOME

You won't be leaving your Runner for the entire battle against Mad Mel, so pick a color you're willing to die in. The machine gun remains the best choice of Runner weaponry for solo players, but skilled turret operators can use rocket launchers with similar success in co-op games.

Once you drive over the ramp to Mad Mel's Racetrack, there's no escape. If your vehicle is destroyed, you'll have little hope of victory on foot. (You can generate a new Runner once you're revived at the New-U pole). Fight conservatively; if your Runner is seriously damaged while fighting the first wave of Bandit Outriders, don't kill the last one until you've given your shields time to fully regenerate by racing around the course

If you do die early and end up being revived outside, don't be in too much of a hurry to charge back into the arena. One fun trick is to climb up the ramp on foot and snipe out all the remaining bandits from a position of relative safety. If you have great aim and a high-powered rifle, you can even take out the boss this way!

Mad Mel makes his debut after the first batch of outriders has been destroyed, and he brings a second batch with him. Don't turn your guns on Mel's tricked-out Runner until you've wiped out all of his men; if you can clear the battlefield of all other opponents, you can freely circle the racetrack to stay ahead of Mad Mel's rockets and regenerate your shields.

While rocket-launcher users must get close to fire accurately, machine-gunners should fight Mad Mel from as far away as possible. As long as you keep moving, his rockets are a lot less accurate at long distances than your bullets. And if Mel gets close enough to ram you, his far heavier vehicle is almost certain to come out on top—when he gets close, don't hesitate to hit the nitro and peel out of the way. If he does manage to smash your runner, all you can do is bail out, reach for your rocket launcher, and hope for the best.

KING OF CLAP

	LEVEL	HEALTH	XP	WEAK POINT	RESISTANCES	SHIELDS
MAD MEL	21	?	?	Head	None	None

Mad Mel is one of those car guys, and drives everywhere he goes, even to get the mail. In fact, he's never been seen outside of his armored vehicle, leading some to speculate that he is actually trapped inside, unable to move.

REPORT MAD MEL'S DEATH TO HELENA PIERCE

When Mad Mel falls, the gates to his arena will re-open for good. Drive southeast to find the Claptrap at the gate to New Haven, who gives you permission to pass. The road out of Dahl Headland leads straight to the gates of New Haven, where you can dismount and follow your waypoint to Helena Pierce. Helena may not have a lot of kind words for you, but a Storage Deck Upgrade that unlocks your final quick-key weapon slot is thanks enough.

KING
OF CLAP

3-1 CIVILIZATION, AT LAST!

QUESTS:

1 Power To The People

2 Claptrap Rescue: New Haven (optional)

3 Is T.K. O.K.? (optional)

4 Like A Moth To Flame (optional)

RAMPAGE OF THE SIREN PHOENIX

IF YOU HAVE LILITH'S PHOENIX SKILL, KILL THE WEAKEST ENEMY IN THE GROUP, THEN START RUSHING AROUND ENEMIES WHILE THE SKILL IS ACTIVE TO LIGHT THE REST ON FIRE. YOU MAY GO DOWN IN THE PROCESS, BUT MOST LIKELY AT LEAST ONE OF THE ENEMIES WILL DIE (IF NOT MORE) AND YOU'LL GET YOUR SECOND WIND.

—PATRICK DEUPREE, LEAD PROGRAMMER

new HAVEN

Welcome to the city of New Haven, the central hub of your journeys for a long time to come. The first priority is to get in good with Helena Pierce, who calls the shots around here. Once you've won her over, start picking up missions from New Haven's other residents.

COLLECT THE FIRST BATCH OF NEW HAVEN QUESTS

When you report Mad Mel's death to Helena Pierce, she asks, well... *demands* that you prove your worth by completing the "Power To The People" mission. The bounty board has several additional missions to offer, including "Like A Moth To Flame," "King Tossing," and "Corrosive Crystal Harvest." Track Scooter down in the garage due west of Helena's office, and he'll throw in the "Is T.K. O.K.?" quest. There are plenty of other New Haven residents you can talk to, but at the moment, the only one with a mission is the damaged Claptrap that's flailing and whimpering beside the bounty board. As you might have guessed, he's looking for help with the quest "Claptrap Rescue: New Haven."

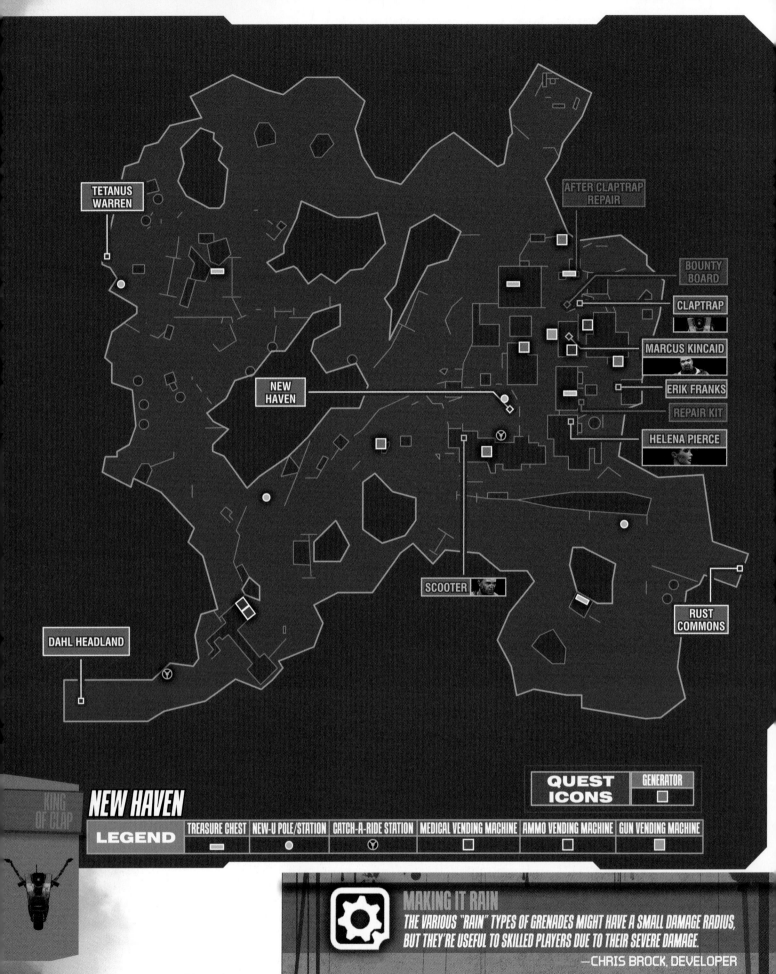

TETANUS WARREN

AFTER CLAPTRAP REPAIR

BOUNTY BOARD

CLAPTRAP

MARCUS KINCAID

ERIK FRANKS

REPAIR KIT

HELENA PIERCE

NEW HAVEN

SCOOTER

RUST COMMONS

DAHL HEADLAND

QUEST ICONS | GENERATOR

NEW HAVEN

LEGEND	TREASURE CHEST	NEW-U POLE/STATION	CATCH-A-RIDE STATION	MEDICAL VENDING MACHINE	AMMO VENDING MACHINE	GUN VENDING MACHINE

MAKING IT RAIN

THE VARIOUS "RAIN" TYPES OF GRENADES MIGHT HAVE A SMALL DAMAGE RADIUS, BUT THEY'RE USEFUL TO SKILLED PLAYERS DUE TO THEIR SEVERE DAMAGE.

—CHRIS BROCK, DEVELOPER

LOCATE THE NEW HAVEN GENERATORS

Someone needs to flip the switches on New Haven's five generators, and all of its residents are too busy looking at their boots and leaning against railings to help. The first generator is in Scooter's garage, just a few steps away from the lazy hick himself. After flipping the switch, head west to the main road out of town, where you'll quickly discover the West Gate generator just outside of New Haven's main entrance.

The third generator is on the east side of town, south of the building with Dr. Zed's vending machine. Hmm… a sparking generator, two gas-filled barrels, and a propane tank. What could possible go wrong? Flip the switch and run for dear life. (Ideally, you should detonate the barrels first, but that's less fun.)

The rooftop generator is on the building with the orange water tower and a guy leaning against an upper railing. There's a staircase on the west side of the building that should make the roof easy to reach. Instead of dropping back down after you turn on the generator, cross the plywood bridge that connects this rooftop to the building to the north. Jump a railing to a building north of that and raid a gun-filled **silver chest**. From the north edge of the roof, you can detect the red glow of the North Gate generator. Leap over the wall to the east and you'll land right by it.

MISSION TAG

1 POWER TO THE PEOPLE

LEVEL 20

- Scooter's power on (1)
- West Gate power on (1)
- Tenement power on (1)
- Rooftop power on (1)
- North Gate power on (1)

Client: Helena Pierce
Turn on generators around New Haven

You've got some nerve, Vault Hunter, strutting into New Haven like the world owes you something. Well, I've got news for you. You pull your own weight here, or you die. Before I lift one finger to help you on your mad quest for the Vault, you're going to do something for me. The last electrical storm blew out New Haven's power grid. Scooter tells me the equipment is fixed now, but someone needs to go reactive all the generators. That's where you come in.

REWARDS: 2,376 XP + $2,411

2 CLAPTRAP RESCUE: NEW HAVEN

LEVEL 21
- ■ *Repair Kit (1)*

Client: Claptrap

Find the repair kit and repair this Claptrap.

You've discovered another malfunctioning Claptrap robot. You noticed that there were some discarded Claptraps rusting on the scrap heaps around town. Perhaps some spare parts could be salvaged from those.

REWARDS: 1,380 XP + STORAGE DECK UPGRADE

COLLECT A SECOND BATCH OF NEW HAVEN QUESTS

Completing "Power To The People" triggers a whole flood of new missions, none of which is worth pursuing until your current slate is clear. But you might as well grab them now: Helena Pierce provides your next main storyline quest, "Seek Out Tannis." The Bounty Board is updated with "Scavenger: Submachine Gun" and "Hidden Journal: Rust Commons." Scooter adds "Scooter's Used Car Parts" and "Up To Our Ears." Finally, a new client offers his first quest, one that's easy to miss since Claptrap never radios in to tell you about it. Speak to Marcus Kincaid (in the building with the ammo and gun vending machines) for "Firepower: All Sales Are Final."

GRAB A REPAIR KIT AND STILL MORE GUNS

Take the stairs up the building between Helena Pierce's office and Marcus Kincaid's shop. Jump on top of the washing machine and, from there, to the roof with the radar dish. There's a **silver chest** up top, and if you look down from the east edge of the roof, you can spot a small balcony below. Drop down there and grab the Repair Kit for the "Claptrap Rescue: New Haven" quest.

Bring the kit to the Claptrap and he rewards you with the usual Storage Deck Upgrade. Follow him as he celebrates his renewed vigor, and he'll punch down a wall to reveal a third **silver chest**!

KING OF CLAP

BEATING THE RESPAWN
IF YOU FIND YOURSELF STARVED FOR INVENTORY SPACE, HEALTH, OR AMMO, FAST TRAVEL BACK TO TOWN. SELL THOSE EXTRA ITEMS YOU DON'T NEED, CHECK STORES FOR NEW FEATURED ITEMS, THEN FAST TRAVEL RIGHT BACK. IF YOU'RE QUICK ENOUGH, THE AREAS YOU'VE ALREADY CLEARED WON'T BE REPOPULATED YET.

—KEITH SCHULER, MISSION GURU

CHEESING UP AMMO

IF YOU FIND A CLASS-MOD DECK WITH AN AMMO REGENERATION ATTRIBUTE, HOLD ON TO IT EVEN IF YOU PREFER YOUR CURRENT DECK. TEMPORARILY EQUIP THE AMMO REGEN DECK WHEN YOU FIND YOURSELF LOW ON AMMO. SIT TIGHT AND GAIN PRECIOUS BULLETS WITHOUT HAVING TO SCROUNGE FOR DROPS, THEN RE-EQUIP YOUR USUAL DECK BEFORE GOING BACK INTO COMBAT.

—KALE MENGES, DEVELOPER

RETURN TO FYRESTONE TO CHECK ON T.K.

If you've completed all of the T.K. quests in Chapter 1, Scooter will offer the "Is T.K. O.K.?" quest. Even if you aren't in the mood to return to Fyrestone, you should go there anyway; this quest offers a large reward and only takes a minute or two to complete. (It is kind of a downer, though.)

Use the Fast Travel station to warp to Fyrestone, then make your way to T.K.'s cabin. The front door is wide open… and the news is not good. Brighten your spirits by taking a look at T.K.'s southern porch, where he's left a brand-new **red chest** for you!

MISSION TAG

3 IS T.K. O.K.?

LEVEL 21

■ T.K. checked on (1)

Client: Scooter
Check on T.K. Baha for Scooter.

I just got a call from my good buddy, T.K. Baha. You met him right? Blind as a bat in heat, and twice as loony. He'll watch your back in a fight, though. Just make sure you yell a lot so's he knows where you're standin'. Anyway, he called me, but he didn't say nothin'. That coot never calls unless he's got a reason, y'know? Would you go check on him? Make sure a skag didn't eat his other leg or something'.

REWARDS: 6,072 XP + $8,102 + GRENADE MOD

A LITTLE DAB WILL DO YA

IN A CO-OP GAME, YOU CAN BE A REAL TEAM PLAYER BY EQUIPPING A CORROSIVE WEAPON. THE NEXT TIME YOUR TEAM FACES A HORDE OF BAD GUYS, SPLASH SOME ACID ON EACH ENEMY—EVERY SHOT FROM YOUR TEAMMATES WILL HURT THEM EVEN MORE!

—MIKE MCVAY, QA LEAD

4 LIKE A MOTH TO FLAME

LEVEL 21

- ■ *1st Torch lit (1)*
- ■ *2nd Torch lit (1)*
- ■ *3rd Torch lit (1)*
- ■ *Mothrakk killed (1)*

Client: New Haven Bounty Board
Light the torches and kill Mothrakk.

Over in the Arid Badlands, just east of Shine Gravel Processor, people have been disappearing in the night. Some say they're being carried away by a monster rakk, one the locals call "Mothrakk." She seems to be attracted to fire, and that's how we're going to lure her out. Light the three torches I've set up, and when she shows up, you take her down.

REWARDS: 8,280 XP + $8,102 + SHOTGUN

BRING DOWN THE DEADLY MOTHRAKK

While you're in the neighborhood, you might as well take a crack at the "Like A Moth To Flame" quest. You need a good sniper rifle and plenty of ammo, so stock up in Fyrestone, then generate a Runner with a mounted machine gun. Drive west past the Zephyr Substation, then hang a left as you would to reach the Lost Cave. The hill with the torches is just south of the cave entrance. When all three are lit, head for the turret and wait for Mothrakk to appear. If you're lucky, you can catch it with a spray of machine-gun fire as it flies in to greet you.

Mothrakk's preferred mode of attack is to circle directly overhead, raining fireballs down upon you. Once it enters the battlefield, your Runner won't be much use, so bail out and look for cover. You won't find any near the torches, but the Catch-A-Ride to the north has a nice fireproof roof. Stand near this safe cover and shoot Mothrakk with a sniper rifle, which has the best combination of power, accuracy, and bullet speed for hitting airborne targets. When you see the fireballs start dropping, step under the roof and wait them out. Then snipe her again as she circles around for the next bombing run.

When you fire the final bullet, Mothrakk pops like a piñata, scattering the usual high-level boss drops over a large area. Try to track where her body falls so you can gather up all of that sweet loot.

MOTHRAKK	LEVEL	HEALTH	XP	WEAK POINT	RESISTANCES	SHIELDS
	29	10	40	None	⚡ ☣ 🔥	None

This giant horror rules the skies over the Arid Badlands, and is known to carry off people and the occasional car, mostly at night.

3-2 (OPTIONAL): THE WARREN OF MAD KING WEE WEE

Patricia Tannis is digging for Vault clues in the east, but this is a fine opportunity to head west instead, into the Tetanus Warren kingdom of King Wee Wee. All of the Tetanus Warren quests are optional, but they're a great way to level up—and the rewards of a Corrosive Artifact, a Storage Deck Upgrade, and several **red chests** help sweeten the deal even more!

QUESTS:

1. Corrosive Crystal Harvest (optional)
2. Claptrap Rescue: Tetanus Warrens (optional)
3. King Tossing (optional)

CUT A PATH THROUGH THE OUTSKIRTS OF NEW HAVEN

There's no way to drive to the Tetanus Warren entrance, so ditch your Runner a short distance outside of town and walk the rest of the way. Every hut you pass is a potential bandit spawn point, so proceed very slowly and cautiously; these foes prefer to fight from a distance, so a sniper rifle or rocket launcher can be very effective here. However, there are also plenty of psychos in the mix, so keep a shotgun handy, too. In multiplayer games, one player should handle the sniping while the rest protect the sniper from psycho rushes.

As you approach the warren, take a quick detour under the giant, rusty, curved-metal supports. There's a **silver chest** among the garbage. That's it for loot outside, but you'll find plenty more chests once you pass through the nearby entrance into the Warren itself.

CLAIM CRYSTALS FROM THE ARMORED SPIDERANTS

As in the original "Crystal Harvest" quest, you collect your 50 Corrosive Crystals by attacking the large crystal formations found throughout the warren. Unlike the Lost Cave, you won't have to clear a path of enemies to reach each and every one of them; the warren is relatively quiet. Don't get complacent, though; there are plenty of Spiderants lurking beneath the earth, just waiting to burrow up as soon as they have you surrounded.

KING WEE WEE

REPAIR KIT

CLAPTRAP

NEW
HAVEN

TETANUS
WARRENS

TETANUS WARREN

QUEST ICONS	CRYSTAL
	◇

LEGEND	TREASURE CHEST	NEW-U POLE/STATION	MEDICAL VENDING MACHINE	AMMO VENDING MACHINE
	▬	●	☐	☐

The pack of Spiderantlings that strikes after the first crystal and before the second is easily beaten. Unfortunately, the larger Spiderants to come, such as the Badass Spiderant Zapper and Badass Spiderant Burner, are much tougher beasts. Their carapace makes them virtually impervious to headshots, so you must aim for the weakpoint on their rear abdomen.

In multiplayer games, make a habit of surrounding the larger Spiderants so that someone always has a clear shot at the back. Spiderants are a bit trickier in single-player games, although Soldiers can mimic this technique by throwing down a turret and rushing past the spider to surround it, while Sirens can Phasewalk past the spider and quickly shotgun it or assassin-strike it from behind. Other characters will have a tougher time getting behind these foes, but it isn't absolutely necessary to do so. The abdomen does stick out a little bit higher than the Spiderant's head, so you can hit it with highly accurate weapons even when it's facing you.

1 CORROSIVE CRYSTAL HARVEST

LEVEL 21

■ *Corrosive Crystals (50)*

Client: New Haven Bounty Board
Harvest Corrosive Crystals in the Tetanus Warrens

Corrosive Elemental Artifacts allow you to customize your skills with the power of acid. The key component for such an artifact is the Corrosive Crystal. I can fashion an artifact for you, but you'll need to provide the crystals. Go to the Tetanus Warrens and shoot the Crystal Clusters to break them apart. Watch out for the bandits that have taken over the cave.

REWARDS: 5,520 XP + $2,700 + CORROSIVE ARTIFACT

RAID THE BANDIT OUTPOSTS FOR RED CHESTS

After a long, straight tunnel, you come to a four-way chamber with a wounded Claptrap. After accepting the "Claptrap Rescue: Tetanus Warren" quest, you can go in three different directions. To proceed toward the Repair Kit and King Wee Wee, head northwest—you'll eventually loop around and end up passing through the northeast anyway. Directly west, behind Claptrap, is a heavily guarded bandit camp that you're free to ignore. There are no quest items inside, but there is a **red chest**.

2 CLAPTRAP RESCUE: TETANUS WARRENS

LEVEL 21

■ *Repair Kit (1)*

Client: Claptrap
Find the repair kit and repair this Claptrap.

You've discovered another defunct Claptrap robot. Could there be an unused repair kit somewhere in here?

REWARDS: 1,380 XP + STORAGE DECK UPGRADE

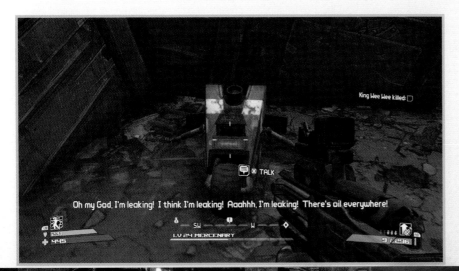

3 KING TOSSING

LEVEL 21

■ *King Wee Wee killed (1)*

Client: New Haven Bounty Board
Go to Tetanus Warrens and kill King Wee Wee

The Tetanus Warrens is a series of interconnected hollows under loose piles of rusting scrap metal. As if that weren't dangerous enough, one of the biggest threats to New Haven makes his home there. King Wee Wee is angry, drunken, and surrounded by a legion of followers. I'm offering a fat reward for someone to end his terrible reign.

REWARDS: 5,244 XP + $5,401 + UNIQUE WEAPON

If you decide it's worth the trouble, jump atop the shipping crates and snipe the two guards on the far side. After that, the doors burst open and all hell breaks loose. Jump back to where your Claptrap is, and wait to either side of the entrance to blow away any psychos that come rushing out. You can then peek through the entrance to pick off any stragglers, ducking back behind cover to restore your shields when needed.

After claiming the treasure from the bandit fort, continue down the northwest path until it forks again. Hang a right, to find a second **red chest**—once again guarded by poor, peaceful bandits who were simply minding their own business. Catch the sentries unawares, then move in quickly and gun down the reinforcements as they pour out of the two tents to the left of the chest.

BRING DOWN THE BANDIT SHANTYTOWN

Return to the New-U pole and continue north. You're about to stumble into an entire bandit shantytown, so prepare to fall back to one of the metal barricades in the hallway that can provide good cover to crouching snipers. After wiping out the foes at the entrance to town, you face another large-scale bandit encounter a short distance to the west, so don't give away your location by shooting crystals or going after the Repair Kit. Keep a low profile so you can snipe multiple foes before the full-blown battle even begins. When it does, keep an eye out for buckets of acid that you can shoot to flush out enemies behind cover, and avoid standing near them yourself.

LEAP FROM THE CANOPIES TO THE REPAIR KIT

The waypoint in the Claptrap Rescue quest points you to a spot near the entrance to the bandit shantytown, but the Repair Kit is nowhere to be seen. It's actually in the web of roots above you, and you need to make a careful series of jumps to reach it. Climb up the metal ramp to the north of the Repair Kit and drop down onto the canvas canopy that's roughly over the boar on the spit.

Dash down the left edge of that canopy to make a running leap to the canopy across the way—the one over the hut marked with a skull. From there, you can make another running jump to a corrugated metal platform set into the south wall, and then it's just a short hop to the Repair Kit. Bring it back to the Claptrap, stopping on the way to explore the cavern in the northwest corner of the map. Several waves of Spiderants guard a handful of crystals and another **red chest** in this area.

END THE REIGN OF KING WEE WEE

The lair of King Wee Wee is beyond the gate at the east end of the bandit shantytown. After what you've been through to reach him, King Wee Wee is a pushover. In fact, you could *literally* just push him over with melee strikes. A safer strategy, though, would be to snipe him until he comes after you, then finish him off at short range. Pin him between two fast-firing weapons (from two players, or a Soldier and his turret) or circle around him to throw off the aim of his boomerang axe while you pulp his face with a shotgun.

THE SPY

DAMAGE	65
ACCURACY	86.7
FIRE RATE	8.3
MAGAZINE	36
ELEMENT	None

High quality zoom, low kick + critical hit bonus!

+35% Critical Hit Damage

+30% Recoil Reduction

When King Wee Wee dies, he drops a relatively weak shield called "Wee Wee's Super Booster"— if it has any special powers, we sure can't figure out what they are. You'll probably find a more fitting reward in the **red chest** in his secret chamber to the southeast. When you're done looting, head west and leap off of the platform into the Spiderant- and Scythid-infested swamp below. If you've completed your crystal collection, you can dash straight past the bugs and back to New Haven.

At the bounty board, you receive the Corrosive Artifact, as well as a high-accuracy, very low-power submachine gun called "The Spy."

CLAPTRAP DANCE OFF

The mad scientist from the "Hidden Journals" quest tree remains on Pandora, and isn't far from town. Her newest excavation site is in the Rust Commons West, a vast mire of garbage located east of New Haven. As long as you're hip dip in Rust-Commons filth, you might as well pursue the five optional quests from the New Haven bounty board, Scooter, and Marcus.

QUESTS:

1. Seek Out Tannis
2. Up To Our Ears (optional)
3. Hidden Journal: Rust Commons West (optional)
4. Scooter's Used Car Parts (optional)
5. Firepower: All Sales Are Final (optional)
6. Scavenger: Submachine Gun (optional)

UNCLOG THE RUST COMMONS SUMP STATION

Generate a Runner with a machine gun, and drive east to the Rust Commons gates, where a Claptrap will greet you and let you through. The road out of New Haven forks to the north and east, but a gate blocks Runners from proceeding more than a few meters down the north road. So drive east instead, then turn left (north) at your earliest opportunity. When you do, you'll find yourself looking over the Rust Commons Sump Station, as unusually large and possibly flaming rakks dive-bomb your Runner. These Badass Rakks are a pain on foot, but can be easily bested by a skilled machine-gun turret operator (and the Runner's auto-targeting feature is quite skilled, indeed).

Park your Runner in front of the outhouse-sized chapel just east of the spot labeled "Sewage Pipes," and mow down any Spiderants that happen to be about. Look west toward the pipes that are your target in the "Up To Our Ears" quest. Shoot out the clogs with a good sniper rifle or rocket launcher, or save ammo by slowly picking away at them with the Runner's mounted turret.

If you hope to recover the **red chest** on the Sump Station catwalk, turn your guns on the bandit guards before you leave that perfect sniping spot. Drive down the hill to the west to finish off the bandits and claim your prize.

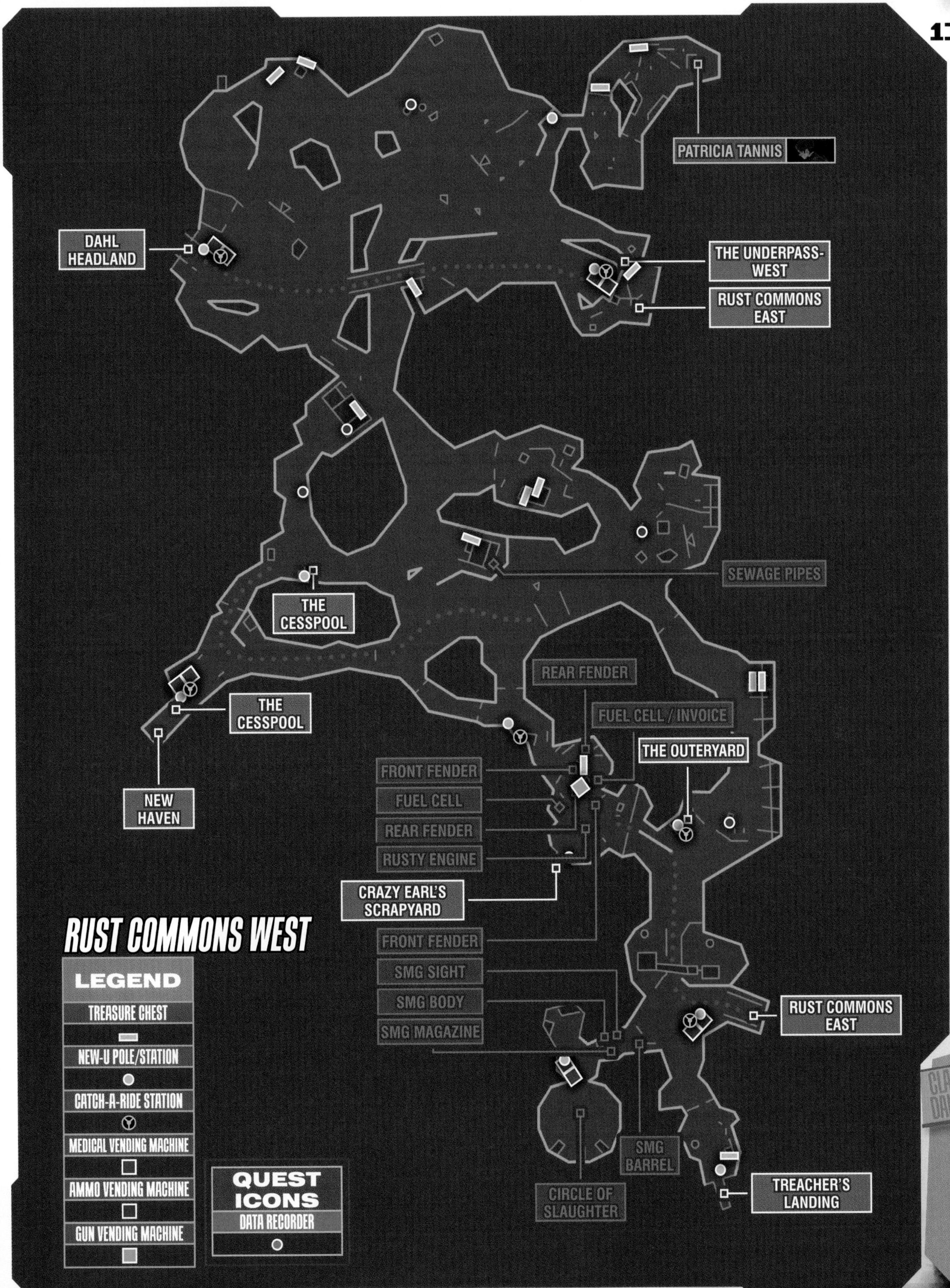

RUST COMMONS WEST

PATRICIA TANNIS

DAHL HEADLAND

THE UNDERPASS-WEST

RUST COMMONS EAST

SEWAGE PIPES

THE CESSPOOL

THE CESSPOOL

NEW HAVEN

REAR FENDER

FUEL CELL / INVOICE

THE OUTERYARD

FRONT FENDER

FUEL CELL

REAR FENDER

RUSTY ENGINE

CRAZY EARL'S SCRAPYARD

FRONT FENDER

SMG SIGHT

SMG BODY

SMG MAGAZINE

RUST COMMONS EAST

SMG BARREL

CIRCLE OF SLAUGHTER

TREACHER'S LANDING

LEGEND

TREASURE CHEST

NEW-U POLE/STATION

CATCH-A-RIDE STATION

MEDICAL VENDING MACHINE

AMMO VENDING MACHINE

GUN VENDING MACHINE

QUEST ICONS
DATA RECORDER

CLAPTRAP DANCE OFF

1 SEEK OUT TANNIS

LEVEL 21

- *Claptrap talked to (1)*
- *Tannis found (1)*

Client: Helena Pierce
Talk to Tannis at her dig site

If you insist on continuing your mad pursuit of the Vault, you should visit Patricia Tannis. I spoke with her about you, and she seemed eager to meet you. If you hurry, you might find her out at her dig site. Talk to Claptrap along the way, and he'll open the gate for you.

REWARDS: 2,760 XP + $2,700

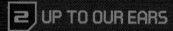

2 UP TO OUR EARS

LEVEL 21

- *Pipe 1 clear (1)*
- *Pipe 2 clear (1)*

Client: Scooter
Destroy the blockage in 2 pipes at the Rust Commons Sump Station

Man! You wouldn't believe the crap I have to put up with. And when I say crap I mean honest to goodness crap! Seems as though bandits overran the Rust Commons Sump Station and killed the personnel. Now the dang pipes are clogged! With all that slurry trickling through tons of vermin-infested, rusting metal, it gets saturated with very unpleasant debris, if you know what I mean. We need it fixed immediately, or we'll be up to our ears in who-knows-what.

REWARDS: 5,520 XP + $8,102 + COMBAT RIFLE

SCOUR THE CESSPOOL FOR DATA RECORDERS

Drive west from the Sump Station, following the river of muck. Don't let the Rakk attacks divert your attention from the barrels of explosive and toxic goo floating in the water; they'll detonate if you bump into them, possibly destroying your Runner in the process.

To your left is the Cesspool Arena, where players in multiplayer games can compete in more of the PvP deathmatch action they enjoyed in the Fyrestone Coliseum. The Cesspool features a new underground sewer map that offers plenty of fun ambush spots. Even if you aren't interested in the arena, you should still stop in and trigger the New-U Station inside, which makes for a convenient Fast Travel stop.

Drive north from the Cesspool, carefully running down Spiderants while avoiding the acid-filled barrels. You'll soon see a small shack to your right, marked by one of those mutant sunflowers and a lot of Vault-themed graffiti. Inside is an objective from the "Hidden Journal: Rust Commons West" quest—a data recorder from Patricia Tannis, chronicling Day 457 of her search for the Vault and accelerating descent into madness.

ZOMBIES EAT BRAINS.

SkagZilla ate your Mom.....

Continue north to a second Sump Station. Drive beneath it to lure out the bandits, then run and gun down as many of them as you can. The next data recorder is on the ground-level platform east of the Sump Station, and there's a **red chest** on the catwalks of the station's upper level.

FIGHT RAKKINISHU FOR THE THIRD RECORDER

The northern plateau of Rust Commons West is filled with Spiderant nests. If you leave your Runner, you'll quickly find yourself surrounded by the eternally re-spawning arachnids. You can rack up piles of XP and maybe a few Class Mods and artifacts (from the Badass varieties), but the Spiderants

never stop coming, forcing you to flee sooner or later. If they take down your Runner, you can find a Catch-A-Ride at either the east or west ends of the map.

Your first stop should be in the northwest corner of the map, where you'll find two high-level **red chests** that are only a few steps away from each other; one under a red canopy and the other behind the nearby defense tower. With an army of Spiderants hot on your tail, you can't afford to be selective—just grab everything out of the boxes and sort it out later.

Next, head for the abandoned camp toward the center of the plateau to find the next data recorder (it's the first in chronological order, so if you set your active quest to "Hidden Journal: Rust Commons West," the waypoint leads you right to it). The camp is usually free of Spiderants, but only because these are the hunting grounds of a high-level, fire-breathing rakk called "Rakkinishu." Move to your turret and do as much damage as you can before its flames endanger your Runner, then bail out and finish it off on foot. The fallen Rakkinishu drops the "Cracked Sash"—a shield with low capacity, but a very high recharge rate. The recorder is in the small, tented box between the two huts.

CLAPTRAP DANCE OFF

RAKKINISHU	LEVEL	HEALTH	XP	WEAK POINT	RESISTANCES	SHIELDS
	25	6	24	None	⚡ ☣ 🔥	None

Few dare tread where this lone rakk casts its grim shadow over the northern reaches of the Western Rust Commons.

- *Journal Day 224 (1)*
- *Journal Day 321 (1)*
- *Journal Day 457 (1)*
- *Journal Day 481 (1)*
- *Journal Day 493 (1)*

Client: New Haven Bounty Board
Download 5 Journal Entries from Data Recorders in Rust Commons West.

This is Patricia Tannis, calling for anyone with two brain cells to rub together. I hid five of my Data Recorders in Rust Commons West, but now I've decided I want them back. Listen to each one, and your ECHO device will record them. Once you have all five recordings, upload them to the bounty board.

REWARDS: 6,000 XP + $20,328

RAID THE RED CHESTS OF THE EAST PLATEAU

Head to the southwest corner of the plateau, and visit the New-U Station to save your progress and create a handy Fast Travel point (this one's called "The Underpass - West"). Follow the mountain path south of the tunnel to reach the lookout above the entrance to the Rust Commons East area. A handful of rakks and another **red chest** await you there.

Still not enough loot for you? Drive east down the road from the New-U Station and stop before you cross the bridge. You'll find a small settlement to the left, the home of a level-25 Badass Psycho, a creature that does not enjoy the company of visitors. What it does enjoy is using the **red chest** on his property as bait, so don't go for the loot until the psycho has emerged from its tent and has been firmly punished for a lack of hospitality.

FIND TANNIS AT THE PLATEAU EXCAVATION SITE

The trail to Tannis's excavation site is just north of "The Underpass - West" outpost. The entrance is narrow, so ditch your ride and hoof it up the mountain pass. The rakks have made a home in the ruins, and it's not uncommon to see them perched peacefully beneath the eerie, shimmering arches. You

know they'll attack you at some point, so blow one away with a sniper rifle and be ready to shotgun the rest when they fly in for revenge. As you head east, traveling the ruins loop in a counterclockwise direction, you also encounter several Spiderants. Use your action skills to exploit the weak point in their abdomens.

Tannis awaits you to the east, in the only building in the ruins. She signs off on your "Seek Out Tannis" mission and gives you the "Meet 'Crazy' Earl" mission in return. The entrance to his scrapyard is at the faraway southern end of the Rust Commons West map, but there's still plenty to do between here and there.

KING OF CLAP

Instead of leaving the way you came, continue along the ruins loop by heading west, walking along the north wall. Leap onto the northernmost white stone platform where it meets the wall, and follow it until you see the first **red chest**. Drop down to the ledge beneath you, and leap from there to the chest. A second **red chest** lies just to the east; if you're very lucky, you may even find a super-rare Eridian Weapon in one of them!

PICK UP THE REMAINING RECORDERS ON THE EASTERN ROAD

Return to your Runner and head south, traveling beneath the bridge and onto the river of sewage. Hang a left at the Sump Station where you found the second recorder, and head east along the steep road through a heavily populated bandit town. If you choose to stop and fight, you'll find two **silver chests** for your troubles; one inside the southernmost building, and the other just outside of the same building. If you punch the nitro before you hit the speed bump on your way out, you can catch some serious hang time—a nice way to earn the hang-time challenges, if you haven't already.

You land outside of a second bandit encampment, literally located in the shadow of a smoldering dump. Gun down the bandits, then grab the second-to-last data recorder from a crate along the west wall of the compound.

Drive southeast from the bandit camp until you hit a barrier that forces you to abandon your Runner and proceed on foot. A dozen or so high-level Spiderants spring from the water to attack you, but they're close enough to the entrance that you can run back to your Runner and blow away the whole lot of them with the turret. Finish off any survivors as you travel back through the muck to the stairs that have been set into the east wall. They lead to a viewing platform with a pair of **silver chests**.

4 SCOOTER'S USED CAR PARTS

LEVEL 21

- ☐ *Front fender (2)*
- ☐ *Rear fender (2)*
- ☐ *Fuel cell (2)*
- ☐ *Rusty engine (1)*

Client: Scooter
Collect all the vehicle parts and return to Scooter.

Scooter here. Somebody's been really hard on the Runners lately, and we're not going to see a shipment of replacement parts anything soon. There are probably plenty of spare parts we could salvage out in the Commons. Take this list and return with the parts, and I'll pay for 'em.

REWARDS: 4,140 XP + $10,803

CLAPTRAP DANCE OFF

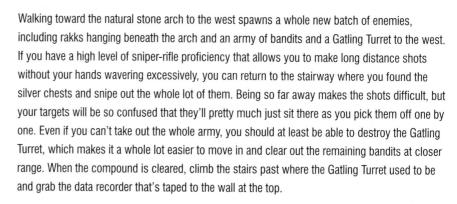

Walking toward the natural stone arch to the west spawns a whole new batch of enemies, including rakks hanging beneath the arch and an army of bandits and a Gatling Turret to the west. If you have a high level of sniper-rifle proficiency that allows you to make long distance shots without your hands wavering excessively, you can return to the stairway where you found the silver chests and snipe out the whole lot of them. Being so far away makes the shots difficult, but your targets will be so confused that they'll pretty much just sit there as you pick them off one by one. Even if you can't take out the whole army, you should at least be able to destroy the Gatling Turret, which makes it a whole lot easier to move in and clear out the remaining bandits at closer range. When the compound is cleared, climb the stairs past where the Gatling Turret used to be and grab the data recorder that's taped to the wall at the top.

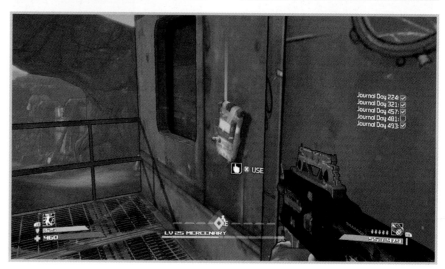

COLLECT THE SUBMACHINE GUN PARTS

The junkyard is just a few steps to the west from that last recorder. There you'll find Scooter's car parts, Marcus's shipping invoice, and the entrance to Crazy Earl's Scrapyard. First, however, grab a Runner and take a quick detour south. Hang a right after you pass under the bridge, and park your Runner at the sign with the five yellow bullets.

All five submachine gun parts are right in front of you, but you must dispense with their bandit guardians. First, snipe out the few bandits hanging around near the gate. As you proceed past the shipping crates, turn your sights to the cliff above and to the right, then prepare to catch the next wave of bandits as they come running toward the edge. Look to the gate from time to time, so you won't be caught unawares when it opens and a handful of psychos rush out. (Incidentally, the ammo vending machine on the other side of the gate sells level 4 ammo upgrades—but they run you an outrageous $60,256 a piece!

☐ THE SMG BARREL IS ATOP THE SHIPPING CRATE, JUST PAST THE ENTRANCE. CLIMB UP THE GARBAGE PILE TO THE LEFT TO REACH A HEIGHT FROM WHICH YOU CAN JUMP ONTO THE CRATE.

☐ THE SMG MAGAZINE IS JUST IN FRONT OF THE BLUE BUILDING, INSIDE AN ABANDONED TIRE.

☐ CLIMB UP THE HILL IN THE AREA WITH THE NEW-U POLE AND VENDING MACHINES, THEN WALK ONTO THE ROOF OF THE BLUE BUILDING FROM THERE. DROP CAREFULLY DOWN THE SOUTH LEDGE OF THE ROOF TO LAND NEAR THE SMG BODY.

☐ JUMP ATOP THE GREY, CHIMNEY-LIKE COLUMN AT THE EAST END OF THE LEDGE WHERE YOU FOUND THE SMG BODY, THEN JUMP EAST TO THE THIN METAL OUTCROPPING OF THE NEIGHBORING BUILDING. YOU CAN LEAP FROM THERE TO THE PLATFORM WHERE THE SMG SIGHT RESTS ATOP A PURPLE COT.

SCAVENGE FOR RUNNER PARTS AND TRADE SECRETS

Return north to the crossroads where you got the Runner, and head west to find the entrance to the junkyard. You face a massive ambush inside, so repeat the trick you used against the Spiderants; park your Runner right against the blockade: run inside to get everyone's attention, then sprint back to your Runner's turret to gun them down. If it's too far to auto-target, then manually blast the Gatling Turret on the distant rooftop.

Move carefully through the ruins, using your sniper rifle to pick off stray bandits who somehow missed the firefight earlier. There's a second Gatling Turret on the far side of the roof. Ease out under the roof and position yourself so the turret is shooting the edge, but is still vulnerable to your sniper fire.

The invoice for the "Firepower: All Sales Are Final" quest is under that same roof. Scooter's car parts are also here, scattered throughout the junkyard. They're typically in plain sight, and your waypoint or map could guide you to them. Note that one of the parts is atop the building with the vending machines and Gatling Turrets, so make a running leap from the tire pile to get up there. The final part is on top of a shipping crate, and you'll need to jump from the nearby half-buried shipping crate to reach it.

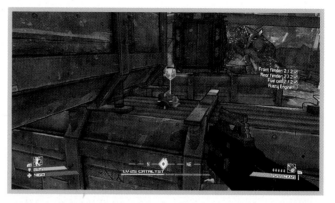

With five completed quests to report, you're probably eager to return to New Haven. Rather than running back, though, leave the junkyard via the southwest exit to Crazy Earl's Scrapyard. A New-U Station at the entrance to the scrapyard allows you to Fast Travel back to New Haven, and then right back to the scrapyard when you're ready to begin your next mission.

3-4 DOING CRAZY EARL'S DIRTY WORK

Crazy Earl is every bit the deranged coot you'd expect him to be, and he ain't givin' no one nothin' for free. If you want that piece of the Vault Key, you'll have to be Crazy Earl's errand boy for as long as he can think of stuff he wants done. Fortunately, all of his tasks involve shooting scores upon scores of bandits, and there are worse ways to pass the time.

QUESTS:

1. Meet "Crazy" Earl
2. Claptrap Rescue: Earl's Scrapyard (optional)
3. Get Off My Lawn!
4. Today's Lesson: High Explosives
5. Hair Of The Dog

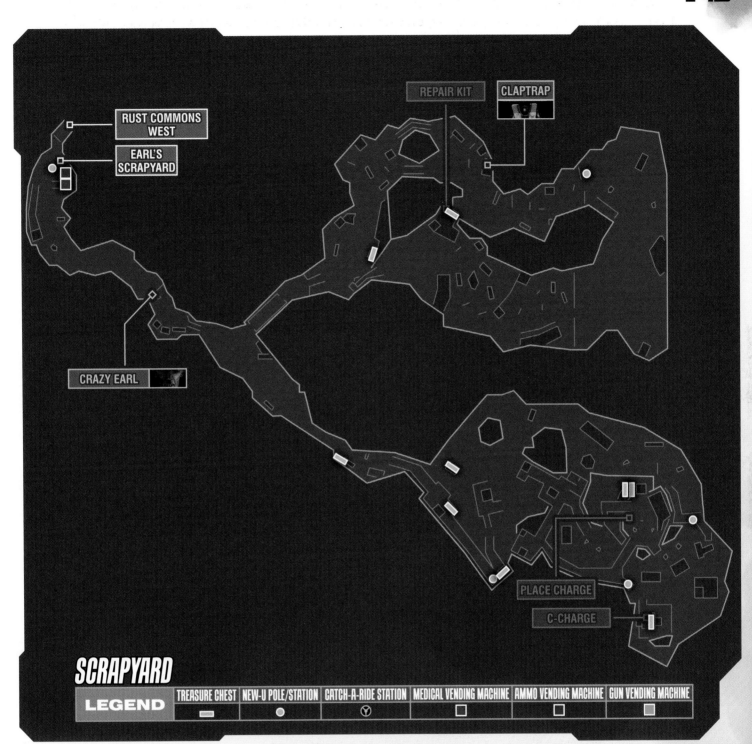

RUST COMMONS WEST

EARL'S SCRAPYARD

REPAIR KIT

CLAPTRAP

CRAZY EARL

PLACE CHARGE

C-CHARGE

SCRAPYARD

LEGEND	TREASURE CHEST	NEW-U POLE/STATION	CATCH-A-RIDE STATION	MEDICAL VENDING MACHINE	AMMO VENDING MACHINE	GUN VENDING MACHINE
	▬	●	Ⓨ	☐	☐	☐

SEEK HIGHER GROUND

VERTICALITY IS YOUR BEST ADVANTAGE IN BORDERLANDS. YOU OFTEN CAN'T EVADE ENEMIES BY RUNNING AROUND THEM, BUT IF YOU JUMP ONTO A ROCK OR PLATFORM, YOU CAN GET A FEW SHOTS IN BEFORE THEY'RE CLOSE ENOUGH TO HIT YOU.

— NICHOLAS WILSON

CLAPTRAP DANCE OFF

TREACHER'S LANDING

KING OF CLAP

TREACHER'S LANDING

LEGEND	TREASURE CHEST	NEW-U POLE/STATION	MEDICAL VENDING MACHINE	AMMO VENDING MACHINE
	▬	●	☐	☐

GET A PAIR OF PLOT MISSIONS FROM CRAZY EARL

Crazy Earl has built a wall near the entrance to the Scrapyard, but the explosive tanks leaning against it suggest an obvious way around it. Earl is in the small house on the other side; he won't come out and he sure as hell won't let you in, but he offers you the "Get Off My Lawn!" and "Today's Lesson: High Explosives" missions through a hole in the door.

You won't have to travel far to find the three Spiderants Earl wants killed; they spawn just a few steps to the southeast. The path through the Scrapyard forks shortly after that encounter—the rest of your quest goals are in the region to the southeast, and a wounded Claptrap is the main draw in the northeast part of the map.

SPIDERANT TARGETING
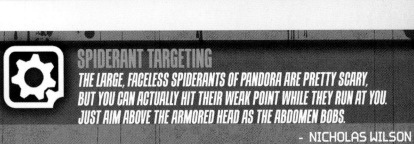

THE LARGE, FACELESS SPIDERANTS OF PANDORA ARE PRETTY SCARY, BUT YOU CAN ACTUALLY HIT THEIR WEAK POINT WHILE THEY RUN AT YOU. JUST AIM ABOVE THE ARMORED HEAD AS THE ABDOMEN BOBS.

— NICHOLAS WILSON

 MISSION TAGS

1 MEET "CRAZY" EARL

LEVEL 22

■ *Path cleared (1)*

Client: Patricia Tannis
Go to the Scrapyard and blow up an entrance to meet Crazy Earl.

Have you met the bearded turtle yet? Crazy Earl? He hides from me, in his Scrapyard to the south. Any time I want to see him, I have to blow a hole in his junk pile. Anyway, he has a piece of the Vault key, along with most of my underwear. The details of that transaction are unimportant, just get that artifact back.

REWARDS: 2,880 XP + $3,025

2 CLAPTRAP RESCUE: SCRAPYARD

LEVEL 22

■ *Repair Kit (1)*

Client: Claptrap
Find the repair kit and repair this Claptrap.

You've discovered another defunct Claptrap robot. Could there be an unused repair kit somewhere in this scrap heap?

REWARDS: 1,440 XP + STORAGE DECK UPGRADE

LEVEL 22

- Bandits killed (25)
- Spiderants killed (3)

Client: Crazy Earl

Kill bandits and spiderants.

You want a favor from me? Well, pick my nose and I'll pick yours, as the saying goes. I got trespassers crawlin' all over my property here. They got their eye on my treasure. You get out there and start exterminatin' interlopers. Then we'll see about whatever it was you wanted.

REWARDS: 4,320 XP + $3,025

4 TODAY'S LESSON: HIGH EXPLOSIVES

LEVEL 22

- C-Charge (1)
- C-Charge placed (1)

Client: Crazy Earl

Collect Earl's C-Charges, then plant them and set them off.

Those bandit assholes stole my C-Charges! The explosives must be around their camp somewhere. You're gonna teach them a lesson. They want my C-Charges? Fine. We'll shove 'em up their asses and set 'em off. You steal Earl's stuff, you get blasted to hell.

REWARDS: 7,200 XP + $9,075

SAVE THE SCRAPYARD CLAPTRAP

Saving the Claptrap is optional, but a quick visit to the northeast region takes only a few minutes and pays off quite nicely with a Storage Deck Upgrade and two **red chests**. Use the cover provided by the shipping crates to move through the small bandit squads as you proceed north, and continue along the north wall when the path briefly splits. You face several Bruisers after emerging from the thin forked path, so try to take one out quickly with a sniper rifle and then back up to lure the remaining foes into the thin path for one-at-a-time thumpings.

Follow the north wall to the wounded Claptrap and talk to him to accept the quest. The waypoint directs you to a clearly visible Repair Kit just to the south, on the upper level of the map. There's no need to complete the loop of the entire northeast region; you can actually leap right to it. Jump atop

the refrigerator that's half-buried in the rubble, and from there to the twisted metal directly to your south. Walk along the metal until you're high enough to jump to the platform with the **red chest** and the Repair Kit.

You'll have plenty of company up there, so do as much damage as you can while crouching behind the red chest, then fall back down and pick off your pursuers from below. When the bandits have exhausted their charge, jump back up, snipe out the stragglers, and collect your loot. In addition to the red chest you used as cover, there's a second **red chest** just to the southwest.

Give the Repair Kit to the Claptrap and return to the Scrapyard crossroads. You can stay and explore the rest of the northeast area if you want, but there isn't anything else in it for you.

TRAVEL SOUTHEAST TO THE BANDIT PIT

To get back to Earl's errands, head southwest from his house, using the open shipping crate as cover to gun down enemy bandits as they emerge from their hut. After raiding a **silver chest**, use the locker beside the hut to get on its roof, and from there to a ledge with a trash pile. (You can often find really good loot in the Scrapyard trash piles.)

Continue southwest to an elevated platform that has "ambush" written all over it. When the bandits do emerge from their hut, blast the barrels around it to greet them with a burst of something nasty. Then gun them down where you stand; there's no usable cover that isn't dangerously close to exploding barrels. When the coast is clear, open the first **silver chest** and then head down the ramp to the southwest to find a second **silver chest** and a New-U pole. Then head right back up to the entrance to the bandit camp, and make a running leap to the **red chest** on the elevated platform to the north.

RECLAIM CRAZY EARL'S C-CHARGE

The pit is a tricky area to navigate. The bandits have built their main camp far above the pit, and left only a single usable entrance. With so many structures at such different heights, your auto-map won't be much help. Basically, you want to travel along the north wall of the pit, avoiding unnecessary encounters with the skags—there's really no end to them. Eventually you'll come across a fortified bandit wall with a New-U pole on top. Take out the bandits from below, then use the path of garbage beneath the metal supports to get atop the wall and leap over. Make your way to the open-roofed building to the southwest, but don't expect to get near it without triggering a flood of bandits and psychos from every other doorway. Fall back to the shipping crates near the wall and use them as cover. After picking off the bandit guardians from afar, return to the open-roofed building to find the C-Charge beside a **silver chest**.

5 | HAIR OF THE DOG

LEVEL 23

■ Bottles of Booze (24)

Client: Crazy Earl
Collect Bottles Of Booze from the bandits at Treacher's Landing.

One more thing. I'm all outta booze. You wanna get my alien whatsit? You're gonna go pick up a new supply from the bandits out at Treacher's Landing. They brew a mean moonshine out there. Don't know what's in it, but who cares? Those bandits don't part with it willingly, of course. That's why you're going, and not me!

REWARDS: 4,950 XP + $5,082

SCRAPYARD

LEGEND	TREASURE CHEST	NEW-U POLE/STATION

DETONATE THE CHARGE IN THE BANDIT CAMP

Head northwest to reach the only ramp to the higher level, and fight your way into the bandit camp. Continue through two platforms, then turn left and ascend a steep ramp to the southwest. Watch out for the pair of explosive barrels at the top of the ramp—they won't hold for long when bandits begin emerging from the shacks to fire at you.

After ascending the ramp, turn left and walk through a small shack. Head up the platform to your right to trigger a New-U pole, and take cover behind the railing there as you scope out the heart of the bandit camp, to the north. Snipe any targets you can, then rush the bridge to take out the survivors.

Insert the C-Charge into the glowing green spot against a water tower, and then move out of the way—it detonates after only a few seconds. The explosion blows off the roof and wall of a nearby shack, exposing a bandit weapons cache that includes a pair of **red chests**. Take your fill of the loot, and then leap off the west edge of the bandit's elevated camp and make your way back to Earl.

FOLLOW EARL'S NEXT WHIM TO TREACHER'S LANDING

Your reward for completing Earl's first two errands is being asked to take on a third: The "Hair Of The Dog" mission. This one takes place in a new area known as Treacher's Landing, so you must leave Crazy Earl's Scrapyard through the Rust Commons West exit, then head east to the Catch-A-Ride. Generate a Runner and drive it south until you hit a bandit camp. You could easily run past the startled bandits and into the Treacher's Landing exit at its south point, but if you hope to open the **silver chest** atop the lookout tower, it's hard to avoid a fight. Run around outside the bandit camp to spawn some Spiderants, and then charge into the camp and up the lookout tower ramp, shotgunning anyone in your way. The Spiderants will keep the bandits occupied while you snipe at them from the tower.

KING OF CLAP

There isn't anywhere specific you need to go in Treacher's Landing. Each bandit has a bottle of hooch, and drops it, along with the rest of their loot when killed. However, you must travel a fair distance into Treacher's Landing before you can kill enough bandits to fill Crazy Earl's 24-bottle order, so

you might as well make a loop of the area to find some **red chests** and earn an unusual achievement/trophy.

After the initial bandit encampment, which is home to a pair of **silver chests**, head south under the elevated platforms to the first boardwalk area. Proceed through the boardwalk to the natural island in the center of the map to find a New-U pole and the first **red chest** on an elevated watch tower. There are two more **red chests** in the long concrete pier to the south, but that area is heavily guarded, and we'll be coming back to it soon anyway.

GET ON A BOAT!

Proceed east through a second boardwalk area, detonating the many toxic barrels and propane tanks to do a bit of extra damage to your foes. When you return to dry land, you'll see several signs directing you to the left—go right instead. Follow the beach through a small cove and to a pier that doesn't appear on the game's auto-map. It leads to a boat with a **red chest**, and when you step on board, you'll unlock the peculiar "You're on a boat!" achievement/trophy. You're on a boat! You're on a boat! Everyone look at you, 'cause you're sailing on a boat!

Ahem. Anyway, return to solid ground and head north to complete the loop and find a third **red chest** at the end. No need to cut through the Rust Commons again; you can Fast Travel directly from the entrance of the area to Crazy Earl's Scrapyard, where Earl admits he never had the Vault Key piece after all.

WAIT A MINUTE. . .
I WAS TOTALLY WRONG EARLIER. THIS PAGE IS CLEARLY THE BEST. SORRY.
- MATTHEW ARMSTRONG, GAME DIRECTOR

A "MARKET CORRECTION" FOR ONE-EYED JACK (OPTIONAL)

After fessing up about the Vault Key, Earl gives you "The Next Piece" and "Earl Needs Food… Badly" missions. But there's plenty more to do before taking on Krom; for example, remember the series of "Firepower" missions you were doing for New Haven's Marcus Kincaid? Well, now is a good time to bring that quest tree to its bitter end.

QUESTS:

1 Firepower: Market Correction (optional)

2 Firepower: Plight Of The Middle Man (optional)

3 Jack's Other Eye (optional)

3-5 MISSION TAG

1 FIREPOWER: MARKET CORRECTION

LEVEL 21

☐ *Ammo Dumps destroyed (6)*

Client: Marcus Kincaid
Destroy the ammo dumps.

I believe that One-Eyed Jack is storing a recent ammo shipment in his warehouse. We can't have that! When there's too much supply, there's no demand. Prices go down, and nobody profits. So I want you to go to the warehouse and trigger a little "market correction" by destroying the ammo dumps. You'll need explosives or elemental weapons, which are, of course, available at any of my stores for a reasonable price!

REWARDS: 5,520 XP + $10,803 + SUBMACHINE GUN

DESTROY ONE-EYED JACK'S BANDIT-TOWN AMMO DUMPS

If you haven't yet collected the "Firepower: Market Correction" quest from Marcus Kincaid, go talk with him in New Haven. With the quest in your Mission Log, Fast Travel to The Underpass - West, and outfit a Runner with a rocket launcher. Drive it under the bridge to the south and hang the first left up the steep hill to the bandit town with two **silver chests**. That's where One-Eyed Jack warehouses his extra munitions.

Get a few Spiderants on your tail, then drive all the way through town and hang a U-turn at the other side. While the Spiderants keep the bandits on the west busy, your rocket launcher can take care of the ones on the east. Return to the west to avenge the fallen Spiderants, then turn your attention to the six ammo crates Marcus hired you to destroy. There's one outside of the building with the two **silver chests**, and two inside. The fourth is atop the building to the northwest, and the final two are outside of the building atop the small hill in the northeast corner of town. You can set the crates aflame with a few blasts from your rocket launcher, or a good shot from any weapon with elemental properties. They explode a few seconds later, so don't park too close!

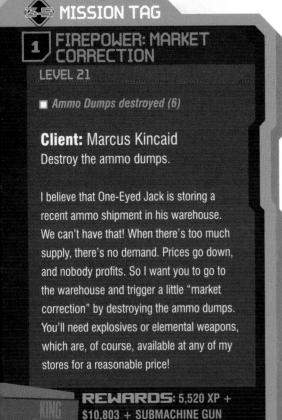

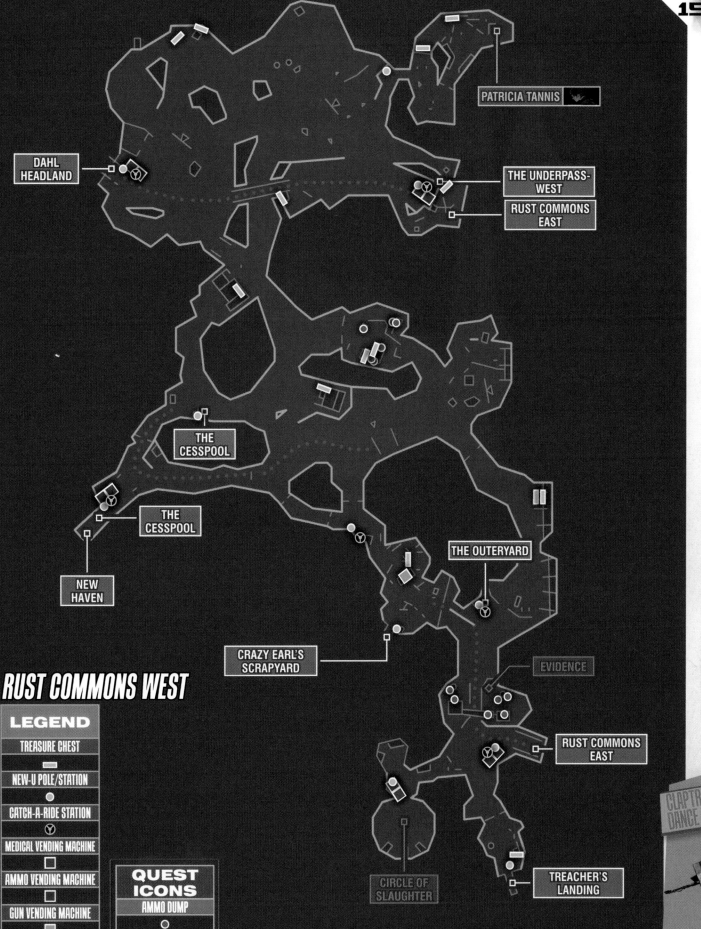

PATRICIA TANNIS

THE UNDERPASS-WEST

RUST COMMONS EAST

DAHL HEADLAND

THE CESSPOOL

THE CESSPOOL

NEW HAVEN

THE OUTERYARD

CRAZY EARL'S SCRAPYARD

EVIDENCE

RUST COMMONS EAST

CIRCLE OF SLAUGHTER

TREACHER'S LANDING

RUST COMMONS WEST

LEGEND

TREASURE CHEST	
NEW-U POLE/STATION	●
CATCH-A-RIDE STATION	Ⓨ
MEDICAL VENDING MACHINE	□
AMMO VENDING MACHINE	□
GUN VENDING MACHINE	▪

QUEST ICONS
AMMO DUMP
○

CLAPTRAP DANCE OFF

2 FIREPOWER: PLIGHT OF THE MIDDLEMAN

LEVEL 23

- Caches destroyed (6)
- Evidence found (1)

Client: Marcus Kincaid
Destroy Weapon Caches and find evidence.

I need to know who exactly is supplying the bandits. The invoice you found was a good start, but we need more. I'm sure you can find some of the original shipping crates, and that will provide the evidence we need. While you're at it, destroy One-Eyed Jack's weapon caches. There is too much of my competitor's product out there! We'll show them what happens when they try to cut out the middleman!

REWARDS: 6,000 XP + $6,776 + COMBAT RIFLE

3 JACK'S OTHER EYE

LEVEL 23

- Jack's Other Eye (1)

Client: Helena Pierce
Kill One-Eyed Jack, and bring back his eye as proof.

What did you and Marcus do? One-Eyed Jack is madder than hell, and my sources tell me he's going to take it out on New Haven. Our only chance is to kill him before he strikes. This is your fault. You fix it.

REWARDS: 6,000 XP + $10,164 + UNIQUE GUN

WREAK MORE HAVOC ON THE BANDIT WEAPON CACHES

Drive to the nearby Cesspool New-U Station and Fast Travel to New Haven. When you report the news, Marcus Kincaid throws you a random submachine gun and a new mission: "Firepower: Plight Of The Middleman." Fast Travel back to the Rust Commons, but this time choose The Outeryard New-U Station to get as close as possible to your next target in the southern part of the map.

The bandit compound is extremely close, just south of the Catch-A-Ride and up the hill to the west (in front of the bridge that crosses over the road). You don't need a Runner, but it makes it easier to kill the first batch of foes.

Destroy the first two weapon caches outside of the building (one by the neighboring hut), then enter the building, head up the ramp, and cross a bridge to the other side. Destroy the third cache on the bridge itself, and the fourth cache on the ground floor of the building on the other side. Destroy the final two caches in the courtyard, and examine an empty crate to the north to find the evidence Marcus Kincaid was looking for.

PUT ONE-EYED JACK OUT OF BUSINESS FOR GOOD

When you report to Marcus Kincaid, he considers the matter settled. Helena Pierce, however, is far from satisfied; your little rampage has led One-Eyed Jack to declare war on New Haven. Speak to her to get the "Jack's Other Eye" mission, which involves returning to the bandit town from the "Market Correction" mission to settle matters with Jack.

The Underpass - West is the closest access point, and a fine place to pick up a Runner. Drive into town and do as much damage as you can with your vehicle, then bail out before the bandits can destroy it. Find some cover atop a building, and snipe out as many of Jack's men as you can without exposing yourself to Jack's eerily accurate white energy blasts.

One-Eyed Jack typically hangs out in the canopied patio at the west end of town. If you avoid engaging him for long enough, he lowers his gun and looks away, allowing you to get the jump on him when you're ready to resume hostilities. A Hunter with a good sniper rifle (a fast-firing one is ideal) can squeeze out a shot or two, and then finish him off with a Bloodwing strike. A Siren can Phasewalk behind him and go for the kill with melee strike (for assassins) or shotgun headshots. Other classes must simply fight it out; use a shock attack to take out his shield, then pummel him with the Soldier's turret or the Berserker's rage state.

You get that gun, the Madjack, when One-Eyed Jack dies. It's a revolver that fires as fast as you can pull the trigger, and its bouncy projectiles ricochet off the environment. Don't forget that you must also pick up **Jack's Other Eye** to prove his death to Helena Pierce. When you bring it to her, she throws in The Sentinel, a worthless level 7 combat rifle.

CLAPTRAP DANCE OFF

ONE-EYED JACK

LEVEL	HEALTH	XP	WEAK POINT	RESISTANCES	SHIELDS
24	6	12	Head	None	Yes

Nobody knows where One-Eyed Jack came from. Marcus suspects that he's a black market weapons dealer, and that his bandit persona is simply a front. It is rumored that he lost his eye in a poker game, to an inside straight flush.

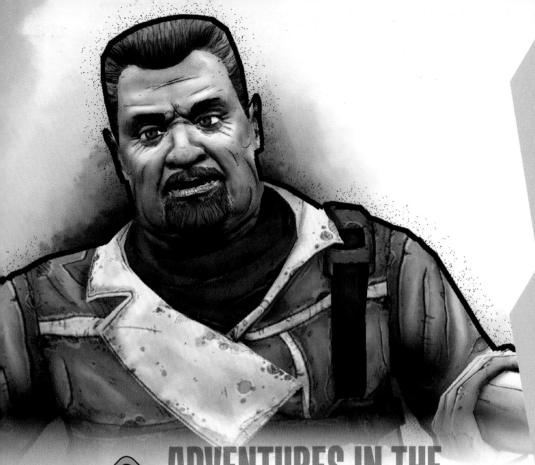

MADJACK	
DAMAGE	96
ACCURACY	94.8
FIRE RATE	3.1
MAGAZINE	6
ELEMENT	None

Fools! They called me maaaaad!

1.6x Weapon Zoom

THE SENTINEL	
DAMAGE	98
ACCURACY	90.3
FIRE RATE	7.7
MAGAZINE	12
ELEMENT	None

A worthless level 7 rifle

+13% Reload Speed

3-6 ADVENTURES IN THE MIDDLE OF NOWHERE (OPTIONAL)

None of the quests in this section is a plot mission, but it's necessary to pass through the Rust Commons East to reach Krom's Canyon, so you might as well poke around a bit first. Before departing, mop up some unfinished business in New Haven with the "Missing Persons" quest. Then head to Rust Commons East to see if you can get that Middle Of Nowhere bounty board back online.

QUESTS:

1. Missing Persons (Optional)
2. Middle Of Nowhere No More: Investigate (Optional)
3. Middle Of Nowhere No More: Fuses? Really? (Optional)
4. Middle Of Nowhere No More: Small Favor (Optional)
5. Middle Of Nowhere No More: Scoot On Back (Optional)
6. Altar Ego: Burning Heresy (Optional)
7. Hidden Journal: Rust Commons East (Optional)
8. Scavenger: Shotgun (Optional)

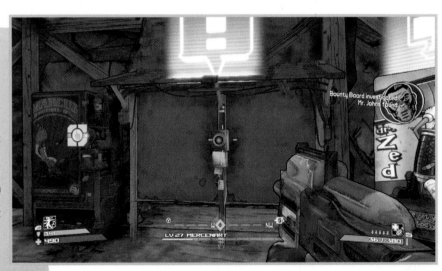

KING OF CLAP

KROM'S
CANYON

SHOTGUN
MAGAZINE

JOURNAL
DAY 684

DRAWBRIDGE

SHOTGUN BODY

SHOTGUN BARREL

SHOTGUN STOCK

RUST COMMONS
WEST

HUDSON JOHNS

OLD HAVEN

MIDDLE OF
NOWHERE

JOURNAL
DAY 718

JOURNAL
DAY 653

BOUNTY BOARD

JOURNAL
DAY 616

TRASH COAST

STACY VON KOFSKY

RUST COMMONS
EAST

RUST COMMONS
WEST

THE CAULDRON

SOUTH
DRAWBRIDGE

DRAWBRIDGE

JOURNAL
DAY 578

LEGEND

TREASURE CHEST

NEW-U POLE/STATION

CATCH-A-RIDE STATION

MEDICAL VENDING MACHINE

AMMO VENDING MACHINE

GUN VENDING MACHINE

QUEST
ICONS

FUSE

CLAPTRAP
DANCE OFF

MISSION TAG

1 MISSING PERSONS

LEVEL 24

☐ *Shawn Stokely found (1)*

Client: New Haven Bounty Board
Search for evidence of Shawn Stokely's
fate around New Haven.

Is anyone out there willing to help me? I'm
trying to find my cousin, Shawn Stokely,
and his son, Jed. They both live here in
New Haven, but they haven't been home or
responded to my calls for weeks. Jed was a
troubled young man and I think he may have
run away again. Shawn must've gone after
him, and now I'm fearing the worst. Anyone,
please, search around New Haven and find
out what happened to my cousin.

REWARDS: 1,560 XP + $3,794

The first is in the abandoned town directly
east of the entrance, atop the largest building
(the one with the gun vending machine).
Jump from the building's back porch onto a
washing machine, from there onto the lower
roof, and then to the main roof.

Return the way you came, toward the
entrance to the Rust Commons West, and
turn left onto the dirt road that leads up a hill
to a compound with a large radar dish. You'll
find two **red chests**; one placed along the
east wall of the main building, and another
in a shack atop the steep ramp to the west.

Return to your Runner and head south along
the main road, past the Pandora billboard.
When the paved road turns east to head
through a tunnel, keep going straight and
continue instead onto a dirt road that leads
to a ramshackle, elevated structure.
A ramp on the right side of the fence takes
you to the Middle of Nowhere New-U Station,
a full set of vending machines, and the broken
bounty board. Read the board, then cross the
plywood bridge near the dumpster to meet
Mr. Johns.

KING OF CLAP

FIND SHAWN STOKELY AT THE ENTRANCE TO NEW HAVEN

Head southwest from New Haven, down the main road where you first entered the city. Climb
up the steep ramp near the entrance to the Dahl Headland to find Shawn Stokely in the room
on the far side of the platform. Read his journal to complete the "Missing Persons" quest and
immediately receive the follow-up quest, "Two Wrongs Make A Right." We'll pursue that in the
next section; for now, concentrate on your business in Krom's Canyon.

LOCATE THE MIDDLE OF NOWHERE BOUNTY BOARD

It's time to visit the Rust Commons East, which is every bit as vast and full of quests as its
western counterpart. To get there, Fast Travel to The Underpass - West, generate a Runner,
and drive it east through the giant pipe. To reach the bounty board, follow the road until it forks, and
then head due south. You might as well hit a few easy **silver** and **red chests** on the way.

SEARCH THE DUMP FOR BOUNTY BOARD FUSES

After signing off on your quest from Helena, Mr. Johns gives you the "Middle Of Nowhere No More: Fuses? Really?" quest. To complete it, drive north, back through the abandoned town, and then northwest to a dump you can only enter on foot. The fuses are in the glowing trash piles, so give each one you see a good kick. Small, fast-moving Scythids will torment you as you search; center your fire on the orange Bursting Scythids to cause explosions that scatter the whole pack.

Return the fuses to Mr. Johns, and he asks you to kill time hunting Spiderants while he repairs the board. You can complete that mission in all of 20 seconds by driving around the field northwest of town until Spiderants spawn, and then running them down or blasting them with your turret. Avoid driving into the big ones, which can do a lot of damage to your Runner.

MISSION TAG

2 MIDDLE OF NOWHERE NO MORE: INVESTIGATE
LEVEL 24

- ☐ *Bounty Board investigated (1)*
- ☐ *Mr. Johns founds (1)*

Client: Helena Pierce

Find the Middle of Nowhere bounty board and Mr. Johns.

A once popular fuel depot in the Rust Commons was abandoned a while ago. People have taken to calling it the "Middle of Nowhere." There was a Bounty Board out there, but it doesn't work anymore. Go take a look at the board and see if you can find its custodian, Mr. Johns. If you were to get the board working again, you might find several jobs left over from before the malfunction.

REWARDS: 4,680 XP + $3,794 + CLASS MOD

CHECK THE BOUNTY BOARD AND REPORT TO HELENA

When the board is up and running, Hudson Johns gives you his final quest: "Middle of Nowhere: Scoot On Back." All that involves is returning to Helena for an easy payday. Fast Travel to New Haven to cross that off the list, then come back and check out the quests on the Middle of Nowhere bounty board: "Altar Ego: Burning Heresy," "Circle Of Slaughter: Meat And Greet," "Scavenger: Shotgun," and "Hidden Journal: Rust Commons East." The "Circle Of Slaughter" arena-battle quests (which take place back in Rust Commons West) are probably a little too tough at this point in the game. The other three missions, however, are all local and can be easily completed at your current level.

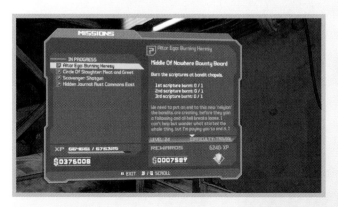

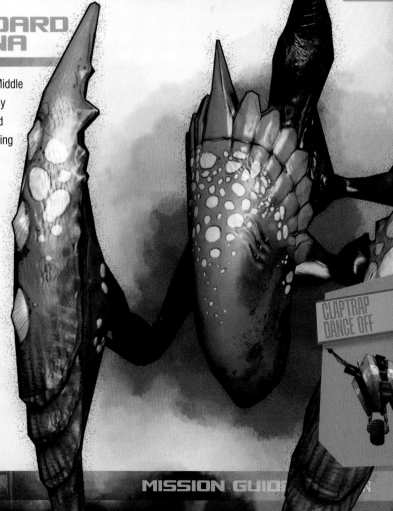

3 MIDDLE OF NOWHERE NO MORE: FUSES? REALLY?

3 MIDDLE OF NOWHERE NO MORE: FUSES? REALLY?

LEVEL 24

■ Bounty Board Fuses (3)

Client: Hudson Johns

Collect fuses and return to Hudson Johns.

The bounty board is missing a fuse, of all things. Who uses fuses these days, anyhow? That's the problem, really. They're hard to come by, seeing as most people have thrown 'em all out. Not like Marcus sells 'em; can't kill anyone with one. Even if you find one, it probably won't work. If you find three, there ought to be one in the bunch that will work. I'd sure appreciate it if you could find some and bring 'em to me.

REWARDS: 6,240 XP + $15,178

4 MIDDLE OF NOWHERE NO MORE: SMALL FAVOR

LEVEL 24

■ Spiderants killed (5)

Client: Hudson Johns

Kill off the spiderants for Hudson Johns.

While I get these fuses assembled and working for the bounty board, I need a small favor. Some spiderants are causing a ruckus nearby. Exterminate the bugs and when you're done I should have the fuse ready for the bounty board. You scratch my back... ya know what I mean?

REWARDS: 6,240 XP + $15,178

COLLECT THE FINAL JOURNALS OF PATRICIA TANNIS

Since they're all fairly close to each other, you might as well pick up the journals in chronological order. Generate a Runner from the Catch-A-Ride directly beneath the bounty board, and drive south until you find the raised drawbridge that's blocking off the east side of the Commons. You'll spot an overturned cardboard box behind one of the drawbridge supports; flip it over and grab the first recorder.

Drive back through the swamp to the north, then pull off when you spot the steep, grassy incline on your left. A large mushroom is growing at the top of the hill, sheltering the second recorder.

Continue to travel north, and then follow the river as it bends to the east. You'll spot a small camp on the west bank with a **red chest** and an army of guardian Spiderants. If you don't feel like dealing with them, you can run in and grab the loot pretty quickly; the third recorder is under the cot that's been propped against the boulder, directly behind the **red chest**.

Travel north and park your Runner near a second raised drawbridge. The fourth recorder is atop the watchtower, although you won't be able to see it until you kick down the loose board that's hiding it.

To find the final recorder, return to the Middle of Nowhere and search in the building behind Mr. Johns—it's squeezed between a crate and the wall.

PUT THE BANDIT SCRIPTURES TO THE TORCH

There are bandit chapels to the north, east, and south, and you can set them aflame in any order you choose. The waypoint suggests starting at the north, so drive your Runner through the shallow, Spiderant-infested lake near the entrance to Rust Commons West and set the first book of scriptures ablaze. Park your Runner near the altar so you can make a hasty retreat from the ever-spawning Spiderants.

Follow the main road south and then east through the tunnel. You'll spot the fenced-off second altar on the left side of the road. Set the holy book ablaze and prepare to be rushed from all directions by a bunch of seriously pissed-off Burning Psychos. No time to watch the scriptures burn; hop in your Runner and hightail it out of there!

5 MIDDLE OF NOWHERE NO MORE: SCOOT ON BACK

LEVEL 24

- [ ] *Helena talked to (1)*

Client: Hudson Johns
Return to Helena with the good news.

Thanks for helpin' me get the board back up and runnin'. Be sure to check it for jobs. Next time you're in New Haven, you ought to ask Miss Helena or that loser Scooter to come out and pay me a visit. I'd sure like to see them again.

REWARDS: ,432 XP + $11,383 + SHIELD

6 ALTAR EGO: BURNING HERESY

LEVEL 24

- [ ] *1st scripture burnt (1)*
- [ ] *2nd scripture burnt (1)*
- [ ] *3rd scripture burnt (1)*

Client: Middle Of Nowhere Bounty Board
Burn the scriptures at bandit chapels.

We need to put an end to this new "religion" the bandits are creating, before they gain a following and all hell breaks loose. I can't help but wonder what started the whole thing, but I'm paying you to end it. I want you to destroy the scriptures that they preach at each of their altars.

REWARDS: 6,240 XP + $7,589 + SHIELD

MISSION TAGS

7 HIDDEN JOURNAL: RUST COMMONS EAST

LEVEL 26

- ■ *Journal Day 578 (1)*
- ■ *Journal Day 616 (1)*
- ■ *Journal Day 653 (1)*
- ■ *Journal Day 684 (1)*
- ■ *Journal Day 718 (1)*

Client: Middle Of Nowhere
Bounty Board

Download 5 Log Entries from Data Recorders in Rust Commons East.

This is Patricia Tannis, calling for anyone with two brain cells to rub together. I hid five of my Data Recorders in Rust Commons East, but now I've decided I want them back. Listen to each one, and your ECHO device will record them. Once you have all five recordings, upload them to the bounty board.

REWARDS: 6,719 XP + $28,560

8 ALTAR EGO: SCAVENGER: SHOTGUN

LEVEL 24

- ■ *Shotgun Body (1)*
- ■ *Shotgun Magazine (1)*
- ■ *Shotgun Stock (1)*
- ■ *Shotgun Barrel (1)*

Client: Middle Of Nowhere
Bounty Board

Find all of the shotgun parts.

There are components to a shotgun scattered around. If you find all of these components, I can reassemble the weapon for you. Bring me the Body, Magazine, Stock, and Barrel.

REWARDS:
3,588 XP + SHOTGUN

KING OF CLAP

The final altar is south of the Middle of Nowhere outpost, on the east bank of the river. This time, a pack of Scythids handle the ambushing, but they aren't difficult to escape.

COLLECT SHOTGUN PARTS AT KROM'S CANYON DAM

After completing your final act of religious persecution at the southern altar, follow the river northeast until you hit a gated-off dam with a Catch-A-Ride and a New-U pole. The entrance to Krom's Canyon (the location of your next plot mission) is just to the northeast, and the Shotgun parts are scattered around the dam.

☐ JUMP UP THE MAKESHIFT STAIRWAY OF CRATES ON THE OTHER SIDE OF THE CATCH-A-RIDE TERMINAL. THE SHOTGUN MAGAZINE IS AT THE TOP.

☐ CROSS THE BRIDGE OVER THE DAM. THE SHOTGUN STOCK IS IN PLAIN SIGHT ATOP A CRATE.

☐ USE THE CRATES WHERE YOU FOUND THE SHOTGUN STOCK TO JUMP TO THE ROOF OF THE BUILDING, WHERE YOU'LL FIND THE SHOTGUN BARREL BETWEEN THE WIRES.

☐ LOOK TO THE NORTHEAST, AND YOU'LL SEE THE SHOTGUN BODY ATOP THE WALL AT THE EDGE OF THE DAM. LEAP FROM THE ROOFTOP WHERE YOU FOUND THE SHOTGUN STOCK TO THE CYLINDRICAL SILVER TANK, AND FROM THERE TO THE BODY.

Bring the pieces back to the bounty board for a random, high-quality shotgun. Hopefully it won't have all of its value wrapped up in a super-fancy scope like this one did. Grrrrr…

VAULT KEY 2: THE WRATH OF KROM

Your expedition to Krom's Canyon begins in the Rust Commons East, where you must fight through Krom's compound at Flood Lock. Then it's into Krom's Canyon itself, where Krom and his piece of the Vault Key await to the left… and Reaver, a Claptrap, and a case of skag meat to the right.

QUESTS:

1. Earl Needs Food… Badly (Optional)
2. Claptrap Rescue: Krom's Canyon (Optional)
3. Two Wrongs Make A Right (Optional)
4. The Next Piece

RUN KROM'S GAUNTLET AT THE RUST COMMONS LAKEBED

In the Rust Commons East, make your way to the dam at the north end of the river (where you found the parts in the "Scavenger: Shotgun" quest), and walk northeast past the floodgates. When you step off the cracked concrete of the dam, grab your sniper rifle and scan the fortifications ahead. You'll spot a Gatling Turret and a Rocket Turret, both of which can be easily destroyed from your current position

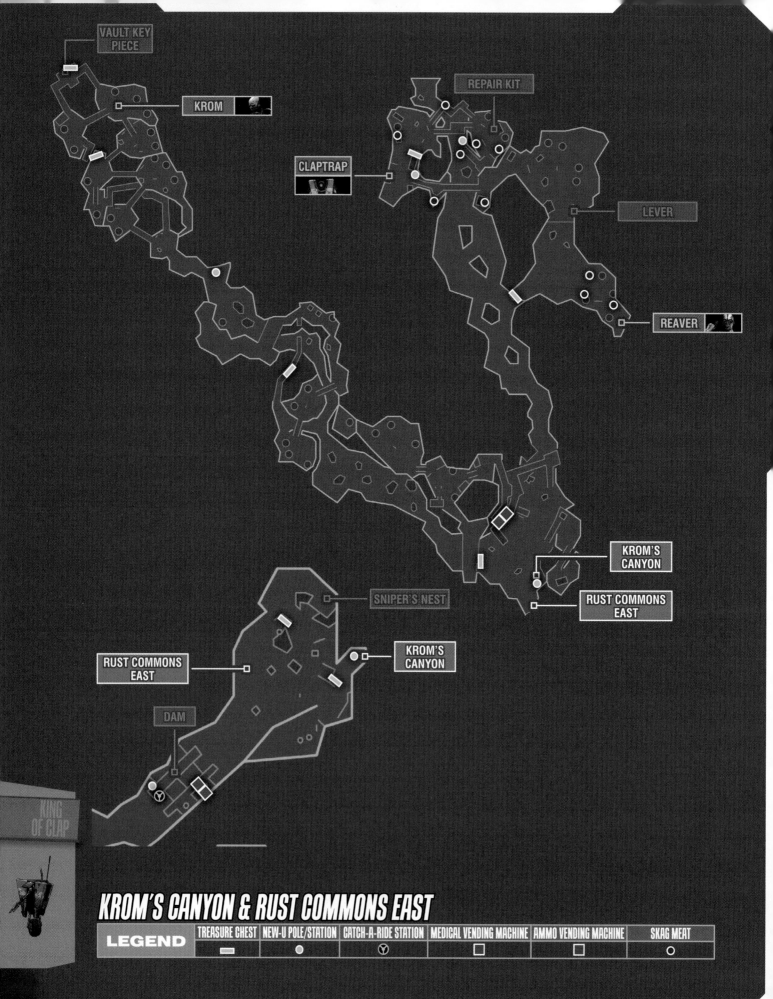

VAULT KEY PIECE

KROM

REPAIR KIT

CLAPTRAP

LEVER

REAVER

KROM'S CANYON

RUST COMMONS EAST

SNIPER'S NEST

RUST COMMONS EAST

KROM'S CANYON

DAM

KING OF CLAP

KROM'S CANYON & RUST COMMONS EAST

LEGEND	TREASURE CHEST	NEW-U POLE/STATION	CATCH-A-RIDE STATION	MEDICAL VENDING MACHINE	AMMO VENDING MACHINE	SKAG MEAT
	▬	●	Ⓨ	□	□	○

Taking out the automated turrets is a good start, but the lakebed is still a deathtrap. There's a sniper nest to the north and a manned turret to the east, and if you fight from the lakebed you'll be pelted from all directions. But if you take that northern sniper nest, you can use it to turn the tables on Krom's men. To get there, run along the west wall and up the curved hill trail. There's a Bruiser and a few other foes up there, so hit them hard—toss a grenade or two, run around their cover, and let rip with a fast-firing, large-capacity submachine gun. After you've dealt with the immediate threats, be ready to turn and shoot any other bandits who may have followed you up.

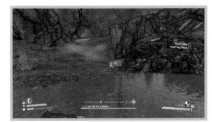

The sniper's nest provides a safe but distant sniping position. Don't stand too close to the edge, where you are exposed to enemy fire from the manned turret to the east. Stay a few feet back, pick a target in the lakebed, and take your shot. Sometimes you'll score the hit, and sometimes you won't—that's fine, too. Once your targets figure out where you're firing from, they may come rushing up to get you, right into the warm embrace of your shotgun.

When the coast seems clear of bandits, ease out to the edge of your sniper nest and look to the east, where a bandit in a manned turret presents your final obstacle. Position yourself so that his bullets are hitting the rock wall behind you, and search your bag of tricks for a solution. If you can't get a clear shot at the bandit operator with a sniper rifle, try a rocket launcher—it won't do much damage to the resilient turret, but the explosions will eventually kill the operator. With all the bandits out of the way, you're free to check out the two **silver chests**, pick up all the dropped items in the lakebed, and make your way to Krom's Canyon.

 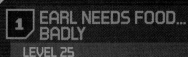

1 EARL NEEDS FOOD... BADLY

LEVEL 25

■ *Canned skag meat (10)*

Client: Crazy Earl
Collect cans of skag meat from Krom's Canyon, then return to Earl.

Hey, if you've got nothing better to do with your time, you can go get me some dinner. I'm talkin' about the best food on Pandora, canned skag meat! Only problem is, Krom likes it too, and he hijacked my entire supply! Make yourself useful! Go on out to Krom's Canyon and hijack it back.

REWARDS: 9,720 XP + $21,250

2 CLAPTRAP RESCUE: KROM'S CANYON

LEVEL 25

■ *Repair kit (1)*

Client: Claptrap
Find the repair kit and repair this Claptrap.

You've discovered a defunct Claptrap here. It looks like the bandits were pretty rough on him. Perhaps there is a repair kit nearby?

REWARDS: 1,620 XP + STORAGE
DECK UPGRADE

3 TWO WRONGS MAKE A RIGHT

LEVEL 25

☐ *Reaver killed (1)*

Client: New Haven Bounty Board
Eliminate Reaver and report back to New Haven.

Shawn's cousin will be devastated to hear about this. It seems that this "Reaver" character needs to be taught a little respect for his elders. If he joined Krom's men, he'll probably be found in Krom's Canyon. Find him, and mete out some old-fashioned discipline. Then return to New Haven and report what happened.

REWARDS:  5,670 XP + $8,500

4 THE NEXT PIECE

LEVEL 25

☐ *Krom killed (1)*
☐ *Vault Key Piece (1)*

Client: Crazy Earl
Get Krom's piece of the Vault Key and return to Tannis.

You want my alien doo-dad? It was stolen from me by one tough-ass bandit, a bastard by the name of Krom. If you're stupid enough to take him on, you'll find him to the northeast, in Krom's Canyon. Just follow the river north and past Flood Lock. If you get it back from him, you and that Tannis woman do whatever you want with it. I'm done with it.

REWARDS: 6,480 XP + $8,500

KING OF CLAP

SCAVENGE FOR SKAG MEAT IN THE NORTHWEST CANYON

While Krom is waiting in the northwest, the rest of the side quests are set in the northeast region. We'll tackle those first, but feel free to skip ahead if you have urgent business with Krom.

As you begin the long trek northeast, you can take a quick detour to a **red chest** by climbing up the second ramp on your right, and following a maze of platforms to the west. It's probably a good idea to gear up, since you won't find much of value in the canyon basin—just scattered bandits and a whole lot of Spiderants.

The first can of skag meat is just before the New-U pole at the north end of the basin. After grabbing it, move quietly up the ramp to the southwest and get the jump on the bandits on the ledge above. Clear the area, then take a position near the bridge across the canyon and get ready to meet the enemy reinforcements from the other side.

Grab the next can of skag meat, then ascend the ramp to the northwest to find the third can and a prime sniping spot. When it's safe to proceed, cross to the ledge on the west side and pick up a fourth can in plain sight. Approaching it often triggers a psycho ambush from the south, so get ready to greet them when you hear the music change.

FIND A REPAIR KIT FOR THE DAMAGED CLAPTRAP

When you discover the Claptrap on the east ledge, accept its mission and backtrack to the west ledge. Look to the sky, and you'll see the Repair Kit hanging from a tall scaffolding. Leap onto the, um, giant wheeled-mailbox-looking thing to the left of the red hut, and from there to the red hut itself. It's tricky, but you can just barely pull off a running leap from the roof of the red hut to the tilted platform with the Repair Kit; jump again as soon as you land to avoid slipping right back off the ledge.

Once rescued, the grateful Claptrap pounds a door into a nearby shed, revealing an otherwise inaccessible **red chest**. Thanks, Claptrap!

CONTINUE THE SKAG MEAT HARVEST

You should have four cans of skag meat in your backpack as you leave the Claptrap to take the southeast bridge across the Canyon. The fifth can will be to your right as you approach the bridge, but don't go there to grab it until after you've already dealt with the onslaught of psychos rushing at you from the other side. After mowing them down, find cover and snipe out the rest of the bandits from across the canyon.

Grab the fifth can and cross the bridge to collect the sixth in the campsite to your right. The waypoint for seventh can seems to be directing you back toward a lower ledge, but only because it's on top of one of the buildings on that level. The only way to reach it is to jump from the rocks at your current clifftop position.

You face a large and well-fortified bandit band when you attempt to push eastward, so grab some cover and pick them off one at a time—attempts to rush them will be met with heavy resistance from a band of bruisers. After wiping out the bandits, you discover a patchwork fence and a lever that opens it. All three cans are on the other side of that fence, but you won't be able to just waltz in and grab them if you've accepted the "Two Wrongs Make A Right" quest, as this is the home of the deadly Reaver.

BATTLE REAVER FOR CANNED MEAT—AND REVENGE!!!

When you lift the fence, you'll find yourself face-to-face with a small bandit army. Your foes stand there dumbfounded for a moment, so use those precious seconds to fall back and grab some cover; do not face them all at once.

As you approach the huts at the southern end of the map, Reaver slithers out from the boarded-up mine. You don't want him to have any friends left on the battlefield when that happens, so proceed slowly and meticulously through his camp, gunning down his henchmen first.

When Reaver does make his debut, switch to a fast-firing automatic weapon with a large clip. Reaver typically wears some sort of elemental-burst shield, so keep your distance when the shield-energy bar hits zero. Once the shield pops, rush in and keep your finger on the trigger. Without the protection of his henchmen, Reaver cannot line up a shot. Once you've burned through your clip, use your action skill to finish the job.

The spoils include the Reaver's Edge rifle, Reaver's shield, and the last three cans of skag meat. When you're done scavenging, leave Reaver's camp by dropping off the ledge to the southwest and take the shortcut marked by a loot-filled **red chest**.

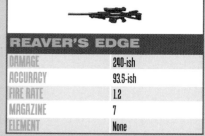

REAVER'S EDGE	
DAMAGE	240-ish
ACCURACY	93.5-ish
FIRE RATE	1.2
MAGAZINE	7
ELEMENT	None

The cutting edge

+19% Recoil Reduction

+150% Critical Hit Damage

REAVER	LEVEL	HEALTH	XP	WEAK POINT	RESISTANCES	SHIELDS
	27	10	20	Head	None	Yes

Jed Stokely lived with his adopted father in New Haven, until the day he decided to murder his old man and join the bandits, taking the name 'Reaver'. He is notorious, even among the bandits, for having a chip on his shoulder and daddy issues.

The long canyon basin that extends northwest from the entrance is home to small bands of bandits and psychos, who are skilled at using the boulder-strewn terrain to pop out at you from all directions. When the path forks, head to the left, blast a few bandits, and look to the right to find a well-concealed cave that holds a **red chest**. You can jump from the broken bridge at the end of the cave and continue up the basin, or go back to the fork and head left, taking the high road at the cliff's edge. The basin route is far less scenic, but much quicker. There are only a handful of enemies, but you'll be vulnerable to attacks from above, so move quickly and aggressively through it. If you take the high road, keep an eye out for bandits on the cliffs above in addition to the ones in your way.

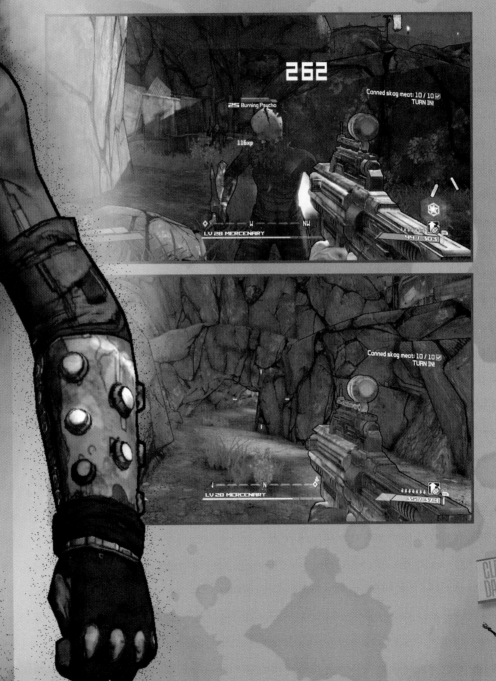

DESTROY KROM'S TURRET, ONE WAY OR ANOTHER

When daylight finally breaks through the shadowy canyon basin, Krom is just ahead. After the introductory cinematic, take partial cover behind the canyon wall and use a scope to scout ahead. At the top of the fortress, there's a small window with the barrel Krom's Turret sticking out—this is the boss you've come to defeat. And if you have a powerful and accurate sniper rifle or rocket launcher, you can actually kill Krom right here and now. Find a spot where the rocks block most of Krom's attacks, then fire at the turret as fast as you can; it quickly becomes apparent whether or not you're doing enough damage to overwhelm the turret's regenerative abilities. If you're having trouble landing accurate shots, keep trying from various spots as you draw closer to Krom.

Players without sufficient long-range weaponry have little choice but to rush Krom's fortress, get inside his hidey-hole, and finish him off face to face. Crisscross from platform to platform. As you traverse the bridge to each new one, quickly move into a position that puts a cliff wall, hut, or some other obstacle between you and Krom's turret. As long as there's something tall and sturdy to your north, you can pick off the scattered bandits and psychos without worrying about rockets from above. Don't miss the explosive barrels that have been conveniently placed in the centers of each platform for your bandit-slaying convenience.

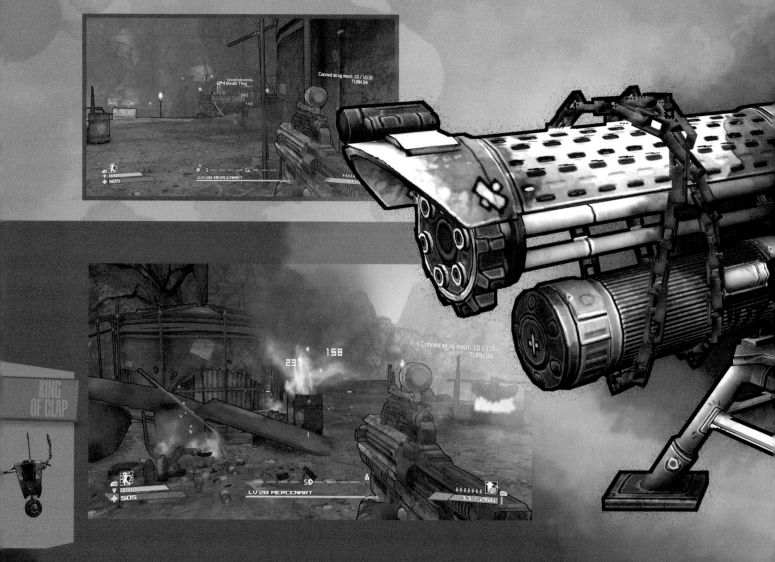

KING OF CLAP

When you finally reach Krom, dash around his wooden structure and then up to the ramp that leads to his turret. Do not step on to the ramp, though—crouch *beside* it, close enough to Krom that his shots pound harmlessly into the platform while you can still target him freely. Needless to say, that's game over for Krom.

When the smoke clears, help yourself to the guns in Krom's **red chest**, the Vault Key Piece, and the pile of cash in the **silver chest**. Krom also drops a unique Shock pistol that has burst fire. It's a long walk back to the entrance to the Rust Commons East, but you can cut it short by choosing to Exit and then reload.

LEVEL	HEALTH	XP	WEAK POINT	RESISTANCES	SHIELDS
25	5	15	Head	None	Yes

KROM

Like Flynt, Krom worked as a prison warden for Dahl until the prisons were abandoned and the convicts set free. His real name is Leslie, which he always hated and changed as soon as Flynt set him up as second in command.

3-8 THE JAYNISTOWN AFFAIR — PART ONE

Jaynistown occupies the southeast corner of the Rust Commons East. The region has long been isolated by a pair of raised drawbridges, but now that that a Vault Key Piece apparently lies on the other side of those bridges, Patricia Tannis is highly motivated to help you with that problem. In addition to the six Janistown plot missions, the surrounding area hosts another six side quests.

QUESTS:

1. Relight The Beacons (optional)

2. A Bug Problem (optional)

3. Green Thumb (optional)

4. Jaynistown: Secret Rendezvous

5. Jaynistown: A Brother's Love

6. Altar Ego: The New Religion (optional)

COLLECT THE FIRST BATCH OF JAYNISTOWN QUESTS

After claiming the Vault Key Piece from Krom, bring it to Patricia Tannis's excavation site in the Rust Commons West. She arranges the "Jaynistown: Secret Rendezvous" mission, which allows you to pass the raised drawbridges in the Rust Commons East.

Crazy Patty isn't the only one with interests in Jaynistown. In New Haven, Helena Pierce has two new missions for you, as well; "Smoke Signals: Investigate Old Haven" will have to wait for a while, but "Relight The Beacons" is an easy payday. The Middle of Nowhere Bounty Board offers "A Bug Problem" and, assuming you've completed the last Altar Ego quest, "Altar Ego: The New Religion."

Besides the usual suspects, there's also a new client with business across the bridge. Drive through the mire south of the Middle of Nowhere, and stop at the small shack surrounded by mutant sunflowers. The owner, a Mr. Stance Von Kofsky, offers you the "Green Thumb" quest.

KING OF CLAP

RUST COMMONS EAST

KROM'S CANYON

DRAWBRIDGE

RUST COMMONS WEST

HUDSON JOHNS

OLD HAVEN

RETCHING SEEPS SAMPLE

MIDDLE OF NOWHERE

BOUNTY BOARD

OLD LYNNE ABBEY

VALVE

PIPE SHUT-OFF

TAYLOR KOBB

CLAPTRAP

STACY VON KOFSKY

TRASH COAST

THE CAULDRON

RUST COMMONS WEST

JAYNIS KOBB

SOUTH DRAWBRIDGE

DRAWBRIDGE

CLAPTRAP DANCE OFF

FETID CAULDRON SAMPLE

LEGEND	TREASURE CHEST	NEW-U POLE/STATION	CATCH-A-RIDE STATION	MEDICAL VENDING MACHINE	AMMO VENDING MACHINE	GUN VENDING MACHINE	BEACON
	▭	●	Ⓨ	☐	☐	☐	●

1 RELIGHT THE BEACONS

LEVEL 27

- ☐ *North Ridge beacon activated (1)*
- ☐ *Overlook beacon activated (1)*

Client: Helena Pierce
Reactivate both beacon towers.

While Dahl still maintained a strong presence on Pandora, they operated two interplanetary beacons, used by interstellar craft for navigation and communication. Recently, bandits have taken up residence around the beacon stations, shutting them down in the process. Somebody needs to get out there and clean the bandit infestation out of those stations, and reactivate the beacons.

REWARDS: 10,440 XP + $15,993
+ SNIPER RIFLE

2 A BUG PROBLEM

LEVEL 27

- ☐ *Retching Seeps sample (1)*
- ☐ *Widowmaker killed (1)*
- ☐ *Fetid Cauldron sample (1)*
- ☐ *Helob killed (1)*

Client: Middle Of Nowhere
Bounty Board
Collect sulfur samples and kill Helob and Widowmaker.

Given the plant growth I've observed outside of New Haven, I suspect there is a component in the sulfur springs which acts as fertilizer for Pandora's native flora. To test my theory, I need samples both from The Retching Seeps and The Fetid Cauldron. I'd do it myself, but each location is guarded by a nasty spiderant! Eliminate these nuisances, and I'll be able to conduct further tests without the need for assistance.

REWARDS: 6,960 XP + $21,324
+ SHOTGUN

LIGHT THE FIRST BEACON BEFORE YOU CROSS THE BRIDGE

From the Middle of Nowhere, drive north. When you return to the main road back to Rust Commons West, hang a U-turn and travel up the hill to the bandit compound with the radar dish. Punch through the bandit guards toward the west end of the compound to reach the terminal that relights the beacon. There are two **red chests** here—one on the east side of the main building, and the other atop the watchtower northeast of the beacon terminal.

That concludes your business on this side of the map, so drive south and have the Claptrap lower the drawbridge to Jaynistown. As you cross, you'll see Jaynistown on your left, your rendezvous spot with Tyler Kobb to the northeast, and the Fetid Cauldron in the southeast.

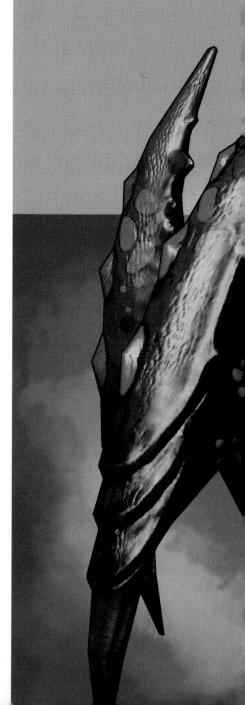

SQUASH HELOB IN THE FETID CAULDRON

The Fetid Cauldron is one of the two sites you must visit in the "A Bug Problem" quest. Drive southeast from the drawbridge and collect your sample from the shimmering Spiderant nest. That's all the provocation Helob needs as it leaps out of the earth to attack you.

Treat Helob like any other Spiderant, using your action skills to dish out devastating strikes to the abdomen. Helob is a better jumper than the rest of its kind, so keep moving and it won't land on you. When it lands nearby, jump up to avoid the shockwave.

The other option is to fight from your Runner, which makes it easy to avoid Helob's leaps and crushes any other Spiderants that get in your way. (You won't earn as much XP as you would fighting on foot, however.) If your level is in the high 20s, your Runner is at full shields, and you're in a single-player game, then you can probably kill Helob by just driving over it—this causes some damage to your Runner, but it should survive. If you're at a lower level or in a multiplayer game, use your turret to soften up Helob as much as possible before going in for the kill.

HELOB

LEVEL	HEALTH	XP	WEAK POINT	RESISTANCES			SHIELDS
28	11	22	Abdomen	⚡	☣	🔥	None

One of the deadliest Spiderants, Helob has learned a leap attack that allows him to catch low-flying rakk and more effectively ambush prey on the ground.

RENDEZVOUS WITH THE BROTHERS KOBB

Park your Runner and walk through the gap in the rocks north of the platform with the Catch-A-Ride and New-U Station. Taylor Kobb is expecting you, so you shouldn't encounter any resistance on the way. Talk to Taylor to complete "Jaynistown: Secret Rendezvous" and begin "Jaynistown: A Brother's Love."

To complete Taylor's mission, you must cross the street to the single entrance to Jaynistown, then hunt down his brother within. Jaynis typically hangs out near the large building in the west part of town, but does roam a bit, so it's hard to say exactly where you'll encounter him. (The waypoint is always fixed on the center of town, and won't help you find Jaynis.)

Snipe out whatever bandits you can from the entrance, then make your way north, where a ramp allows you to ascend a building to the first of four gun chests (a **silver chest**, in this case). That building offers a good position from which to snipe the remaining foes, and you can proceed west from there, and then south, to where you may be able to get a shot at Jaynis.

Jaynis wields a powerful and fast-firing, but highly inaccurate, combat rifle known as "The Meat Grinder." Fight him from as far away as possible; the accuracy of your sniper rifle always gives you the edge over his scattershot attacks.

With Jaynis dead, the bandits should cease respawning, allowing you to collect the three other chests at your leisure. Most are in plain sight, but the red chest to the southwest is behind a gate that won't open until an event that occurs a bit later in the game. If you want the chest now, follow the gate north, where you can slip behind it and walk along a thin railing to reach it.

JAYNIS KOBB

LEVEL	HEALTH	XP	WEAK POINT	RESISTANCES	SHIELDS
27	6	12	Head	None	Yes

Jaynis and Taylor Kobb have hated each other since birth. They've never overtly fought one another, opting instead to employ poison, traps, and assassins to do the other in.

THE MEAT GRINDER

DAMAGE	90-ish
ACCURACY	23.9-ish
FIRE RATE	6.7
MAGAZINE	86
ELEMENT	None

War is in your blood

+62 Magazine Size

+70% Damage

+12% Fire Rate

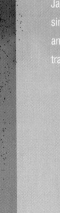

3 GREEN THUMB

LEVEL 29

- ■ *Valve (1)*
- ■ *Water pump turned off (1)*

Client: Stance Von Kofsky
Find a valve somewhere, then use it to turn off the water pump.

The flowers around here may not look pretty, but they're actually a pretty destructive force, and they grow just about anywhere there's water. So you can probably understand why a broken water pipe is such a problem. Please fix it, before the flowers run me out of my home! Find a valve somewhere, then use it to turn off the water pump.

REWARDS: 7,439 XP + $20,062 + SHOTGUN

LIGHT THE OVERLOOK BEACON NORTH OF JAYNISTOWN

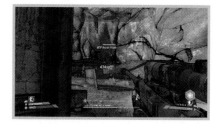

Drive across the street to give Taylor the news. He has your next plot mission "Jaynistown: Spread The Word," which takes place in New Haven. However, before Fast Traveling back, clear your slate of optional quests in the Jaynistown area.

Drive north toward the fork split. To find the next beacon in the "Relight The Beacons" quest, head left through the stone arch and park at the barrier outside of the compound. After an initial batch of psychos, you mainly face soldiers who are intelligent enough to hold their ground and fire from afar. Run to the central building and take cover behind a corner, then ease out to blast the soldiers one at a time.

Circle to the west side of the building to find one **red chest**, then head north to find the beacon control panel and a **silver chest** on the overlook platform.

KILL THE ABBEY BANDITS AND COLLECT THEIR PAMPHLETS

Return to the fork, and head east through the pipe this time. A quick left turn on the other side leads to the Old Lynne Abbey, which has become the holy land of the religious cult in the Altar Ego quest tree.

The religious tracts you seek are not inside the building, but in the hands of the cult members themselves. Gun down the dozen or so devout Psychos who charge after you take a few steps into the abbey grounds, then sift through their remains to collect the six pamphlets. That completes the quest, but don't leave without assaulting the church in the name of Pandora's one true god: **red chest** loot!

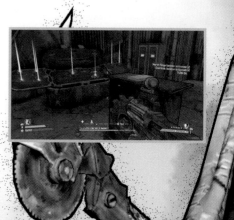

SHUT OFF THE WATER IN JAYNISTOWN

Continue northeast down the road toward the Abbey until you see a tent to your right, near a party of wandering Bandits. Run them down, then head under the canopy to grab the **Valve** for the "Green Thumb" quest.

Drive that back to Jaynistown and follow the pipe to the northwest building, where it connects to a bank of rusty machinery. A conveniently placed staircase leads right to the spot where the Valve snaps into place, completing the quest.

4 JAYNISTOWN: SECRET RENDEZVOUS

LEVEL 27

- ☐ *Claptrap talked to (1)*
- ☐ *Taylor Kobb found (1)*

Client: Patricia Tannis

Cross the drawbridges and talk to Taylor Kobb, outside of Jaynistown.

I'm reading traces of Eridian artifact activity out of the Trash Coast, so we're going there next. It's across the drawbridges, so talk to one of the Claptraps there. Pierce has already given you the necessary credentials. It's a little shady, but I've arranged for a meeting with a bandit named Taylor Kobb. The bandits of Jaynistown control access to the Trash Coast, but he says he can get us in.

REWARDS: 3,840 XP + $5,331

5 JAYNISTOWN: A BROTHER'S LOVE

LEVEL 27

- ☐ *Jaynis Kobb killed (1)*

Client: Taylor Kobb

Kill Jaynis Kobb in Jaynistown.

My brother Jaynis is the leader of Jaynisown, and he's turned he place into a hive of scum and villainy. It wasn't always that way. Good people used to live in that town, but his thugs chased them all away. When I protested, he exiled me, his own brother! It ain't right, and the people of that town deserve better. Jaynis needs to be "removed" from office. Violently.

REWARDS: 6,264 XP + $10,662

6 ALTAR EGO:
THE NEW RELIGION

LEVEL 27

■ *Pamphlets (6)*

Client: Middle Of Nowhere Bounty
Board

Collect pamphlets from the bandits at Old
Lynne Abbey.

You know Old Lynne Abbey, up on the
Overlook? That place has been abandoned
since we pulled out of New Haven, but some
bandits recently took the place over, and are
now proselytizing and handing out pamphlets
to anyone who'll listen. I doubt those nut jobs
have really found religion. We need to grab
some of those pamphlets and figure out what
they're up to.

REWARDS: 6,960 XP + $5,331

SOLVE THE BUG PROBLEM IN THE RETCHING SEEPS

Return to that northeast road and follow it past the tent where you found the Valve. When you
spot the New-U pole and the entrance to Old Haven, hang a left and roll down the hill toward
the second drawbridge. It isn't hard to spot a **silver chest** in the oil-processing
facility to your right, but claiming it is another matter entirely; your presence
immediately sparks a bloody three-way war between yourself, the bandits,
and an army of Spiderants.

Continue west until you spot the shimmering Spiderant hole where you
can collect the Retching Seeps sample. Before you do this, though, turn
your attention to the shack and watchtower a few steps to the west. Wipe
out the resident bandits to head off their interference, then grab a second
silver chest atop the tower.

WIDOWMAKER	LEVEL	HEALTH	XP	WEAK POINT	RESISTANCES	SHIELDS
	28	18	36	Abdomen	⚡☣	None

Widowmaker is so-named because it has killed every would-be exterminator that ever
attempted to kill it. It's known to burrow in the ground and catch prey by surprise.

Be ready for a fight when you collect the sample—the Widowmaker will soon
be upon you. This foe is quite a bit heartier than Helob, but isn't much tougher
to beat. If you stand still when it burrows underground, Widowmaker should
rise from the earth with its back turned toward you, providing a nice opportunity
to pummel its abdomen with a long spray of submachine gun or combat-rifle
fire. Prepare to jump when it retaliates with an attack of its own, and you should
have little trouble surviving. If you do take some hard hits, remember that you
can always retreat to your Runner and simply run it down.

KING
OF CLAP

See, this is why assassins negotiate the price *before* they pull the trigger. After all you've done for Taylor, the gate to the Trash Coast remains locked, and you're still stuck running his errands. You're no closer to finding the next Vault Key Piece, and this whole Jaynistown affair is only gonna get messier…

QUESTS:

1. Altar Ego: Godless Monsters (optional)
2. Jaynistown: Spread The World
3. Jaynistown: Getting What's Coming To You
4. Jaynistown: Unintended Consequences
5. Dumpster Diving For Great Justice (optional)
6. Jaynistown: Cleaning Up Your Mess

3-9 MISSION TAG

1 ALTAR EGO: GODLESS MONSTERS

LEVEL 29

☐ *Slither killed (1)*

Client: Middle Of Nowhere Bounty Board

Go to the Trashy Knoll, find Slither, and kill it.

After looking at those pamphlets you collected, I'm fairly certain there's something interesting out there. Their crude drawings show stick figures gathered around some kind of monster named "Slither." Maybe if you kill their "god," they'll abandon this whole religious scheme?

REWARDS: 8,369 XP + $20,062 + UNIQUE GUN

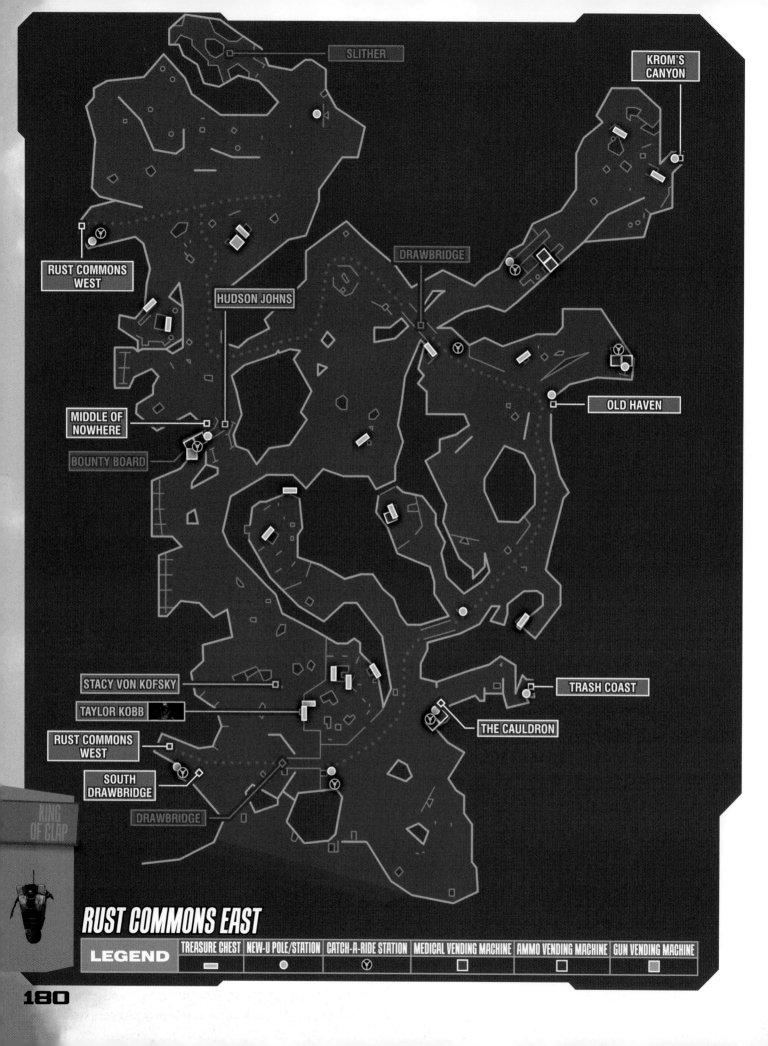

SLITHER

KROM'S CANYON

DRAWBRIDGE

RUST COMMONS WEST

HUDSON JOHNS

OLD HAVEN

MIDDLE OF NOWHERE

BOUNTY BOARD

STACY VON KOFSKY

TAYLOR KOBB

TRASH COAST

THE CAULDRON

RUST COMMONS WEST

SOUTH DRAWBRIDGE

DRAWBRIDGE

KING OF CLAP

RUST COMMONS EAST

LEGEND	TREASURE CHEST	NEW-U POLE/STATION	CATCH-A-RIDE STATION	MEDICAL VENDING MACHINE	AMMO VENDING MACHINE	GUN VENDING MACHINE
	▬	●	Ⓨ	☐	☐	▪

TETANUS WARREN

AFTER CLAPTRAP
REPAIR

BOUNTY
BOARD

NEW
HAVEN

MARKUS KINCAID

ERIK FRANKS

HELENA PIERCE

DAHL HEADLAND

SCOOTER

RUST
COMMONS

QUEST ICONS | DUMPSTER

NEW HAVEN

LEGEND | TREASURE CHEST | NEW-U POLE/STATION | CATCH-A-RIDE STATION | MEDICAL VENDING MACHINE | AMMO VENDING MACHINE | GUN VENDING MACHINE

CLAPTRAP
DANCE OFF

SLAY THE GOD OF THE BANDIT FAITH

When you turn in "Altar Ego: The New Religion" at the Middle Of Nowhere bounty board, you receive the final quest in the series: "Altar Ego: Godless Monsters." If you're prepared to face down the might of an angry god, you might as well do it now; hop into your Runner and drive to the northwest corner of the map, where you collected the Fuses not long ago.

When you approach the center of the eerily quiet Trashy Knoll, a burst of flame heralds the descent of a god. And out comes, uh… a scythid? Yeah, it's unusually colorful. And fast. And pretty strong for one of these beasts. But really, the mighty Slither is a threat to no one.

Blow Slither away, then sift through the loot—it drops some pretty sweet stuff, for a bug. Another interesting prize awaits at the bounty board when you report your victory. The Dove is a pitifully weak repeater, but it never runs out of ammo and never needs to reload.

SLITHER	LEVEL	HEALTH	XP	WEAK POINT	RESISTANCES	SHIELDS
	28	8	16	Entire Body	None	None

Some of the more impressionable bandits formed a cult of worship and sacrifice around this mutant scythid. As a result, Slither has become a man-eater, albeit a contented and well-fed man-eater.

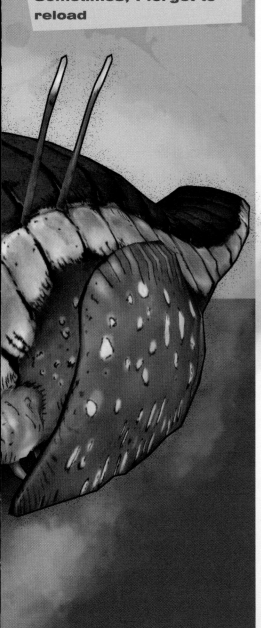

THE DOVE

DAMAGE	55
ACCURACY	87.2
FIRE RATE	~3.7
MAGAZINE	INFINITE!
ELEMENT	None

Sometimes, I forget to reload

Erik Franks stands outside the easternmost building in New Haven. Speaking to him completes the "Jaynistown: Spread The Word" quest, and unlocks the next step: Jaynistown: Getting What's Coming To You." But Erik seems less interested in the successful coup than the fate of his girly mags, and asks for your help with the "Dumpster Diving For Great Justice" side quest, as well.

First, collect your reward! Leave town and travel to the dead-end gate at the north end of the map to find a large shipping crate full of… Red chests? Eridian Weapons? Scantily clad women? It certainly couldn't be an obvious ambush, could it? Yep… it is. Gun down the Mutant Midget Psycho inside the crate, then swing left and blow away a bunch of low-level bandits as they leap over the wall. Really, Taylor? You thought that would work?

Opening the crate unlocked the "Jaynistown: Unintended Consequences" mission, which you can complete by having a quick chat with Helena Pierce. She agrees that Taylor Kobb must die, and sends you on your way with the final mission of this whole sordid affair: "Jaynistown: Cleaning Up Your Mess."

DUMPSTER DIVING FOR ERIK'S LOST PORN

To complete Erik Frank's "Dumpster Diving For Great Justice" quest, you'll need to search five dumpsters in the outskirts of New Haven. The waypoints point you toward them, but in a less than ideal order that make the quest take longer than necessary. So instead of running northwest after the first waypoint, leave the city through its main entrance and search the dumpster on the outside of its southwest wall. Turn to the southwest and walk beneath the curved metal awning to find the next dumpster.

Head back toward New Haven and hang a right at the main road. Blast your way through the bandit camp just south of the entrance to the Rust Commons West, then search the dumpster a few steps south of the camp.

The final three dumpsters are in the heavily bandit-infested region in the northwest sector of the map. Head northwest from the entrance to the city of New Haven, toward the waypoint. Climb the garbage pile past the hut beneath another metal awning and, after surviving a Mutant Midget Psycho onslaught, turn left at the toilet. The dumpster is on a downward slope to the west.

Follow the waypoint north, walking along the garbage pile to avoid a fight with the bandits to the west. The waypoint leads right to the fifth dumpster.

You cannot avoid a fight on your way to the final dumpster, which is directly to your west, just southeast of the entrance to the Tetanus Warrens.

INFILTRATE THE NEWLY FORTIFIED TAYLORTOWN

Perhaps having heard that his assassination attempt has failed, Taylor Kobb has figured out that you're coming for him. Accordingly, he's made a few changes in Taylortown: More bandits, automated turrets on the roofs, and a series of scrap-metal walls designed to guide you into an elaborate ambush.

Taylor assumes you'll be coming through the main entrance, but you can quash his plans by finding another way in. Climb up the watchtower outside of town, and jump from the ramp railing onto the natural rock wall that borders the town. That puts you even higher than the rooftops, allowing you to snipe out the two turrets with ease and rain death upon the bandits hoping to ambush you.

The waypoint directs you to that lifeguard tower-shaped building at the west end of town; the one you had to walk on the other side of the fence to reach. Thanks to some newly constructed walls, you can now only approach this building directly from the east. Head that way now; the walls may be forcing you into an ambush, but they also prevent the bandits to the north and south from interfering.

4 JAYNISTOWN: UNINTENDED CONSEQUENCES
LEVEL 27

■ *Report to Helena Pierce (1)*

Client: Erik Franks
Report to Helena Pierce in New Haven.

Something is fishy here. You'd better go talk to Helena Pierce. Your liberation of Jaynistown may have had unintended consequences.

REWARDS: 3,480 XP

5 DUMPSTER DIVING FOR GREAT JUSTICE
LEVEL 27

■ *Erik Franks found (1)*

Client: Erik Franks
Search dumpsters around New Haven to recover Erik's, uh, valuables.

You seem like someone who can keep a secret. You see, my wife can be quick to anger, and we had, uh, a disagreement. In her rage, she took something of great value to me and threw it away. Go check the dumpsters outside of town. I think you'll know what you're looking for when you find it. I know it's asking a lot, but keep this just between you and me, okay? I'll make it worth your while.

REWARDS: 3,828 XP + $31,987

KILL THE NEW BOSS, SAME AS THE OLD BOSS

When you approach Taylor's building, a burst of flames heralds the rise of some rocket turrets on the roofs of the neighboring buildings. A pair of Badass Bruisers also join Taylor Kobb in the frontal assault. Move to the left, taking shelter behind the south wall of the south building. That keeps the far turret from targeting you, and causes the rockets from the turret atop the south building to detonate harmlessly on the roof. Hold your ground there and prepare to shotgun blast or machinegun the Badass Bruisers when they come around the corner.

Once the bandits are gone, move south until you can take out the top of the turret above your building. Try to stay in the blind spots of the northern turret as you face Taylor Kobb. He's packing a powerful rocket launcher, but it's not a very effective weapon at close range. Move in and pound him with fast-firing weapons to keep him on the ropes. Berserkers can pummel him when they get close, while Soldiers are advised to drop a turret and keep him pinned. Sirens should first use their Phasewalk ability to get in a position to destroy the north turret, and then to get behind Taylor Kobb.

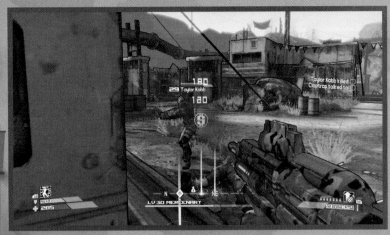

KING
OF CLAP

TAYLOR KOBB

LEVEL	HEALTH	XP	WEAK POINT	RESISTANCES	SHIELDS
29	6	12	Head	None	Yes

The enmity between the Kobb brothers has only served to make them stronger and more clever as they outwit or overcome each attempt on their lives.

Your parting gift from Taylor Kobb is The Roaster, an excellent flame-type rocket launcher that can hold two rounds at once. You can also re-raid the red chest from his command center (it now seems to hold higher-level loot than it did before), and find a new **silver chest** behind the building directly to the north.

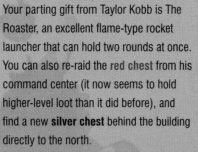

The final phase of the "Jaynistown: Cleaning Up Your Mess" mission is gaining access the Trash Coast. Head up the mountain trail behind the camp where you first met Taylor Kobb to find his belligerent Claptrap standing guard at the entrance to the coast. With Taylor dead, he reluctantly allows you through, launching the next plot mission: "Another Piece Of The Puzzle." Pass through the gate to visit the New-U Station at the entrance to the Trash Coast, then Fast Travel back to New Haven and collect a new batch of side quests before you proceed.

6 JAYNISTOWN: CLEANING UP YOUR MESS

LEVEL 29

- ☐ *Taylor Kobb killed (1)*
- ☐ *Claptrap talked to (1)*

Client: Helena Pierce
Kill Taylor Kobb, then talk to his Claptrap.

An idiot Vault Hunter follows the direction of an insane archaeologist, and the result is disaster. Jaynis was no angel, but under Taylor's rule, Jaynistown is a greater threat than ever. You caused this mess, so you can clean it up by killing Taylor Kobb. If reaching the Trash Coast is so blasted important, his hacked Claptrap should allow you to pass once he's dead.

REWARDS: 13,391 XP + $20,062

THE ROASTER	
DAMAGE	398
ACCURACY	93.2
FIRE RATE	0.9
MAGAZINE	2
ELEMENT	Fire x 4

Highly effective vs. Flesh

Chance to light enemies on fire

Gonna cook someone today

Very high Elemental Effect chance

3-10 RETURN TO TREACHER'S LANDING (OPTIONAL)

After completing the "Jaynistown: Getting What's Coming To You" quest, Claptrap reveals two new quests: "Wanted: Fresh Fish" from the New Haven bounty board, and "I've Got A Sinking Feeling…" from Scooter. Your time in New Haven is drawing to an end, so this is a good time to revisit Treacher's Landing for this pair of missions, and to finally challenge that Circle of Slaughter quest tree, as well.

QUESTS:

1. Wanted: Fresh Fish (optional)
2. I've Got A Sinking Feeling… (optional)
3. Circle Of Slaughter: Meat And Greet (optional)
4. Circle Of Slaughter: Round 1 (optional)
5. Circle Of Slaughter: Round 2 (optional)
6. Circle Of Slaughter: Final Round (optional)

FISH IN TREACHER'S LANDING, BORDERLANDS-STYLE

Once you've collected the quests from Scooter and the New Haven bounty board, Fast Travel to Treacher's Landing. Use the ammo vending machine at the entrance to ensure you have plenty of rockets; your Rocket Launcher comes in quite handy for both of the quests.

After fighting your way through a reinvigorated band of bandits at the entrance, you'll begin to discover fishing poles with shimmering floaters in the platforms to the south. Toss a grenade at the floater or, better yet, blast it with a rocket—four dead fish will flop into the water for you to collect! If you run out of explosives, it's possible to catch fish by firing with other weapons into the water around the floater, but it requires a lot of ammunition to hit all four fish per floater when you're firing blind.

Don't worry if you miss a fish or two; there are six fishing spots (marked as "Fish Bomb" on our map), for a total of 24 fish to catch.

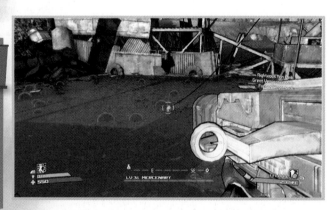

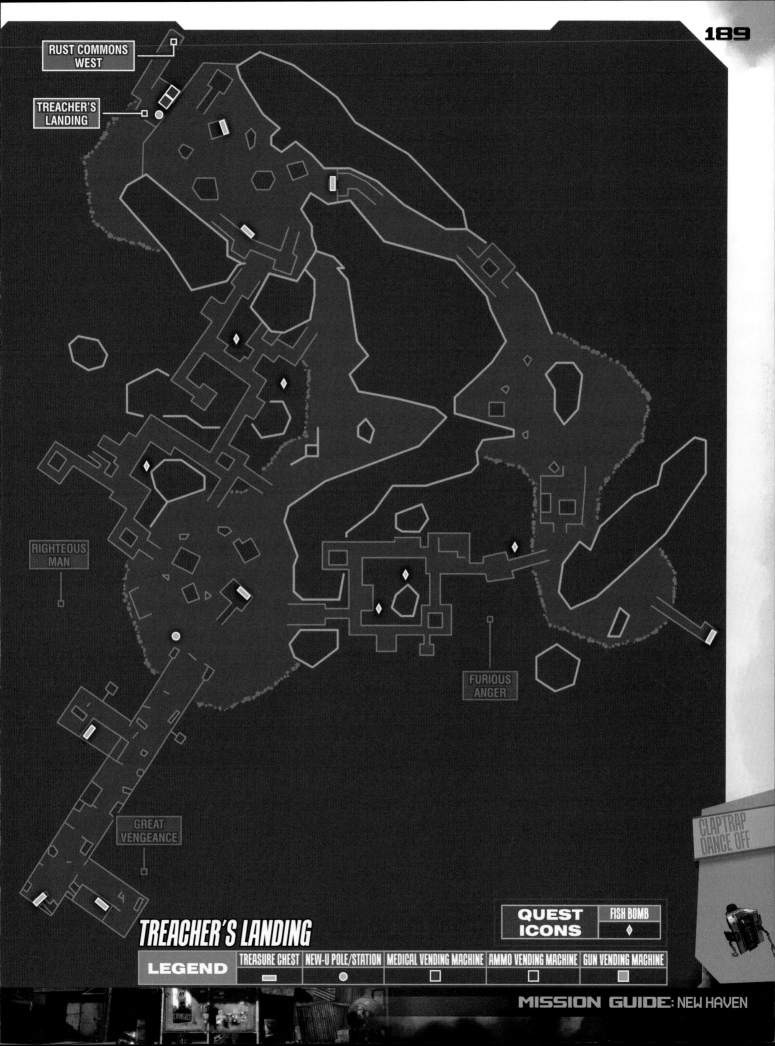

RUST COMMONS
WEST

TREACHER'S
LANDING

RIGHTEOUS
MAN

FURIOUS
ANGER

GREAT
VENGEANCE

CLAPTRAP
DANCE OFF

TREACHER'S LANDING

QUEST ICONS	FISH BOMB
	◇

LEGEND	TREASURE CHEST	NEW-U POLE/STATION	MEDICAL VENDING MACHINE	AMMO VENDING MACHINE	GUN VENDING MACHINE
	▭	●	☐	☐	☐

1 WANTED: FRESH FISH

LEVEL 27

■ Fresh Fish (20)

Client: New Haven Bounty Board

Throw grenades into the water around Treacher's Landing, and pick up the fish that float to the surface. Bring them back to the New Haven bounty board.

Fish are a rarity in the sludge you find around the Rust Commons, but they're out there and I'm willing to pay for them. There's no bait, lures, or nets that can catch the bastards, though. Your best bet is to go to the docks at Treacher's Landing and drop a grenade into the water. Grab whatever fish float to the surface, and watch out for the bandits.

REWARDS: 6,960 XP + $21,324 + UNIQUE GUN

2 I'VE GOT A SINKING FEELING...

LEVEL 27

■ Righteous Man sunk (1)
■ Great Vengeance sunk (1)
■ Furious Anger sunk (1)

Client: Scooter

Sink the Righteous Man, Great Vengeance, and Furious Anger.

The bandits have a new weapon. They've built three gunboats, and they're using them to stage raids along the entire coastline. It's got to stop. I'm putting up a bounty for anyone who'll go to Treacher's Landing and sink those things.

REWARDS: 17,400 XP + $26,656 + ROCKET LAUNCHER

SEND THE RIGHTEOUS MAN TO THE BOTTOM OF THE SEA

Travel along the boardwalk of platforms instead of cutting through the central peninsula. When you reach the southwest end of the boardwalk, you begin taking fire from a mounted turret in the water to the south— that's the Righteous Man, the first of the three bandit ships Scooter asked you to sink.

Move to the platforms on your right or left, where metal railings provide some cover. Use a Rocket Launcher (or, if you don't have one, a sniper rifle) to blow away the turret. That should leave the ship defenseless as you target the shimmering fuel tank on its aft deck. One good shot at that should spell the end for the Righteous Man.

HUNT FOR SHIPS AND LOOT ON THE TREACHER'S LANDING PIER

After triggering the New-U pole on the central peninsula, head southwest down the concrete pier. You face several bandits along the way, so use your sniper rifle to catch them unawares and keep a shotgun handy for when Bruisers suddenly appear around a corner.

About a third of the way down the pier, a building comes into view on your right. Use a pile of crates along its north wall to reach the roof with **silver chest**—the first of three. From there, proceed to the east wall of the pier to get a good look at the Great Vengeance bandit ship. A rocket blast or two sends it to the bottom of the sea.

Continue to the end of the pier. This springs an ambush from a team of bandits hiding in the shipping crates. Fighting them is worth the risk, as there are two more **silver chests** in the area. One is atop the building to the east and, once again, there's an easy stack of crates leading to the roof. The silver chest atop the shipping crates at the end of the pier is a bit trickier, though. You must jump from the propane tank or bridge supports onto the east shipping crate, then leap from there to the west shipping crate, where you can hop off of a much smaller box to reach the treasure.

SINK THE FURIOUS ANGER AND FINISH YOUR FISH COLLECTION

From the pier, head east to the second network of platforms. Follow the southern edge until you have a clear shot at the Furious Anger, which is docked much closer to the shore than the previous two boats. It hosts a nearly indestructible manual turret, but it should be easy to pick off the bandit at the switch. Alternatively, you could run east until you have a clear shot at the engine in the back, and destroy that to take the whole thing out.

The last three floaters are in the second network of platforms, allowing you to also polish off "Wanted: Fresh Fish." You're now free to return to New Haven and collect rocket launchers as additional awards for completing both quests. "Wanted: Fresh Fish" earns you The Leviathan, a Gearbox-made launcher that's relatively weak, but can hold six rounds and fires in a parabolic art that can be useful for hitting enemies behind cover. Scooter's gift is a random rocket launcher that just might be good enough to supplant The Roaster as your go-to big gun.

LEVIATHAN (GEARBOX)	
DAMAGE	404
ACCURACY	91.7
FIRE RATE	1.2
MAGAZINE	6
ELEMENT	None

It rises!

2.7x Weapon Zoom

SURVIVE CHUCK DURDEN'S CIRCLE OF SLAUGHTER

The Circle of Slaughter is in the Rust Commons West, in the small town-like area where you collected Submachine Gun pieces for the "Scavenger: Submachine Gun" quest. The quickest way to reach it now is to warp to "The Outeryard," generate a ride, and then drive due south until you see the sign with the five yellow bullets.

3 CIRCLE OF SLAUGHTER: MEAT AND GREET

LEVEL 26

■ *Chuck Durden met (1)*

Client: Middle Of Nowhere Bounty Board
Talk to Chuck Durden.

Think you've got what it takes to be a gladiator? Forget those puny Circle Of Death events my weakling brother puts on, this is where you'll find the REAL action! Talk to Chuck Durden, if you think you got what it takes.

REWARDS: 1,007 XP

4 CIRCLE OF SLAUGHTER: ROUND 1

LEVEL 26

■ *Round survived (1)*

Client: Chuck Durden
It's kill or be killed!

All you gotta do is survive. All my pets have to do is tear you in half. See you soon, in one piece or maybe two.

REWARDS: 6,719 XP + $14,280

CLAPTRAP DANCE OFF

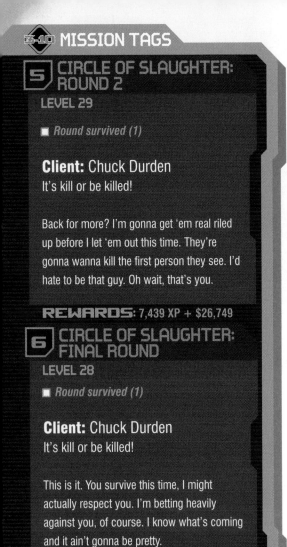

LEVEL 29

■ *Round survived (1)*

Client: Chuck Durden

It's kill or be killed!

Back for more? I'm gonna get 'em real riled up before I let 'em out this time. They're gonna wanna kill the first person they see. I'd hate to be that guy. Oh wait, that's you.

REWARDS: 7,439 XP + $26,749

6 CIRCLE OF SLAUGHTER: FINAL ROUND

LEVEL 28

■ *Round survived (1)*

Client: Chuck Durden

It's kill or be killed!

This is it. You survive this time, I might actually respect you. I'm betting heavily against you, of course. I know what's coming and it ain't gonna be pretty.

REWARDS: 7,200 XP + $35,825 + SUBMACHINE GUN

You battle highly trained bandits in this area instead of skags, so it's important to find and hold good cover. After passing through the gate into the coliseum, run to the right and catch the first cage full of bandits as it's lowered onto the field; greet your noble competitors with a spray of machine-gun fire or a series of shotgun blasts, then run to the left and take cover behind the pile of tires. This spot, between the right and center cages, is the best of the many bad cover options available to you. It's prudent to stand far back from the tires to gun down psychos and bruisers as they maneuver around them. Move directly behind the tires when it's time to pick off the more levelheaded bandits, who will have taken in the center of the arena.

In the second round, go straight for the spot with the tires between the cages, as the first batch of enemies (typically bruisers) emerge from a cage in the center. Greet them with a handful of grenades, then fall back against the wall of their cage, where you can wait for them to meander over to you. These foes are powerful, but slow, so just wait until one rounds the corner before you throw your Bloodwing, drop a Scorpio Turret, or enter a berserker rage.

Before attempting the third and final round, stock up on grenades at the vending machine. You need a full supply of them to flush out the very conservative and tenacious bandits hiding behind the metal barriers in the arena's center. These foes pick away at you while their bruiser brethren attack directly.

Meet the bruisers with a flame, shock, or corrosive attack as they spring from their cages, then fall back to your usual position up against a wall so that only half the bandits have a clear shot at you. The bruisers are a serious pain here; use your action skills and deadliest weapons to kill them

as soon as possible, even if that means charging them and unloading multiple shotgun blasts in their faces. Between bruiser attacks, switch to a sniper rifle to pick off distant bandits from the relative safety of your tire pile.

THE GUARDIAN ANGEL'S TRASH-COAST CHALLENGE

The Trash Coast Chamber of Commerce may want to look into a new name for their region. Sure, there are massive piles of garbage around every corner, but this strip of shoreline east of Jaynistown has more scenic beauty than its name would suggest. Alas, there's no time for relaxing on the beach; The Guardian Angel's vague "challenge" awaits you to the north, and there are several side quests to pursue in the bandit-infested south.

QUESTS:

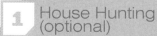

1. House Hunting (optional)
2. Claptrap Rescue: Trash Coast (optional)
3. Bait And Switch (optional)
4. Earl's Best Friend (optional)
5. Another Piece Of The Puzzle

1 HOUSE HUNTING

LEVEL 27

■ *Bleeder killed (1)*

Client: Middle of Nowhere Bounty Board
Go to the Trash Coast and kill Bleeder.

I live in New Haven, but I can't stand having a woman in charge anymore. So, I found a nice bit o' waterfront property out in the Trash Coast. Trouble is, there's a bunch o' them scythid whatever-the-hells ranging around outside, including a really tough one I called Bleeder. Kill them scythids, especially Bleeder, and I'll be able to get the hell away from this place.

REWARDS: 6,960 XP + $15,993 + GUN

CHOOSE YOUR PATH: NORTH OR SOUTH

Before chasing the next Vault Key Piece to the Trash Coast, pay a visit to Crazy Earl and the Middle of Nowhere bounty board to pick up the "Earl's Best Friend," "House Hunting," and "Bait And Switch" side quests. Then Fast Travel to the Trash Coast to consider a pair of options: Head north for the climactic battle of this chapter, or venture south to pursue all three side quests and rescue a wounded Claptrap. Our walkthrough covers the southern region first, but feel free to skip ahead to the northern trek if you're in the mood for a major boss fight.

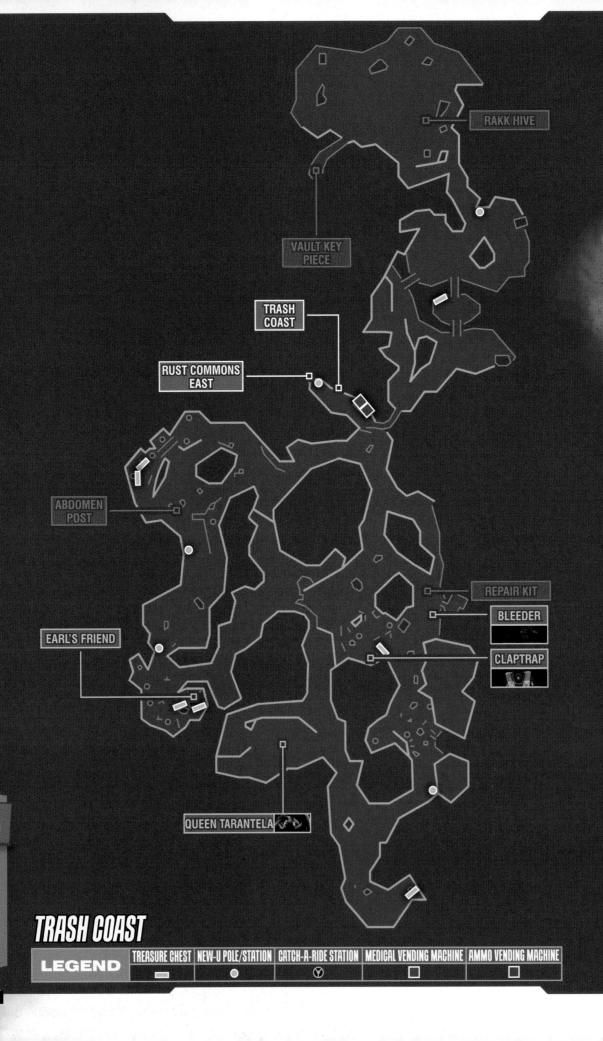

RAKK HIVE

VAULT KEY
PIECE

TRASH
COAST

RUST COMMONS
EAST

ABDOMEN
POST

REPAIR KIT

BLEEDER

EARL'S FRIEND

CLAPTRAP

QUEEN TARANTELA

TRASH COAST

LEGEND	TREASURE CHEST	NEW-U POLE/STATION	CATCH-A-RIDE STATION	MEDICAL VENDING MACHINE	AMMO VENDING MACHINE
	▬	●	ⓨ	☐	☐

KILL BLEEDER AND BOOST THE LOCAL REAL-ESTATE VALUES

To begin the "House Hunting" quest, make your way east toward the shoreline, then follow it south until you see the lovely beach house just offshore. The area is crawling with scythids, and you must blow them all away before Bleeder makes its dramatic debut from the spawning hole at the center of the wildflowers.

When Bleeder is hurling globules of blood, there's little you can do to protect yourself except run away or find cover until it stops. Then it's payback time… Pummel it with a shotgun or fast-firing weapon as you match its movements to keep it from moving too close or too far away.

BLEEDER

LEVEL	HEALTH	XP	WEAK POINT	RESISTANCES	SHIELDS
28	14	56	Entire Body	None	None

Bleeder is an enigma; a crime against all natural law. How can any living thing bleed for days and not die?

2 CLAPTRAP RESCUE: TRASH COAST

LEVEL 27

- ■ *Repair Kit (1)*

Client: Claptrap

Find the repair kit and repair this Claptrap.

You've discovered another defunct Claptrap robot. Could there be an unused repair kit somewhere out here?

REWARDS: 1,740 XP + STORAGE DECK UPGRADE

3 BAIT AND SWITCH

LEVEL 27

- ■ *Queen Abdomen (1)*
- ■ *Abdomen swapped (1)*

Client: Middle of Nowhere Bounty Board

Collect a Queen Spiderant Abdomen and swap it for the bandits'.

Attempts at human habitation along the Trash Coast have always failed, because spiderants overwhelm anyone who tries to live there. The bandits managed it, though, by placing a Queen Spiderant Abdomen in the middle of their camp. I want you to take an abdomen from a rival Queen, then replace the bandits' with that one. Let's see if the spiderants will do our dirty work for us.

REWARDS: 6,960 XP + $13,328 + GUN

FIND CLAPTRAP AND PIPE-WALK TO ITS REPAIR KIT

A sprawling camp lies west of the beachfront home, where bandits wage perpetual war against the indigenous Larva Crab Worms. Riling up the worms and making a mad run through the camp is a risky, but fun, way to pit your foes against each other. A more practical solution, however, is to just methodically pick off the bandits so you can help yourself to their **red chest** and wounded Claptrap.

The waypoint that marks the Repair Kit's location leads back toward the beach, but do you really think the developers would make it that easy? Nope. The Repair Kit is atop the giant pipe that travels from the western cliffs to dump water outside the beach house, and you must find a way to get on top of it.

The only way to do this without making a loop of the whole area is to climb the lookout tower in the northern part of the camp, and then jump from there onto the garbage pile to the northeast. The steep slope sends you sliding down the garbage pile, but landing above a large piece of debris that's sticking out of the pile halts your slide and allows you to jump again. Get sufficient elevation to jump onto the boulder that runs beneath the pipe, then hop gingerly from there onto the pipe itself. Tap your movement control lightly to maintain balance as you walk down the center of the slippery pipe.

After repairing the Claptrap and collecting the reward, you can get back on the pipe and follow it to the upper cliffs to the west, which allows you to cut out the bandit- and spiderant-infested southern coastline entirely. However, there is a **red chest** down there, so loot hunters should continue the scenic tour.

BATTLE QUEEN TARANTELLA AT SPIDERANT FALLS

If you decided to take the long route, venture south along the shoreline until you hit the grassy ledge at the southwest tip of the map. That's where you'll find the **red chest**, but you must contend with a seemingly endless number of high-level Spiderants to reach it. Kill only the enemies essential to your quest (unless you're farming for XP), then grab the loot and get out of there. Passing through an archway of roots to the northwest takes you into a wide meadow dominated by a sludge-colored waterfall. Players who took the pipe from the bandit city end up north of this spot and must, therefore, head south to reach it.

At the falls, walk along the ledge at the south end of the map to attain a prime sniping spot for dealing with the spiderants below. Prepare to kill a ton of them before the Queen Tarantella (your target in the "Bait And Switch" quest) makes her appearance. If she doesn't spawn even after you've downed all the other spiderants on the field, you may need to go down to the basin to lure her out. You can then run right back up to your ledge and send a bunch of sniper rounds into her abdomen. When you go to search her body for the abdomen quest item, keep a shotgun handy for her newborn spiderant babies.

RESCUE EARL'S FRIEND FROM THE BANDIT ARENA

Head north and, when you see the giant pipe again, turn left and follow the west wall until it takes a turn to the south, back toward the waterfall. At that point, continue due west to a bandit camp set in a lovely patch of grass and wildflowers. Kill a few bandits, then make your way into the cage-fighting arena to the east. Earl's best friend is there; all you need to do is press the button outside his cage and he finds his way back to Earl independently. Don't miss the **red chest** south of the arena!

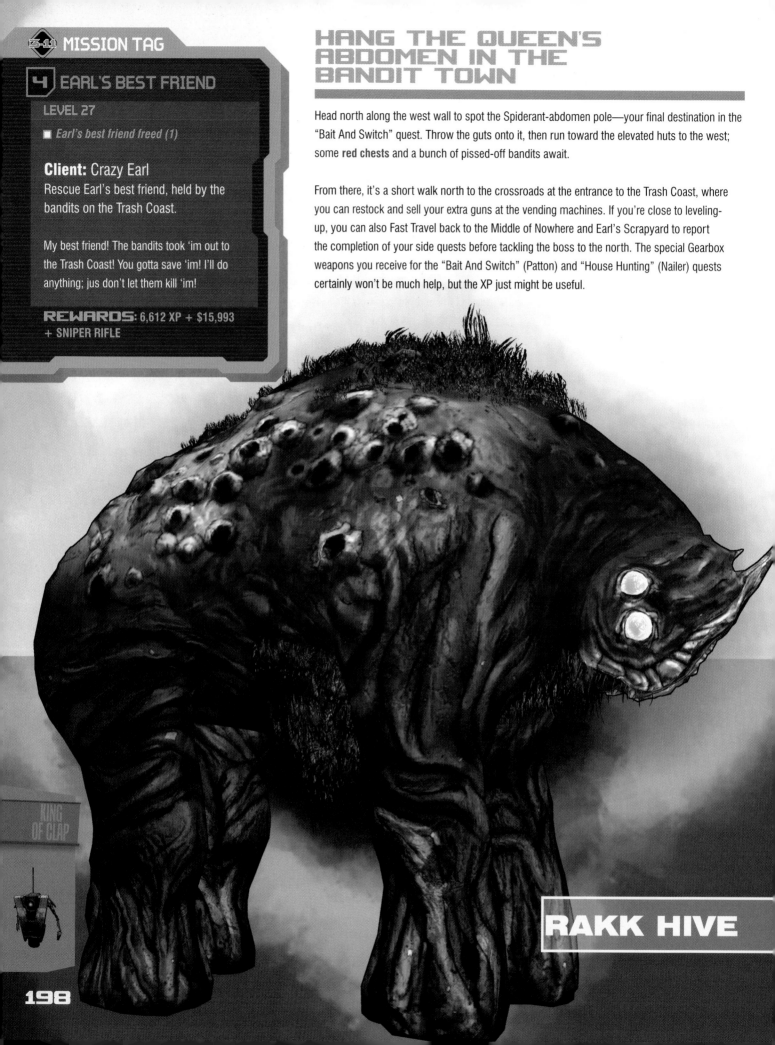

4 EARL'S BEST FRIEND

LEVEL 27

☐ *Earl's best friend freed (1)*

Client: Crazy Earl

Rescue Earl's best friend, held by the bandits on the Trash Coast.

My best friend! The bandits took 'im out to the Trash Coast! You gotta save 'im! I'll do anything; jus don't let them kill 'im!

REWARDS: 6,612 XP + $15,993 + SNIPER RIFLE

HANG THE QUEEN'S ABDOMEN IN THE BANDIT TOWN

Head north along the west wall to spot the Spiderant-abdomen pole—your final destination in the "Bait And Switch" quest. Throw the guts onto it, then run toward the elevated huts to the west; some **red chests** and a bunch of pissed-off bandits await.

From there, it's a short walk north to the crossroads at the entrance to the Trash Coast, where you can restock and sell your extra guns at the vending machines. If you're close to leveling-up, you can also Fast Travel back to the Middle of Nowhere and Earl's Scrapyard to report the completion of your side quests before tackling the boss to the north. The special Gearbox weapons you receive for the "Bait And Switch" (Patton) and "House Hunting" (Nailer) quests certainly won't be much help, but the XP just might be useful.

RAKK HIVE

KING OF CLAP

NAILER	
DAMAGE	282
ACCURACY	97.3
FIRE RATE	1.4
MAGAZINE	6
ELEMENT	None

Thwack!

+17% Recoil Reductions

1.8x Weapon Zoom

+150% Critical Hit Damage

PATTON	
DAMAGE	264
ACCURACY	91.7
FIRE RATE	1.9
MAGAZINE	6
ELEMENT	None

May God have mercy upon my enemies, because I won't.

MEET THE GUARDIAN ANGEL'S "CHALLENGE" TO THE NORTH

Aside from a red chest and the Spiderants that guard it, there's little of interest in the lovely lagoon area north of the entrance to the Trash Coast. Use the pleasant walk to recharge your shields, HP (if you have an HP-regenerating shield), and ammo (if you have an ammo-regenerating Class Mod). After tripping the New-U pole to the north, make your way into the red canopied tent to find no less than seven grey chests filled with ammo. If that's not a hint that something big is coming, we don't know what is. Load up your guns, then step into the open field to the north where the gargantuan Rakk Hive teems with vicious activity.

The Rakk Hive spits gas-grenades from its mouth, shoots two varieties of rakks out of its back, and can deliver a powerful seismic stomp to the area around it. Your primary weapon should be fast-firing and accurate, as you'll want to stand a fair distance away from the beast while still maintaining a good chance of hitting its eyes. Not only does a shot to the eyes score critical damage, but aiming for them also forces you to fight from the Rakk Hive's side, where you'll be safest from its attacks.

You can dodge its direct strikes, but the beasts that the Rakk Hive unleashes soon circle back at you. The more rakks that spawn, the more dangerous they are—especially the yellow and orange Kamikaze Rakks, which explode on impact. Blast these menacing creatures from afar with your primary weapon to detonate them early. A shotgun fired at close range should be sufficient against the white Defender Rakks, which are heartier, but less powerful. Impending rakk strikes are the best times to use the action skill of Soldiers, Sirens, and Berserkers, but Hunters should probably save their Bloodwing for the Rakk Hive itself.

While keeping the rakk population under control is important, you certainly don't want to exterminate them entirely, as they provide an endless source of Second Winds. As soon as you fall, isolate the nearest flock of rakks in the sky and begin firing with your primary weapon. It's hard to be accurate at this distance, but you should score enough lucky hits to bring one down, allowing you to resume the fight against the hive.

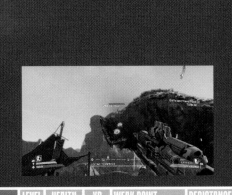

LEVEL	HEALTH	XP	WEAK POINT	RESISTANCES	SHIELDS
28	80	160	Eyes	None	None

It is uncertain whether the rakk and the Rakk Hive have a symbiotic or parasitic relationship. Either way, it's really, really disgusting.

5 ANOTHER PIECE OF THE PUZZLE
LEVEL 27

☐ *Challenge overcome (1)*
☐ *Vault Key Piece (1)*

Client: Guardian Angel
Recover another Vault Key Piece from the Trash Coast.

The Guardian Angel spoke cryptically of a challenge that awaits in the Trash Coast, and Tannis thinks another piece of the Vault Key can be found there. Given the way things have worked out so far, you're probably going to need to overcome this mysterious challenge before you'll be able to obtain the third fragment of the Vault Key and return it to Tannis.

REWARDS: 10,440 XP + $15,993

BRING THE VAULT KEY PIECE TO TANNIS

When the Rakk Hive collapses, look toward the rocky wall to the southwest and locate a circular barrier of yellow organic matter. Get closer to investigate—but not too close, or you'll be caught in the flame jet of the rakk that bursts from it! Don't waste ammo trying to shoot it down; it's just there to open the path for you.

Inside the rakk's tunnel is a small flock of its cousins—and a **silver chest** that contains the next Vault Key Piece! You must take that piece to a Fast Travel station, warp to The Underpass - West, and then bring it to Patricia Tannis. She provides your final quest mission for the chapter: "Not Without My Claptrap."

3-12 SMOKE SIGNALS OVER OLD HAVEN

Helena Pierce asked you to check in at Old Haven a while ago, but things came up and, well… we never really got around to it. That's just as well, because now you must go there, as Patricia Tannis can't resume her search for the Vault Key Pieces without the help of some precious Claptrap. While we're searching for him, we can solve Helena's mystery and maybe even find a bandit treasure for ourselves.

QUESTS:

KING OF CLAP

1 Smoke Signals: Investigate Old Haven (optional)

2 Smoke Signals: Shut Them Down (optional)

3 Bandit Treasure: Three Corpses, Three Keys (optional)

4 Claptrap Rescue: Old Haven (optional)

5 No Without My Claptrap

6 Bandit Treasure: X Marks The Spot (optional)

OLD HAVEN

RUST COMMONS EAST

DYING BANDIT

1ST BANDIT KEY

BANDIT STRONGBOX

APARTMENT DISTRICT SMOKE SIGNAL

2ND BANDIT KEY

ROOFTOP SMOKE SIGNAL

REPAIR KIT

JUNKYARD SMOKE SIGNAL

CANAL DISTRICT SMOKE SIGNAL

BUTTON

3RD BANDIT KEY

CLAPTRAP

CLAPTRAP DANCE OFF

OLD HAVEN

LEGEND	TREASURE CHEST	NEW-U POLE/STATION	CATCH-A-RIDE STATION	MEDICAL VENDING MACHINE	AMMO VENDING MACHINE	GUN VENDING MACHINE

1 | SMOKE SIGNALS: INVESTIGATE OLD HAVEN

LEVEL 28

☐ *Investigate Old Haven (1)*

Client: Helena Pierce
Infiltrate Old Haven and investigate the smoke signals.

Now that the bridges are open, we've noticed four columns of smoke rising from Old Haven. We believe these are bandit distress calls, since they don't have free access to ECHOnet. It could be a trap, but we can't risk ignoring a problem that's worse than the bandits themselves. I'm offering a reward to anyone who will scout Old Haven and find out what's going on.

REWARDS: 6,120 XP + $11,941

GATHER SIDE QUESTS IN OLD HAVEN ITSELF

To reach Old Haven, Fast Travel to the Rust Commons East and take a Runner to the entrance on the east side of the map, near the northern drawbridge. You won't have to go far to complete the "Smoke Signals: Investigate Old Haven" quest; examining the dead bodies in the very first room finishes the job. Examine them again to send the news to Helena Pierce and immediately receive the follow-up quest "Smoke Signals: Shut Them Down."

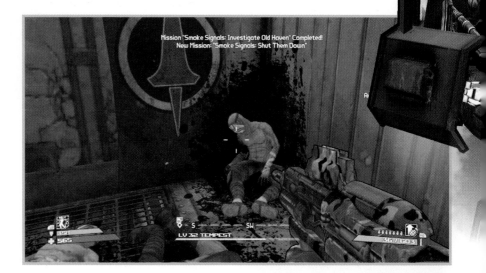

After exiting that first room, travel along the north wall of Old Haven to find more dead bandits. One of them grants you the "Bandit Treasure: Three Corpses, Three Keys" mission before dropping the key that begins this quest.

PREPARE AN ACID SHOWER FOR THE CRIMSON LANCE

Old Haven is a wide-open area. There are no barriers preventing you from going directly to any point of the city, so it's easy to pursue all of the quests at once. But the city is under heavy guard from the Crimson Lance, powerful new enemies that come heavily armored and are vulnerable only to armor-eating corrosive weaponry. If you have any corrosive weapons or Grenade Mods in your possession, seriously consider equipping them, even if their stats are significantly worse than the other weapons at your disposal. Hitting a Crimson Lance soldier with a corrosive effect will eat away at its armor, and also inflict enough recurring damage that you can often just take cover and wait for them to die.

If you don't have any good weapons, you should at least be able to equip a Corrosive Artifact to give your action skill those properties. Sirens may want to go so far as to re-spec their characters to max out their Spark and Venom skills.

Be especially wary of Crimson Lance engineers, who can deploy Scorpio Turrets just like our own Soldier class. Now you can get a taste of what it feels like to be double-teamed by a single opponent—it isn't much fun. Tag the engineer with some acid and get behind cover until he dies or his turret runs out of steam. Remember that the turret can only fire in an arc of around 120 degrees, so it's harmless if you're behind or to the side of it.

SHUT DOWN THE ROOFTOP AND JUNKYARD SMOKE SIGNALS

Start in the northwest and make a loop of the city to make an efficient route through Old Haven. Head southeast beneath the colored-triangle banner that signals the end of the Old Haven-entrance safety zone and the beginning of constant resistance from the Crimson Lance. Hang an immediate right, then turn right again so that you're heading due west. After surviving your first Crimson Lance encounter, use the staircase in the yard of the house to your right to get atop

the roof (this is a good way to rush any surviving snipers). Continue west along the rooftops, climbing each staircase you find. You'll soon find yourself at the source of the Rooftops smoke signal; just pull the green lever to shut it down.

Continue traveling south down the network of rooftops as far as you can. Then look westward toward a stairway back down to the ground level; this is where you'll spot an easy **silver chest**. Continue to follow the western wall south, into the junkyard area. Pull a lever to shut down another smoke signal, then leave the junkyard the way you came.

 A RULE TO DIE BY

AS A GENERAL RULE, TRY TO USE FIRE DAMAGE FOR BANDITS, CORROSIVE DAMAGE FOR CRIMSON LANCE, AND SHOCK DAMAGE FOR GUARDIANS.

—JONATHAN HEMINGWAY, GAME DESIGNER

3-12 MISSION TAG

2 SMOKE SIGNALS: SHUT THEM DOWN

LEVEL 28

- Apartment District (1)
- Canal District (1)
- Junkyard (1)
- Rooftops (1)

Client: Helena Pierce

Shut down the four smoke signals in Old Haven, then return to Helena Pierce.

Steele has made good on her earlier threats. The Crimson Lance now consider you as much an enemy as any bandit. If they're going to be killing indiscriminately, you need to defuse their little trap before New Haven residents get hurt. Fight your way through Old Haven and put out their smoke signals. I'll reward you well once the job is done.

REWARDS: 6,480 XP + $29,854 + CLASS MOD

CLAPTRAP DANCE OFF

COLLECT A BANDIT KEY IN THE CANAL DISTRICT

3 BANDIT TREASURE: THREE CORPSES, THREE KEYS

LEVEL 28

- ◼ *1st Bandit Key (1)*
- ◼ *2nd Bandit Key (1)*
- ◼ *3rd Bandit Key (1)*
- ◼ *Strongbox found (1)*

Client: Dead Bandit

Search Old Haven for keys and a locked strongbox.

One of the bandits is breathing his last few ragged breaths. He opens his hand, holding what appears to be a strongbox key. He wheezes, "find brothers… two more… keys… Lance get nothin'" He coughs and then lies still.

REWARDS: 10,800 XP + $5,970

4 NOT WITHOUT MY CLAPTRAP

LEVEL 28

- ◼ *Claptrap freed (1)*

Client: Patricia Tannis

Rescue Claptrap in Old Haven.

Once our Vault Key is completed, it will lead us to the location of the Vault. There's just one more piece, and my sources tell me that Baron Flynt has it. He lives on a giant digging machine in the Salt Flats. Wait. The gate to the Salt Flats won't open unless you find the silly little Claptrap doorman. My sources tell me he's trapped inside Old Haven, so maybe you'd better go and get him out of there first. Otherwise, I'll be stuck here with you.

REWARDS: 10,800 XP + $5,970

KING OF CLAP

Continue to travel south after leaving the junkyard, toward a pair of shipping crates divided by a rusty steel railing. This is a good point from which to pick off the automated Gatling Turrets to the southeast (any weapon will do, it needn't be corrosive) and any Crimson Lancers with their heads sticking out of cover.

When the coast is relatively clear, drop into the empty canal to the southwest and climb up a staircase to the other side. You emerge at the scene of another bandit slaughter. The third Bandit Key shimmers among the bodies.

SAVE THE CLAPTRAP AND DOUSE THE NEXT FIRE

The crates piled at the corner of the building should make it easy to snipe at the many Crimson Lancers who have joined you on this side of the moat. If you position yourself carefully, the crates will even block the shots from incoming turrets as you destroy them. Hold this position until the area is completely clear, as you still have quite a bit of business here.

There's a **red chest** beneath the stairs to the east. Just beyond that is a switch that lowers a door to free the Claptrap you've come to save. Speak to it after pressing the button, and it signs off on your "Not Without My Claptrap" mission and replaces it with one promisingly titled "The Final Piece."

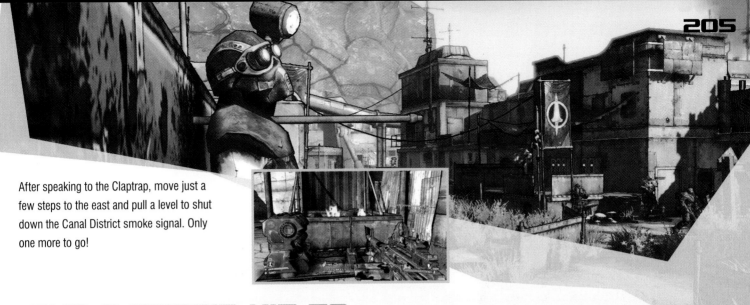

After speaking to the Claptrap, move just a few steps to the east and pull a level to shut down the Canal District smoke signal. Only one more to go!

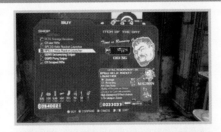

FIND A REPAIR KIT TO SAVE ANOTHER CLAPTRAP

Leap back across the canal and head west, back toward the junkyard. Across the street from the junkyard entrance, there's an open building surrounded by silver metal barricades. Enter from the west to discover a **silver chest** and a wounded Claptrap that entrusts you with the "Claptrap Rescue: Old Haven" quest. (We'd have stopped in earlier, but he only seems to appear after completing "Not Without My Claptrap.") While you're here, you may want to circle around the building and enter it from the east to access a gun vending machine that usually sells something with corrosive properties.

Follow the canal to the east, then turn north toward the building marked by the Repair Kit waypoint. Use the staircase on the building to the south of the waypoint, and make a running leap from there to the first-story roof of the designated building. A **silver chest** is up there, along with the repair kit in a room to the right.

FINISH OFF YOUR QUESTS IN THE APARTMENT DISTRICT

Complete the loop by traveling north along the east wall to reach the scene of the final bandit slaughter (with the second Bandit Key) after scattered opposition.

CLAPTRAP DANCE OFF

5 CLAPTRAP RESCUE: OLD HAVEN

LEVEL 28

■ *Repair Kit (1)*

Client: Claptrap

Find the repair kit and repair this Claptrap.

You've discovered another defunct Claptrap robot. Could there be an unused repair kit somewhere in this town?

REWARDS: 1,800 XP + STORAGE DECK UPGRADE

6 BANDIT TREASURE: X MARKS THE SPOT

LEVEL 28

■ *Stash found (1)*

Client: Dead Bandit

Go to the Dahl Headland and recover the bandit treasure.

The ragged map in the strongbox marks a location in the Dahl Headland. The bandit's dying wish was that his treasure not fall into the hands of the Crimson Lance. You feel duty-bound to grant the man's final request by taking it for yourself.

REWARDS: 7,200 XP + $29,854

You'll have a harder time proceeding north to the Apartment District Smoke Signal. It's guarded by Crimson Lance soldiers, who can pour out of all of the neighboring buildings, as well as mounted turrets on the roofs. Proceed slowly between cover to avoid triggering new reinforcements before you can take out the ones that have already spawned.

SEARCH FOR THE LOOT IN THE CITY CENTER

All of the quest goals are scattered near the outside walls, but there's plenty to find in the center of city. Many buildings have red and silver chests on their roofs, and it's something of a puzzle to figure out how to reach them.

To get the chests on the buildings northwest of where you found the repair kit, make your way to the east side of the larger building. Look for the scene shown in our screenshot below, where you can jump from the blue garbage receptacle to a green tarp-covered crate, and from there to a roof. Walk along that rooftop to grab one **red chest**, then return to the area with the garbage receptacle and tarp-covered crate, and make a flying leap to the north to land on a metal awning that connects to the northeast roof of the same building. From there, step out onto the canopy that connects this building to one to the north, then ease up on the ledge on either side of that canopy until you're high enough to jump onto the slumping center of the canopy above. It's a tricky jump, but the reward of a second **red chest** is well worth it.

Use similar tricks to claim the remaining chests in the area. Instead of looking for ways up to the roofs with the chests, seek access to neighboring buildings, then leap from there to your prize. For example, you can jump from the southern building (which has a stairway) to the **silver chest** on the building west of the previous two.

The chest north of that, which is on a second-story roof, is a little bit trickier. Once again, start from the building to its south, where you can jump on a row of lockers to reach a lower floor with a stairway. From there, jump north, through the broken railing on the balcony. There's a **red chest** right around the corner.

FOLLOW THE BANDIT MAP TO HIDDEN TREASURE

On your way out of town, return to the area where you found the first bandit corpse. Bring your keys to the shimmering door of the nearby building, and take a look at the map inside to complete the "Bandit Treasure: Three Corpses, Three Keys" quest and begin "Bandit Treasure: X Marks The Spot."

The map is, well... not a lot of help. But your quest waypoint certainly is! Warp to Lucky's Last Chance Watering Hole and generate a Runner. Drive it north by northwest until you reach the ends of the earth (literally), then look down over the ledge to spot a small structure built into the side of the cliff. Drop down onto it and use your keys to get inside. In addition to the cash for completing the quest, you'll find a **red chest** that contains random, but always high-rarity, weapons. An easy ramp leads back to your Runner.

4-1 THE FINAL PIECE OF THE PUZZLE

Patricia Tannis claims that the final piece of the Vault Key is in the hands of Baron Flynt, a bandit lord who sits like a James Bond villain atop a massive digging machine in the Salt Flats. Once you get his attention, he's happy to invite you in for a cordial chat and several rocket-shotgun blasts to the face.

QUESTS:

1. The Final Piece

2. Scavenger: Machine Gun (optional)

3. Claptrap Rescue: The Salt Flats (optional)

salt FLATS

THE DEVIL'S
FOOTSTOOL

THE
DESCENT

CLAPTRAP

MAGAZINE

BARREL

ELEVATOR

STOCK

THE BACK
DOOR

BODY

REPAIR KIT

THE SALT FLATS

RUST COMMONS
EAST

CLAPTRAP
DANCE OFF

CRIMSON
ENCLAVE

SALT FLATS

LEGEND	TREASURE CHEST	NEW-U POLE/STATION	CATCH-A-RIDE STATION	ENTRANCE	MEDICAL VENDING MACHINE	AMMO VENDING MACHINE	GUN VENDING MACHINE
	—	●	Ⓨ	●	☐	☐	☐

MISSION TAGS

1 THE FINAL PIECE

LEVEL 30

- ■ *Bandit patrols destroyed (4)*
- ■ *Thor infiltrated (1)*
- ■ *Baron Flynt killed (1)*

Client: Patricia Tannis

Take back the final piece of the Vault Key from Baron Flynt.

The little Claptrap doorman is freed, so you should now be able to enter the Salt Flats. Talk to the Claptrap once he's at the gate. It is time to go after Baron Flynt, who punched my dog and stole a piece of the Vault Key. Did I mention he lives on a giant digging machine in the Salt Flats? He calls himself the leader of all the bandits. You'd like him, I think.

REWARDS: 15,360 XP + $29,959

2 SCAVENGER: MACHINE GUN

LEVEL 30

- ■ *Machine Gun Body (1)*
- ■ *Machine Gun Magazine (1)*
- ■ *Machine Gun Stock (1)*
- ■ *Machine Gun Barrel (1)*

Client: Middle Of Nowhere
Bounty Board

Find all of the machine gun parts.

There are components to a machine gun scattered around. If you find all of these components, I can reassemble the weapon for you. Bring me the Body, Cylinder, Sight, and Barrel.

REWARDS: 4,416 XP +
COMBAT RIFLE

GATHER LOOT AS YOU EXPLORE THE SALT FLATS

The rescued Claptrap meets you at the Salt Flats gate in the Rust Commons East, northeast of the entrance to Old Haven. While you're in the area, pay a visit to the Middle Of Nowhere to collect the last-ever bounty board side quest: "Scavenger: Machine Gun."

The Salt Flats is a huge area, so you'll definitely want a Runner to explore it. Treasure hunters shouldn't miss the **red chest** in the small bandit camp west of the entrance—it's at the top of their lookout tower. Next, visit the bandit camp on the east side of the map to grab two more **red chests**. The psychos are a cinch to clear out with a Runner and the chests are easily accessible, so this is a nice treasure stop to visit every time you load up your game.

The game's third and final arena, The Devil's Footstool, can be found at the northern tip of the Salt Flats. This one offers an open desert battlefield scattered with ruins that provide plenty of cover. There isn't much of interest here for solo players, but there is a New-U station where you can establish a Fast Travel point for later.

KILL BANDIT OUTRIDERS TO CATCH FLYNT'S EYE

The Machine Gun parts, the broken Claptrap, and Baron Flynt are all inside of the bandit stronghold that surrounds Thor, the giant digging machine at the center of the Salt Flats. There's no way inside without Flynt's permission, so get his attention by circling the property in search of his Bandit Outriders, and destroying at least four of them.

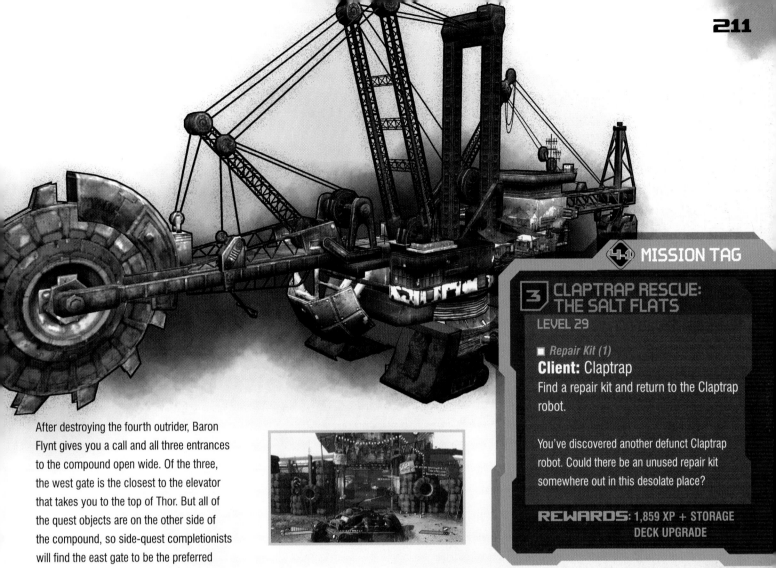

MISSION TAG

3 CLAPTRAP RESCUE: THE SALT FLATS
LEVEL 29

■ *Repair Kit (1)*
Client: Claptrap
Find a repair kit and return to the Claptrap robot.

You've discovered another defunct Claptrap robot. Could there be an unused repair kit somewhere out in this desolate place?

REWARDS: 1,859 XP + STORAGE DECK UPGRADE

After destroying the fourth outrider, Baron Flynt gives you a call and all three entrances to the compound open wide. Of the three, the west gate is the closest to the elevator that takes you to the top of Thor. But all of the quest objects are on the other side of the compound, so side-quest completionists will find the east gate to be the preferred point of entry.

GATHER THE MACHINE GUN PIECES

☐ CLIMB UP THE RUSTY PLATFORM DIRECTLY TO THE RIGHT AS YOU ENTER THROUGH THE EAST GATE. THE MACHINE GUN BARREL IS AT THE TOP.

☐ SOUTHWEST OF THE EAST GATE ARE TWO HUTS, A PAIR OF SHIPPING CRATES, AND SOME RUSTY SIDING THAT HAS BEEN ARRANGED INTO A U-SHAPED FORMATION. ENTER THE "U" FROM THE NORTH, THEN JUMP ON THE PILE OF CRATES AND CARDBOARD BOXES TO GET ATOP THE SHIPPING CRATE. THE MACHINE GUN STOCK IS UP THERE.

☐ THE MACHINE GUN BODY RESTS ATOP A WATER TANK SITUATED BETWEEN THE EAST ENTRANCE AND THE VENDING MACHINES. MOVE BETWEEN THE TWO SHIPPING CRATES DIRECTLY NORTH OF THE WATER TANKS TO SPOT A PAIR OF BARRELS THAT CAN BE USED TO JUMP ATOP ONE OF THE CRATES. LEAP TO THE WATER TANKS FROM THERE TO CLAIM THE THIRD PIECE.

☐ THE MACHINE GUN MAGAZINE IS ON A HUT NORTH OF WHERE YOU FOUND THE MACHINE GUN BODY. YOU CAN EASILY REACH THE ROOF BY JUMPING FROM THE NEARBY METAL AND CONCRETE BARRICADE.

SAVE THE WOUNDED CLAPTRAP

There's another whimpering Claptrap just west of where you found the Machine Gun Magazine. The Repair Kit is in the southeast corner of Thor, near where you found the Machine Gun Stock. You'll find it in a garbage pile cordoned off by more metal and concrete barricades, beneath an old mattress.

Fight your way through scattered bandit psychos and killers to make your way to the west entrance of the compound. There's a **red chest** on a platform just south of the west gate, as well as a pair of **grey chests**, filled with ammo. Head directly east from the gate to enter the cavern that runs beneath Thor to find yet another **red chest**, along with a New-U pole and the elevator to the top.

HANZ

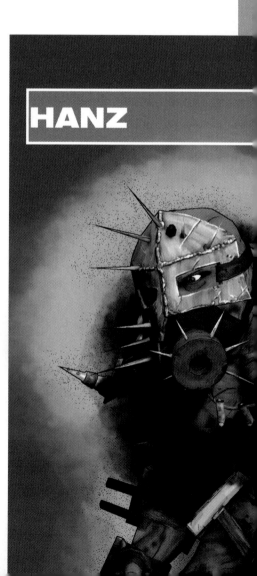

SURVIVE THREE WAVES OF FLYNT'S HENCHMEN

After stepping off of the elevator and receiving a taunting ECHO call from Baron Flynt, a door rises on the other side of Thor, unleashing an ungodly number of angry psychos. It's hard to survive them all at once, so hit as many as you can with an action skill that's enhanced by a corrosive or flaming artifact, and count on the continuing damage to provide easy Second Wind kills. After wiping out the first wave, another door opens, unleashing a smaller group led by a hearty Badass Psycho.

Once the second wave of foes has been slain, an elevator at the center of the battlefield lifts, and Baron Flynt's bodyguards enter the battlefield. The blade-wielding Hanz rushes in to fight at close range while the more cautious Franz covers him from afar with a machine gun. You can throw a wrench into their two-man show by running into the room from which the first batch of psychos emerged—the half-open door is too low for Hanz to squeeze through, so he cannot reach you while you blast Franz. Hanz won't be completely helpless, though; he can still throw grenades, and he almost surely will. Use a sniper rifle or an accurate, powerful combat rifle to gun down Franz, but don't use the scope or you won't be able to spot the incoming grenades in time to dodge them. When Franz is dead, you can slay the poor, ungainly Hanz at your leisure.

LEVEL	HEALTH	XP	WEAK POINT	RESISTANCES	SHIELDS
30	15	20	Head	None	None

Years ago, Hanz was a hardcore LARPer. That is, until he was convicted for decapitating a man pretending to be an elf. He was imprisoned on Pandora, but was later set free by Baron Flynt. He has served as Flynt's bodyguard ever since. No relation to Franz.

FRANZ

LEVEL	HEALTH	XP	WEAK POINT	RESISTANCES	SHIELDS
30	18	25	Head	None	Yes

Franz once ran the best tattoo parlor in New Haven, but was imprisoned after a piercing went horribly wrong and left three dead. Baron Flynt set him free, and he has served as Flynt's bodyguard and enforcer ever since. No relation to Hanz.

CLAPTRAP DANCE OFF

TAKE BARON FLYNT'S LIFE AND BOOM STICK

Once Hanz and Franz fall, Baron Flynt and a handful of other bandits appear on the upper levels of the tower. You can reach them from the ramps on the other side, but take this opportunity to do as much sniper-rifle damage as possible instead. Try to eliminate Flynt's henchmen first, but keep him in your sights to dodge his shots. Flynt is using some sort of rocket-firing shotgun, and while the projectiles it fires move quickly, they're clearly visible and can be easily avoided when fighting from long range. If you do get hit with a rocket, or Flynt's henchmen manage to wear away your shields, go back into the room where you hid from Hanz to recharge in peace.

Instead of running up after Flynt, snipe at him and his henchmen until he gets fed up and comes down to you. You can then fight him in the center of the spacious lower platform, where you can fire while circling him constantly. As long as you're moving, Flynt will have a hard time landing a rocket shot.

BARON FLYNT	LEVEL	HEALTH	XP	WEAK POINT	RESISTANCES	SHIELDS
	30	12	12	Head	⚡ ☣ 🔥	Yes

Flynt once worked for Dahl as a prison warden on Pandora. When Dahl abandoned the operation, he was left to fend for himself, along with a prison full of starving convicts. He freed these desperate men, and with them formed a tribe of bandits. He now leads them from his base aboard Thor, an abandoned mining vehicle.

BOOM STICK

DAMAGE	~400
ACCURACY	0
FIRE RATE	~4
MAGAZINE	6
ELEMENT	None

Beyond Groovy

~+600% Damage

+600% Burst Fire Count

~+75% Fire Rate

The weapon Flynt drops when he dies seems to be different than the one he used in the battle. The Boom Stick is similar to Sledge's Shotgun, but even more ludicrous. It has a power of roughly 400, an accuracy of 0, and it fires its entire load of six explosive pellets every time the trigger is pulled. The Boom Stick could turn a cow into ground beef at pointblank range, but could also just as easily whiff completely against a foe standing 10 yards away. It's difficult to use in most combat situations, but when dying at melee range, there's no more satisfying way to earn a Second Wind.

COLLECT THE FINAL... WAIT, WHAT?!

Use the ramps on Thor's side to reach a garbage pile on top, where an elevator rises to present you with a familiar **silver chest**. Open it and you'll find… nothing. This was all a wild goose chase arranged by Patricia Tannis. This revelation concludes "The Final Piece" mission and begins the "Get Some Answers" mission. The next step is to penetrate deep into Crimson Lance territory and track down Patricia Tannis.

Speaking of the Crimson Lance, a full assault force of these guys awaits when you ride the elevator back to the surface. The bastards have sealed the west and north gates, so you must now fight your way to the east gate at the opposite end of the camp. Don't forget to equip your corrosive weapons and artifacts, and make ample use of your action skill to escape alive.

If your Runner isn't waiting at the east gate, grab one at the Catch-A-Ride just outside the sealed north gate. Drive to the New-U station at the southern crossroads so you can Fast Travel back to the Middle of Nowhere. Redeem those Machine Gun parts for a high-quality Combat Rifle—you're gonna need one.

INFILTRATE THE CRIMSON ENCLAVE

If you've taken the time to explore the distant reaches of the Salt Flats, you probably noticed the giant gate to the southwest that's under heavy Crimson Lance guard. This seems like a logical entrance to Crimson Lance territory, but those who take on the task of crossing these defenses will find only a locked gate (and a **red chest** as a consolation prize).

The real entrance to the Crimson Fastness is through a small cave called "The Back Door," which is just northwest of that heavily guarded gate. The Back Door is a straightforward underground passage that, until you reach the end, is guarded only by Spiderants. You can easily run past these creatures if you want, but battling the high-level elemental varieties is a good way to get the level 3 artifacts that are only available as monster drops. You'll also find three **red chests** in the Back Door, all in plain sight along the main passage.

MASTER MCCLOUD

CRIMSON
FASTNESS

THE SALT
FLATS

THE BACKDOOR

LEGEND	TREASURE CHEST	NEW-U POLE/STATION	CATCH-A-RIDE STATION	MEDICAL VENDING MACHINE	AMMO VENDING MACHINE	GUN VENDING MACHINE
	▬	●	ⓨ	☐	☐	☐

HEART OF STEELE
LOOK UP TO THE OBSERVATION ROOM AT THE VERY BEGINNING OF YOUR BATTLE
WITH MASTER MCCLOUD. . .

—GRAEME TIMMINS, LEAD LEVEL DESIGNER

10110 CANNON	
DAMAGE	~850
ACCURACY	91.7
FIRE RATE	0.4
MAGAZINE	Infinite
ELEMENT	None

0100111101001101010000111

TURN THE TABLES ON MASTER MCCLOUD

There's a button on a crate at the end of the cave. Press it and you suddenly find yourself in a massive arena, facing Master McCloud and two Lance Royal Guards.

Master McCloud is packing an Eridian blaster that is likely the single most powerful weapon you've ever encountered. Fortunately, its projectiles travel slowly, so if you fight from across the room, you'll have plenty of time to dodge. Poor tactician that he is, Master McCloud happily holds his ground and attempts to play a game of Eridian whack-a-mole as you move between cover dispensing with his men.

The Lance Royal Guards are heavily armored, so soften them up with corrosive grenades, corrosive action skills, or corrosive weapons fire. Beyond that, this battle is all about positioning; choose cover that provides protection from Master McCloud and one of the guardsmen while you focus on the third.

Once you're alone with Master McCloud, he becomes a little more adventurous, and moves in on your position. He also begins to deploy Scorpio Turrets, although you can easily dodge them simply by moving to the massive blind spot on their sides and continuing to sidestep the energy blasts from there. After tagging him with some acid, fight back with an accurate long-range weapon; the closer you must get to score a hit, the higher the odds that McCloud will surprise you with a blast from his gun. Stay nimble, and that gun will soon be yours!

CLAPTRAP DANCE OFF

MASTER MCCLOUD

LEVEL	HEALTH	XP	WEAK POINT	RESISTANCES	SHIELDS
31	15	45	Head	None	None

Master McCloud sees himself as a star-hopping, interplanetary hero. Given half a chance, he will regale anyone with tales of his many exploits. This probably explains why he has been stationed on a remote dustball like Pandora, as far from Atlas HQ as humanly possible.

4-2 BEHIND ENEMY LINES

You've been betrayed by one ally and cut off from the others. Now you're stuck in the Crimson Fastness, surrounded by heavily armored stooges as the window of Vault opportunity is closing fast. All you can do is search for Patricia Tannis in hopes that a solution presents itself. And if not, well, there's always revenge…

QUESTS:

1 Get Some Answers

2 Claptrap Rescue: Crimson Fastness (optional)

3 Find The ECHO Command Console

4 Reactive The ECHO Comm System

RESCUE THE CRIMSON FASTNESS CLAPTRAP

You won't go unnoticed in the Crimson Fastness for long. In the room past the entrance with the vending machines and New-U Station, clouds of steam hide a handful of foes and an automated turret. Move east instead of south, gunning down the handful of guards around the staircase, and use that to get onto a railing that allows you to move south toward the turret without passing through its range of fire. At the south end of the room, use the doorway to block the turret's fire as you step out just far enough to destroy it.

Turn your attention to the wailing blue Claptrap, the only survivor of an apparent Claptrap holocaust. To complete his repair quest, you must travel to the heavily guarded, split-level room to the east. Surprise one roaming guard with a Boom Stick blast to the head, and use your action skill to help take out the other guards on the upper level. Stay away from the railings until you're ready to kill the lower-floor enemies with sniper headshots from above. The Repair Kit is in plain sight on the ground floor.

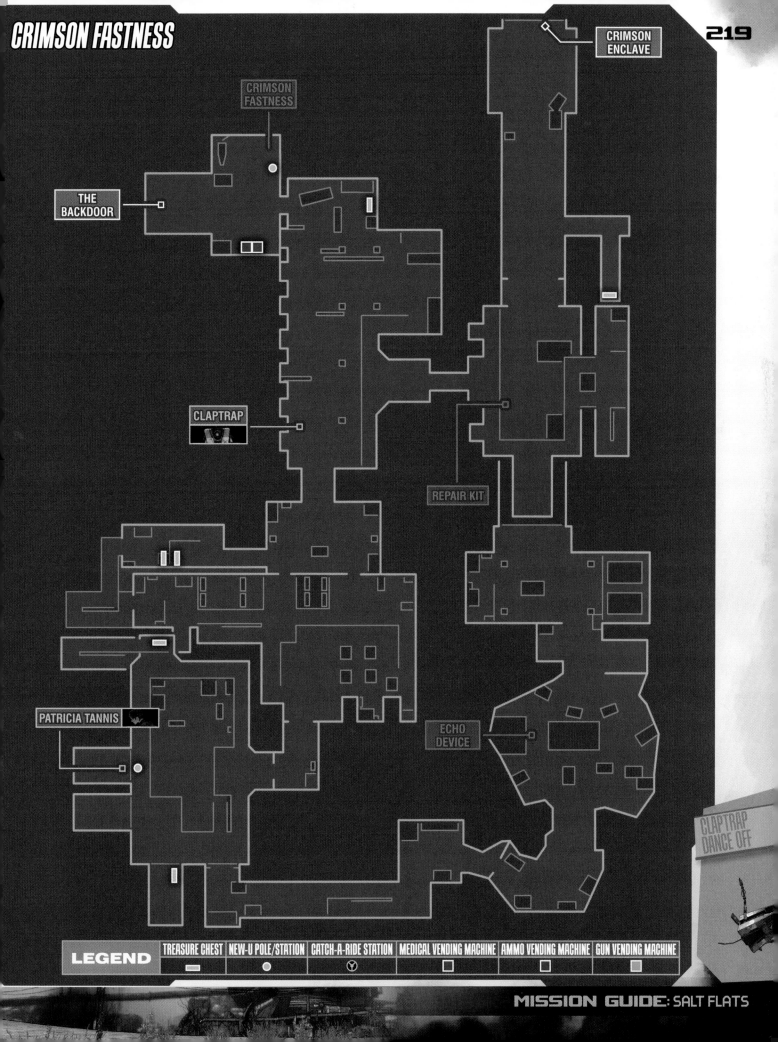

CRIMSON FASTNESS

CRIMSON
ENCLAVE

CRIMSON
FASTNESS

THE
BACKDOOR

CLAPTRAP

REPAIR KIT

PATRICIA TANNIS

ECHO
DEVICE

CLAPTRAP
DANCE OFF

LEGEND	TREASURE CHEST	NEW-U POLE/STATION	CATCH-A-RIDE STATION	MEDICAL VENDING MACHINE	AMMO VENDING MACHINE	GUN VENDING MACHINE

CRIMSON FASTNESS

THE SALT
FLATS

CRIMSON ENCLAVE

LEGEND	TREASURE CHEST	NEW-U POLE/STATION	CATCH-A-RIDE STATION	MEDICAL VENDING MACHINE	AMMO VENDING MACHINE	TRANSMITTER CONSOLE
	—	●	Ⓨ	☐	☐	◈

USE SECRET PASSAGES TO BYPASS THE GUARDS

The grateful Claptrap opens a secret passage that not only leads to two **red chests**, but also allows you to slip past the guards in the barracks to the south. To avoid a fight, take the passage to the upper level of the barracks and, when the catwalk is free of guards, use the green panel on your right to open the door to another passage. You won't miss out on any red or silver chests in the barracks—just the XP you would have earned from a good Crimson Lance slaughter.

FIGHT YOUR WAY TO PATRICIA TANNIS'S... CELL?

The second passage leads to the upper level of a Crimson Lance prison. With Tannis stuck on the lower floor, you can't avoid a fight—but you have the high ground and the railings should provide decent cover.

On the ground floor, Patricia Tannis gives you an Explosive Artifact and a new mission: "Find The ECHO Command Console." Speaking with her will also open the door to a nearby cell where you can grab a **red chest**.

1 GET SOME ANSWERS

LEVEL 30

■ *Tannis Found (1)*

Client: Patricia Tannis
Find Tannis, wherever she may be.

Tannis has betrayed you. Who knows what motivates that babbling bitch, but it's a sure bet she's fled her dig site. It's time to take back your Vault key and get some answers. First, you'll need to figure out where she's hiding.

REWARDS: 15,360 XP + ARTIFACT

2 CLAPTRAP RESCUE: CRIMSON FASTNESS

LEVEL 30

■ *Repair Kit (1)*

Client: Claptrap
Find a repair kit and return to the Claptrap robot.

You've discovered another defunct Claptrap robot. Could there be an unused repair kit somewhere out here?

REWARDS: 1,920 XP + STORAGE DECK UPGRADE

Your next target is the ECHO Console in the southwest part of the complex. As you enter the hallway south of the prison, you'll spot a few guards with their backs turned and the targeting light of a distant turret. Get the jump on them with a grenade or two and they should pose little trouble. You then have two options when it comes to the turret. You can either use a crate as cover as you detonate the turret from afar or crouch-walk into the nearby ventilation shaft and use that to travel to the other end of the hallway. The ventilation shaft ends directly above the turret, where you can easily position yourself so the corner of the shaft is blocking its shots.

Use the ECHO Console to complete your current mission, which gives way to "Reactive the ECHO Comm System." To complete that one, you must activate the Transmitter Consoles in three Crimson Lance installations of the Crimson Enclave area to the north.

PUNCH THROUGH THE CRIMSON LANCE DEFENSIVE LINE

As you head north to the exit of the compound, a siren blares and a blast door rises to reveal a trio of Badass Engineers. These foes are heavily armored and have the ability to drop Scorpio Turrets, which they use immediately upon spotting you. This is a fun time to be a Siren, since you can Phasewalk right through them, and either find the staircase to the north and snipe them from above, or just keep running until you're out of the compound. (Don't miss the **red chest** in the alcove on the way out!)

Other classes should immediately get behind the palette of crates to protect themselves from the turrets, then fall back to more distant cover and prepare to shoot the engineers when they come a-searching. The sluggish engineers make an easy target for McCloud's Eridian cannon.

ROOT ON THE GUARDIANS AS THEY BATTLE THE LANCE

You exit the compound to find the Crimson Lance locked in open warfare with an army of Guardians. Remember them? The deadly, but frail, Guardians have nearly all of their defensive strength in their shields, so shock weapons are ideal against them. It requires a close-range shotgun blast or a highly accurate weapon to pull off a critical-damage headshot, though, as the tiny heads that jut out of their torsos are tough targets to hit.

In the battle raging outside of the Crimson Fastness, the Crimson Lance seem to have the upper hand. But don't let that stop you from targeting both sides for some easy XP. Snipe from afar to escape your foes' notice for as long as possible.

ACTIVATE TRANSMITTER #1 IN NORTHERN COMPOUND

To find the first transmitter compound, head northwest from the entrance to the Crimson Enclave, then veer northeast when the path forks. This area remains in Crimson Lance hands, so corrosive weapons serve you better than those that deal shock damage; you may want to keep your best of each type quick-keyed from now on. Move slowly between cover, and stay to the southwest of the shipping crate to remain out of the Gatling Turret's line of fire. Once you've mopped up the guards, peek around the shipping crate to destroy the turret.

All three of the transmitter compounds are unmanned, so you can explore their interiors without fear of a Crimson Lance ambush. The console is at the end of the second-floor hallway, and there's a **red chest** on the roof.

3 FIND THE ECHO COMMAND CONSOLE

LEVEL 31

■ *ECHO console found (1)*

Client: Patricia Tannis
Find the ECHO command console.

It's probably impossible to take back the Vault Key or open the Vault now. Let's focus on something else instead. Let's bring the ECHO system back online. The Lance locked it down, but I know how we can bring it back, since I pretty much invented it. I wrote some instructions on the back of this paper towel. Find the ECHO command console, and follow my instructions.

REWARDS: 3,960 XP

4 REACTIVATE ECHO COMM SYSTEM

LEVEL 31

■ *Transmitter Console activated (3)*

Client: Patricia Tannis
Reactivate Transmitter Consoles.

The notes Tannis gave you are rambling and disjointed, and appear to be written in the form of an argument with either an invisible cellmate or a rat. However, she also mentions reactivating three network transmitter consoles in three separate buildings, then returning to this main control console.

REWARDS: 9,900 XP

CLAPTRAP DANCE OFF

ACTIVATE TRANSMITTER #2 IN THE SOUTHERN COMPOUND

Return to the area with the vending machines, and then travel south to find the second transmitter compound. It's a little harder to find cover from the Gatling Turret outside this one, so destroy it from afar with a sniper rifle or rocket launcher. You can then use all the shipping crates to your left as cover while you approach the building, which will allow you to pick off the remaining guards without exposing yourself to attacks from the roof.

The ground-level door is locked from the inside, so you must use the stairs on the side of the building to reach the roof, then descend to the second floor from there. Continue down to the ground floor to find this compound's **red chest**.

ACTIVATE TRANSMITTER #3 IN THE WESTERN COMPOUND

Travel northwest from the southern compound to reach a bridge where a pitched battle is being fought between the Crimson Lance and Guardian forces. When you tire of being a spectator, take a position near the defense tower on the east side of the bridge and pick off the survivors.

As you approach the compound, rush behind the shipping crate to protect yourself from the nearby turret. It's hard to find a spot from which you can detonate it safely, so step into its path of fire, then use your action skill and a grenade or two to smash it. Recharge behind your shipping crate and peek out to shoot the compound's many guards one at a time, gradually cracking the compound's tough defenses. A good corrosive or flaming

rocket launcher would be a godsend against the more distant targets. When the coast is clear, activate the final transmitter and grab yourself some loot from the **red chest** on the roof.

KING OF CLAP

RETURN TO THE CRIMSON FASTNESS COMMAND CONSOLE

To finish the quest, return to the ECHO Command Console at the Crimson Fastness. Once again, you must punch through the line of Badass Engineers outside the terminal, but this time you can get upstairs to blast them from above, where you're too high for their turrets to hit. At the Command Console, you complete your current quest and get a new one: "Find Steele." To do that, return to the Crimson Enclave and head toward the northern compound. When the road splits, head down the northwest fork, generate a Runner, and then drive it to the end of the road. There you'll find the gate that connects to the Salt Flats, now open at last.

THE ICY TREK TO THE VAULT

The Vault is opening and Helena Steele has a significant head start. At least that saves you the trouble of having to find it, since you can follow her trail of Crimson Lance stooges through a new Salt Flats passage, an excavation site carved into the side of a mountain, and a snowy promontory. Only your Guardian Angel knows what you'll find at the end.

QUESTS:

1. Find Steele
2. Destroy The Destroyer
3. Bring The Vault Key To Tannis

FOLLOW STEELE THROUGH A NEW MOUNTAIN PATH

After entering the Salt Flats from the Crimson Enclave, drive northeast along the main road. You soon discover that a new trail has been carved into the mountains to the north. It's too thin for your Runner, so ditch it and continue on foot. You won't find any red or silver chests in this new region of the Salt Flats, but you will encounter a squad of Crimson Lancers guarding their most precious discovery—a path to the Vault known simply as "The Descent." If you don't feel like fighting, you can make a mad dash to the west, leap over the ledge, and land right at the start of The Descent.

CLAPTRAP DANCE OFF

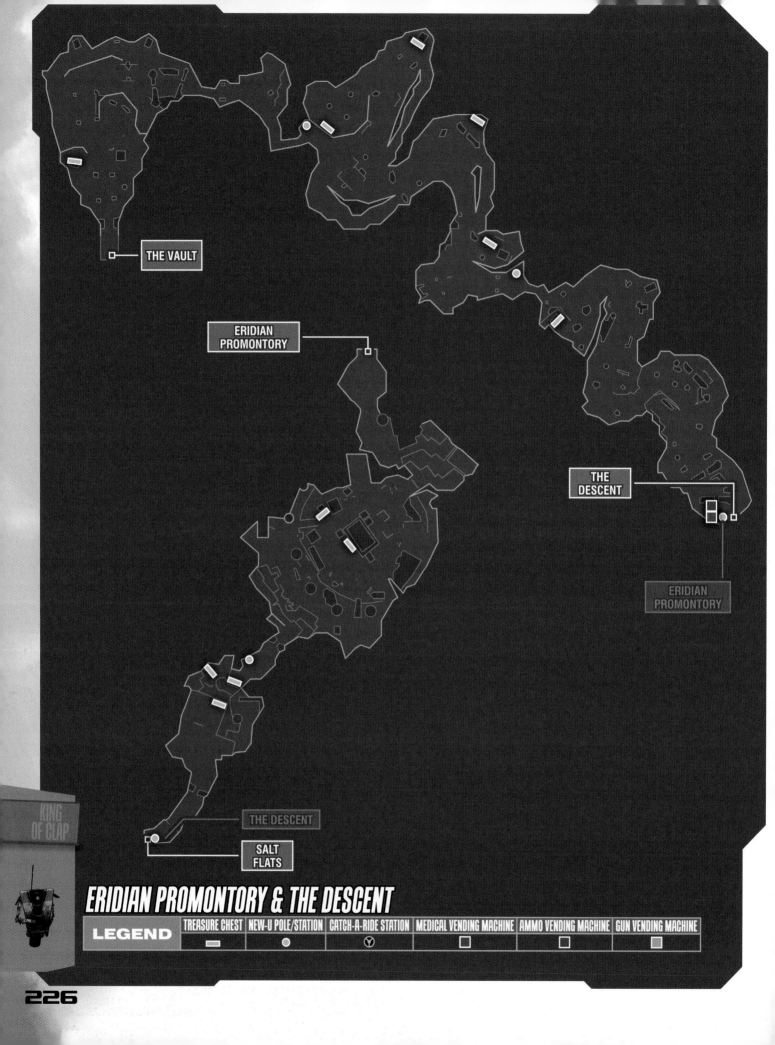

THE VAULT

ERIDIAN
PROMONTORY

THE
DESCENT

ERIDIAN
PROMONTORY

THE DESCENT

SALT
FLATS

ERIDIAN PROMONTORY & THE DESCENT

LEGEND	TREASURE CHEST	NEW-U POLE/STATION	CATCH-A-RIDE STATION	MEDICAL VENDING MACHINE	AMMO VENDING MACHINE	GUN VENDING MACHINE
	▬	●	Ⓨ	▢	▢	▢

Upon entering The Descent, large flocks of native Trash Feeder birds take to the skies. They're no threat to you, but if you take a shot at one, the entire flock retaliates. With a good shotgun or automatic weapon, you can then plow through them to easily complete the "Conveyor of Death" challenge, which involves killing 25 enemies in rapid succession.

Don't get so caught up in your wildlife slaughter that you overlook the actual threat of an impending Guardian attack. Take aim at the flying, shock-firing Sera Guardians to get them out of your hair before more powerful Guardians can enter the battlefield to challenge you at melee range.

After clearing out the Guardians, you find a **red chest** in plain sight at a well-lit altar. Directly west of that altar, several platforms have been cut into the western wall, allowing you to carefully jump to a second **red chest**. The quality of weapons in these chests has increased dramatically in this area, so if you feel underpowered, this might be a good time to repeat the Exit-Reload trick until you get something that proves effective against the many Guardians ahead.

⊹ MISSION TAGS

1 FIND STEELE

LEVEL 31

☐ *Steele found (1)*

Client: Patricia Tannis
Find Steele and take back the Vault Key.

I know where the Vault is, and so does Steele. She took my Vault Key. You know, the one you worked so hard to get for me? Well, she took it. That albino bitch is going to open the Vault unless you can somehow find her and beat her to it. I'm marking a waypoint at the location of the Vault. I don't have to tell you what to do, do I?

REWARDS: 20,400 XP

2 DESTROY THE DESTROYER

LEVEL 32

☐ *Destroyer defeated (1)*

Client: Guardian Angel
Defeat the Destroyer.

Do you feel that I betrayed you? Do not. I am possessed of a sight that allows me to look forward and backward along the timeline, and the release of this creature was inevitable. There was only one chance for this dimension's continued existence. A hero. Someone who was at the right place, at the right time, and strong enough to push back. I have given you the unique opportunity to defend the existence of all that you know. Go! Fight! Be that hero! I will help you however I can.

REWARDS: 28,560 XP

3 BRING THE VAULT KEY TO TANNIS

LEVEL 32

■ *Destroyer defeated (1)*

Client: Patricia Tannis
Grab the Vault Key and return to Tannis at her Rust Commons dig site.

The Vault Key won't work again for another two hundred years, so it is now effectively useless. Tannis has volunteered to become the caretaker of the key and may even pay well for it.

REWARDS: 17,136 XP + $234,885

DESCEND INTO THE ATLAS EXCAVATION SITE

The path to the bottom begins at a downward slanting slab south of the altar. Note that the path involves several steep drops, so once you go down, there's no coming back up. (There will be Fast Travel stations ahead, though, so this is not a point of no return.) You could certainly survive a dramatic plunge from the top to the bottom, but traveling through the spiral of ledges set against the canyon walls will ensure that you don't miss the **gray ammo chest** or **silver gun chest** along the way.

When you reach the bottom, follow the tunnel northeast to a massive excavation site where the Crimson Lance are meeting heavy resistance from Guardians. It would be nice to stay neutral, but the flying Sera Guardians will likely notice you and begin aiming in your direction. Pick them off first, and let the Badass Guardians on the ground mop up the Crimson Lance.

You face several newly spawned Crimson Lance soldiers as you descend into the basin, so move slowly and be ready for attacks that could come from any direction. Once you've cleared the battlefield, help yourself to some new guns from the two **red chests**, then refill them with ammo from the plentiful **grey chests**.

TREAD GINGERLY TO THE ERIDIAN PROMONTORY

Approach the metal door to the northeast and it rises to reveal several Crimson Lance guards. At the same time, new guards begin to enter the basin from the north, making it a challenge to clear the basin area again. If you don't feel like a fight, a mad dash past the guards and through the metal door should work fine; the Crimson Lance tend not to follow.

There are no enemies in the final stretch of The Descent, but there are plenty of bottomless pits. Always look before you leap to reach the Eridian Promontory safely.

SLAY THE VAULT'S STAUNCHEST GUARDIANS

At the entrance to the Eridian Promontory you'll find a pair of vending machines and one last New-U station. If you need to Fast Travel back to a bounty board or something, this is the time to do it.

The Guardians begin their assault a few steps to the north. Their ranks now include projectile-hurling Arch Guardians, so long-range sniper tactics are no longer as effective; keep moving to stay ahead of their shots.

The Crimson Lance appear as you proceed up the trail, but they're outmatched by the Guardians this time. Exploit their distraction to score some long-range headshots off against them, but be ready to switch to a short-range weapon when the Guardians rush in for revenge.

AVAIL YOURSELF OF SOME LAST-CHANCE LOOT

As you approach the first New-U pole, follow the west wall to make sure you don't miss a tiny Crimson Lance camp that holds the area's first **red chest**. There's also a **silver chest** past the New-U pole, in a second small camp to the east. But you'll need to punch through a group of Principal and Arch

Guardians to reach it. There are a few Crimson Lance soldiers in the camp, so it's a good idea to run past the Guardians, lead them into the camp, and then drop off the ledge near the New-U pole. That should keep the bulk of the Guardians distracted so that you can battle them one or two at a time. As you proceed north from the silver chest, walk along the eastern rim of the trail so that you don't miss another **red chest** at the cliff's edge.

ASCEND TO THE MOUTH OF THE VAULT

After claiming that second **red chest**, proceed west along the elevated southern wall to snipe at the Guardians and Crimson Lance soldiers fighting below. When the battle ends, search the area to the north for two more **red chests** before proceeding west toward the Vault.

The large area outside the Vault is full of Guardians. Many are Sera Guardians, who perch calmly atop the columns until they're attacked, making it easy to snipe them out first. They're the weakest of the Guardians, so abandon the Sera hunt as soon as a more deadly variety appears. Scour the area for

ammo before continuing into the Vault; you're going to need a lot of it, particularly for mid-range weapons like Submachine Guns, Combat Rifles, and Handguns.

DESTROY THE DESTROYER

Inside the Vault, you meet the mighty Destroyer. This massive beast has four main modes of attack, but its tongue-whips and shockwaves can be easily dodged if you fight from far enough away. The broken arches with the Crimson Lance flags mark the ideal distance and provided solid cover.

The Destroyer can also unleash a pink energy beam from its eye, which deals devastating amounts of damage, but cannot penetrate the rubble on the battlefield. The eye beam is preceded by the sound of a high-pitched intake of breath, giving you just enough time to get behind cover. However, hiding won't protect you from the explosive spikes that are lobbed by the Destroyer's four purple tentacles. Stay close enough to cover that you can get behind it within a second or two, but strafe constantly to avoid being targeted by the spikes whenever the purple tentacles are out.

The Destroyer has several weak points, but your primary target should be the purple pustules on the spike-throwing tentacles. Doing enough damage to those destroys the tentacle, damaging the Destroyer and weakening its offense. Destroyed tentacles grow back, but that's a good thing—you always want one or two of them on the battlefield, because they're your only hope of getting a Second Wind if the boss takes you down. When the Destroyer is down to its last pair of tentacles, leave them alive and switch to targeting the weak points on its mouth, eyes, and tongue.

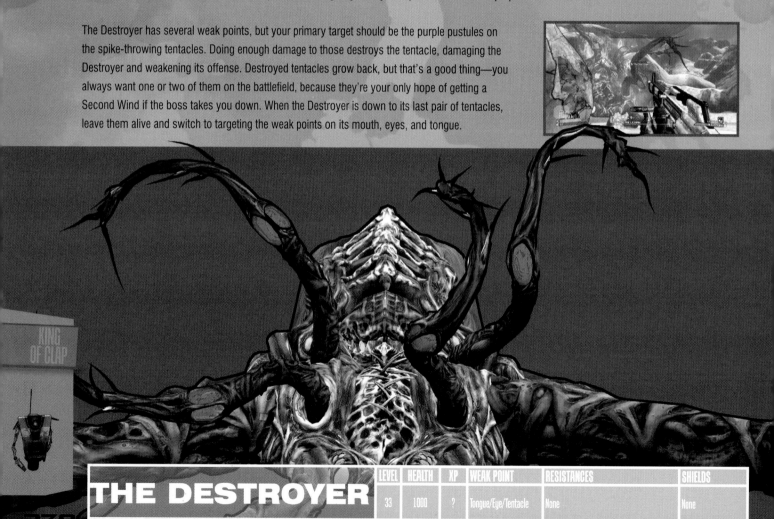

KING OF CLAP

THE DESTROYER	LEVEL	HEALTH	XP	WEAK POINT	RESISTANCES	SHIELDS
	33	1000	?	Tongue/Eye/Tentacle	None	None

COMPLETE YOUR FINAL TASK,
AND BEGIN IT ALL ANEW

The Destroyer is dead and the credits have rolled, but the game isn't over quite yet. You have one final plot mission: "Bring The Vault Key To Tannis." Grab the fallen key and use the Vault's New-U station to warp to the Underpass - West, and hike up to Patricia Tannis's old excavation site. Give her the goods and, well… that's it.

If you still have unfinished quests to complete, you can do them now. But if you're ready to move on to bigger and better things, exit your game and load it up again. You'll be given the option of choosing Playthrough 1, to continue your current game, or Playthrough 2 to begin a new one. If you choose Playthrough 2, you'll restart the game from the moment you got off the bus at Fyrestone. However, this time you begin with all of your accumulated levels, items, and skills. The enemies you face will be much higher level, and so will the guns you acquire. The odds of finding Eridian weapons also increases significantly.

Congratulations… and good luck!

From Gearbox Software, comes the first expansion to the Role Playing Shooter of the Year

BORDERLANDS™

An all new storyline. Join the Vault Hunters as they try to solve the mystery of who the hell is making all these flippin' zombies!

Tons of new creatures to fight! Crawling Torsos, Were-Skags, and Exploding Tankensteins!

So much to do and explore! Visit the Jakobs weapon factory, the Ruins of Dead Haven, and much more!

the Zombie Island of Dr Ned

Mission CHECKLIST

CHAPTER 1: MISSIONS IN THE ARID BADLANDS AREA

MISSION TYPE	NAME	PREREQUISITE	CLIENT	LEVEL	WALKTHROUGH SECTION
Plot Mission 01	Fresh Off The Bus	-	Guardian Angel	2	1-1
Plot Mission 02	The Doctor Is In	PM01	Dr. Zed	2	1-1
Plot Mission 03	Skags At The Gate	PM02	Dr. Zed	2	1-1
Plot Mission 04	Claptrap Rescue	PM03	Claptrap	2	1-1
Plot Mission 05	Fix'er Upper	PM04	Dr. Zed	2	1-1
Plot Mission 06	Blinding Nine-Toes	PM05	Dr.Zed	2	1-1
Plot Mission 07	Nine-Toes: Meet T.K. Baha	PM06	Dr. Zed	3	1-2
Plot Mission 08	Nine-Toes: T.K.'s Food	PM07	T.K. Baha	2	1-2
Plot Mission 09	Got Grenades?	PM08	T.K. Baha	2	1-2
Plot Mission 10	Nine-Toes: Take Him Down	PM09	T.K. Baha	4	1-2
Plot Mission 11	Nine-Toes: Time To Collect	PM10	T.K. Baha	7	1-2
Plot Mission 12	Job Hunting	PM11	Dr. Zed	7	1-2
Side Mission 01	Hidden Journal: The Arid Badlands	PM12	Fyrestone B.B.	13	1-5
Side Mission 02	T.K. Has More Work	PM12	T.K. Baha	10	1-3
Side Mission 03	T.K.'s Life And Limb	SM02	T.K. Baha	7	1-3
Side Mission 04	By The Seeds Of Your Pants	SM02	T.K. Baha	9	1-3
Side Mission 05	Why Are They Here?	PM12	Fyrestone B.B.	7	1-3
Plot Mission 13	Catch-A-Ride	PM12	Scooter	7	1-4
Plot Mission 14	Bone Head's Theft	PM13	Scooter	10	1-4
Side Mission 06	Claptrap Rescue: Safe House	PM14	Claptrap	14	1-6
Side Mission 07	Claptrap Rescue: The Lost Cave	PM14	Claptrap	15	1-7
Side Mission 08	Get A Little Blood On The Tires	PM14	Fyrestone B.B.	10	1-4
Plot Mission 15	The Piss Wash Hurdle	PM14	Scooter	10	1-4
Side Mission 09	Shock Crystal Harvest	PM15	Fyrestone B.B.	15	1-7
Plot Mission 16	Return to Zed	PM15	Scooter	10	1-4
Plot Mission 17	Sledge: Meet Shep	PM16	Dr. Zed	10	1-4
Side Mission 10	Braking Wind	PM16	Shep Sanders	10	1-5
Side Mission 11	Get The Flock Outta Here	PM16	Shep Sanders	10	1-5
Plot Mission 18	Sledge: The Mine Key	PM17	Shep Sanders	10	1-5
Side Mission 12	Scavenger: Sniper Rifle	PM18	Fyrestone B.B.	11	1-6
Side Mission 13	The Legend Of Moe And Marley	PM18	Fyrestone B.B.	15	1-6
Side Mission 14	Circle Of Death: Meat And Greet	PM18	Fyrestone B.B.	11	1-7
Side Mission 15	Circle Of Death: Round 1	SM14	Rade Zayben	11	1-7
Side Mission 16	Circle Of Death: Round 2	SM15	Rade Zayben	15	1-7
Side Mission 17	Circle Of Death: Final Round	SM16	Rade Zayben	18	1-7
Plot Mission 19	Sledge: To The Safe House	PM18	Shep Sanders	14	1-6
Side Mission 18	What Hit The Fan	PM19	Shep Sanders	13	1-7
Side Mission 19	Scavenger: Combat Rifle	PM19	Fyrestone B.B.	15	1-7
Plot Mission 20	Sledge: Battle For The Badlands	PM19	Shep Sanders	17	1-8
Side Mission 20	Insult To Injury	PM20	Fyrestone B.B.	15	1-9
Side Mission 21	Find Bruce McClone	PM20	Fyrestone B.B.	15	1-9
Side Mission 22	Product Recall	SM22	Fyrestone B.B.	15	1-9
Side Mission 23	Schemin' That Sabotage	PM20	Fyrestone B.B.	18	1-9

CHAPTER 2: MISSIONS IN THE DAHL HEADLAND AREA

MISSION TYPE	NAME	PREREQUISITE	CLIENT	LEVEL	WALKTHROUGH SECTION
Plot Mission 21	Leaving Fyrestone	PM20	Dr. Zed	18	2-1
Side Mission 24	Big Game Hunter	PM21	Ernest Whitting	20	2-2
Plot Mission 22	Getting Lucky	PM21	Ernest Whitting	18	2-1
Plot Mission 23	Powering The Fast Travel Network	PM22	Lucky Zaford	20	2-1
Side Mission 25	Fuel Feud	PM23	Lucky's B.B.	18	2-2
Side Mission 26	Well There's Your Problem Right There	PM23	Lucky's B.B.	18	2-2
Side Mission 27	Death Race Pandora	PM23	Lucky's B.B.	20	2-2
Side Mission 28	Scavenger: Revolver	PM23	Lucky's B.B.	20	2-2
Side Mission 29	Ghosts Of The Vault	PM23	Lucky's B.B.	20	2-2
Plot Mission 24	Road Warriors: Hot Shots	PM23	Lucky Zaford	18	2-1
Plot Mission 25	Road Warriors: Bandit Apocalypse	PM24	Lucky Zaford	20	2-3

KING OF CLAP

MISSION TYPE	NAME	PREREQUISITE	CLIENT	LEVEL	WALKTHROUGH SECTION
Side Mission 30	Claptrap Rescue: New Haven	PM25	Claptrap	21	3-1
Side Mission 31	Claptrap Rescue: Tetanus Warren	PM25	Claptrap	21	3-2
Side Mission 32	Corrosive Crystal Harvest	PM25	New Haven B.B.	21	3-2
Side Mission 33	King Tossing	PM25	New Haven B.B.	21	3-2
Side Mission 34	Is T.K. O.K.?	PM25	Scooter	21	3-1
Side Mission 35	Like A Moth To Flame	PM25	New Haven B.B.	21	3-1
Plot Mission 26	Power To The People	PM25	Helena Pierce	20	3-1
Side Mission 36	Up To Our Ears	PM26	Scooter	21	3-3
Side Mission 37	Scooter's Used Car Parts	PM26	Scooter	21	3-3
Side Mission 38	Hidden Journal: Rust Commons West	PM26	New Haven B.B.	23	3-3
Side Mission 39	Scavenger: Submachine Gun	PM26	New Haven B.B.	23	3-3
Side Mission 40	Firepower: All Sales Are Final	PM26	Marcus Kincaid	21	3-3
Side Mission 41	Firepower: Market Correction	SM40	Marcus Kincaid	21	3-5
Side Mission 42	Firepower: Plight Of The Middle Man	SM41	Marcus Kincaid	23	3-5
Side Mission 43	Jack's Other Eye	SM42	Helena Pierce	23	3-5
Plot Mission 27	Seek Out Tannis	PM26	Helena Pierce	21	3-3
Plot Mission 28	Meet "Crazy" Earl	PM27	Patricia Tannis	22	3-4
Side Mission 44	Claptrap Rescue: Scrapyard	PM28	Claptrap	22	3-4
Plot Mission 29	Get Off My Lawn!	PM28	Crazy Earl	22	3-4
Plot Mission 30	Today's Lesson: High Explosives	PM29	Crazy Earl	22	3-4
Plot Mission 31	Hair Of The Dog	PM30	Crazy Earl	23	3-4
Side Mission 45	Claptrap Rescue: Krom's Canyon	PM31	Claptrap	25	3-7
Side Mission 46	Earl Needs Food[e]Badly	PM31	Crazy Earl	25	3-7
Side Mission 47	Missing Persons	PM31	New Haven B.B.	24	3-6
Side Mission 48	Two Wrongs Make A Right	SM47	New Haven B.B.	25	3-7
Side Mission 49	Middle Of Nowhere No More: Investigate	PM31	Helena Pierce	24	3-6
Side Mission 50	Middle Of Nowhere No More: Fuses? Really?	SM49	Hudson Johns	24	3-6
Side Mission 51	Middle Of Nowhere No More: Small Favor	SM50	Hudson Johns	24	3-6
Side Mission 52	Middle Of Nowhere No More: Scoot On Back	SM51	Hudson Johns	24	3-6
Side Mission 53	Scavenger: Shotgun	SM52	Middle of Nowhere B.B.	24	3-6
Side Mission 54	Altar Ego: Burning Heresy	SM52	Middle of Nowhere B.B.	24	3-6
Side Mission 55	Circle Of Slaughter: Meat and Greet	SM52	Middle of Nowhere B.B.	26	3-10
Side Mission 56	Circle Of Slaughter: Round 1	SM55	Chuck Durden	26	3-10
Side Mission 57	Circle Of Slaughter: Round 2	SM56	Chuck Durden	29	3-10
Side Mission 58	Circle Of Slaughter: Final Round	SM57	Chuck Durden	28	3-10
Side Mission 59	Hidden Journal: Rust Commons East	SM52	Middle of Nowhere B.B.	26	3-6
Plot Mission 32	The Next Piece	PM31	Crazy Earl	25	3-7
Side Mission 60	Altar Ego: The New Religion	PM32, SM52	Middle of Nowhere B.B.	27	3-8
Side Mission 61	Altar Ego: Godless Monsters	SM60	Middle of Nowhere B.B.	29	3-9
Side Mission 62	A Bug Problem	PM32, SM52	Middle of Nowhere B.B.	27	3-8
Side Mission 63	Relight The Beacons	PM32, SM52	Helena Pierce	27	3-8
Side Mission 64	Green Thumb	PM32	Stance Von Kofsky	29	3-8
Side Mission 65	Smoke Signals: Investigate Old Haven	PM32	Helena Pierce	28	3-12
Side Mission 66	Smoke Signals: Shut Them Down	SM65	Helena Pierce	28	3-12
Side Mission 67	Claptrap Rescue: Old Haven	PM32	Claptrap	28	3-12
Side Mission 68	Bandit Treasure: Three Corpses, Three Keys	PM32	Dead Bandit	28	3-12
Side Mission 69	Bandit Treasure: X Marks The Spot	SM68	Dead Bandit	28	3-12
Plot Mission 33	Jaynistown: Secret Rendezvous	PM32	Patricia Tannis	27	3-8
Plot Mission 34	Jaynistown: A Brother's Love	PM33	Taylor Kobb	27	3-8
Side Mission 70	Dumpster Diving For Great Justice	PM34	Erik Franks	27	3-9
Plot Mission 35	Jaynistown: Spread The Word	PM34	Taylor Kobb	27	3-9
Plot Mission 36	Jaynistown: Getting What's Coming To You	PM35	Erik Franks	27	3-9
Side Mission 71	I've Got A Sinking Feeling[e]	PM36	Scooter	27	3-10
Side Mission 72	Wanted: Fresh Fish	PM36	New Haven B.B.	27	3-10
Plot Mission 37	Jaynistown: Unintended Consequences	PM36	Erik Franks	27	3-9
Plot Mission 38	Jaynistown: Cleaning Up Your Mess	PM37	Helena Pierce	29	3-9
Side Mission 73	Bait And Switch	PM38	Middle of Nowhere B.B.	27	3-11
Side Mission 74	Claptrap Rescue: Trash Coast	PM38	Claptrap	27	3-11
Side Mission 75	Earl's Best Friend	PM38	Crazy Earl	27	3-11
Side Mission 76	House Hunting	PM38	Middle of Nowhere B.B.	27	3-11
Plot Mission 39	Another Piece Of The Puzzle	PM38	Guardian Angel	27	3-11
Plot Mission 40	Not Without My Claptrap	PM39	Patricia Tannis	28	3-12

CHAPTER 4: MISSIONS IN THE SALT FLATS AREA

MISSION TYPE	NAME	PREREQUISITE	CLIENT	LEVEL	WALKTHROUGH SECTION
Side Mission 77	Claptrap Rescue: The Salt Flats	PM40	Claptrap	29	4-1
Side Mission 78	Scavenger: Machine Gun	PM40	Middle of Nowhere B.B.	30	4-1
Plot Mission 41	The Final Piece	PM40	Patricia Tannis	30	4-1
Side Mission 79	Claptrap Rescue: Crimson Fastness	PM41	Claptrap	31	4-2
Plot Mission 42	Get Some Answers	PM41	Patricia Tannis	30	4-2
Plot Mission 43	Find The ECHO Command Console	PM42	Patricia Tannis	31	4-2
Plot Mission 44	Reactivate The ECHO Comm System	PM43	Patricia Tannis	31	4-2
Plot Mission 45	Find Steele	PM44	Patricia Tannis	31	4-3
Plot Mission 46	Destroy The Destroyer	PM45	Guardian Angel	32	4-3
Plot Mission 47	Bring The Vault Key To Tannis	PM46	Patricia Tannis	32	4-3

CLAPTRAP
DANCE OFF

Challenges CHECKLIST

12 Days of Pandora	Master the technology of Pandora	5,000XP
(12 Assault Rifle Kills, 11 Pistol kills, 10 Shotgun kills, 9 SMG kills, 8 Sniper Rifle Kills, 7 Melee kills, 6 Critical hit kills, 5 Explosive kills, 4 Shock kills, 3 Incendiary kills, 2 Faces melted, 1 Grenade kill)		

Headhunter	Kill 50 Human enemies	1,000 XP
Not Really a People Person	Kill 250 Human enemies	2,000 XP
Misanthrope	Kill 1,000 Human enemies	5,000 XP
War Criminal	Kill 2,500 Human enemies	20,000 XP

Lucky Shot!	Kill 100 enemies with Critical Hits	1,000 XP
Crack Shot	Kill 250 enemies with Critical Hits	2,000 XP
Don't You Ever Miss?	Kill 1,000 enemies with Critical Hits	5,000 XP
Brain Surgeon	Kill 2,500 enemies with Critical Hits	20,000 XP

Relentless	Kill 5 enemies in succession with no more than 7 seconds between each kill	500 XP
Chain Killer	Kill 10 enemies in succession with no more than 7 seconds between each kill	1,000 XP
Killing Spree	Kill 15 enemies in succession with no more than 7 seconds between each kill	2,000 XP
Conveyor of Death	Kill 25 enemies in succession with no more than 7 seconds between each kill	5,000 XP

Action Hero	Kill 50 enemies using your Action Skill	1,000 XP
Beware! Mad Skills!	Kill 250 enemies using your Action Skill	2,000 XP
Why do you even carry a gun?	Kill 1,000 enemies using your Action Skill	5,000 XP
Your Kung Fu is Best	Kill 2,500 enemies using your Action Skill	20,000 XP

Seasoned Killer	Kill 500 enemies	1,000 XP
Numb to the Voice	Kill 1,000 enemies	2,000 XP
Terror of Pandora	Kill 4,000 enemies	5,000 XP
I am become Death...	Kill 10,000 enemies	20,000 XP

Pocket Change	Earn 10,000 Dollars	1,000 XP
Money, It buys Happiness	Earn 250,000 Dollars	2,000 XP
The Rich get Richer	Earn 1,000,000 Dollars	5,000 XP
How Much For The Planet?	Earn 9,999,999 Dollars	20,000 XP

Duelist	Win 10 Duels	500 XP
Smack Down!	Win 50 Duels	1,000 XP
Bragging Rights	Win 250 Duels	2,000 XP
Invincible	Win 1,000 Duels	5,000 XP

Skag Slayer	Kill 50 Skags	1,000 XP
SIT! STAY! PLAY DEAD!	Kill 250 Skags	2,000 XP
I hate dogs	Kill 1,000 Skags	5,000 XP
You Are The Skagpocalypse	Kill 2,500 Skags	20,000 XP

Spiderant Slayer	Kill 50 Spiderants	1,000 XP
Bug Crusher	Kill 250 Spiderants	2,000 XP
I hate bugs	Kill 1,000 Spiderants	5,000 XP
The Exterminator	Kill 2,500 Spiderants	20,000 XP

Rakk Slayer	Kill 50 Rakk	1,000 XP
If it flies, it dies	Kill 250 Rakk	2,000 XP
Rakk Flak	Kill 1,000 Rakk	5,000 XP
If I can't fly, no one flies	Kill 2,500 Rakk	20,000 XP

What is that thing?	Kill 50 Guardians	1,000 XP
The Vault is mine	Kill 250 Guardians	2,000 XP
Xenophobe	Kill 1,000 Guardians	5,000 XP
Dominant species	Kill 2,500 Guardians	20,000 XP

Spray and Prey	Get 50 kills with Combat Rifles	1,000 XP
Size matters	Get 250 kills with Combat Rifles	2,000 XP
Make Chunks	Get 1,000 kills with Combat Rifles	5,000 XP
One Man Army	Get 2,500 kills with Combat Rifles	20,000 XP

Draw!	Get 50 kills with Pistols	1,000 XP
Size doesn't matter	Get 250 kills with Pistols	2,000 XP
No one's laughing now	Get 1,000 kills with Pistols	5,000 XP
Pistolero	Get 2,500 kills with Pistols	20,000 XP

KING OF CLAP

Get off my lawn!	Get 50 kills with Shotguns	1,000 XP
Taste the red mist	Get 250 kills with Shotguns	2,000 XP
Instant Autopsy	Get 1,000 kills with Shotguns	5,000 XP
Buckshot Legend	Get 2,500 kills with Shotguns	20,000 XP

Boom	Get 50 kills with Launchers	1,000 XP
BOOM	Get 250 kills with Launchers	2,000 XP
KaBOOM!	Get 1,000 kills with Launchers	5,000 XP
KA BOOOOOOOOM!!!!	Get 2,500 kills with Launchers	20,000 XP

Rat a Tat!	Get 50 kills with SMGs	1,000 XP
So many little holes...	Get 250 kills with SMGs	2,000 XP
Bullet Hose	Get 1,000 kills with SMGs	5,000 XP
Human Tsunami	Get 2,500 kills with SMGs	20,000 XP

One Shot, One Kill	Get 50 kills with Sniper Rifles	1,000 XP
I'll wait back here...	Get 250 kills with Sniper Rifles	2,000 XP
Brain Ventilator	Get 1,000 kills with Sniper Rifles	5,000 XP
Finger of God	Get 2,500 kills with Sniper Rifles	20,000 XP

Punchy	Get 50 kills with Melee	1,000 XP
Brawler	Get 250 kills with Melee	2,000 XP
Boxer	Get 1,000 kills with Melee	5,000 XP
Heavyweight Champion	Get 2,500 kills with Melee	20,000 XP

Hot! Too Hot!	Get 100 kills with Incendiary attacks	1,000 XP
Toasty!	Get 250 kills with Incendiary attacks	2,000 XP
Plays with matches	Get 1,000 kills with Incendiary attacks	5,000 XP
Pyromaniac	Get 2,500 kills with Incendiary attacks	20,000 XP

Zap!	Get 100 kills with Shock attacks	1,000 XP
Nikola is a friend of mine	Get 250 kills with Shock attacks	2,000 XP
Puts forks in sockets	Get 1,000 kills with Shock attacks	5,000 XP
Shocker	Get 2,500 kills with Shock attacks	20,000 XP

Chemistry Rocks!	Get 100 kills with Corrosive attacks	1,000 XP
Why is the floor all gooey?	Get 250 kills with Corrosive attacks	2,000 XP
Mixes household chemicals	Get 1,000 kills with Corrosive attacks	5,000 XP
Chemist	Get 2,500 kills with Corrosive attacks	20,000 XP

Boom goes the Dynamite!	Get 100 kills with Explosive attacks	1,000 XP
Too bad about the Tinnitus	Get 250 kills with Explosive attacks	2,000 XP
Crosses border for fireworks	Get 1,000 kills with Explosive attacks	5,000 XP
Demolitionist	Get 2,500 kills with Explosive attacks	20,000 XP

Road Rage	Kill 25 Enemies with a vehicle	1,000 XP
Vehicular Manslaughter	Kill 150 Enemies with a vehicle	2,000 XP
School bus Driver	Kill 500 Enemies with a vehicle	5,000 XP
Hell on Wheels	Kill 1,000 Enemies with a vehicle	20,000 XP

What's in here?	Open 50 Lootable objects	1,000 XP
Scavenger	Open 250 Lootable objects	2,000 XP
Wilderness Survivor	Open 1,000 Lootable objects	5,000 XP
No stone unturned	Open 5,000 Lootable objects	20,000 XP

Ooo! Shiney!	Open 5 Chests	1,000 XP
Treasure Hunter	Open 25 Chests	2,000 XP
Swag Master	Open 100 Chests	5,000 XP
Envy of Pirates	Open 500 Chests	20,000 XP

How much for the gun?	Sell 50 Items	1,000 XP
Gun runner	Sell 100 Items	2,000 XP
Arms dealer	Sell 400 Items	5,000 XP
Merchant of Death	Sell 1,200 Items	20,000 XP

Impulse buyer	Buy 5 Items	1,000 XP
Good Consumer	Buy 50 Items	2,000 XP
I want it all!	Buy 200 Items	5,000 XP
Self-contained economy	Buy 500 Items	20,000 XP

Lots of shots	Shoot 2,000 Times	1,000 XP
Keep firing	Shoot 10,000 Times	2,000 XP
Who made that man a gunner?	Shoot 25,000 Times	5,000 XP
I fired every bullet ever	Shoot 100,000 Times	20,000 XP

Hang Time	Get 2 seconds of vehicle hang time	500 XP
Airborne	Get 3 seconds of vehicle hang time	1,000 XP
This is not a flight simulator	Get 4 seconds of vehicle hang time	2,000 XP
Orbit Achieved	Get 5 seconds of vehicle hang time	5,000 XP

CLAPTRAP DANCE OFF

No matter how much time you've spent with Borderlands so far, you're probably aware of the game's lofty promise of containing millions of weapons—over 15 million to be exact. You're probably also wondering how that's even possible, and curious as to how anyone can wrap their head around such a vast collection. This chapter sets out to answer those two questions. Not only are we going to lift the hood and take a peek at what's going on behind the scenes to make those numbers possible, but we're also going to break it all down and show you some foolproof tips on how to quickly—and accurately—ascertain the value of a weapon just by its name.

Of course, firearms aren't the only pieces of equipment you'll come to rely on in the quest for the Vault. This chapter also covers Shields, Class Decks, Storage Deck Updates, and Grenade Mods. And be sure to flip ahead to our "Gun Catalog" sample about 400 choice weapons from all nine manufacturer's product lines.

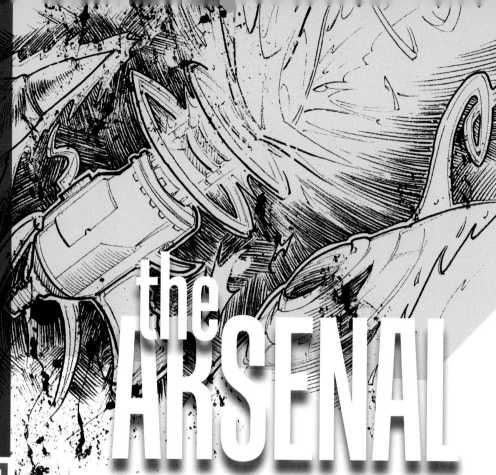

the ARSENAL

WEAPONS 101
SEMI-RANDOM WEAPON GENERATION

The first thing to understand about how the weapon system in *Borderlands* works is that every weapon you encounter—whether it be in a vending machine, a Skag Pile, a weapons crate, or dropped by a slain enemy—is generated instantaneously, and somewhat randomly, based on a number of factors. These include your character's level, class & skills, what type of enemy you killed (in the case of loot drops), where you are in the game's mission structure, and which character you are playing as. Each weapon is assembled on the fly within the game engine by combining a random selection of components from within a half-dozen different parts categories. Each weapon consists of the following parts: body, grip, magazine, barrel, sight, stock, and a specific material (sights and stocks are optional on some models). Many also have accessories, and these come in numerous varieties.

THE COMPONENTS

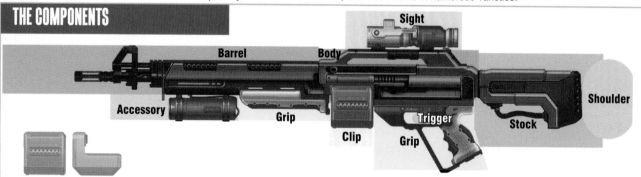

THIS ILLUSTRATION OF A COMBAT RIFLE IDENTIFIES THE DIFFERENT COMPONENTS THAT GO INTO ASSEMBLING A SINGLE WEAPON. EACH MANUFACTURER HAS A NUMBER OF PROPRIETARY OPTIONS FOR ITS COMPONENTS (EXCLUDING "SHOULDER" AND "TRIGGER").

Stock	Higher quality stocks provide more stability and accuracy. Smaller stocks and stockless weapons achieve faster reloads and equip speed.
Body	Affects the weapon's firing rate and damage rating.
Barrel	The type of barrel used affects weapon damage ratings and accuracy.
Magazine	Better magazines yield increases in magazine size, reload speed, and equip speed.
Scope	A scoped weapon offers various degrees of zoom, dependent on the quality of the scope.
Materials	Higher quality materials yield different looks and stronger manufacturer bonuses.
Accessory	Provide a range of benefits from Elemental Effects to damage and stability bonuses, and much, much more.

KING OF CLAP

The Math

This semi-random assembling of the weapon, the assigning of statistical values, and ultimately the generation of its name all happens on the spot, during the fraction of a second it takes for the weapon to spawn in the game environment—all the while making sure that the game experience remains balanced for the player. Try not to spend too much time thinking about that, as doing so may very well cause your head to explode.

If you consider that there are nine weapons manufacturers in the game, all producing roughly five different types of weapons apiece, and each of those is comprised of a half-dozen components, of which there are myriad options, it becomes a bit clearer how the game can have over 15 million weapons.

But now it's time to blow the cover off this system and help you crack the code: not every weapon has a unique name. In fact, there are countless weapons with the same name—even legendary weapons—that simply have different statistical values or bonuses, but are otherwise the same. Generally speaking, of course…

DECIPHERING WEAPON NAMES

Every weapon has a full-length name that appears on the battlefield when the weapon spawns, and a somewhat shorter name that appears on the inventory screen once the weapon is in your Backpack. The full length name contains the manufacturer's name and grade, an alphanumeric code, and a descriptive adjective or two. Each part of this name reveals a clue regarding the weapon's value before you even glance at the stats. Let's break it down one piece at a time: Manufacturer Grade, Alphanumeric Serial Number, and Descriptive Model Name…

Manufacturer Grade

Each of the nine gun manufacturers builds weapons within six different grade classifications, and each weapon grade corresponds to a range of weapon levels. The player can only equip weapons that are of an equal or lesser level to that of the character. It stands to reason that the majority of gun you encounter will be within the grade that corresponds to your character, but there are exceptions. Skag Piles, for example, are often filled with low-grade weapons, regardless the character's level. The following table shows the grade breakdown for each manufacturer, based on weapon level.

WEAPON LEVEL	TEDIORE	VLADOF	DAHL	S&S MUNITIONS	MALIWAN	TORGUE	JAKOBS	ATLAS	HYPERION
0	Cheap	Surplus	Rusty	Old	Obsolete	Weaksauce	Plywood	Puny	Substandard
1 to 12	-	-	-	-	-	-	-	-	-
13 to 21	Value	Peasants	Mercenary	Revised	Standard	Power	Classic	Champion	Valde
22 to 30	Special	Peoples	Soldier	Upgraded	Sterling	Force	Vintage	Heroic	Melior
31 to 39	Super	Workers	Freelancer	Enhanced	Prototype	Excellent	Choice	Herculean	Ultra
40 to 48	Limited	Soldiers	Veteran	Faultless	Paradigm	Awesome	Antique	Legendary	Magnus
50	Supreme	Patriots	Elite	Perfect	Pure	Ultimate	Original	Titan	Optimus

DING! LEVEL 50 SUPREMACY!

Once you reach Level 50 in the game (likely on your second playthrough), the entire game rebalances itself to Level 50 and every enemy you encounter and weapon you acquire will be Level 50. In this chapter and the **Gun Catalog** section of this guide that follows, we focus on the weapons you see during your *initial* playthrough. Those who do manage to max their level during the initial playthrough will be happy to note that the weapons you get will be just like the level 48 examples shown in our Gun Catalog, only better! If you can believe it!

The names in the previous table above won't be shown once the weapon is inside your Backpack—the weapon level is clearly visible—but knowing what this list of names corresponds to is the first step in quickly ascertaining the value of a weapon on the ground. Weapon level is *not* the most important factor in deciding which gun to equip—certainly not—but you'll eventually reach a point where it's simply not worth your effort to pick up low-level equipment. Although even low-level weapons can be sold for some profit, those weapon names listed in the first row (level 1 to 12) are considered to be each manufacturer's lowest quality product. As you continue to play the game and gain a better feel for the perks of each of the manufacturers, you'll likely come to prefer weapons from a certain make and the names given to the various grades will begin to have more meaning to you.

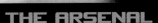

PUNY WEAKSAUCE #$&%!

It's worth pointing out that weapons of average quality between level 1 and 12 do not get a grade name. Only the manufacturer's name precedes the alphanumeric model code and other descriptors. However, some low level weapons are of such low quality that they're given the manufacturer's corresponding garbage-grade. When you see a weapon with any of these overtly negative names (e.g. Rusty, Old, Plywood, Substandard) you can go ahead and leave it on the ground—it's hardly worth the effort to carry it to a vending machine. Chances are you'll just drop it to make room for something better before you get there anyway.

Alphanumeric Serial Numbers

The second part of each weapon's name is its alphanumeric code. In general, the longer this serial number, the better the weapon. This model code is a combination of letters and numbers that are linked behind the scenes to various parts of the weapon. For example, each weapon's body contributes a specific portion of that alphanumeric code. There are far too many weapon bodies and codes to list, but fortunately that's not the case with the other half of this code. The last portion of the code is linked directly to the weapon material. Each manufacturer has three materials that they use to build their guns. The rarer the material used in building the weapon, the more pronounced the manufacturer's unique bonuses are.

The following table lists the three materials code for each manufacturer in increasing rarity. The rarer the material, the higher quality the weapon and the bigger boost that weapon receives from the manufacturer's inherent traits.

RARITY	TEDIORE	VLADOF	DAHL	S&S MUNITIONS	MALIWAN	TORGUE	JAKOBS	ATLAS	HYPERION
Common	-	-	-	-	-	-	-	-	-
Slightly Rare	-A	/V2	U	.2	B	-	ZZ	-	.W
Very Rare	-B	/V3	D	.3	C	-	XX	-	.G

TRADE SECRETS

All nine manufacturers refrain from linking a model code to their most common materials, but Torgue and Atlas take it one step further. Although they do have three distinct materials, they keep the use of higher grade materials a secret. Whereas you can always be sure that a weapon bearing Vladof's "/V3" suffix has been made of the highest-grade materials, there's no way to tell when it comes to Torgue and Atlas.

Descriptive Model Names

The third and final piece of the weapon name is the part that that reveals the most qualitative information, provided you know what the dozens of possible adjectives mean. As mentioned earlier, the weapon's name is generated only after the game engine analyzes the quality of the parts used to build the weapon and the statistical values assigned to things like firing rate, zoom, melee damage, etc. Each weapon type has its own unique vocabulary used to describe the overlying properties. This portion of the name is typically two words long (the prefix and the title) unless the weapon is very basic, in which case it may have less. The prefix describes the quality and/or statistical bonus, while the title is a specific name given to a particular trait for that given weapon type. This sounds confusing now, but we've put together some tables that should shed some light on this.

UNDERSTANDING WEAPON NAMING TABLES

The following tables list the possible prefixes and titles for each weapon type. A weapon can have any of the prefixes (or none) and any of the titles (or none), but no weapon can have more than one prefix or title. Legendary weapons can still have any of the prefixes, but their title is determined by the unique manufacturer-specific part that was included in the build. For example, a weapon may be called a "Wicked Needler" if it has mainly very high quality parts and a high rate of fire. That same weapon may be called a "Wicked Firehawk" if Maliwan's Firehawk accessory was included in the build. Legendary titles supersede regular titles.

REPEATER PISTOLS

PREFIXES

PREFIX	CAUSE	EFFECT
-	Default	None
Bad	High Quality Parts	Bonus Damage
Cruel	Higher Quality Parts	Bonus Damage
Wicked	Highest Quality Parts	Bonus Damage
Fanged	Blade Accessory	Piercing Melee Damage
Stabilized	Stability Accessory	Increased Damage, Better Accuracy
Sighted	Laser Sight Accessory	High Accuracy
Double	Double Shot Accessory	Two Projectiles, Lower Accuracy

LEGENDARY TITLES

MANUFACTURER	LEGENDARY TITLE	UNIQUE COMPONENT	EFFECT
Tediore	Protector	Body	Free Ammo
Dahl	Hornet	Accessory	2-Shot Burst with Corrosive Damage
Vladof	Rebel	Magazine	Big Clip, Fast Reload
S&S Munitions	Gemini	Accessory	Split Shot
Maliwan	Firehawk	Accessory	Bonus Fire Tech
Torgue	Violator	Barrel	3 Projectile, 3-Shot Burst
Hyperion	Invader	Scope	12-Shot Burst While Zoomed
Atlas	Troll	Accessory	Regenerates Health

TITLES

TITLE	DEFINING CHARACTERISTIC
Repeater	Default
Swatter	High Accuracy
Peashooter	Low Damage
Needler	Fast Rate of Fire
Raptor	High Quality
Lacerator	Penetration Damage

HANDGUN-TYPE WEAPON IN THE PISTOL FAMILY THAT FEATURES AUTOMATIC FIRE, ALBEIT AT A SLOWER RATE THAN OTHER FULLY-AUTOMATIC WEAPONS. EIGHT MANUFACTURERS BUILD REPEATER PISTOLS.

MACHINE PISTOLS

PREFIXES

PREFIX	CAUSE	EFFECT
-	Default	None
Mean	High Quality Parts	Bonus Damage
Grim	Higher Quality Parts	Bonus Damage
Vile	Highest Quality Parts	Bonus Damage
Fanged	Blade Accessory	Piercing Melee Damage
Stabilized	Stability Accessory	Increased Damage, Better Accuracy
Sighted	Laser Sight Accessory	High Accuracy
Double	Double Shot Accessory	Two Projectiles, Lower Accuracy
Cold	Cold Accessory	Slower, Powerful Bullets

LEGENDARY TITLES

MANUFACTURER	LEGENDARY TITLE	UNIQUE COMPONENT	EFFECT
Vladof	Vengeance	Barrel	Bullets Penetrate Shields
S&S Munitions	Vanatos	Magazine	Big Magazine, Low Kick
Hyperion	Reaper	Accessory	Huge Melee Damage, Health Steal

TITLES

TITLE	DEFINING CHARACTERISTIC
Machine Pistol	Default
Fury	Lower Accuracy, Big Magazine
Torment	High Damage, Bonus Tech
Rage	Fast Rate of Fire, Burst Fire

HANDGUN-TYPE WEAPON IN THE PISTOL FAMILY THAT UTILIZES BURST FIRE. EACH SQUEEZE OF THE TRIGGER FIRES A RAPID BURST OF BULLETS, BUT THE GUN IS NOT FULLY-AUTOMATIC LIKE THE REPEATER PISTOL. ONLY THREE MANUFACTURERS OFFER A LINE OF MACHINE PISTOLS.

REVOLVER PISTOLS

PREFIXES

PREFIX	CAUSE	EFFECT
-	Default	None
Brutal	High Quality Parts	Bonus Damage
Primal	Higher Quality Parts	Bonus Damage
Savage	Highest Quality Parts	Bonus Damage
Bladed	Blade Accessory	Piercing Melee Damage
Bloody	-	High Damage
Swift	-	High Rate of Fire, Lower Kick, Faster Recovery
Raw	-	Low Accuracy, Fast Fire Rate

LEGENDARY TITLES

MANUFACTURER	LEGENDARY TITLE	UNIQUE COMPONENT	EFFECT
Tediore	Equalizer	Body	Free Ammo
Dahl	Anaconda	Barrel	Accurate, Good Damage
Maliwan	Defiler	Accessory	Corrosive Damage
Jakobs	Unforgiven	Barrel	Super Accurate, Critical Hit Bonus, Slow Recovery
Atlas	Chimera	Accessory	Random Damage Types

TITLES

TITLE	DEFINING CHARACTERISTIC
Revolver	Default
Viper	High Accuracy
Law	High Rate of Fire
Justice	High Damage
Razor	Bonus Melee Damage
Masher	Shotgun Firing

REVOLVER PISTOLS ARE THE CLASSIC HANDGUN-TYPE WEAPON AND FEATURE THE SLOWEST RATE OF FIRE. EACH SQUEEZE OF THE TRIGGER FIRES A LONE SLUG, BUT WITH ABOVE-AVERAGE ACCURACY AND DAMAGE. FIVE MANUFACTURERS OFFER THESE GUNS.

THEY'RE LEGENDARY FOR A REASON

ALWAYS TEST OUT GUNS THAT HAVE A SLOGAN OF SOME KIND IN THEIR DESCRIPTION; SLOGANS OR CATCHPHRASES USUALLY INDICATE A SERIOUSLY COOL OR UNIQUE BONUS UNDER THE HOOD.

– KALE MENGES, DEVELOPER

PREFIXES

PREFIX	CAUSE	EFFECT
Combat	Default	None
Battle	High Quality Parts	Bonus Damage
War	Higher Quality Parts	Bonus Damage
Genocide	Highest Quality Parts	Bonus Damage
Jagged	Blade Accessory	Bonus Melee Damage
Frenzied	Frenzy Accessory	High Rate of Fire
Terrible	Terrible Accessory	High Damage
Riot	Riot Grip	High Rate of Fire, Low Accuracy
Hunter's	-	High Accuracy, More Zoom

LEGENDARY TITLES

MANUFACTURER	LEGENDARY TITLE	UNIQUE COMPONENT	EFFECT
Tediore	Defender	Body	Free Ammo
Dahl	Bulldog	Magazine	More Ammo, Faster Reload
Torgue	Friendly Fire	Accessory	Smile Pattern, Incendiary Tech
Jakobs	Striker	Barrel	Higher Accuracy, Critical Hit Bonus
Atlas	Hydra	Accessory	Fan Pattern

TITLES

TITLE	DEFINING CHARACTERISTIC
Shotgun	Default
Shredder	Many Projectiles
Scattergun	Low Accuracy
Carnage	Fires Mini-Rockets
Matador	Low Accuracy, High Rate of Fire

COMBAT SHOTGUNS ARE LIKE TRADITIONAL SHOTGUNS. THEY FIRE A SINGLE SHELL WITH EACH PULL OF THE TRIGGER AND HAVE A DELIBERATE, SLOW RATE OF FIRE WITH HIGH DAMAGE. FIVE MANUFACTURERS BUILD COMBAT SHOTGUNS.

PREFIXES

PREFIX	CAUSE	EFFECT
Assault	Default	None
Grievous	High Quality Parts	Bonus Damage
Lethal	Higher Quality Parts	Bonus Damage
Fatal	Highest Quality Parts	Bonus Damage
Spiked	Blade Accessory	Bonus Melee Damage
Raging	Raging Accessory	High Rate of Fire
Painful	Painful Accessory	High Damage
Riot	Riot Grip	High Rate of Fire, Low Accuracy
Angry	-	Faster Reload, Slight Magazine Increase

LEGENDARY TITLES

MANUFACTURER	LEGENDARY TITLE	UNIQUE COMPONENT	EFFECT
Vladof	Hammer	Accessory	Hammer Pattern, Explosive
Maliwan	Plague	Accessory	High Corrosive Tech
S&S Munitions	Crux	Accessory	Cross Pattern
Hyperion	Butcher	Barrel	5-Shot Burst, 50% Chance of Free Shot

TITLES

TITLE	DEFINING CHARACTERISTIC
Shotgun	Default
Brute	Higher Damage
Sweeper	Low Accuracy, More Pellets
Death	Higher Accuracy

ASSAULT SHOTGUNS ARE THE CLOSEST THING TO A FULLY-AUTOMATIC SHOTGUN YOU'RE GOING TO FIND. HOLD THE TRIGGER AND LET THE METHODICAL STRING OF BURSTS RING OUT. THERE ARE FOUR MANUFACTURERS CURRENTLY OFFERING A LINE OF ASSAULT SHOTGUNS.

PREFIXES

PREFIX	CAUSE	EFFECT
Patrol	Default	None
Violent	High Quality Parts	Bonus Damage
Hostile	Higher Quality Parts	Bonus Damage
Malevolent	Highest Quality Parts	Bonus Damage
Relentless	Relentless Accessory	High Rate of Fire
Ruthless	Ruthless Accessory	Low Kick
Double	Double Shot Accessory	Two Projectiles, Lower Accuracy
Twisted	Twisted Accessory	Spiral Pattern

LEGENDARY TITLES

MANUFACTURER	LEGENDARY TITLE	UNIQUE COMPONENT	EFFECT
Tediore	Savior	Body	Free Ammo
Dahl	Wildcat	Magazine	Huge Clip, Low Accuracy
Maliwan	HellFire	Accessory	Every Shot Incendiary
Torgue	Gasher	Barrel	High Damage
Hyperion	Bitch	Barrel	Critical Hit Bonus

TITLES

TITLE	DEFINING CHARACTERISTIC
SMG	Default
Bruiser	High Damage
Stinger	High Rate of Fire, Low Kick
Anarchy	Low Accuracy, 3 Wild Projectiles, Rare
Vector	No Kick, Fast Reload, Good Firing Rate
Thumper	Single Shot, High Damage

THESE HANDHELD MACHINE GUNS ARE FULLY-AUTOMATIC AND SUPPLY AN EXCELLENT BLEND OF ACCURACY, RATE OF FIRE, AND DAMAGE. THEY ALSO PROVIDE VERY FAST RELOAD TIMES AND LOW RECOIL. FOUR MANUFACTURERS OFFER A LINE OF PATROL SMG WEAPONS.

KING OF CLAP

COMBAT RIFLES

PREFIXES

PREFIX	CAUSE	EFFECT
Scoped	Default	None
Battle	High Quality Parts	Bonus Damage
War	Higher Quality Parts	Bonus Damage
Genocide	Highest Quality Parts	Bonus Damage
Intense	Intense Accessory	Bonus Accuracy
Deathly	Deathly Accessory	High Damage, Low Kick
Short	-	Low Damage, Low Kick, Fast Reload
Punishing	-	Higher Damage

LEGENDARY TITLES

MANUFACTURER	LEGENDARY TITLE	UNIQUE COMPONENT	EFFECT
Tediore	Guardian	Body	Free Ammo
Dahl	Raven	Barrel	5-Shot Burst
Hyperion	Destroyer	Barrel	Ricochet Bullets

TITLES

TITLE	DEFINING CHARACTERISTIC
Rifle	Default
Stomper	High Damage
Cobra	High Accuracy
Pounder	Single Shot, High Damage

COMBAT RIFLES FIRE A SHORT BURST OF HIGH-CALIBER ROUNDS AT VERY HIGH ACCURACY AND SPEED. THESE RIFLES ARE FAST TO RELOAD AND WELL-SUITED FOR MEDIUM RANGE ASSAULTS. THREE MANUFACTURERS BUILD COMBAT RIFLES.

SNIPER RIFLES

PREFIXES

PREFIX	CAUSE	EFFECT
-	Default	None
Solid	High Quality Parts	Bonus Damage
Hard	Higher Quality Parts	Bonus Damage
Fearsome	Highest Quality Parts	Bonus Damage
Rolling	Rolling Accessory	Fast Reload
Heavy	Heavy Accessory	Bonus Damage
Long	Long Accessory	Higher Accuracy
Liquid	Firing Rate	High Rate of Fire, Reload, Fast Recovery
Distant	Accuracy	Bonus Accuracy, Less Kick

LEGENDARY TITLES

MANUFACTURER	LEGENDARY TITLE	UNIQUE COMPONENT	EFFECT
Maliwan	Volcano	Accessory	Incendiary Tech, Spawns Secondary Explosions
Jakobs	Skullmasher	Barrel	Critical Hit Bonus, Knockback
Atlas	Cyclops	Scope	More Zoom, Critical Hit Bonus, Faster Projectiles

TITLES

TITLE	DEFINING CHARACTERISTIC
Sniper Rifle	Default
Thunder	High Damage
Hawkeye	High Accuracy

SNIPER RIFLES FIRE A SINGLE BULLET AT A VERY HIGH ACCURACY AND SPEED OVER LONG DISTANCES. THEY HAVE SLOW RATES OF FIRE AND CAN BE SLOW TO RELOAD, BUT PACK TREMENDOUS STOPPING POWER. THREE MANUFACTURERS MAKE SNIPER RIFLES.

SEMI-AUTO SNIPER RIFLES

PREFIXES

PREFIX	CAUSE	EFFECT
Semi-Auto	Default	None
Solid	High Quality Parts	Bonus Damage
Hard	Higher Quality Parts	Bonus Damage
Fearsome	Highest Quality Parts	Bonus Damage
Brisk	Brisk Accessory	High Rate of Fire
Sober	Sober Accessory	Bonus Accuracy
Deep	Deep Accessory	Bonus Damage
Vicious	Fast Reload	Max Accuracy, Fast Recovery

LEGENDARY TITLES

MANUFACTURER	LEGENDARY TITLE	UNIQUE COMPONENT	EFFECT
Dahl	Penetrator	Barrel	Fully Automatic Firing
S&S Munitions	Orion	Accessory	Ricochet Shock Tech
Torgue	Cobra	Accessory	Big Explosions
Hyperion	Executioner	Magazine	5-Shot Burst While Zoomed, 10-Shot Clip

TITLES

TITLE	DEFINING CHARACTERISTIC
Assault Sniper	Default
Driver	High Damage, Knockback
Lance	High Accuracy
Wrath	High Tech Bonus

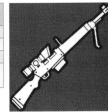

THESE SEMI-AUTOMATIC SNIPER RIFLES DON'T PACK THE OVERWHELMING POWER OF A NORMAL SNIPER RIFLE, BUT THEY HAVE A MUCH HIGHER FIRING RATE AND FILL THE VOID BETWEEN COMBAT RIFLES AND SNIPER RIFLES. FOUR MANUFACTURERS OFFER A LINE OF SEMI-AUTO SNIPER RIFLES.

CLAPTRAP DANCE OFF

PREFIXES

PREFIX	CAUSE	EFFECT
Rocket	Default	None
Big	High Quality Parts	Bonus Damage
Massive	Higher Quality Parts	Bonus Damage
Colossal	Highest Quality Parts	Bonus Damage
Recoilless	Recoilless Accessory	Lower Kick
Evil	Evil Accessory	High Firing Rate, Bonus Accuracy
Devastating	Devastating Accessory	Bonus Damage
Spread	Spread Barrel	Fan Pattern
Triple	Triple Barrel	3-Shot Burst
Helix	Helix Barrel	Helix Pattern

LEGENDARY TITLES

MANUFACTURER	LEGENDARY TITLE	UNIQUE COMPONENT	EFFECT
Vladof	Mongol	Barrel	Rapid Fire
Maliwan	Rhino	Barrel	Spawns Explosions in Flight
Torgue	Redemption	Barrel	Super Big Rocket, Slow
Hyperion	Nidhogg	Barrel	Ranged Auto Explode: 60 Yards

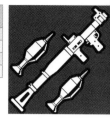

TITLES

TITLE	DEFINING CHARACTERISTIC
Launcher	Default
Destructor	Super Big Rocket, Slow, High Damage
Harpoon	High Speed Projectiles, High Accuracy

ROCKET LAUNCHERS ARE SHOULDER-MOUNTED WEAPONS OF MASS-DESTRUCTION. THEY FIRE AN ENORMOUSLY POWERFUL ROCKET THAT DETONATES ON CONTACT. FOUR MANUFACTURERS CURRENTLY BUILD ROCKET LAUNCHERS.

ELEMENTAL TECHNOLOGIES

Many of the weapons you'll encounter in *Borderlands* have what are known collectively as Elemental Effects. These elemental properties are not unlike the magic attacks you've likely experienced in traditional role-playing games, but there are some key differences to how they behave here. There are four Elemental Effects:

 INCENDIARY: A FIRE ATTACK THAT BURNS FLESH AND IS MOST EFFECTIVE AGAINST UNARMORED CREATURES AND BANDITS.

 SHOCK: AN ELECTRICITY-BASED ATTACK THAT CAUSES HIGH DAMAGE TO SHIELDS AND IS VERY EFFECTIVE AGAINST GUARDIANS.

 CORROSIVE: A TOXIC SPLASH ATTACK THAT EATS AWAY AT ARMOR TO DELIVER HIGH DAMAGE—VERY EFFECTIVE AGAINST THE CRIMSON LANCE.

 EXPLOSIVE: AN EXPLOSION THAT INFLICTS DAMAGE TO ALL ENEMIES IN THE VICINITY.

It's important to understand that not every shot fired from the weapon emits the Elemental Effect. There are four levels of Elemental Technology and the higher the level, the better the chance for each shot fired to have a special effect, such as exploding or lighting an enemy on fire. Also, higher levels result in an increased chance for larger, more powerful explosions. The Elemental Tech level appears as a multiplier beside the corresponding icon.

Elementally, My Dear Watson

Each weapon type also has its own unique nuance with respect to how it handles Elemental Effects. Understanding these differences will help you know what to expect when trying to compare a combat rifle with Incendiary x3 and, say, a sniper rifle with Shock x2. Here's what we discovered after extensive detective work:

SNIPER RIFLES: Charge up their elemental abilities between each shot. The more time between your shots the more likely the next shot will have an elemental effect. In a fire fight this means that the first shot you fire into the fray is very likely to explode and deal a lot of elemental damage, but if you start firing your sniper rifle rapidly, then your chances of getting an elemental effect are decreased.

REVOLVER PISTOLS: These are the "gamblers gun" when it comes to elemental effects. Almost every shot will have a small elemental effect, but you have a small chance for a spectacular elemental effect based on the multiplier. The odds and the power of the spectacular elemental effects both increase with higher elemental levels.

 **PATROL SMG:** Have a small chance for each shot to explode with the appropriate element. Higher Elemental Levels increase the odds.

 MACHINE PISTOLS: Similar to combat rifles in that the first few shots in the burst are more likely to fire special elemental shots. Hit your mark with the first few shots in the burst.

 REPEATER PISTOLS: Have a small chance for each shot to explode with the appropriate element. Higher Elemental Levels increase the odds.

 COMBAT RIFLES: More likely to fire special elemental shots with the early shots in the burst. Try to make sure your first few shots hit their mark.

SHOTGUNS: These weapons are all-or-nothing when it comes to elemental effects. Either every pellet in the shot is elementally charged or none of them are. The higher the Elemental Level, the greater your chances are of firing an elementally charged blast.

 **ROCKET LAUNCHERS:** Always level 4 Elemental Tech and provide a big explosion of elemental damage with each shot. They are, after all, rocket launchers.

ERIDIAN WEAPONS

There's one more type of weapon that hasn't been addressed yet, and that's the incredibly rare set of Eridian weapons. These alien-bred guns are unlike anything seen by the other manufacturers, and not just in looks and abilities. These weapons generate their own energy-based ammunition. There are a number of different Eridian weapons, with thousands of combinations of parts and statistical ratings, just like any other make. Eridian weapons don't have as many parts options as some of the other manufacturers and they only have one material. Their weapon names are a combination of a binary-based serial number and a descriptive title.

SMG BLASTERS

TITLE	EFFECT
Eridian Blaster	Plasma Gun
Mercurial Blaster	High Rate of Fire Plasma Gun
Wave Blaster	Wave Form Plasma Gun, Shock Damage
Ball Blaster	Plasma Gun, Homing Projectiles

SHOTGUN

TITLE	EFFECT
Thunder Storm	Lightning Shotgun

CANNON

TITLE	EFFECT
Cannon	Energy-Based Launcher

DAMAGE ISN'T EVERYTHING
WHEN COMPARING WEAPONS, DON'T ASSUME THAT HIGHER DAMAGE IS ALWAYS BETTER. EXTRA POWER IS WORTHLESS IF YOU CAN'T HIT YOUR TARGET.

— ROB HEIRONIMUS, TECHNICAL DESIGNER

CLAPTRAP DANCE OFF

ADDITIONAL EQUIPMENT

The Vault Hunters in Pandora have some amazing skills at their disposal, and even better firepower, but they wouldn't stand a chance of surviving their journey without some additional protective gear. Fortunately for them, weapons aren't the only equipment they encounter. There are also Shields, Class Decks, Grenade Mods, and Elemental Artifacts. This section discusses each of these valuable accessories.

INCREASED CAPACITY

There are also Ammo Deck Updates, Storage Deck Updates, and Equipment Slot upgrades to purchase and earn. These upgrades can be purchased at vending machines, gained by repairing broken Claptraps, and awarded for reaching milestones in the main mission structure. See the **Survival Basics** chapter of this guide for details.

ORB SHIELDS

MANY SHIELDS GIVE OFF A POWERFUL BLAST WHEN DEPLETED. TAKE COVER QUICKLY SO THEY CAN RECHARGE.

Every weapons manufacturer (excluding Jakobs) and two more named Anshin and Pangolin make a vital piece of equipment known as an Orb Shield. This shield absorbs all damage you incur until depleted, thereby offering an incredible life-saving service. Shields come in a variety of shapes and sizes and many boast unique properties. Regardless of type or manufacturer, all shields have a Capacity and Recharge Rate. Capacity is the amount of damage the shield can absorb before being depleted and the Recharge Rate is the speed at which the shield recharges. It's important to take cover and escape the immediate threat as soon as the shield is depleted so that it can recharge—it won't recharge while you continue to take damage!

Shields are named in a very similar fashion to weapons. Each name consists of a manufacturer's name and grade, an alphanumeric serial number generated by the body and left and right wings of the shield, and then a descriptor and title. There are over 11,000 different shields, although many of these shields only differ in statistical values. The weapons manufacturers use the same grades to reflect the level of their product. Here's a look at what Anshin and Pangolin's product grades are called. Note that shields and other equipment don't have a garbage grade and only come in forms that are worth having, relatively speaking.

SHIELD LEVEL	ANSHIN	PANGOLIN
1 to 12	-	-
13 to 21	Expert	Leather
22 to 30	Select	Mail
31 to 39	Impeccable	Buckler
40 to 48	Exemplar	Shield
50	Immaculate	Plate

ORB SHIELDS: PREFIXES

PREFIX	EFFECT
Orb	Default
Balanced	Good Quality
Symmetrical	High Quality
Sterling	Higher Quality
Harmonious	Highest Quality
Reinforced	Good Max Capacity
Hardened	High Max Capacity
Unbreakable	Higher Max Capacity
Impenetrable	Highest Max Capacity
Quick Charge	Good Recharge Speed
Accelerated	High Recharge Speed
Rapid	Higher Recharge Speed
Alacritous	Highest Speed

ORB SHIELD: TITLE

TITLE	DEFINING CHARACTERISTIC
Shield	Default

Assuming the Orb Shield is made with enough quality parts to warrant a name other than "Shield," it will get one of three unique titles from the corresponding manufacturer. The better the quality of the shield, the more unique the name and the stronger the effect. In the following table, shields with unique title 3 have stronger effects than those with unique title 2, and so on.

ORB SHIELDS: UNIQUE TITLES

MANUFACTURER	UNIQUE TITLE 1	UNIQUE TITLE 2	UNIQUE TITLE 3	EFFECT
Tediore	Healing Shield	Restorative Shield	Panacea	Health Regen
Dahl	Neutralizing Shield	Dilution	Hazmat	Corrosive Resist
Vladof	Guerilla Shield	Skirmisher Shield	Ambush Shield	Recharge Rate
S&S Munitions	Acidburst Shield	Acid Wave	Acid Nova	Corrosive Blast on Depletion
Maliwan	Shockburst Shield	Shock Wave	Shock Nova	Shock Blast on Depletion
Torgue	Fireburst Shield	Fire Wave	Fire Nova	Incendiary Blast on Depletion
Hyperion	Thermal Shield	Asbestic	Endothermic	Fire Resistant
Atlas	Grounded Shield	Anionic Shield	Cationic	Shock Resistant
Anshin	Tough Guy	Muscleman	Macho	Increases Max Health
Pangolin	Unyielding Shield	Enduring Shield	Fortified Shield	Increases Max Shield Capacity

CLASS DECKS

USE THE COMPARE FEATURE TO STUDY THE DIFFERENCES BETWEEN CLASS MODS IN DIFFERENT JOBS. IT HELPS TO EQUIP THE ONE THAT BOOSTS THE SKILLS YOU'RE ALREADY INVESTED IN.

Each of the four characters has a total of seven different Class Decks that can be equipped to strengthen their skills and weapons capabilities along a specific job or class, such as "Rifleman" for Roland or "Firefly" for Lilith. Four of these Class Decks boost the character's abilities personally and three offer team benefits. Class Decks can be swapped out at any time, just like a Shield or Grenade Mod.

There are over 28,000 available Class Decks per character. As with Orb Shields, each Class Deck is comprised of a manufacturer grade and body, a left and right side, and a material. The body determines the class and the other components determine the eventual statistical boosts that will be received for equipping it. The name of the Class Deck simply states the Skill associated with the Class Deck, such as "Heavy Gunner Class Mod." Refer to the "Vault Hunters" chapter of this guide for a full listing of each available Class Deck type per character.

GRENADE MODS

As was the case with Orb Shields, every manufacturer except Jakobs makes what are known as Grenade Mods. When equipped, Grenade Mods add Elemental Effects to the standard Protean Grenades and also often add special physical properties to them, transforming them into proximity mines, "Bouncing Betties," contact grenades, or even a type known as "Transfusion," which steals health from enemies. There are 198 total variants of Grenade Mods, but many of the differences are purely statistical and rely entirely on the manufacturer and grade. Most grenades with an Elemental Effect are Explosive by nature, but there is a chance that the other Elemental Effects will be selected during the on-the-fly generation of the Grenade Mod.

CONTACT: Explode after touching an enemy.

PROXIMITY MINE: Wait to explode until an enemy gets close.

BOUNCING BETTIE: Pop up into the air before exploding.

STICKY: Attach to surfaces and then explode after a few seconds.

MIRV: Throw out several more grenades upon exploding.

RAIN: Throw themselves into the air and fire down on unsuspecting enemies below.

LONGBOW: Teleport to their destination and explode.

TRANSFUSION: Steal health from enemies and heal you.

RUBBERIZED: Bounce off all surfaces and explode when they touch an enemy.

GRENADE MODS BY MANUFACTURER

MANUFACTURER					NON-ELEMENTAL
Tediore	Contact	-	-	-	-
Vladof	Proximity Mine	Proximity Mine	Proximity Mine	Proximity Mine	-
Dahl	Bouncing Bettie	Bouncing Bettie	Bouncing Bettie	Bouncing Bettie	-
S&S Munitions	Sticky	Sticky	Sticky	Sticky	-
Maliwan	-	Contact	Contact	Contact	-
Torgue	MIRV	MIRV	MIRV	MIRV	-
Atlas	Rain	Rain	Rain	Rain	-
Hyperion	Longbow	Longbow	Longbow	Longbow	-
Anshin	-	-	-	-	Transfusion
Pangolin	Rubberized	Rubberized	Rubberized	Rubberized	-

ELEMENTAL ARTIFACTS

The final piece of equipment left to discuss is the Elemental Artifact. These valuable entities are equipped on the Skills Screen in the empty slot next to the character's Action Skill and add an Elemental Effect to the character's Action Skill. Elemental Artifacts come in all four varieties—Explosive, Incendiary, Corrosive, and Shock—and add various levels of Elemental damage to the Action Skill. For example, equipping a Shock Artifact to Roland's Scorpio Turret adds Shock damage to each shot fired from the Scorpio Turret.

FIRING SHOCK-BASED PROJECTILES WITH THE SCORPIO TURRET MAY NOT BE NECESSARY AGAINST SKAGS, BUT IT WILL HELP A LOT AGAINST GUARDIANS!

All Elemental Artifacts are produced by the Eridian company and are comprised of an Eridian grade, an element, a body, and the left and right sides. The individual differences between Elemental Artifacts is slight and all four characters can acquire Elemental Artifacts in each of the four elements. You receive your first Elemental Artifact as a reward before leaving Fyrestone. Be on the lookout for extras and always consider the type of enemy you're going up against and change your Elemental Artifact accordingly.

TEDIORE

GUN CATALOG ★ ★ ★

REPEATER PISTOLS

TEDIORE MAKES ROUGHLY 81,000 VARIETIES OF REPEATER PISTOLS.

BLR REPEATER

LEVEL	BUY	SELL
-	$315	$45

DAMAGE	ACCURACY	FIRE RATE	MAGAZINE	ELEMENTAL
7	74.2	3.3	12	-

- ☐ +50% RELOAD SPEED
- ☐ 1.8X WEAPON ZOOM

RF4-A CRUEL REPEATER

LEVEL	BUY	SELL
13	$4,375	$625

DAMAGE	ACCURACY	FIRE RATE	MAGAZINE	ELEMENTAL
33	79.2	3.0	16	-

- ☐ +100% MELEE DAMAGE
- ☐ +46% RELOAD SPEED
- ☐ +5% DAMAGE
- ☐ 2.6X WEAPON ZOOM

TK5-B WICKED REPEATER

LEVEL	BUY	SELL
22	$37,450	$5,350

DAMAGE	ACCURACY	FIRE RATE	MAGAZINE	ELEMENTAL
55	76.2	4.7	18	-

- ☐ +60% RELOAD SPEED
- ☐ +6% DAMAGE
- ☐ 3.1X WEAPON ZOOM

HRD WICKED REPEATER

LEVEL	BUY	SELL
31	$89,768	$12,824

DAMAGE	ACCURACY	FIRE RATE	MAGAZINE	ELEMENTAL
95	85.0	2.4	12	-

- ☐ +50% RELOAD SPEED
- ☐ +28% DAMAGE
- ☐ 4.1X WEAPON ZOOM

LEGENDARY WEAPON
PRO4-A WICKED PROTECTOR

LEVEL	BUY	SELL
40	$1,689,877	$241,411

DAMAGE	ACCURACY	FIRE RATE	MAGAZINE	ELEMENTAL
135 (x2)	74.4	5.5	19	-

- ☐ +46% RELOAD SPEED
- ☐ +16 AMMO REGENERATION
- ☐ 4.7X WEAPON ZOOM

THE *PROTECTOR* GENERATES ITS OWN AMMUNITION.

AMMO IS NO LONGER AN ISSUE!

BLR5-B WICKED REPEATER

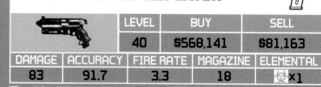

LEVEL	BUY	SELL
40	$568,141	$81,163

DAMAGE	ACCURACY	FIRE RATE	MAGAZINE	ELEMENTAL
83	91.7	3.3	18	☢ x1

- ☐ +60% RELOAD SPEED
- ☐ -16% DAMAGE

KING OF CLAP

> **A SOLDIER ONLY HAS TO CARRY HIS GUN, I CARRY MY WHOLE FAMILY**

WHY TEDIORE?

FIREPOWER FOR THE COMMON MAN

Tediore's Model Lines	
LEVEL	LINE
1 to 12	Cheap
13 to 21	Value
22 to 30	Special
31 to 39	Super
40 to 48	Limited
50	Supreme

Tediore was founded on the principle that no family should be without the protection that an affordable, lightweight firearm provides. Whether you're planning on taking little Billy out to the fields for his first pheasant hunt or you need to chase some trouble off your front porch, Tediore will be there for you. Over the years, Tediore has built a reputation among the working class men and women of this land for providing fast-reloading weapons that anyone, on any budget, can afford. So the next time you're headed down to the Save-N-Save, why not put a little peace of mind in the cart and grab yourself a Tediore? Tediore's pistols, shotguns, sub-machine guns and rifles can be found at major retailers nationwide.

TEDIORE

TEDIORE

RF BLAST REPEATER

	LEVEL	BUY	SELL
	48	$441,504	$63,072

DAMAGE	ACCURACY	FIRE RATE	MAGAZINE	ELEMENTAL
79	74.2	3.0	12	x1

- ☐ +50% RELOAD SPEED
- ☐ 2.6X WEAPON ZOOM

TK4-A WICKED LACERATOR

	LEVEL	BUY	SELL
	48	$1,909,845	$272,835

DAMAGE	ACCURACY	FIRE RATE	MAGAZINE	ELEMENTAL
107	79.2	7.7	16	-

- ☐ +200% MELEE DAMAGE
- ☐ +46% RELOAD SPEED
- ☐ -13% DAMAGE
- ☐ 3.1X WEAPON ZOOM

REVOLVER PISTOLS

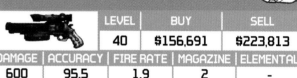

TEDIORE MAKES ROUGHLY 97,200 VARIETIES OF REVOLVER PISTOLS.

RV12

	LEVEL	BUY	SELL
	-	$280	$40

DAMAGE	ACCURACY	FIRE RATE	MAGAZINE	ELEMENTAL
12	88.8	1.3	6	-

- ☐ +57% RELOAD SPEED
- ☐ 1.6X WEAPON ZOOM

AX10-A SAVAGE JUSTICE

	LEVEL	BUY	SELL
	40	$156,691	$223,813

DAMAGE	ACCURACY	FIRE RATE	MAGAZINE	ELEMENTAL
600	95.5	1.9	2	-

- ☐ +127% DAMAGE
- ☐ +62% RELOAD SPEED
- ☐ +46% ACCURACY
- ☐ 4.2X WEAPON ZOOM

DL1-A SAVAGE REVOLVER

	LEVEL	BUY	SELL
	13	$9,282	$1,326

DAMAGE	ACCURACY	FIRE RATE	MAGAZINE	ELEMENTAL
103	87.3	1.0	6	-

- ☐ +100% MELEE DAMAGE
- ☐ +46% RELOAD SPEED
- ☐ +25% DAMAGE
- ☐ 2.3X WEAPON ZOOM

RV21 BRUTAL RAZOR

	LEVEL	BUY	SELL
	48	$719,418	$102,774

DAMAGE	ACCURACY	FIRE RATE	MAGAZINE	ELEMENTAL
310	86.4	1.3	6	-

- ☐ +200% MELEE DAMAGE
- ☐ +24% RELOAD SPEED
- ☐ -5% DAMAGE
- ☐ 2.3X WEAPON ZOOM

MAL230-B SAVAGE MASHER

	LEVEL	BUY	SELL
	22	$44,751	$6,393

DAMAGE	ACCURACY	FIRE RATE	MAGAZINE	ELEMENTAL
53 (x7)	82.5	1.6	3	-

- ☐ +40% RELOAD SPEED
- ☐ -61% DAMAGE
- ☐ 2.8X WEAPON ZOOM

DL330-A SAVAGE REVOLVER

	LEVEL	BUY	SELL
	48	$1,928,955	$275,565

DAMAGE	ACCURACY	FIRE RATE	MAGAZINE	ELEMENTAL
289	93.1	1.0	3	x2

- ☐ +50% RELOAD SPEED
- ☐ 2.8X WEAPON ZOOM

KLR300 SAVAGE REVOLVER

	LEVEL	BUY	SELL
	31	$142,814	$20,402

DAMAGE	ACCURACY	FIRE RATE	MAGAZINE	ELEMENTAL
201	91.3	1.2	6	x2

- ☐ +44% RELOAD SPEED
- ☐ 3.7X WEAPON ZOOM

KING OF CLAP

LEGENDARY WEAPON
EQ20-B SAVAGE EQUALIZER

	LEVEL	BUY	SELL
	40	$689,339	$98,477

DAMAGE	ACCURACY	FIRE RATE	MAGAZINE	ELEMENTAL
21.8	90.4	1.6	6	x2

- ☐ +57% RELOAD SPEED

THE *EQUALIZER* GENERATES ITS OWN AMMUNITION.

UNENDING FIREPOWER!

COMBAT SHOTGUNS

TEDIORE MAKES ROUGHLY 82,900 VARIETIES OF COMBAT SHOTGUNS.

SG11 CHEAP SCATTERGUN

	LEVEL	BUY	SELL
	-	$357	$51

DAMAGE	ACCURACY	FIRE RATE	MAGAZINE	ELEMENTAL
6 (x11)	26.9	0.7	6	-

- ☐ +58% RELOAD SPEED
- ☐ 1.5X WEAPON ZOOM
- ☐ +2 PROJECTILES FIRED

ZX240-B GENOCIDE SHOTGUN

	LEVEL	BUY	SELL
	22	$62,412	$8,916

DAMAGE	ACCURACY	FIRE RATE	MAGAZINE	ELEMENTAL
47 (x9)	58.5	1.3	6	-

- ☐ +35% RELOAD SPEED
- ☐ 2.7X WEAPON ZOOM

SPR900-A GENOCIDE MATADOR

	LEVEL	BUY	SELL
	13	$11,753	$1,679

DAMAGE	ACCURACY	FIRE RATE	MAGAZINE	ELEMENTAL
35 (x12)	17.1	0.8	12	-

- ☐ +150% MELEE DAMAGE
- ☐ +3 PROJECTILES FIRED
- ☐ +14% RELOAD SPEED
- ☐ 2.2X WEAPON ZOOM

SG240 BATTLE CARNAGE

	LEVEL	BUY	SELL
	48	$735,840	$105,120

DAMAGE	ACCURACY	FIRE RATE	MAGAZINE	ELEMENTAL
518	51.3	0.7	6	-

- ☐ +24% RELOAD SPEED
- ☐ 1.5X WEAPON ZOOM

Holy crap! It shoots rockets!

BA 350 GENOCIDE SHOTGUN

	LEVEL	BUY	SELL
	31	$204,015	$29,145

DAMAGE	ACCURACY	FIRE RATE	MAGAZINE	ELEMENTAL
153 (x9)	43.8	0.6	2	-

- ☐ +55% RELOAD SPEED
- ☐ 3.6X WEAPON ZOOM

BA 350-A GENOCIDE MATADOR

	LEVEL	BUY	SELL
	48	$3,256,673	$465,239

DAMAGE	ACCURACY	FIRE RATE	MAGAZINE	ELEMENTAL
182 (x12)	17.1	0.7	2	🔥x1

- ☐ +57% RELOAD SPEED
- ☐ +3 PROJECTILES FIRED

SG1 COMBAT SCATTERGUN

	LEVEL	BUY	SELL
	40	$189,917	$27,131

DAMAGE	ACCURACY	FIRE RATE	MAGAZINE	ELEMENTAL
67 (x11)	26.9	0.7	6	-

- ☐ +52% RELOAD SPEED
- ☐ 1.5X WEAPON ZOOM
- ☐ +2 PROJECTILES FIRED

LEGENDARY WEAPON
DEF900-B GENOCIDE DEFENDER

	LEVEL	BUY	SELL
	40	$1,032,983	$147,569

DAMAGE	ACCURACY	FIRE RATE	MAGAZINE	ELEMENTAL
82 (x9)	37.7	1.0	12	⚡x2

- ☐ +20% RELOAD SPEED

THE *DEFENDER* GENERATES ITS OWN AMMUNITION.

I CAN DO THIS ALL DAY...

CLAPTRAP DANCE OFF

TEDIORE

TEDIORE

COMBAT RIFLES

CR SCOPED RIFLE

	LEVEL	BUY	SELL
	4	$679	$97

DAMAGE	ACCURACY	FIRE RATE	MAGAZINE	ELEMENTAL
15	85.4	10.0	12	-

☐ +41% RELOAD SPEED ☐ 1.4X WEAPON ZOOM

CR-B GENOCIDE POUNDER

	LEVEL	BUY	SELL
	40	$631,267	$90,181

DAMAGE	ACCURACY	FIRE RATE	MAGAZINE	ELEMENTAL
160	91.7	3.3	6	⚡x1

☐ +58% RELOAD SPEED ☐ 2.0X WEAPON ZOOM

TCH320-A GENOCIDE RIFLE

	LEVEL	BUY	SELL
	13	$10,430	$1,490

DAMAGE	ACCURACY	FIRE RATE	MAGAZINE	ELEMENTAL
47	91.0	13	18	-

☐ +30% RELOAD SPEED ☐ 2.0X WEAPON ZOOM

TCH30 GENOCIDE RIFLE

	LEVEL	BUY	SELL
	48	$1,243,571	$177,653

DAMAGE	ACCURACY	FIRE RATE	MAGAZINE	ELEMENTAL
133	88.8	13.0	12	🔥x2

☐ +41% RELOAD SPEED ☐ 2.4X WEAPON ZOOM

HLK400-B GENOCIDE POUNDER

	LEVEL	BUY	SELL
	22	$103,026	$14,718

DAMAGE	ACCURACY	FIRE RATE	MAGAZINE	ELEMENTAL
146	91.4	3.0	6	-

☐ +50% RELOAD SPEED ☐ 2.4X WEAPON ZOOM
☐ +114% DAMAGE

AR50 GENOCIDE COBRA

	LEVEL	BUY	SELL
	31	$246,932	$35,276

DAMAGE	ACCURACY	FIRE RATE	MAGAZINE	ELEMENTAL
92	93.6	15.0	12	☣x1

☐ +41% RELOAD SPEED ☐ 3.2X WEAPON ZOOM

HLK420-A GENOCIDE COBRA

	LEVEL	BUY	SELL
	48	$4,885,013	$697,859

DAMAGE	ACCURACY	FIRE RATE	MAGAZINE	ELEMENTAL
249	94.1	7.7	18	-

☐ +19% RELOAD SPEED ☐ +46% ACCURACY
☐ +49% RECOIL REDUCTION ☐ 3.2X WEAPON ZOOM

LEGENDARY WEAPON
GRD12-A WAR GUARDIAN

	LEVEL	BUY	SELL
	40	$406,931	$58,133

DAMAGE	ACCURACY	FIRE RATE	MAGAZINE	ELEMENTAL
156	86.5	7.7	18	-

☐ +40% RELOAD SPEED ☐ 1.4X WEAPON ZOOM
☐ +16 AMMO
   REGENERATION

THE *GUARDIAN* GENERATES ITS OWN AMMUNITION.

HOLD YOUR GROUND... FOREVER

KING OF CLAP

★ ★ ★ ★ ★ ★ ★

PATROL SMG

TEDIORE MAKES ROUGHLY 174,900 VARIETIES OF SUB-MACHINE GUNS.

TD VIOLENT THUMPER

LEVEL	BUY	SELL
-	$721	$103

DAMAGE	ACCURACY	FIRE RATE	MAGAZINE	ELEMENTAL
12	77.5	2.8	18	-

- ☐ +49% RELOAD SPEED
- ☐ 1.7X WEAPON ZOOM
- ☐ +34% DAMAGE

TEK330-B MALEVOLENT SMG

LEVEL	BUY	SELL
22	$54,089	$7,727

DAMAGE	ACCURACY	FIRE RATE	MAGAZINE	ELEMENTAL
47	87.2	10.8	36	-

- ☐ +63% RELOAD SPEED
- ☐ +2% DAMAGE
- ☐ +51% RECOIL REDUCTION
- ☐ 2.9X WEAPON ZOOM

RF440 TWISTED BRUISER

LEVEL	BUY	SELL
31	$370,398	$52,914

DAMAGE	ACCURACY	FIRE RATE	MAGAZINE	ELEMENTAL
102	77.5	9.3	82	-

- ☐ +19% RELOAD SPEED
- ☐ +54 MAGAZINE SIZE
- ☐ +55% DAMAGE
- ☐ 3.9X WEAPON ZOOM

HX 550-B MALEVOLENT BRUISER

LEVEL	BUY	SELL
40	$1,939,714	$277,102

DAMAGE	ACCURACY	FIRE RATE	MAGAZINE	ELEMENTAL
108	85.3	12.5	46	☣x2

- ☐ +30% RELOAD SPEED
- ☐ +23% DAMAGE

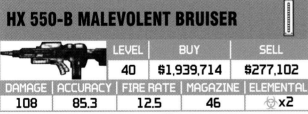

KKA22-A HOSTILE BRUISER

LEVEL	BUY	SELL
13	$6,629	$947

DAMAGE	ACCURACY	FIRE RATE	MAGAZINE	ELEMENTAL
38	74.5	8.3	28	-

- ☐ +35% RELOAD SPEED
- ☐ 2.4X WEAPON ZOOM
- ☐ +36% DAMAGE

LEGENDARY WEAPON
SV4-A MALEVOLENT SAVIOR

LEVEL	BUY	SELL
40	$2,065,966	$295,138

DAMAGE	ACCURACY	FIRE RATE	MAGAZINE	ELEMENTAL
122	90.9	10.8	55	-

- ☐ +14% RELOAD SPEED
- ☐ 4.3X WEAPON ZOOM
- ☐ +16 AMMO REGENERATION

THE *SAVIOR* GENERATES ITS OWN AMMUNITION.

HALLELUJAH

TD200 MALEVOLENT THUMPER

LEVEL	BUY	SELL
48	$1,273,573	$181,939

DAMAGE	ACCURACY	FIRE RATE	MAGAZINE	ELEMENTAL
133 (x2)	65.0	2.8	21	-

- ☐ +33% RELOAD SPEED
- ☐ 1.7X WEAPON ZOOM
- ☐ +22% DAMAGE

CLAPTRAP DANCE OFF

TEDIORE

GUN CATALOG

DAHL'S MODEL LINES

LEVEL	LINE
1 TO 12	SURPLUS
13 TO 21	MERCENARY
22 TO 30	SOLDIER
31 TO 39	FREELANCER
40 TO 48	VETERAN
50	ELITE

REPEATER PISTOLS

DAHL MAKES ROUGHLY 71,200 VARIETIES OF REPEATER PISTOLS.

HRD5D WICKED REPEATER

LEVEL	BUY	SELL
2	$3,101	$443

DAMAGE	ACCURACY	FIRE RATE	MAGAZINE	ELEMENTAL
19	76.2	2.4	18	-

- ☐ -16% RECOIL REDUCTION
- ☐ +69% DAMAGE
- ☐ +100% MELEE DAMAGE
- ☐ 4.1X WEAPON ZOOM

RF4 U WICKED REPEATER

LEVEL	BUY	SELL
25	$30,702	$4,386

DAMAGE	ACCURACY	FIRE RATE	MAGAZINE	ELEMENTAL
79 (x2)	75.6	2.8	19	-

- ☐ -18% RECOIL REDUCTION
- ☐ +34% DAMAGE

BLR REPEATER

LEVEL	BUY	SELL
16	$4.340	$620

DAMAGE	ACCURACY	FIRE RATE	MAGAZINE	ELEMENTAL
34	80.0	3.3	12	-

- ☐ +23% RECOIL REDUCTION
- ☐ 1.8X WEAPON ZOOM

TK5D WICKED REPEATER

LEVEL	BUY	SELL
34	$98,798	$14,114

DAMAGE	ACCURACY	FIRE RATE	MAGAZINE	ELEMENTAL
62 (x2)	64.2	4.3	14	-

- ☐ +42% RECOIL REDUCTION
- ☐ 3.1X WEAPON ZOOM
- ☐ -25% DAMAGE

DAHL

KING OF CLAP

MERCS CHOOSE DAHL BECAUSE THEY ONLY GET PAID IF THEY SURVIVE.

NEED TO CLEAR A ROOM? GET A DAHL.

WHY DAHL?

DAHL HAS BEEN OUTFITTING THE DEFENDERS OF FREEDOM FOR OVER A CENTURY, AND ISN'T ABOUT TO STOP ANYTIME SOON. WE'VE BUILT OUR COMPANY ON THE FOUNDATION THAT DEAD CUSTOMERS CAN'T BE REPEAT CUSTOMERS—KEEPING YOU ALIVE IS IN OUR BEST INTEREST! WE ALSO KNOW THAT THOSE OF YOU DOING THE GOVERNMENT'S SECRET DIRTY WORK HAVE ENOUGH TO CONTEND WITH AND DON'T NEED TO FIGHT YOUR WEAPON, TOO. THAT'S WHY WE AT DAHL HAVE STRIVED TO MANUFACTURE THE SMOOTHEST AND MOST STABLE WEAPONS ON THE MARKET. AND WHEN YOU GET SURROUNDED—AND YOU WILL—YOU'LL BE GLAD TO KNOW YOUR DAHL HAS BEEN PRECISION MACHINED TO REMAIN AS ACCURATE DURING SUSTAINED FIRE AS HUMANLY POSSIBLE. SO MAKE SURE YOU TAKE A DAHL WITH YOU THE NEXT TIME YOU GO ON ASSIGNMENT. IT JUST MIGHT BRING YOU BACK.

CLAPTRAP DANCE OFF

DAHL

HRD BAD REPEATER

	LEVEL	BUY	SELL
	43	$317,933	$45,419

DAMAGE	ACCURACY	FIRE RATE	MAGAZINE	ELEMENTAL
121	76.7	2.9	12	-

- ☐ +5% RECOIL REDUCTION
- ☐ +12% DAMAGE
- ☐ 2.6X WEAPON ZOOM

BLR4 U WICKED REPEATER

	LEVEL	BUY	SELL
	43	$572,276	$82,468

DAMAGE	ACCURACY	FIRE RATE	MAGAZINE	ELEMENTAL
91	80.8	3.1	16	⚡ x1

- ☐ +12% RECOIL REDUCTION
- ☐ 3.1X WEAPON ZOOM

TK WICKED LACERATOR

	LEVEL	BUY	SELL
	48	$2,260,167	$322,881

DAMAGE	ACCURACY	FIRE RATE	MAGAZINE	ELEMENTAL
131	86.7	4.3	12	-

- ☐ +38% RECOIL REDUCTION
- ☐ +200% MELEE DAMAGE
- ☐ +7% DAMAGE
- ☐ 4.7X WEAPON ZOOM

LEGENDARY WEAPON
RF5D WICKED HORNET

	LEVEL	BUY	SELL
	48	$3,516,800	$502,400

DAMAGE	ACCURACY	FIRE RATE	MAGAZINE	ELEMENTAL
207	76.2	7.9	18	☣ x2

- ☐ 4.1X WEAPON ZOOM

THE *HORNET* OFFERS A TWO-SHOT CORROSIVE BURST THAT DOES UNUSUALLY HIGH DAMAGE.

FEEL THE STING

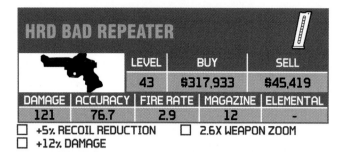

REVOLVER PISTOLS
DAHL MAKES ROUGHLY 97,200 VARIETIES OF REVOLVER PISTOLS.

MAL10D SAVAGE JUSTICE

	LEVEL	BUY	SELL
	-	$1,127	$161

DAMAGE	ACCURACY	FIRE RATE	MAGAZINE	ELEMENTAL
23	92.6	1.9	6	-

- ☐ +24% RECOIL REDUCTION
- ☐ +12% ACCURACY
- ☐ +33% DAMAGE
- ☐ 3.7X WEAPON ZOOM

KLR10 PRIMAL MASHER

	LEVEL	BUY	SELL
	16	$8,561	$1,223

DAMAGE	ACCURACY	FIRE RATE	MAGAZINE	ELEMENTAL
43 (x7)	73.3	1.2	6	-

- ☐ -123% RECOIL REDUCTION
- ☐ -57% DAMAGE
- ☐ 1.6X WEAPON ZOOM

LEGENDARY WEAPON
AX220 U SAVAGE ANACONDA

	LEVEL	BUY	SELL
	25	$87,920	$12,560

DAMAGE	ACCURACY	FIRE RATE	MAGAZINE	ELEMENTAL
262	94.7	1.9	6	-

- ☐ +35% RECOIL REDUCTION
- ☐ +67% DAMAGE
- ☐ 1.6X WEAPON ZOOM

THE *ANACONDA* OFFERS VERY HIGH DAMAGE AND EQUALLY HIGH ACCURACY.

LONG AND STRONG

KING OF CLAP

DAHL

RV31D SAVAGE RAZOR

	LEVEL	BUY	SELL
	34	$194,859	$27,837

DAMAGE	ACCURACY	FIRE RATE	MAGAZINE	ELEMENTAL
240	904	1.3	6	-

- ☐ +52% RECOIL REDUCTION
- ☐ +200% MELEE DAMAGE
- ☐ +9% DAMAGE
- ☐ 2.3X WEAPON ZOOM

KLR PRIMAL REVOLVER

	LEVEL	BUY	SELL
	48	$989,205	$141,315

DAMAGE	ACCURACY	FIRE RATE	MAGAZINE	ELEMENTAL
261	90.0	1.0	6	x1

- ☐ -46% RECOIL REDUCTION
- ☐ -20% DAMAGE
- ☐ 2.8X WEAPON ZOOM

DL13 PRIMAL MASHER

	LEVEL	BUY	SELL
	43	$428,155	$61,165

DAMAGE	ACCURACY	FIRE RATE	MAGAZINE	ELEMENTAL
129 (x7)	71	1	3	-

- ☐ -123% RECOIL REDUCTION
- ☐ -55% DAMAGE
- ☐ 2.8X WEAPON ZOOM

AX320 SAVAGE JUSTICE

	LEVEL	BUY	SELL
	48	$4,346,076	$620,868

DAMAGE	ACCURACY	FIRE RATE	MAGAZINE	ELEMENTAL
409	95.7	1.9	6	-

- ☐ +57% RECOIL REDUCTION
- ☐ +100% MELEE DAMAGE
- ☐ +25% DAMAGE
- ☐ +48% ACCURACY

MAL U SAVAGE LAW

	LEVEL	BUY	SELL
	43	$723,303	$103,329

DAMAGE	ACCURACY	FIRE RATE	MAGAZINE	ELEMENTAL
236	93.6	1.9	6	x2

- ☐ +41% RECOIL REDUCTION
- ☐ 3.7X WEAPON ZOOM

COMBAT SHOTGUNS

DAHL MAKES ROUGHLY 86,400 VARIETIES OF COMBAT SHOTGUNS.

BA 1 BATTLE SHOTGUN

	LEVEL	BUY	SELL
	5	$1,708	$244

DAMAGE	ACCURACY	FIRE RATE	MAGAZINE	ELEMENTAL
16 (x9)	35.0	0.8	6	-

- ☐ +-15% RECOIL REDUCTION
- ☐ 1.5X WEAPON ZOOM

SPR240 U GENOCIDE SHOTGUN

	LEVEL	BUY	SELL
	25	$153,517	$21,931

DAMAGE	ACCURACY	FIRE RATE	MAGAZINE	ELEMENTAL
53 (x9)	72.9	0.9	6	x1

- ☐ +43% RECOIL REDUCTION
- ☐ 4.0X WEAPON ZOOM

SG900 GENOCIDE SHOTGUN

	LEVEL	BUY	SELL
	16	$21,168	$3,024

DAMAGE	ACCURACY	FIRE RATE	MAGAZINE	ELEMENTAL
44 (x9)	50.0	1.3	12	-

- ☐ -4% RECOIL REDUCTION
- ☐ 3.6X WEAPON ZOOM

ZX3500 GENOCIDE CARNAGE

	LEVEL	BUY	SELL
	34	$285,005	$40,715

DAMAGE	ACCURACY	FIRE RATE	MAGAZINE	ELEMENTAL
470	58.5	1.3	2	-

- ☐ +58% RECOIL REDUCTION
- ☐ 1.5X WEAPON ZOOM

HOLY CRAP! IT SHOOTS ROCKETS!

CLAPTRAP DANCE OFF

DAHL

LEGENDARY WEAPON
BA 100 WAR BULLDOG

	LEVEL	BUY	SELL
	43	$846,902	$120,986

DAMAGE	ACCURACY	FIRE RATE	MAGAZINE	ELEMENTAL
120 (x9)	35.0	0.9	20	-

☐ -46% RECOIL REDUCTION
☐ 2.2X WEAPON ZOOM

THE *BULLDOG* HAS AN ENORMOAUS MAGAZINE AND BOASTS A SURPRISINGLY FAST RELOAD SPEED.

ZPR1 U GENOCIDE MATADOR

	LEVEL	BUY	SELL
	43	$1,164,492	$166,356

DAMAGE	ACCURACY	FIRE RATE	MAGAZINE	ELEMENTAL
93 (x12)	22.5	1.6	6	x2

☐ +25% RECOIL REDUCTION   ☐ 2.7X WEAPON ZOOM

ZPR1100D GENOCIDE SHOTGUN

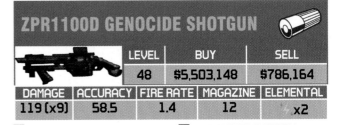

	LEVEL	BUY	SELL
	48	$5,503,148	$786,164

DAMAGE	ACCURACY	FIRE RATE	MAGAZINE	ELEMENTAL
119 (x9)	58.5	1.4	12	x2

☐ +58% RECOIL REDUCTION   ☐ 3.6X WEAPON ZOOM

SPR340 GENOCIDE SHOTGUN

	LEVEL	BUY	SELL
	48	$3,587,234	$512,462

DAMAGE	ACCURACY	FIRE RATE	MAGAZINE	ELEMENTAL
119 (x9)	50.0	0.9	6	x1

☐ -3% RECOIL REDUCTION   ☐ 4.0X WEAPON ZOOM

COMBAT RIFLES
DAHL MAKES ROUGHLY 33,600 VARIETIES OF COMBAT RIFLES.

AR500D GENOCIDE POUNDER

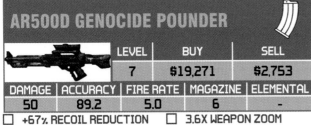

	LEVEL	BUY	SELL
	7	$19,271	$2,753

DAMAGE	ACCURACY	FIRE RATE	MAGAZINE	ELEMENTAL
50	89.2	5.0	6	-

☐ +67% RECOIL REDUCTION   ☐ 3.6X WEAPON ZOOM
☐ +97% DAMAGE

TCH U GENOCIDE RIFLE

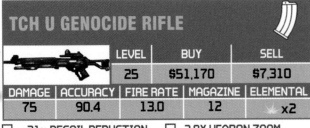

	LEVEL	BUY	SELL
	25	$51,170	$7,310

DAMAGE	ACCURACY	FIRE RATE	MAGAZINE	ELEMENTAL
75	90.4	13.0	12	x2

☐ +21% RECOIL REDUCTION   ☐ 2.0X WEAPON ZOOM

HLK320D GENOCIDE COBRA

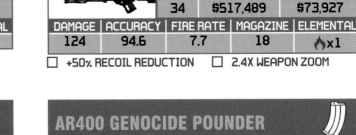

	LEVEL	BUY	SELL
	34	$517,489	$73,927

DAMAGE	ACCURACY	FIRE RATE	MAGAZINE	ELEMENTAL
124	94.6	7.7	18	x1

☐ +50% RECOIL REDUCTION   ☐ 2.4X WEAPON ZOOM

AR400 GENOCIDE POUNDER

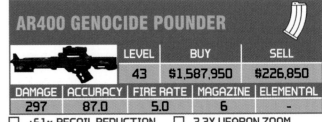

	LEVEL	BUY	SELL
	43	$1,587,950	$226,850

DAMAGE	ACCURACY	FIRE RATE	MAGAZINE	ELEMENTAL
297	87.0	5.0	6	-

☐ +61% RECOIL REDUCTION   ☐ 3.2X WEAPON ZOOM
☐ +106% DAMAGE

KING OF CLAP

LEGENDARY WEAPON
CR38 SCOPED RAVEN

LEVEL	BUY	SELL
16	$19,271	$2,753

DAMAGE	ACCURACY	FIRE RATE	MAGAZINE	ELEMENTAL
51	91.3	10.0	21	-

☐ -8% RECOIL REDUCTION ☐ 1.4X WEAPON ZOOM

LEGENDARY WEAPON
CR780 U GENOCIDE RAVEN

LEVEL	BUY	SELL
43	$3,074,274	$439,182

DAMAGE	ACCURACY	FIRE RATE	MAGAZINE	ELEMENTAL
124	91.7	10.0	21	⚡x2

☐ 1.4X WEAPON ZOOM

THE *RAVEN* FIRES A FIVE-SHOT BURST AND COMES EQUIPPED WITH A LARGER MAGAZINE.

2 MORE BULLETS MAKE ALL THE DIFFERENCE

TCH10D WAR RIFLE

LEVEL	BUY	SELL
48	$940,709	$134,387

DAMAGE	ACCURACY	FIRE RATE	MAGAZINE	ELEMENTAL
213	90.4	13.0	12	-

☐ +17% RECOIL REDUCTION ☐ 1.4X WEAPON ZOOM

HLK2 GENOCIDE COBRA

LEVEL	BUY	SELL
48	$2,119,726	$302,818

DAMAGE	ACCURACY	FIRE RATE	MAGAZINE	ELEMENTAL
173	94.3	7.7	18	x1

☐ +32% RECOIL REDUCTION ☐ +48% ACCURACY

PATROL SMG
DAHL MAKES ROUGHLY 174,900 VARIETIES OF SUB-MACHINE GUNS.

TEK500 MALEVOLENT THUMPER

LEVEL	BUY	SELL
4	$13,279	$1,897

DAMAGE	ACCURACY	FIRE RATE	MAGAZINE	ELEMENTAL
16	91.3	3.6	18	🔥x2

☐ +28% DAMAGE ☐ 4.3X WEAPON ZOOM

RF2 U VIOLENT BRUISER

LEVEL	BUY	SELL
16	$9,408	$1,344

DAMAGE	ACCURACY	FIRE RATE	MAGAZINE	ELEMENTAL
47	80.8	6.4	28	-

☐ -7% RECOIL REDUCTION ☐ 1.7X WEAPON ZOOM
☐ +41% DAMAGE

CLAPTRAP DANCE OFF

DAHL

HX 230D MALEVOLENT STINGER

	LEVEL	BUY	SELL
	25	$74,942	$10,706

DAMAGE	ACCURACY	FIRE RATE	MAGAZINE	ELEMENTAL
82	76.2	14.2	36	-

- ☐ +53% RECOIL REDUCTION
- ☐ +57% DAMAGE
- ☐ +41% FIRE RATE
- ☐ 2.4X WEAPON ZOOM

HX 2 U MALEVOLENT SMG

	LEVEL	BUY	SELL
	48	$1,630,559	$232,937

DAMAGE	ACCURACY	FIRE RATE	MAGAZINE	ELEMENTAL
104	80.8	12.5	28	⬡ x1

- ☐ +38% RECOIL REDUCTION
- ☐ -4% DAMAGE

TD340 MALEVOLENT BRUISER

	LEVEL	BUY	SELL
	34	$306,208	$43,744

DAMAGE	ACCURACY	FIRE RATE	MAGAZINE	ELEMENTAL
93	86.7	12.1	55	-

- ☐ +72% RECOIL REDUCTION
- ☐ +27% DAMAGE
- ☐ 2.9X WEAPON ZOOM

LEGENDARY WEAPON
TEK540D MALEVOLENT WILDCAT

	LEVEL	BUY	SELL
	43	$6,763,407	$966,201

DAMAGE	ACCURACY	FIRE RATE	MAGAZINE	ELEMENTAL
127	39.4	10.8	70	-

- ☐ +62% RECOIL REDUCTION
- ☐ +33% DAMAGE
- ☐ 1.4X WEAPON ZOOM

THE *WILDCAT* MAY NOT BE THE MOST ACCURATE WEAPON IN YOUR ARSENAL, BUT ITS HUGE MAGAZINE MAKES UP FOR IT!

THE ULTIMATE CLOSE QUARTERS FELINE

KKA450 U TWISTED ANARCHY

	LEVEL	BUY	SELL
	43	$2,381,925	$340,275

DAMAGE	ACCURACY	FIRE RATE	MAGAZINE	ELEMENTAL
135 (x4)	35.0	6.9	92	-

- ☐ +41% RECOIL REDUCTION
- ☐ +64% MAGAZINE SIZE
- ☐ 3.9X WEAPON ZOOM

RF100 MALEVOLENT THUMPER

	LEVEL	BUY	SELL
	48	$2,890,538	$412,934

DAMAGE	ACCURACY	FIRE RATE	MAGAZINE	ELEMENTAL
198	91.3	2.5	18	✴ x1

- ☐ -6% RECOIL REDUCTION
- ☐ +81% DAMAGE

KING OF CLAP

SEMI-AUTO SNIPER RIFLES

DAHL MAKES ROUGHLY 14,400 VARIETIES OF SEMI-AUTOMATIC SNIPER RIFLES.

PPZ LIQUID SNIPER

LEVEL	BUY	SELL
4	$1,071	$153

DAMAGE	ACCURACY	FIRE RATE	MAGAZINE	ELEMENTAL
57	94.0	2.4	5	-

- ☐ +38% RECOIL REDUCTION
- ☐ +150 CRITICAL HIT DAMAGE
- ☐ +41% FIRE RATE
- ☐ 1.0X WEAPON ZOOM

LB27 U FEARSOME SNIPER

LEVEL	BUY	SELL
16	$13,699	$1,957

DAMAGE	ACCURACY	FIRE RATE	MAGAZINE	ELEMENTAL
189	92.8	2.0	7	-

- ☐ +17% RECOIL REDUCTION
- ☐ +150 CRITICAL HIT DAMAGE
- ☐ 1.5X WEAPON ZOOM

PPZ30D FEARSOME THUNDER

LEVEL	BUY	SELL
25	$99,197	$14,171

DAMAGE	ACCURACY	FIRE RATE	MAGAZINE	ELEMENTAL
381	96.2	2.1	5	-

- ☐ +57% RECOIL REDUCTION
- ☐ +150 CRITICAL HIT DAMAGE
- ☐ +83% DAMAGE
- ☐ 1.8X WEAPON ZOOM

LEGENDARY WEAPON
LBD FEARSOME PENETRATOR

LEVEL	BUY	SELL
43	$1,094,464	$156,352

DAMAGE	ACCURACY	FIRE RATE	MAGAZINE	ELEMENTAL
363	94.3	3.0	8	x2

- ☐ +61% RECOIL REDUCTION

THE *PENETRATOR* HAS AN EXTENDED MAGAZINE, LOW KICK, AND CAN FIRE ABOUT AS RAPIDLY AS YOU CAN SQUEEZE THE TRIGGER.

PPZ570 U FEARSOME WRATH

LEVEL	BUY	SELL
43	$5,086,522	$726,646

DAMAGE	ACCURACY	FIRE RATE	MAGAZINE	ELEMENTAL
417	97.5	2.4	7	x3

- ☐ +68% RECOIL REDUCTION
- ☐ 2.7X WEAPON ZOOM

PPZ HARD SNIPER

LEVEL	BUY	SELL
48	$1,404,788	$200,684

DAMAGE	ACCURACY	FIRE RATE	MAGAZINE	ELEMENTAL
669	94.0	2.1	5	-

- ☐ +33% RECOIL REDUCTION
- ☐ +150% CRITICAL HIT DAMAGE
- ☐ 1.5X WEAPON ZOOM

LB30 U FEARSOME WRATH

LEVEL	BUY	SELL
48	$1,582,728	$226,104

DAMAGE	ACCURACY	FIRE RATE	MAGAZINE	ELEMENTAL
444	92.8	1.2	5	x4

- ☐ +12% RECOIL REDUCTION
- ☐ 1.8X WEAPON ZOOM

DAHL

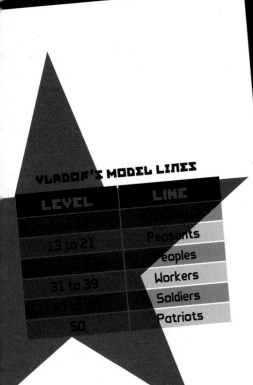

VLADOF'S MODEL LINES

LEVEL	LINE
13 to 21	Peasants
	Peoples
31 to 39	Workers
40 to 49	Soldiers
50	Patriots

THE WEAPONS OF THE REVOLUTION. EVEN OPPRESSION ITSELF FEARS VLADOF.

GUN CATALOG

REPEATER PISTOLS

VLADOF MAKES ROUGHLY 64,800 VARIETIES OF REPEATER PISTOLS.

KING OF CLAP

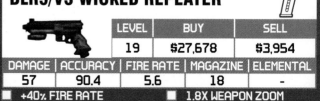

HRD4/V2 WICKED REPEATER

LEVEL	BUY	SELL
10	$4,305	$615

DAMAGE	ACCURACY	FIRE RATE	MAGAZINE	ELEMENTAL
42	83.1	4.1	16	-

- ☐ +18% FIRE RATE
- ☐ +68% DAMAGE

BLR5/V3 WICKED REPEATER

LEVEL	BUY	SELL
19	$27,678	$3,954

DAMAGE	ACCURACY	FIRE RATE	MAGAZINE	ELEMENTAL
57	90.4	5.6	18	-

- ☐ +40% FIRE RATE
- ☐ 1.8X WEAPON ZOOM
- ☐ +27% DAMAGE

VLADOF

LEGENDARY WEAPON
TK6 CRUEL REBEL

	LEVEL	BUY	SELL
	28	$80,290	$11,470

DAMAGE	ACCURACY	FIRE RATE	MAGAZINE	ELEMENTAL
61 (x2)	62.2	5.9	40	-

- ☐ +44% FIRE RATE
- ☐ -9% DAMAGE
- ☐ 2.6X WEAPON ZOOM

NEVER STOP SHOOTING!

THE REBEL HAS THE LARGEST MAGAZINE OF ANY PISTOL AND OFFERS FAST RELOAD SPEED, FIRE RATE, AND GOOD DAMAGE.

TK STATIC REPEATER

	LEVEL	BUY	SELL
	37	$107,842	$15,406

DAMAGE	ACCURACY	FIRE RATE	MAGAZINE	ELEMENTAL
55	74.7	5.8	12	⚡x1

- ☐ +30% FIRE RATE

BLR4/V3 WICKED REPEATER

	LEVEL	BUY	SELL
	46	$922,810	$131,830

DAMAGE	ACCURACY	FIRE RATE	MAGAZINE	ELEMENTAL
109	73.3	5.2	16	☣x1

- ☐ +36% FIRE RATE
- ☐ -7% DAMAGE
- ☐ 4.1X WEAPON ZOOM

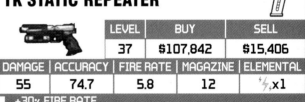

CLAPTRAP DANCE OFF

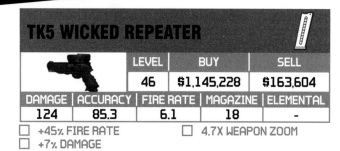

TK5 WICKED REPEATER

	LEVEL	BUY	SELL
	46	$1,145,228	$163,604
DAMAGE	ACCURACY	FIRE RATE	MAGAZINE	ELEMENTAL
124	85.3	6.1	18	-

- ☐ +45% FIRE RATE
- ☐ +7% DAMAGE
- ☐ 4.7X WEAPON ZOOM

BLR4 FANGED REPEATER

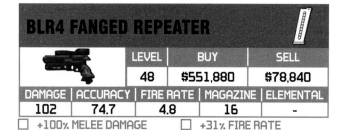

	LEVEL	BUY	SELL
	48	$551,880	$78,840
DAMAGE	ACCURACY	FIRE RATE	MAGAZINE	ELEMENTAL
102	74.7	4.8	16	-

- ☐ +100% MELEE DAMAGE
- ☐ +31% FIRE RATE

LEGENDARY WEAPON
HRD6/V2 WICKED REBEL

	LEVEL	BUY	SELL
	48	$2,182,474	$311,782
DAMAGE	ACCURACY	FIRE RATE	MAGAZINE	ELEMENTAL
220	83.1	4.7	34	-

- ☐ +100% MELEE DAMAGE
- ☐ +29% FIRE RATE
- ☐ +79% DAMAGE

NEVER STOP SHOOTING!

THE **REBEL** HAS THE LARGEST MAGAZINE OF ANY PISTOL AND OFFERS FAST RELOAD SPEED, FIRE RATE, AND GOOD DAMAGE.

MACHINE PISTOLS

VLADOF MAKES ROUGHLY 12,600 VARIETIES OF MACHINE PISTOLS.

TMP2 FANGED RAGE

	LEVEL	BUY	SELL
	10	$2,730	$390
DAMAGE	ACCURACY	FIRE RATE	MAGAZINE	ELEMENTAL
22	74.7	20.3	16	-

- ☐ +100% MELEE DAMAGE
- ☐ +59% FIRE RATE
- ☐ +300% BURST FIRE RATE

BURST FIRE

TMP2/V3 VILE TORMENT

	LEVEL	BUY	SELL
	28	$70,042	$10,006
DAMAGE	ACCURACY	FIRE RATE	MAGAZINE	ELEMENTAL
98	73.3	14.0	18	-

- ☐ +40% FIRE RATE
- ☐ +47% DAMAGE
- ☐ +2 MAGAZINE SIZE
- ☐ 3.1X WEAPON ZOOM

TMP8/V2 COLD TORMENT

	LEVEL	BUY	SELL
	19	$10,388	$1,484
DAMAGE	ACCURACY	FIRE RATE	MAGAZINE	ELEMENTAL
71	78.0	13.2	1484	-

- ☐ +52% RECOIL REDUCTION
- ☐ +37% FIRE RATE
- ☐ +59% DAMAGE
- ☐ +12 MAGAZINE SIZE

TMP2 COLD TORMENT

	LEVEL	BUY	SELL
	37	$115,584	$16,512
DAMAGE	ACCURACY	FIRE RATE	MAGAZINE	ELEMENTAL
140	78.0	12.0	18	-

- ☐ +50% RECOIL REDUCTION
- ☐ +54% DAMAGE
- ☐ +31% FIRE RATE
- ☐ +2 MAGAZINE SIZE

KING OF CLAP

TMP2/V2 VILE TORMENT

	LEVEL	BUY	SELL
	46	$2,633,911	$376,273

DAMAGE	ACCURACY	FIRE RATE	MAGAZINE	ELEMENTAL
137	83.1	15.5	18	🔥x3

☐ +17% DAMAGE   ☐ 4.7X WEAPON ZOOM

TMP8/V2 GRIM RAGE

	LEVEL	BUY	SELL
	48	$1,099,602	$157,086

DAMAGE	ACCURACY	FIRE RATE	MAGAZINE	ELEMENTAL
92	74.7	21.8	26	☣x2

☐ +62% FIRE RATE

BURST FIRE

TMP8/V3 VILE TORMENT

	LEVEL	BUY	SELL
	46	$817,404	$116,772

DAMAGE	ACCURACY	FIRE RATE	MAGAZINE	ELEMENTAL
172	90.4	13.0	28	-

☐ +36% FIRE RATE   ☐ +12 MAGAZINE SIZE
☐ +48% DAMAGE

LEGENDARY WEAPON
TMP2 STABILIZED VENGEANCE

	LEVEL	BUY	SELL
	48	$1,258,292	$179,756

DAMAGE	ACCURACY	FIRE RATE	MAGAZINE	ELEMENTAL
142	90.4	12.7	17	-

☐ +58% RECOIL REDUCTION
☐ +34% FIRE RATE
☐ 1.8X WEAPON ZOOM

THE VENGEANCE PACKS GOOD

DAMAGE AND IS VERY ACCURATE.

BEST OF ALL, ITS BULLETS MAY

IGNORE SHIELDS.

ASSAULT SHOTGUNS

VLADOF MAKES ROUGHLY 23,000 VARIETIES OF ASSAULT SHOTGUNS.

SG10 ASSAULT SWEEPER

	LEVEL	BUY	SELL
	10	$2,156	$308

DAMAGE	ACCURACY	FIRE RATE	MAGAZINE	ELEMENTAL
19 (x9)	23.0	1.8	5	-

☐ +31% FIRE RATE   ☐ +2 PROJECTILES FIRED

ZX330/V2 FATAL SWEEPER

	LEVEL	BUY	SELL
	19	$24,024	$3,432

DAMAGE	ACCURACY	FIRE RATE	MAGAZINE	ELEMENTAL
43 (x9)	6.7	2.2	7	-

☐ +44% FIRE RATE   ☐ +2 PROJECTILES FIRED
☐ +15% DAMAGE   ☐ 1.7X WEAPON ZOOM

CLAPTRAP DANCE OFF

VLADOF

VLADOF

BA 20/V3 FATAL SHOTGUN

	LEVEL	BUY	SELL
	28	$147,259	$21,037

DAMAGE	ACCURACY	FIRE RATE	MAGAZINE	ELEMENTAL
85 (x7)	48.7	1.7	5	-

☐ +26% FIRE RATE   ☐ 2.5X WEAPON ZOOM
☐ +52% DAMAGE

ZPR630 FATAL BRUTE

	LEVEL	BUY	SELL
	37	$880,831	$125,883

DAMAGE	ACCURACY	FIRE RATE	MAGAZINE	ELEMENTAL
149 (x7)	40.8	2.4	7	-

☐ +48% FIRE RATE   ☐ 3.0X WEAPON ZOOM
☐ +98% DAMAGE

SG10/V2 FATAL SHOTGUN

	LEVEL	BUY	SELL
	46	$1,718,514	$245,502

DAMAGE	ACCURACY	FIRE RATE	MAGAZINE	ELEMENTAL
87 (x7)	66.5	1.9	5	x1

☐ +33% FIRE RATE   ☐ 4.0X WEAPON ZOOM

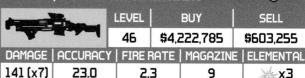

LEGENDARY WEAPON
ZX330/V3 FATAL HAMMER

	LEVEL	BUY	SELL
	46	$4,222,785	$603,255

DAMAGE	ACCURACY	FIRE RATE	MAGAZINE	ELEMENTAL
141 (x7)	23.0	2.3	9	x3

☐ +46% FIRE RATE
☐ 4.5X WEAPON ZOOM

DROP THE HAMMER!

THE HAMMER INFLICTS HIGH DAMAGE, HAS AN EXTENDED MAGAZINE AND SUPERIOR EXPLOSIVE DAMAGE. FIRES IN A SPECIAL PATTERN.

BA 20 GRIEVOUS SWEEPER

	LEVEL	BUY	SELL
	48	$1,027,747	$146,821

DAMAGE	ACCURACY	FIRE RATE	MAGAZINE	ELEMENTAL
145 (x9)	6.7	1.4	5	-

☐ +10% FIRE RATE   ☐ +2 PROJECTILES FIRED
☐ +42% DAMAGE

ZPR630/V2 FATAL SHOTGUN

	LEVEL	BUY	SELL
	48	$3,637,459	$519,637

DAMAGE	ACCURACY	FIRE RATE	MAGAZINE	ELEMENTAL
151 (x7)	48.7	2.5	7	-

☐ +50% FIRE RATE   ☐ 1.7X WEAPON ZOOM
☐ +47% DAMAGE

ROCKET LAUNCHERS

VLADOF MAKES ROUGHLY 44,100 VARIETIES OF ROCKET LAUNCHERS.

RPG10 ROCKET LAUNCHER

LEVEL	BUY	SELL
9	$2,793	$399

DAMAGE	ACCURACY	FIRE RATE	MAGAZINE	ELEMENTAL
139	89.0	1.0	3	-

☐ +31% FIRE RATE   ☐ 1.9X WEAPON ZOOM

SPC21/V2 MASSIVE ROCKET LAUNCHER

LEVEL	BUY	SELL
19	$21,322	$3,046

DAMAGE	ACCURACY	FIRE RATE	MAGAZINE	ELEMENTAL
341	97.3	1.2	2	-

☐ +44% FIRE RATE   ☐ 2.7X WEAPON ZOOM

RWL520/V3 COLOSSAL ROCKET LAUNCHER

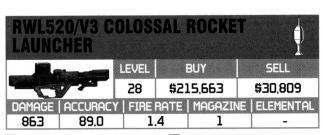

LEVEL	BUY	SELL
28	$215,663	$30,809

DAMAGE	ACCURACY	FIRE RATE	MAGAZINE	ELEMENTAL
863	89.0	1.4	1	-

☐ +51% FIRE RATE   ☐ 3.3X WEAPON ZOOM

RPG760 COLOSSAL ROCKET LAUNCHER

LEVEL	BUY	SELL
37	$573,545	$81,935

DAMAGE	ACCURACY	FIRE RATE	MAGAZINE	ELEMENTAL
701	72.3	3.0	3	⚡x4

☐ +77% FIRE RATE   ☐ 4.3X WEAPON ZOOM

SPC17/V2 COLOSSAL ROCKET LAUNCHER

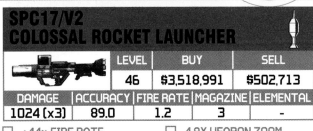

LEVEL	BUY	SELL
46	$3,518,991	$502,713

DAMAGE	ACCURACY	FIRE RATE	MAGAZINE	ELEMENTAL
1024 (x3)	89.0	1.2	3	-

☐ +44% FIRE RATE   ☐ 4.9X WEAPON ZOOM

LEGENDARY WEAPON
RWL20/V3 COLOSSAL MONGOL

LEVEL	BUY	SELL
46	$3,020,108	$431,444

DAMAGE	ACCURACY	FIRE RATE	MAGAZINE	ELEMENTAL
1076	97.3	1.4	9	-

☐ +51% FIRE RATE
☐ 1.9X WEAPON ZOOM

BEWARE THE HORDE!

THE MONGOL SPAWNS A HORDE OF ADDITIONAL ROCKETS. MOST EFFECTIVE AT LONG RANGE.

RPG51 SPREAD ROCKET LAUNCHER

LEVEL	BUY	SELL
48	$1,304,450	$186,350

DAMAGE	ACCURACY	FIRE RATE	MAGAZINE	ELEMENTAL
747	89.0	5.0	5	-

☐ +87% FIRE RATE   ☐ 2.7X WEAPON ZOOM
☐ +500% BURST FIRE COUNT

SPC720/V2 COLOSSAL ROCKET LAUNCHER

LEVEL	BUY	SELL
48	$3,637,459	$519,637

DAMAGE	ACCURACY	FIRE RATE	MAGAZINE	ELEMENTAL
829	89.0	1.2	3	🔥x4

☐ +44% FIRE RATE   ☐ 3.3X WEAPON ZOOM

CLAPTRAP DANCE OFF

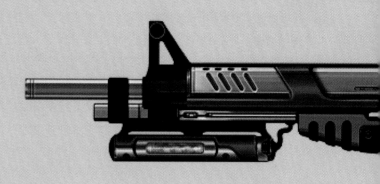

S&S MUNITIONS' MODEL LINES

LEVEL	LINE
1 to 12	Old
13 to 21	Revised
22 to 30	Upgraded
31 to 39	Enhanced
40 to 48	Faultless
50	Perfect

RELOAD: (VERB)
1. SOMETHING YOU DO AFTER YOUR TARGET IS DEAD.

REPEATER PISTOLS

S&S Munitions makes roughly 47,500 varieties of repeater pistols.

LEGENDARY WEAPON
BLR4 WICKED GEMINI

LEVEL	BUY	SELL
4	$2,016	$288

DAMAGE	ACCURACY	FIRE RATE	MAGAZINE	ELEMENTAL
14 (x2)	80.0	4.5	32	-

- [ ] +20 MAGAZINE SIZE
- [ ] -2% DAMAGE
- [ ] 2.6X WEAPON ZOOM

DOUBLE WHAMMY

THE *GEMINI* FIRES A SPLIT SHOT BURST AND IS EQUIPPED WITH AN EXTENDED MAGAZINE.

RF5.2 WICKED REPEATER

LEVEL	BUY	SELL
13	$5,425	$775

DAMAGE	ACCURACY	FIRE RATE	MAGAZINE	ELEMENTAL
38	83.3	2.8	25	-

- [ ] +13 MAGAZINE SIZE
- [ ] +23% DAMAGE
- [ ] 3.1X WEAPON ZOOM

TK4.3 WICKED LACERATOR

LEVEL	BUY	SELL
22	$48,748	$6,964

DAMAGE	ACCURACY	FIRE RATE	MAGAZINE	ELEMENTAL
62	78.7	4.6	24	-

- [ ] +12 MAGAZINE SIZE
- [ ] +200% MELEE DAMAGE
- [ ] +20% DAMAGE
- [ ] 4.1X WEAPON ZOOM

KING OF CLAP

S&S MUNITIONS

HAVING THE LARGEST CLIP SIZES AROUND IS JUST ONE MORE EXAMPLE OF HOW S&S MUNITIONS MERGES SMART DESIGN AND HIGH TECHNOLOGY

the S&S MUNITIONS STORY: the brothers who first founded s&s munitions did so with the goal to not just make a weapon, but to change an industry. As avid outdoorsmen with time in the military, they knew the power of your weapon only mattered when it was loaded. Tired of seeing their clips run dry at the most inopportune times, they set out to develop the highest capacity guns on the market. s&s munitions is now the standard-bearer for large capacity, easy-to-change magazines. today, our commitment to functional technological advancements doesn't end there. s&s munitions also makes some of the most powerful tech weapons on the market. If power and capacity are your concerns, then say yes to s&s.

CLAPTRAP
DANCE OFF

S&S
MUNiTiONS

HRD5 WICKED REPEATER

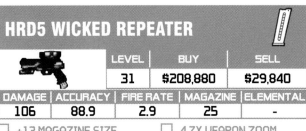

	LEVEL	BUY	SELL
	31	$208,880	$29,840

DAMAGE	ACCURACY	FIRE RATE	MAGAZINE	ELEMENTAL
106	88.9	2.9	25	-

- ☐ +13 MAGAZINE SIZE
- ☐ +43% DAMAGE
- ☐ 4.7X WEAPON ZOOM

BLR4 CAUSTIC REPEATER

	LEVEL	BUY	SELL
	40	$185,171	$26,453

DAMAGE	ACCURACY	FIRE RATE	MAGAZINE	ELEMENTAL
62	80.0	3.3	22	☣x1

- ☐ +10 MAGAZINE SIZE
- ☐ 2.6X WEAPON ZOOM

RF5.3 WICKED REPEATER

	LEVEL	BUY	SELL
	40	$852,208	$121,744

DAMAGE	ACCURACY	FIRE RATE	MAGAZINE	ELEMENTAL
109	92.8	3.8	27	✳x2

- ☐ +15 MAGAZINE SIZE
- ☐ +10% DAMAGE
- ☐ 1.8X WEAPON ZOOM

TK4 DOUBLE REPEATER

	LEVEL	BUY	SELL
	48	$667,772	$95,396

DAMAGE	ACCURACY	FIRE RATE	MAGAZINE	ELEMENTAL
85 (x2)	67.5	4.3	25	-

- ☐ +13 MAGAZINE SIZE
- ☐ 2.6X WEAPON ZOOM

LEGENDARY WEAPON
HRD5.2 WICKED GEMINI

	LEVEL	BUY	SELL
	48	$2,289,308	$327,044

DAMAGE	ACCURACY	FIRE RATE	MAGAZINE	ELEMENTAL
162 (x2)	83.3	2.8	36	-

- ☐ +24 MAGAZINE SIZE
- ☐ +32% DAMAGE
- ☐ 3.1X WEAPON ZOOM

THE *GEMINI* FIRES A SPLIT SHOT BURST AND IS EQUIPPED WITH AN EXTENDED MAGAZINE.

MACHINE PISTOLS

S&S Munitions makes roughly 10,800 varieties of machine pistols.

TMP8.3 VILE MACHINE PISTOL

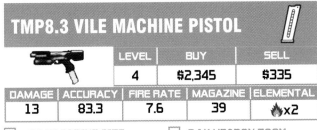

LEVEL	BUY	SELL
4	$2,345	$335

DAMAGE	ACCURACY	FIRE RATE	MAGAZINE	ELEMENTAL
13	83.3	7.6	39	🔥x2

☐ +23 MAGAZINE SIZE ☐ 3.1X WEAPON ZOOM

TMP8.2 VILE TORMENT

LEVEL	BUY	SELL
22	$42,161	$6,023

DAMAGE	ACCURACY	FIRE RATE	MAGAZINE	ELEMENTAL
71	88.9	8.3	39	-

☐ +23 MAGAZINE SIZE ☐ +37% DAMAGE
☐ +100% MELEE DAMAGE ☐ 4.7X WEAPON ZOOM

TMP8.3 COLD TORMENT

LEVEL	BUY	SELL
31	$84,098	$12,014

DAMAGE	ACCURACY	FIRE RATE	MAGAZINE	ELEMENTAL
149	87.2	9.0	42	-

☐ +26 MAGAZINE SIZE ☐ +30% RECOIL REDUCTION
☐ +100% DAMAGE

LEGENDARY WEAPON
TMP88.2 VILE THANATOS

LEVEL	BUY	SELL
40	$823,270	$117,610

DAMAGE	ACCURACY	FIRE RATE	MAGAZINE	ELEMENTAL
112 (x2)	87.3	9.3	74	-

☐ +58 MAGAZINE SIZE ☐ 1.8X WEAPON ZOOM
☐ +12% DAMAGE

LEGENDARY WEAPON
TMP88 VILE THANATOS

LEVEL	BUY	SELL
13	$10,976	$1,568

DAMAGE	ACCURACY	FIRE RATE	MAGAZINE	ELEMENTAL
41	78.7	11.3	64	-

☐ +48 MAGAZINE SIZE ☐ 3.1X WEAPON ZOOM
☐ +34% DAMAGE

BIG TONY SAYS "HI"

THE *THANATOS* IS EQUIPPED WITH AN EXTENDED MAGAZINE AND A FAST RELOAD TIME.

TMP8 GRIM MACHINE PISTOL

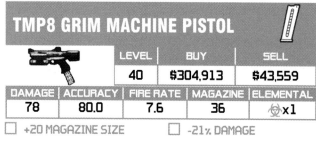

	LEVEL	BUY	SELL
	40	$304,913	$43,559

DAMAGE	ACCURACY	FIRE RATE	MAGAZINE	ELEMENTAL
78	80.0	7.6	36	☣x1

☐ +20 MAGAZINE SIZE   ☐ -21% DAMAGE

TMP8.2 VILE RAGE

	LEVEL	BUY	SELL
	48	$1,610,994	$230,142

DAMAGE	ACCURACY	FIRE RATE	MAGAZINE	ELEMENTAL
105	83.3	19.7	36	🗯x1

☐ +300% BURST FIRE COUNT   ☐ +3.1X WEAPON ZOOM

Burst fire

LEGENDARY WEAPON
TMP88.3 VILE THANATOS

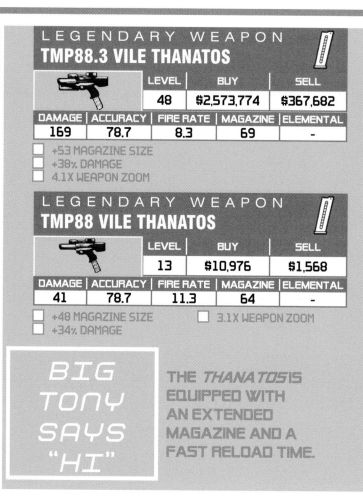

	LEVEL	BUY	SELL
	48	$2,573,774	$367,682

DAMAGE	ACCURACY	FIRE RATE	MAGAZINE	ELEMENTAL
169	78.7	8.3	69	-

☐ +53 MAGAZINE SIZE
☐ +38% DAMAGE
☐ 4.1X WEAPON ZOOM

LEGENDARY WEAPON
TMP88 VILE THANATOS

	LEVEL	BUY	SELL
	13	$10,976	$1,568

DAMAGE	ACCURACY	FIRE RATE	MAGAZINE	ELEMENTAL
41	78.7	11.3	64	-

☐ +48 MAGAZINE SIZE   ☐ 3.1X WEAPON ZOOM
☐ +34% DAMAGE

BIG TONY SAYS "HI"

THE *THANATOS* IS EQUIPPED WITH AN EXTENDED MAGAZINE AND A FAST RELOAD TIME.

ASSAULT SHOTGUNS

S&S Munitions makes roughly 14,400 varieties of assault shotguns.

SG43.3 FATAL SHOTGUN

	LEVEL	BUY	SELL
	4	$3,794	$542

DAMAGE	ACCURACY	FIRE RATE	MAGAZINE	ELEMENTAL
17 (x7)	55.1	1.5	10	-

☐ +5 MAGAZINE SIZE   ☐ 2.5X WEAPON ZOOM
☐ +41% DAMAGE

SPR330 FATAL DEATH

	LEVEL	BUY	SELL
	13	$14,105	$2,015

DAMAGE	ACCURACY	FIRE RATE	MAGAZINE	ELEMENTAL
39 (x7)	74.6	1.0	9	-

☐ +4 MAGAZINE SIZE   ☐ 3.0X WEAPON ZOOM
☐ +50% DAMAGE

KING OF CLAP

ZX530.2 FATAL SHOTGUN

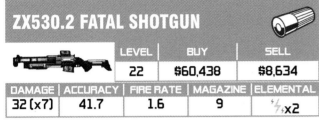

	LEVEL	BUY	SELL
	22	$60,438	$8,634

DAMAGE	ACCURACY	FIRE RATE	MAGAZINE	ELEMENTAL
32 (x7)	41.7	1.6	9	⚡⚡x2

☐ +4 MAGAZINE SIZE   ☐ 4.0X WEAPON ZOOM

SG330.2 FATAL SHOTGUN

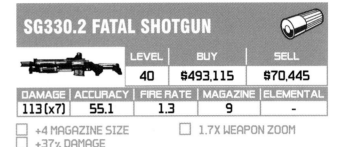

	LEVEL	BUY	SELL
	40	$493,115	$70,445

DAMAGE	ACCURACY	FIRE RATE	MAGAZINE	ELEMENTAL
113 (x7)	55.1	1.3	9	-

☐ +4 MAGAZINE SIZE   ☐ 1.7X WEAPON ZOOM
☐ +37% DAMAGE

BA43 LETHAL SHOTGUN

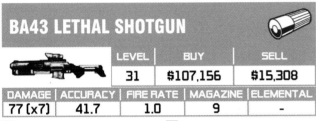

	LEVEL	BUY	SELL
	31	$107,156	$15,308

DAMAGE	ACCURACY	FIRE RATE	MAGAZINE	ELEMENTAL
77 (x7)	41.7	1.0	9	-

☐ +4 MAGAZINE SIZE   ☐ +25% DAMAGE

SPR530.3 FATAL DEATH

	LEVEL	BUY	SELL
	48	$3,908,009	$558,287

DAMAGE	ACCURACY	FIRE RATE	MAGAZINE	ELEMENTAL
151 (x7)	74.6	1.0	10	-

☐ +5 MAGAZINE SIZE   ☐ 2.5X WEAPON ZOOM
☐ +47% DAMAGE

LEGENDARY WEAPON
ZPR43 FATAL CRUX

	LEVEL	BUY	SELL
	40	$716,198	$102,314

DAMAGE	ACCURACY	FIRE RATE	MAGAZINE	ELEMENTAL
135 (x7)	83.3	1.9	16	💥

☐ +11 MAGAZINE SIZE   ☐ +62% DAMAGE

THE *CRUX* IS EQUIPPED WITH AN EXTENDED MAGAZINE AND FIRES A POWERFUL EXPLOSIVE ATTACK IN A SPECIAL PATTERN.

CROSS THEIR HEART, HOPE THEY DIE

CLAPTRAP DANCE OFF

ZX630 FATAL SHOTGUN

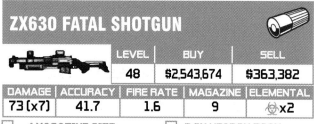

	LEVEL	BUY	SELL
	48	$2,543,674	$363,382

DAMAGE	ACCURACY	FIRE RATE	MAGAZINE	ELEMENTAL
73 (x7)	41.7	1.6	9	☣x2

☐ +4 MAGAZINE SIZE ☐ 3.0X WEAPON ZOOM

SEMI-AUTO SNIPER RIFLES

S&S Munitions makes roughly 6,700 varieties of repeater pistols.

LB570 FEARSOME SNIPER

	LEVEL	BUY	SELL
	13	$15,190	$2,170

DAMAGE	ACCURACY	FIRE RATE	MAGAZINE	ELEMENTAL
167	96.2	1.4	9	-

☐ +4 MAGAZINE SIZE ☐ 2.7X WEAPON ZOOM
☐ +150% CRITICAL HIT DAMAGE

PPZ7 HARD SNIPER

	LEVEL	BUY	SELL
	22	$20,195	$2,885

DAMAGE	ACCURACY	FIRE RATE	MAGAZINE	ELEMENTAL
227	95.0	2.4	9	-

☐ +4 MAGAZINE SIZE ☐ 1.0X WEAPON ZOOM
☐ +150% CRITICAL HIT DAMAGE

LB370.3 FEARSOME SNIPER

	LEVEL	BUY	SELL
	31	$161,119	$23,017

DAMAGE	ACCURACY	FIRE RATE	MAGAZINE	ELEMENTAL
412	95.0	1.4	10	-

☐ +5 MAGAZINE SIZE ☐ 1.5X WEAPON ZOOM
☐ +150% CRITICAL HIT DAMAGE

PPZ470 FEARSOME WRATH

	LEVEL	BUY	SELL
	40	$855,820	$122,260

DAMAGE	ACCURACY	FIRE RATE	MAGAZINE	ELEMENTAL
371	93.6	2.4	9	☣x4

☐ +4 MAGAZINE SIZE ☐ 1.8X WEAPON ZOOM

KING OF CLAP

LB570.2 FEARSOME WRATH

	LEVEL	BUY	SELL
	40	$1,086,239	$155,177

DAMAGE	ACCURACY	FIRE RATE	MAGAZINE	ELEMENTAL
346	96.7	1.4	9	x3

- ☐ +4 MAGAZINE SIZE
- ☐ -2% DAMAGE
- ☐ 2.4X WEAPON ZOOM

LB270.3 FEARSOME SNIPER

	LEVEL	BUY	SELL
	48	$2,490,313	$355,759

DAMAGE	ACCURACY	FIRE RATE	MAGAZINE	ELEMENTAL
643	98.1	1.4	10	-

- ☐ +5 MAGAZINE SIZE
- ☐ +150% CRITICAL HIT DAMAGE
- ☐ 1.0X WEAPON ZOOM

LEGENDARY WEAPON
PPZ470.3 FEARSOME ORION

	LEVEL	BUY	SELL
	4	$10,780	$1,540

DAMAGE	ACCURACY	FIRE RATE	MAGAZINE	ELEMENTAL
75	96.7	2.4	16	x3

- ☐ 2.4X WEAPON ZOOM

LEGENDARY WEAPON
PPZ7 FEARSOME ORION

	LEVEL	BUY	SELL
	48	$6,574,428	$939,204

DAMAGE	ACCURACY	FIRE RATE	MAGAZINE	ELEMENTAL
708	96.2	2.4	15	x4

- ☐ 2.7X WEAPON ZOOM

A HUNTER LIVES AMONG THE STARS...

THE *ORION* IS EQUIPPED WITH AN EXTENDED MAGAZINE AND FIRES A SHOCK ATTACK. ITS RICOCHET SPAWNS ADDITIONAL SHOCK PROJECTILES DEPENDENT ON TECH LEVEL.

CLAPTRAP DANCE OFF

Isn't it time you take your weapons to the next level?
Sure, old-fashioned slug throwers have served you well in the past, but
so did bologna sandwiches. You've grown. Your tastes have changed.
They've refined. It's time you had a gun that evolved with you and
didn't feel like a family heirloom. Maliwan believes in honoring the
past by embracing the future. Every Maliwan weapon is designed by
the skilled technicians in our bleeding-edge laboratories to pack as
much elemental punch as possible. Our staff of artisans crafts each
weapon to look as good as it performs. Maliwan offers a full line of
pistols, shotguns, rifles, and rocket launchers to fit every style.

If it's not elemental, it's not a Maliwan.

REPEATER PISTOLS
Maliwan makes roughly 32,400 varieties of repeater pistols.

BLR C WICKED REPEATER

LEVEL	BUY	SELL
7	$2,821	$403

DAMAGE	ACCURACY	FIRE RATE	MAGAZINE	ELEMENTAL
18	82.9	3.7	12	☣ x3

■ 4.1X WEAPON ZOOM

VERY HIGH ELEMENTAL EFFECT CHANCE

RF4 WICKED REPEATER

LEVEL	BUY	SELL
15	$12,950	$1,850

DAMAGE	ACCURACY	FIRE RATE	MAGAZINE	ELEMENTAL
36	88.9	2.6	16	⚡ x3

■ 4.7X WEAPON ZOOM

HIGH ELEMENTAL EFFECT CHANCE

KING
OF CLAP

TECHNOLOGY WILL SET YOU FREE.

MALIWAN

WHERE FORM MEETS FUNCTION

MALIWAN'S MODEL LINES	
LEVEL	LINE
1 to 12	Obsolete
13 to 21	Standard
22 to 30	Sterling
31 to 39	Prototype
40 to 48	Paradigm
50	Pure

CLAPTRAP
DANCE OFF

TK5 B WICKED REPEATER

	LEVEL	BUY	SELL
	25	$69,083	$9,869

DAMAGE	ACCURACY	FIRE RATE	MAGAZINE	ELEMENTAL
58	88.2	5.5	18	🔥x3

☐ -1% DAMAGE

HIGHER ELEMENTAL EFFECT CHANCE

BLR4 CAUSTIC REPEATER

	LEVEL	BUY	SELL
	43	$289,030	$41,290

DAMAGE	ACCURACY	FIRE RATE	MAGAZINE	ELEMENTAL
68	80.0	3.6	16	☣x2

☐ 2.6X WEAPON ZOOM

HIGH ELEMENTAL EFFECT CHANCE

RF BLAST REPEATER

	LEVEL	BUY	SELL
	43	$238,868	$34,124

DAMAGE	ACCURACY	FIRE RATE	MAGAZINE	ELEMENTAL
83	83.3	2.8	12	💥x2

☐ 1.8X WEAPON ZOOM

HIGHER ELEMENTAL EFFECT CHANCE

TK C WICKED REPEATER

	LEVEL	BUY	SELL
	48	$1,614,256	$230,608

DAMAGE	ACCURACY	FIRE RATE	MAGAZINE	ELEMENTAL
118	82.9	4.0	12	⚡x3

☐ 4.1X WEAPON ZOOM

VERY HIGH ELEMENTAL EFFECT CHANCE

MALIWAN

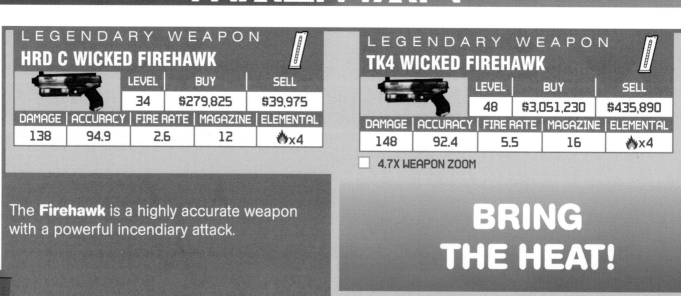

LEGENDARY WEAPON
HRD C WICKED FIREHAWK

	LEVEL	BUY	SELL
	34	$279,825	$39,975

DAMAGE	ACCURACY	FIRE RATE	MAGAZINE	ELEMENTAL
138	94.9	2.6	12	🔥x4

LEGENDARY WEAPON
TK4 WICKED FIREHAWK

	LEVEL	BUY	SELL
	48	$3,051,230	$435,890

DAMAGE	ACCURACY	FIRE RATE	MAGAZINE	ELEMENTAL
148	92.4	5.5	16	🔥x4

☐ 4.7X WEAPON ZOOM

The **Firehawk** is a highly accurate weapon with a powerful incendiary attack.

BRING THE HEAT!

REVOLVER PISTOLS
Maliwan makes roughly 45,000 varieties of revolver pistols.

RV11 B PRIMAL REVOLVER

	LEVEL	BUY	SELL
	-	$532	$76

DAMAGE	ACCURACY	FIRE RATE	MAGAZINE	ELEMENTAL
13	92.5	1.3	6	☣x2

☐ 2.3X WEAPON ZOOM

HIGHER ELEMENTAL EFFECT CHANCE

DL30 C SAVAGE REVOLVER

	LEVEL	BUY	SELL
	15	$11,067	$1,581

DAMAGE	ACCURACY	FIRE RATE	MAGAZINE	ELEMENTAL
99	91.5	1.0	3	⚡x4

☐ 2.8X WEAPON ZOOM

VERY HIGH ELEMENTAL EFFECT CHANCE

MAL200 SAVAGE LAW

	LEVEL	BUY	SELL
	25	$45,465	$6,495

DAMAGE	ACCURACY	FIRE RATE	MAGAZINE	ELEMENTAL
124	94.4	1.9	6	💥x4

☐ -21% DAMAGE   ☐ 3.7X WEAPON ZOOM

HIGH ELEMENTAL EFFECT CHANCE

LEGENDARY WEAPON
KLR300 B PESTILENT DEFILER

	LEVEL	BUY	SELL
	34	$1,003,135	$143,305

DAMAGE	ACCURACY	FIRE RATE	MAGAZINE	ELEMENTAL
598	94.1	1.0	2	☣x4

☐ 4.2X WEAPON ZOOM

GIVE SICK

The **Defiler** inflicts very high damage along with a powerful corrosive attack.

MALIWAN

AX12 C SAVAGE LAW

	LEVEL	BUY	SELL
	43	$940,555	$134,365

DAMAGE	ACCURACY	FIRE RATE	MAGAZINE	ELEMENTAL
287	96.7	1.9	3	x3

☐ +33% FIRE RATE

VERY HIGH ELEMENTAL EFFECT CHANCE

LEGENDARY WEAPON
MAL300 C PESTILENT DEFILER

	LEVEL	BUY	SELL
	48	$2,868,404	$409,772

DAMAGE	ACCURACY	FIRE RATE	MAGAZINE	ELEMENTAL
385	95.2	1.9	6	⊗x4

GIVE SICK

The **Defiler** inflicts very high damage along witha powerful corrosive attack.

RV1 CAUSTIC REVOLVER

	LEVEL	BUY	SELL
	43	$362,285	$51,755

DAMAGE	ACCURACY	FIRE RATE	MAGAZINE	ELEMENTAL
190	91.7	1.3	6	⊗x2

☐ 1.6X WEAPON ZOOM

HIGH ELEMENTAL EFFECT CHANCE

DL230 B SAVAGE REVOLVER

	LEVEL	BUY	SELL
	48	$1,519,777	$217,111

DAMAGE	ACCURACY	FIRE RATE	MAGAZINE	ELEMENTAL
333	90.4	1.0	3	⚡,x3

☐ +2% DAMAGE

HIGHER ELEMENTAL EFFECT CHANCE

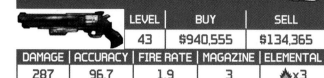

MALIWAN

ASSAULT SHOTGUNS

Maliwan makes roughly 14,400 varieties of assault shotguns.

BA 10 B FATAL SHOTGUN

	LEVEL	BUY	SELL
	6	$3,927	$561

DAMAGE	ACCURACY	FIRE RATE	MAGAZINE	ELEMENTAL
16 (x7)	32.7	1.0	5	⚡,x2

☐ 4.0X WEAPON ZOOM

HIGHER ELEMENTAL EFFECT CHANCE

BA 330 FATAL SHOTGUN

	LEVEL	BUY	SELL
	43	$1,049,601	$149,943

DAMAGE	ACCURACY	FIRE RATE	MAGAZINE	ELEMENTAL
95 (x7)	25.3	1.0	7	🍃x2

☐ +6% DAMAGE   ☐ 3.0X WEAPON ZOOM

HIGH ELEMENTAL EFFECT CHANCE

ZPR330 C FATAL DEATH

	LEVEL	BUY	SELL
	15	$45,934	$6,562

DAMAGE	ACCURACY	FIRE RATE	MAGAZINE	ELEMENTAL
32 (x7)	66.7	1.9	7	⚡,x4

☐ +9% DAMAGE   ☐ 4.5X WEAPON ZOOM

VERY HIGH ELEMENTAL EFFECT CHANCE

SG20 LETHAL SHOTGUN

	LEVEL	BUY	SELL
	25	$43,981	$6,283

DAMAGE	ACCURACY	FIRE RATE	MAGAZINE	ELEMENTAL
46 (x7)	55.1	1.3	5	⊗x3

☐ -6% DAMAGE

HIGH ELEMENTAL EFFECT CHANCE

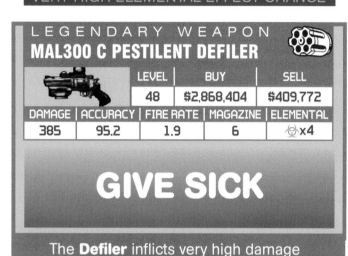
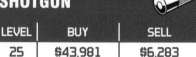

KING OF CLAP

LEGENDARY WEAPON
SPR630 B FATAL PLAGUE

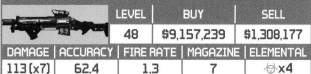

	LEVEL	BUY	SELL
	34	$573,216	$81,888

DAMAGE	ACCURACY	FIRE RATE	MAGAZINE	ELEMENTAL
82 (x7)	75.8	1.07	6	☣x4

The **Plague** packs a powerful corrosive attack with a much higher chance than normal shotguns.

LEGENDARY WEAPON
SG630 C PESTILENT PLAGUE

	LEVEL	BUY	SELL
	48	$9,157,239	$1,308,177

DAMAGE	ACCURACY	FIRE RATE	MAGAZINE	ELEMENTAL
113 (x7)	62.4	1.3	7	☣x4

☐ 4.5X WEAPON ZOOM

BRING
OUT YOUR
DEAD

ZX10 C FATAL SHOTGUN

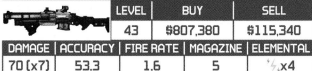

	LEVEL	BUY	SELL
	43	$807,380	$115,340

DAMAGE	ACCURACY	FIRE RATE	MAGAZINE	ELEMENTAL
70 (x7)	53.3	1.6	5	⚡x4

☐ -23% DAMAGE

VERY HIGH ELEMENTAL EFFECT CHANCE

ZPR20 B FATAL SHOTGUN

	LEVEL	BUY	SELL
	48	$3,306,779	$472,397

DAMAGE	ACCURACY	FIRE RATE	MAGAZINE	ELEMENTAL
108 (x7)	63.8	1.9	5	☣x3

☐ 4.0X WEAPON ZOOM

HIGHER ELEMENTAL EFFECT CHANCE

CLAPTRAP DANCE OFF

MALIWAN

PATROL SMG

Maliwan makes roughly 81,000 varieties of patrol sub-machine guns.

TD230 C MALEVOLENT SMG

LEVEL	BUY	SELL
7	$3,451	$493

DAMAGE	ACCURACY	FIRE RATE	MAGAZINE	ELEMENTAL
16	82.9	8.3	36	☣x3

☐ -7% DAMAGE

VERY HIGH ELEMENTAL EFFECT CHANCE

KKA340 MALEVOLENT SMG

LEVEL	BUY	SELL
15	$15,813	$2,259

DAMAGE	ACCURACY	FIRE RATE	MAGAZINE	ELEMENTAL
30	88.9	6.9	55	⚡x3

☐ 2.9X WEAPON ZOOM

HIGH ELEMENTAL EFFECT CHANCE

TEK450 B TWISTED BRUISER

LEVEL	BUY	SELL
25	$157,010	$22,430

DAMAGE	ACCURACY	FIRE RATE	MAGAZINE	ELEMENTAL
66	85.0	10.8	69	☣x4

☐ +26% DAMAGE   ☐ 3.9X WEAPON ZOOM

HIGHER ELEMENTAL EFFECT CHANCE

RF500 C MALEVOLENT THUMPER

LEVEL	BUY	SELL
34	$1,751,505	$250,215

DAMAGE	ACCURACY	FIRE RATE	MAGAZINE	ELEMENTAL
127	89.	2.5	18	🔥x3

☐ +73% DAMAGE   ☐ 4.3X WEAPON ZOOM

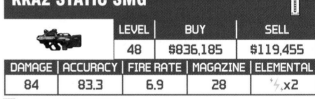

MALIWAN

HX 12 MALEVOLENT SMG

LEVEL	BUY	SELL
43	$1,058,631	$151,233

DAMAGE	ACCURACY	FIRE RATE	MAGAZINE	ELEMENTAL
101	92.8	12.5	28	☣x3

☐ +6% DAMAGE

HIGH ELEMENTAL EFFECT CHANCE

KKA2 STATIC SMG

LEVEL	BUY	SELL
48	$836,185	$119,455

DAMAGE	ACCURACY	FIRE RATE	MAGAZINE	ELEMENTAL
84	83.3	6.9	28	⚡x2

☐ 1.7X WEAPON ZOOM

VERY HIGH ELEMENTAL EFFECT CHANCE

TEK350 ERUPTING SMG

LEVEL	BUY	SELL
48	$2,020,809	$288,687

DAMAGE	ACCURACY	FIRE RATE	MAGAZINE	ELEMENTAL
90	88.9	10.8	46	✸x4

☐ 2.9X WEAPON ZOOM

HIGH ELEMENTAL EFFECT CHANCE

KING OF CLAP

LEGENDARY WEAPON
TD3 B COMBUSTION HELLFIRE

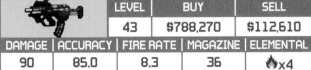

	LEVEL	BUY	SELL
	43	$788,270	$112,610

DAMAGE	ACCURACY	FIRE RATE	MAGAZINE	ELEMENTAL
90	85.0	8.3	36	🔥x4

WE DON'T NEED NO WATER...

The **HellFire** delivers a tremendously powerful incendiary attack.

SNIPER RIFLES
Maliwan makes roughly 16,800 varieties of sniper rifles.

GGN CAUSTIC SNIPER

	LEVEL	BUY	SELL
	7	$1,897	$271

DAMAGE	ACCURACY	FIRE RATE	MAGAZINE	ELEMENTAL
51	96.7	0.6	6	☣x2

☐ 1.0X WEAPON ZOOM

HIGH ELEMENTAL EFFECT CHANCE

VRR29 B ERUPTING SNIPER

	LEVEL	BUY	SELL
	15	$10,794	$1,542

DAMAGE	ACCURACY	FIRE RATE	MAGAZINE	ELEMENTAL
128	96.2	0.8	3	⚡x4

☐ 150% CRITICAL HIT DAMAGE   ☐ 1.5X WEAPON ZOOM

HIGHER ELEMENTAL EFFECT CHANCE

LEGENDARY WEAPON
DVL350 C FEARSOME VOLCANO

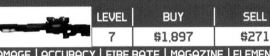

	LEVEL	BUY	SELL
	25	$175,364	$25,052

DAMAGE	ACCURACY	FIRE RATE	MAGAZINE	ELEMENTAL
358	98.1	0.7	6	🔥x4

☐ 1.8X WEAPON ZOOM

PELE DEMANDS A SACRIFICE!

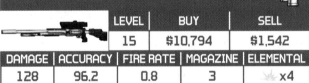
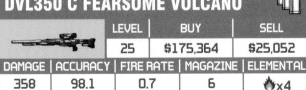

The **Volcano** offers a high firing rate and a powerful incendiary attack.

MALIWAN

GGN40 FEARSOME SNIPER

	LEVEL	BUY	SELL
	34	$265,377	$37,911

DAMAGE	ACCURACY	FIRE RATE	MAGAZINE	ELEMENTAL
317	97.4	0.6	6	⚡x3

☐ 2.4X WEAPON ZOOM

HIGH ELEMENTAL EFFECT CHANCE

VRR590 B COMBUSTION SNIPER

	LEVEL	BUY	SELL
	43	$3,099,894	$442,842

DAMAGE	ACCURACY	FIRE RATE	MAGAZINE	ELEMENTAL
393	98.6	0.8	3	🔥x4

☐ 2.7X WEAPON ZOOM

HIGHER ELEMENTAL EFFECT CHANCE

DVL5 C FEARSOME SNIPER

	LEVEL	BUY	SELL
	43	$1,164,492	$166,356

DAMAGE	ACCURACY	FIRE RATE	MAGAZINE	ELEMENTAL
426	97.3	0.6	6	x3

☐ +150% CRITICAL HIT DAMAGE   ☐ 1.0X WEAPON ZOOM

VERY HIGH ELEMENTAL EFFECT CHANCE

VRR490 B PESTILENT SNIPER

	LEVEL	BUY	SELL
	48	$2,445,177	$349,311

DAMAGE	ACCURACY	FIRE RATE	MAGAZINE	ELEMENTAL
432	97.9	0.8	3	☣x4

☐ 1.8X WEAPON ZOOM

HIGHER ELEMENTAL EFFECT CHANCE

LEGENDARY WEAPON
GGN30 SOLID VOLCANO

	LEVEL	BUY	SELL
	48	$1,400,931	$200,133

DAMAGE	ACCURACY	FIRE RATE	MAGAZINE	ELEMENTAL
551	95.7	0.8	6	🔥x4

PELE DEMANDS A SACRIFICE!

The **Volcano** offers a high firing rate and a powerful incendiary attack.

ROCKET LAUNCHERS
Maliwan makes roughly 18,900 varieties of rocket launchers.

RWL16 COLOSSAL ROCKET LAUNCHER

	LEVEL	BUY	SELL
	7	$6,069	$867

DAMAGE	ACCURACY	FIRE RATE	MAGAZINE	ELEMENTAL
218	91.7	1.0	2	☣x4

☐ 4.3X WEAPON ZOOM

HIGH ELEMENTAL EFFECT CHANCE

SPC50 B COLOSSAL ROCKET LAUNCHER

	LEVEL	BUY	SELL
	25	$61,404	$8,772

DAMAGE	ACCURACY	FIRE RATE	MAGAZINE	ELEMENTAL
396	77.5	2.9	3	🔥x4

☐ +300% BURST FIRE COUNT

HIGHER ELEMENTAL EFFECT CHANCE

KING OF CLAP

RPG270
COLOSSAL ROCKET LAUNCHER

LEVEL	BUY	SELL
15	$27,181	$3,883

DAMAGE	ACCURACY	FIRE RATE	MAGAZINE	ELEMENTAL
347	91.7	0.7	1	⚡x4

☐ 4.9X WEAPON ZOOM

HIGH ELEMENTAL EFFECT CHANCE

RWL10
MASSIVE ROCKET LAUNCHER

LEVEL	BUY	SELL
34	$171,304	$24,472

DAMAGE	ACCURACY	FIRE RATE	MAGAZINE	ELEMENTAL
828	91.7	1.0	2	☣x4

☐ 1.9X WEAPON ZOOM

HIGH ELEMENTAL EFFECT CHANCE

RPG10
HELIX ROCKET LAUNCHER

LEVEL	BUY	SELL
43	$477,736	$68,248

DAMAGE	ACCURACY	FIRE RATE	MAGAZINE	ELEMENTAL
657 (x3)	91.7	0.7	3	⚡x4

☐ 1.9X WEAPON ZOOM

HIGH ELEMENTAL EFFECT CHANCE

RWL570
COLOSSAL ROCKET LAUNCHER

LEVEL	BUY	SELL
48	$7,631,029	$1,090,147

DAMAGE	ACCURACY	FIRE RATE	MAGAZINE	ELEMENTAL
1052	91.7	1.3	3	☣x4

☐ 4.9X WEAPON ZOOM

HIGH ELEMENTAL EFFECT CHANCE

RPG70 B
COLOSSAL ROCKET LAUNCHER

LEVEL	BUY	SELL
48	$1,778,791	$254,113

DAMAGE	ACCURACY	FIRE RATE	MAGAZINE	ELEMENTAL
1036	92.5	0.7	2	⚡x4

☐ 1.9X WEAPON ZOOM

LEGENDARY WEAPON
SPC260 C COLOSSAL RHINO

LEVEL	BUY	SELL
43	$2,766,841	$395,263

DAMAGE	ACCURACY	FIRE RATE	MAGAZINE	ELEMENTAL
1001	93.3	0.9	2	🔥x4

☐ 4.3X WEAPON ZOOM

THE UNSTOPPABLE FORCE

The **Rhino** launches a charging rocket that explodes continuously as it flies.

CLAPTRAP DANCE OFF

MALIWAN

"BRING THE PAIN!"

REPEATER PISTOLS

Torgue makes roughly 75,600 varieties of repeater pistols.

HRD5 WICKED REPEATER

LEVEL	BUY	SELL
10	$4,515	$645

DAMAGE	ACCURACY	FIRE RATE	MAGAZINE	ELEMENTAL
47	82.7	3.0	18	-

- ☐ +87% DAMAGE
- ☐ -12% FIRE RATE

BLR WICKED REPEATER

LEVEL	BUY	SELL
19	$16,772	$2,396

DAMAGE	ACCURACY	FIRE RATE	MAGAZINE	ELEMENTAL
65	90.2	4.1	12	-

- ☐ +46% DAMAGE
- ☐ +100% MELEE DAMAGE
- ☐ +19% FIRE RATE
- ☐ 1.8X WEAPON ZOOM

"KILL 'EM DEADER."

LEGENDARY WEAPON
RF4 CRUEL VIOLATOR

LEVEL	BUY	SELL
28	$61,761	$8,823

DAMAGE	ACCURACY	FIRE RATE	MAGAZINE	ELEMENTAL
47 (x3)	77.5	9.1	16	-

- ☐ -30% DAMAGE
- ☐ +300% BURST FIRE COUNT
- ☐ +63% FIRE RATE

YOUR MOVE, CREEP

KING OF CLAP

THE *VIOLATOR* HAS DEVASTATING POWER AND DEALS A THREE-SHOT BURST THAT FIRES THREE BULLETS PER SHOT.

TORGUE

The next time you go shopping for a new gun, ask yourself one question: Are you a man? If you answer in the affirmative, then you're ready for a Torgue. You see, we at Torgue make guns for real men. Tough guys. Badasses. The kind of guys your dad was and that you hope to be! Torgue doesn't screw around making lightweight toys and we sure as hell aren't concerned with selling you a stylish accessory like those guys in the hip-huggers over at Maliwan. No. We make them tough, and we make them heavy. It's up to you to make 'em dead. Do it with a Torgue.

GUN CATALOG

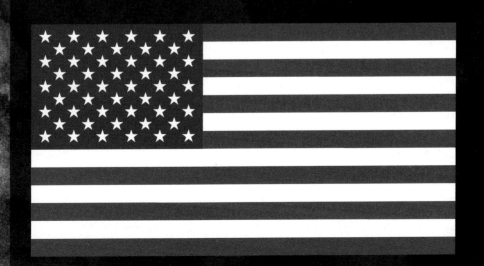

CLAPTRAP
DANCE OFF

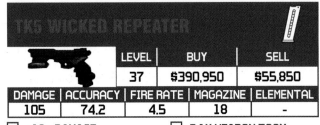

TK5 WICKED REPEATER

	LEVEL	BUY	SELL
	37	$390,950	$55,850

DAMAGE	ACCURACY	FIRE RATE	MAGAZINE	ELEMENTAL
105	74.2	4.5	18	-

- ☐ +16% DAMAGE
- ☐ +25% FIRE RATE
- ☐ 3.1X WEAPON ZOOM

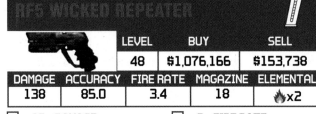

RF5 WICKED REPEATER

	LEVEL	BUY	SELL
	48	$1,076,166	$153,738

DAMAGE	ACCURACY	FIRE RATE	MAGAZINE	ELEMENTAL
138	85.0	3.4	18	🔥x2

- ☐ +13% DAMAGE
- ☐ +3% FIRE RATE

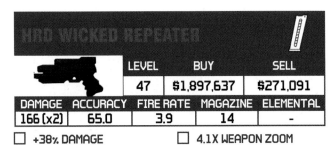

HRD WICKED REPEATER

	LEVEL	BUY	SELL
	47	$1,897,637	$271,091

DAMAGE	ACCURACY	FIRE RATE	MAGAZINE	ELEMENTAL
166 (x2)	65.0	3.9	14	-

- ☐ +38% DAMAGE
- ☐ +14% FIRE RATE
- ☐ 4.1X WEAPON ZOOM

TK WICKED LACERATOR

	LEVEL	BUY	SELL
	48	$2,203,663	$314,809

DAMAGE	ACCURACY	FIRE RATE	MAGAZINE	ELEMENTAL
184	82.7	5.3	12	-

- ☐ +50% DAMAGE
- ☐ +200% MELEE DAMAGE
- ☐ +37% FIRE RATE
- ☐ 1.8X WEAPON ZOOM

BLR STABILIZED REPEATER

	LEVEL	BUY	SELL
	48	$456,059	$65,157

DAMAGE	ACCURACY	FIRE RATE	MAGAZINE	ELEMENTAL
132	77.5	3.9	12	-

- ☐ +23% RECOIL REDUCTION
- ☐ +14% FIRE RATE
- ☐ +8% DAMAGE

COMBAT SHOTGUNS

Torgue makes roughly 77,800 varieties of combat shotguns.

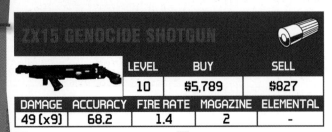

ZX15 GENOCIDE SHOTGUN

	LEVEL	BUY	SELL
	10	$5,789	$827

DAMAGE	ACCURACY	FIRE RATE	MAGAZINE	ELEMENTAL
49 (x9)	68.2	1.4	2	-

- ☐ +121% DAMAGE
- ☐ +46% FIRE RATE

BA 1 GENOCIDE MATADOR

	LEVEL	BUY	SELL
	19	$24,234	$3,462

DAMAGE	ACCURACY	FIRE RATE	MAGAZINE	ELEMENTAL
53 (x12)	26.9	1.0	6	-

- ☐ +150% MELEE DAMAGE
- ☐ +33% DAMAGE
- ☐ +28% FIRE RATE
- ☐ +3 PROJECTILES FIRED

KING
OF CLAP

ZPR1100 GENOCIDE MATADOR

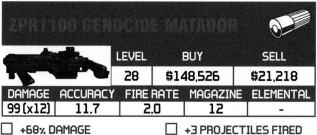

	LEVEL	BUY	SELL
	28	$148,526	$21,218

DAMAGE	ACCURACY	FIRE RATE	MAGAZINE	ELEMENTAL
99 (x12)	11.7	2.0	12	-

- ☐ +68% DAMAGE
- ☐ +63% FIRE RATE
- ☐ +3 PROJECTILES FIRED
- ☐ 2.2X WEAPON ZOOM

SPR15 GENOCIDE SHOTGUN

	LEVEL	BUY	SELL
	47	$2,491,846	$355,978

DAMAGE	ACCURACY	FIRE RATE	MAGAZINE	ELEMENTAL
217 (x9)	43.8	1.0	2	⚡x1

- ☐ +23% FIRE RATE
- ☐ 3.6X WEAPON ZOOM

SG11 STABILIZED SCATTERGUN

	LEVEL	BUY	SELL
	28	$42,966	$6,138

DAMAGE	ACCURACY	FIRE RATE	MAGAZINE	ELEMENTAL
55 (x11)	26.9	1.5	6	-

- ☐ -7% DAMAGE
- ☐ +49% FIRE RATE
- ☐ +2 PROJECTILES FIRED
- ☐ 1.5X WEAPON ZOOM

BA 1100 GENOCIDE CARNAGE

	LEVEL	BUY	SELL
	48	$2,505,132	$357,876

DAMAGE	ACCURACY	FIRE RATE	MAGAZINE	ELEMENTAL
718	51.3	0.9	12	-

- ☐ +557% DAMAGE
- ☐ +17% FIRE RATE
- ☐ +150% MELEE DAMAGE

Holy crap! It shoots rockets!

ZPR1 WAR MATADOR

	LEVEL	BUY	SELL
	48	$1,254,274	$179,182

DAMAGE	ACCURACY	FIRE RATE	MAGAZINE	ELEMENTAL
134 (x12)	26.9	1.7	6	-

- ☐ +150% MELEE DAMAGE
- ☐ +23% DAMAGE
- ☐ +57% FIRE RATE
- ☐ +3 PROJECTILES FIRED

LEGENDARY WEAPON
ZX1 FRIENDLY FIRE

	LEVEL	BUY	SELL
	47	$3,623,102	$517,586

DAMAGE	ACCURACY	FIRE RATE	MAGAZINE	ELEMENTAL
109 (x9)	68.2	1.4	6	🔥x3

- ☐ 4.0X WEAPON ZOOM

THE *FRIENDLY FIRE* SHOOTS A POWERFUL INCENDIARY ATTACK THAT FIRES IN A VERY SPECIAL PATTERN.

HAVE A NICE DAY!

CLAPTRAP DANCE OFF

TORGUE

RF 400 TWISTED THUMPER

	LEVEL	BUY	SELL
	10	$17,773	$2,539

DAMAGE	ACCURACY	FIRE RATE	MAGAZINE	ELEMENTAL
59	77.5	2.9	27	-

- ☐ +166% DAMAGE
- ☐ -184% FIRE RATE
- ☐ -1 MAGAZINE SIZE
- ☐ 3.9X WEAPON ZOOM

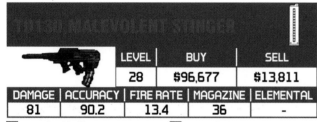

TD130 MALEVOLENT STINGER

	LEVEL	BUY	SELL
	28	$96,677	$13,811

DAMAGE	ACCURACY	FIRE RATE	MAGAZINE	ELEMENTAL
81	90.2	13.4	36	-

- ☐ +37% DAMAGE
- ☐ +38% FIRE RATE
- ☐ +47% RECOIL REDUCTION

TEK250 MALEVOLENT SMG

	LEVEL	BUY	SELL
	47	$1,700,839	$242,977

DAMAGE	ACCURACY	FIRE RATE	MAGAZINE	ELEMENTAL
109	77.5	12.2	46	✦x2

- ☐ +3% DAMAGE
- ☐ +32% FIRE RATE
- ☐ 2.4X WEAPON ZOOM

LEGENDARY WEAPON
KKA4 MALEVOLENT GASHER

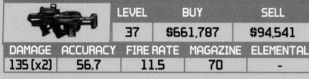

	LEVEL	BUY	SELL
	37	$661,787	$94,541

DAMAGE	ACCURACY	FIRE RATE	MAGAZINE	ELEMENTAL
135 (x2)	56.7	11.5	70	-

- ☐ 67% DAMAGE
- ☐ +300% BURST FIRE COUNT
- ☐ 28% FIRE RATE

TEAR IT UP

THE *GASHER* INFLICTS HIGH DAMAGE
AND FIRES A BURST OF ROUNDS.

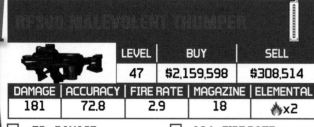

RF500 MALEVOLENT THUMPER

	LEVEL	BUY	SELL
	47	$2,159,598	$308,514

DAMAGE	ACCURACY	FIRE RATE	MAGAZINE	ELEMENTAL
181	72.8	2.9	18	🔥x2

- ☐ +70% DAMAGE
- ☐ -184% FIRE RATE

HX 42 MALEVOLENT STINGER

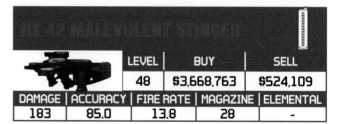

	LEVEL	BUY	SELL
	48	$3,668,763	$524,109

DAMAGE	ACCURACY	FIRE RATE	MAGAZINE	ELEMENTAL
183	85.0	13.8	28	-

- ☐ +68% DAMAGE
- ☐ +40% FIRE RATE
- ☐ +41% RECOIL REDUCTION
- ☐ 3.9X WEAPON ZOOM

KING
OF CLAP

TD530 TWISTED BRUISER

	LEVEL	BUY	SELL
	48	$9,106,062	$1,300,866

DAMAGE	ACCURACY	FIRE RATE	MAGAZINE	ELEMENTAL
144	77.5	9.7	54	☣x4

- ☐ +32% DAMAGE
- ☐ 4.3X WEAPON ZOOM

HX 52 MALEVOLENT STINGER

	LEVEL	BUY	SELL
	19	$145,411	$20,773

DAMAGE	ACCURACY	FIRE RATE	MAGAZINE	ELEMENTAL
76	82.7	15.5	28	-

- ☐ +93% DAMAGE
- ☐ +46% FIRE RATE
- ☐ +20% RECOIL REDUCTION
- ☐ 4.3X WEAPON ZOOM

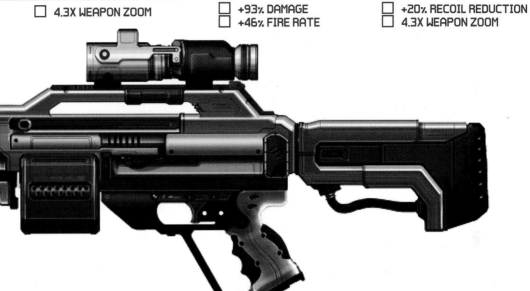

SEMI-AUTO SNIPER RIFLES

Torgue makes roughly 13,500 varieties of semi-automatic sniper rifles.

PPZ20 LIQUID SNIPER

	LEVEL	BUY	SELL
	10	$2,877	$411

DAMAGE	ACCURACY	FIRE RATE	MAGAZINE	ELEMENTAL
119	93.3	2.7	5	-

- ☐ +35% DAMAGE
- ☐ +46% FIRE RATE
- ☐ +150% CRITICAL HIT DAMAGE
- ☐ 1.5X WEAPON ZOOM

LB370 FEARSOME SNIPER

	LEVEL	BUY	SELL
	19	$27,797	$3,971

DAMAGE	ACCURACY	FIRE RATE	MAGAZINE	ELEMENTAL
255	91.8	2.2	7	-

- ☐ +63% DAMAGE
- ☐ +36% FIRE RATE
- ☐ +150% CRITICAL HIT DAMAGE
- ☐ 1.8X WEAPON ZOOM

PPZ40 FEARSOME SNIPER

	LEVEL	BUY	SELL
	28	$211,141	$30,163

DAMAGE	ACCURACY	FIRE RATE	MAGAZINE	ELEMENTAL
407	96.3	2.4	5	-

- ☐ +72% DAMAGE
- ☐ +40% FIRE RATE
- ☐ +150% CRITICAL HIT DAMAGE
- ☐ 2.4X WEAPON ZOOM

PPZ FEARSOME THUNDER

	LEVEL	BUY	SELL
	47	$2,146,816	$306,688

DAMAGE	ACCURACY	FIRE RATE	MAGAZINE	ELEMENTAL
861	97.1	2.4	5	-

- ☐ +102% DAMAGE
- ☐ +40% FIRE RATE
- ☐ +150% CRITICAL HIT DAMAGE
- ☐ 1.0X WEAPON ZOOM

CLAPTRAP DANCE OFF

TORGUE

LB570 FEARSOME COBRA

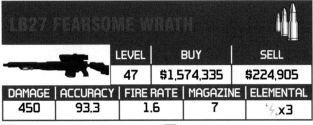

	LEVEL	BUY	SELL
	37	$1,284,752	$183,536

DAMAGE	ACCURACY	FIRE RATE	MAGAZINE	ELEMENTAL
556	94.8	0.9	7	x4

☐ +72% DAMAGE ☐ 2.7X WEAPON ZOOM

I LIKE IT!

THE *COBRA* IS A STAGGERINGLY POWERFUL EXPLOSIVE WEAPON WITH A SLOW RATE OF FIRE.

LB27 FEARSOME WRATH

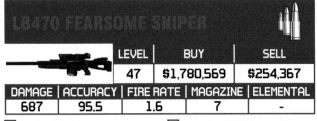

	LEVEL	BUY	SELL
	47	$1,574,335	$224,905

DAMAGE	ACCURACY	FIRE RATE	MAGAZINE	ELEMENTAL
450	93.3	1.6	7	x3

☐ +6% DAMAGE ☐ +12% FIRE RATE

PPZ30 FEARSOME WRATH

	LEVEL	BUY	SELL
	47	$1,825,663	$260,809

DAMAGE	ACCURACY	FIRE RATE	MAGAZINE	ELEMENTAL
522	91.8	2.4	5	x4

☐ +20% DAMAGE ☐ +40% FIRE RATE

LB470 FEARSOME SNIPER

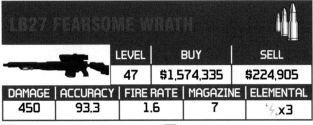

	LEVEL	BUY	SELL
	47	$1,780,569	$254,367

DAMAGE	ACCURACY	FIRE RATE	MAGAZINE	ELEMENTAL
687	95.5	1.6	7	-

☐ +57% DAMAGE ☐ +150% CRITICAL HIT
☐ +12% FIRE RATE DAMAGE
  ☐ 2.4X WEAPON ZOOM

ROCKET LAUNCHERS

Torgue makes roughly 44,100 varieties of rocket launchers.

SPC520 COLOSSAL ROCKET LAUNCHER

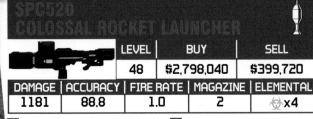

	LEVEL	BUY	SELL
	48	$2,798,040	$399,720

DAMAGE	ACCURACY	FIRE RATE	MAGAZINE	ELEMENTAL
1181	88.8	1.0	2	x4

☐ +32% DAMAGE ☐ +24% FIRE RATE

RWL10 BIG ROCKET LAUNCHER

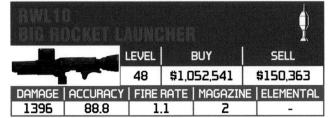

	LEVEL	BUY	SELL
	48	$1,052,541	$150,363

DAMAGE	ACCURACY	FIRE RATE	MAGAZINE	ELEMENTAL
1396	88.8	1.1	2	-

☐ +46% DAMAGE ☐ 1.9X WEAPON ZOOM
☐ +40% FIRE RATE

SPC11
COLOSSAL ROCKET LAUNCHER

LEVEL	BUY	SELL
10	$6,468	$924

DAMAGE	ACCURACY	FIRE RATE	MAGAZINE	ELEMENTAL
338	88.8	1.0	1	-

☐ +76% DAMAGE   ☐ 2.7X WEAPON ZOOM
☐ +32% FIRE RATE

RWL220
COLOSSAL ROCKET LAUNCHER

LEVEL	BUY	SELL
19	$31,990	$4,570

DAMAGE	ACCURACY	FIRE RATE	MAGAZINE	ELEMENTAL
436	72.1	3.1	3	🔥x4

☐ +27% DAMAGE   ☐ 3.3X WEAPON ZOOM

RPG10
HELIX ROCKET LAUNCHER

LEVEL	BUY	SELL
28	$51,555	$7,365

DAMAGE	ACCURACY	FIRE RATE	MAGAZINE	ELEMENTAL
485 (x3)	97.2	0.8	3	-

☐ -6% DAMAGE   ☐ 1.9X WEAPON ZOOM
☐ +14% FIRE RATE

SPC770
COLOSSAL ROCKET LAUNCHER

LEVEL	BUY	SELL
37	$1,892,716	$270,388

DAMAGE	ACCURACY	FIRE RATE	MAGAZINE	ELEMENTAL
743	97.2	5.0	6	-

☐ +6% DAMAGE   ☐ +500% BURST FIRE COUNT
☐ +87% FIRE RATE   ☐ 4.9X WEAPON ZOOM

LEGENDARY WEAPON
RPG21 COLOSSAL REDEMPTION

LEVEL	BUY	SELL
47	$2,226,560	$318,080

DAMAGE	ACCURACY	FIRE RATE	MAGAZINE	ELEMENTAL
2521	88.8	0.8	4	-

☐ +171% DAMAGE   ☐ 2.7X WEAPON ZOOM
☐ +14% FIRE RATE

MONSTER KILL!

THE *REDEMPTION* FIRES A MASSIVE ROCKET THAT MAKES A BIG BANG.

RWL10
COLOSSAL ROCKET LAUNCHER

LEVEL	BUY	SELL
47	$1,533,441	$219,063

DAMAGE	ACCURACY	FIRE RATE	MAGAZINE	ELEMENTAL
1181	88.8	1.1	3	-

☐ +27% DAMAGE   ☐ 1.9X WEAPON ZOOM
☐ +40% FIRE RATE

CLAPTRAP DANCE OFF

TORGUE

JAKOBS

REVOLVER PISTOLS

Jakobs makes roughly 54,000 varieties of revolver pistols.

KLR10

	LEVEL	BUY	SELL
	-	$931	$133

DAMAGE	ACCURACY	FIRE RATE	MAGAZINE	ELEMENTAL
50	93.6	0.7	2	-

☐ +187% DAMAGE   ☐ 3.7X WEAPON ZOOM

DL330 SAVAGE JUSTICE

	LEVEL	BUY	SELL
	31	$108,192	$15,456

DAMAGE	ACCURACY	FIRE RATE	MAGAZINE	ELEMENTAL
300	9+1.7	0.7	3	-

☐ +51% DAMAGE   ☐ 1.6X WEAPON ZOOM

AX20 ZZ SAVAGE JUSTICE

	LEVEL	BUY	SELL
	13	$38,885	$5,555

DAMAGE	ACCURACY	FIRE RATE	MAGAZINE	ELEMENTAL
120	97.0	1.3	6	-

☐ +46% DAMAGE   ☐ +64% ACCURACY
☐ +100% MELEE DAMAGE   ☐ 4.3X WEAPON ZOOM

MAL10 ZZ PRIMAL JUSTICE

	LEVEL	BUY	SELL
	40	$255,311	$36,473

DAMAGE	ACCURACY	FIRE RATE	MAGAZINE	ELEMENTAL
344	92.9	1.3	6	-

☐ +30% DAMAGE   ☐ 2.6X WEAPON ZOOM
☐ +15% ACCURACY

LEGENDARY WEAPON
RV21 XX SAVAGE UNFORGIVEN

	LEVEL	BUY	SELL
	22	$39,389	$5,627

DAMAGE	ACCURACY	FIRE RATE	MAGAZINE	ELEMENTAL
95 (x7)	87.0	0.7	6	-

☐ -31% DAMAGE   ☐ +200% CRITICAL HIT DAMAGE

IT'S A HELLUVA THING...

THE *UNFORGIVEN* OFFERS HIGH DAMAGE, HIGH ACCURACY, AND A LARGE CRITICAL HIT BONUS, BUT IT'S HEAVY, IS SLOW TO FIRE, AND KICKS LIKE A MULE!

FAMILY OWNED
AND OPERATED
FOR

OVER 300 YEARS

"HANDCRAFTED FIREPOWER GOOD ENOUGH FOR MY SON'S SON."

THE JAKOBS FAMILY

HAS BEEN ASSEMBLING QUALITY HANDCRAFTED FIREARMS FOR OVER 300 YEARS. AND THOUGH THE WORLD HAS CHANGED QUITE A LOT SINCE MONTGOMERY'S GRANDFATHER BOLTED ON THE SANDALWOOD GRIP OF THE COMPANY'S FIRST REVOLVER, OUR FAMILY TRADITION AND COMMITMENT TO BUILDING A SUPERIOR PRODUCT IS STILL AS TRUE AS EVER. THE EMPLOYEES AT JAKOBS MIGHT NOT ALL SHARE THE SAME LAST NAME ANYMORE, BUT WE'RE STILL FAMILY. AND WE WANT YOU TO JOIN US. WHEN YOU INVEST IN A JAKOBS, YOU'RE NOT ONLY GETTING THE MOST POWERFUL FIREARM MONEY CAN BUY; YOU'RE ALSO JOINING THE BIGGEST FAMILY OF SATISFIED GUN OWNERS THE WORLD OVER. WHETHER YOU'RE SHOULDERING ONE OF OUR RENOWNED RIFLES OR STARING DOWN THE BARREL OF ONE OF OUR TIMELESS PISTOLS, YOU CAN BE SURE EACH AND EVERY SHOT PACKS THE RELIABILITY AND STRENGTH THAT ONLY A JAKOBS CAN OFFER.

JAKOBS' MODEL LINES

LEVEL	LINE
1 TO 12	PLYWOOD
13 TO 21	CLASSIC
22 TO 30	VINTAGE
31 TO 39	CHOICE
40 TO 48	ANTIQUE
50	ORIGINAL

CLAPTRAP
DANCE OFF

JAKOBS

KLR XX SAVAGE JUSTICE

	LEVEL	BUY	SELL
	40	$746,788	$106,684

DAMAGE	ACCURACY	FIRE RATE	MAGAZINE	ELEMENTAL
779	91.1	0.7	2	-

- ☐ +194% DAMAGE
- ☐ -7% ACCURACY
- ☐ +200% MELEE DAMAGE
- ☐ 2.8X WEAPON ZOOM

AX220 SAVAGE JUSTICE

	LEVEL	BUY	SELL
	48	$2,225,713	$317,959

DAMAGE	ACCURACY	FIRE RATE	MAGAZINE	ELEMENTAL
548	93.6	1.3	6	-

- ☐ +67% DAMAGE
- ☐ +23% ACCURACY
- ☐ 3.7X WEAPON ZOOM

LEGENDARY WEAPON
KLR330 ZZ SAVAGE UNFORGIVEN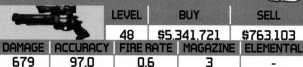

	LEVEL	BUY	SELL
	48	$5,341,721	$763,103

DAMAGE	ACCURACY	FIRE RATE	MAGAZINE	ELEMENTAL
679	97.0	0.6	3	-

- ☐ 107% DAMAGE
- ☐ +200% CRITICAL HIT DAMAGE
- ☐ 4.3X WEAPON ZOOM

IT'S A HELLUVA THING...

THE *UNFORGIVEN* OFFERS HIGH DAMAGE, HIGH ACCURACY, AND A LARGE CRITICAL HIT BONUS, BUT IT'S HEAVY, IS SLOW TO FIRE, AND KICKS LIKE A MULE!

COMBAT SHOTGUNS

Jakobs makes roughly 40,300 varieties of shotguns.

SG15 BATTLE MATADOR

	LEVEL	BUY	SELL
	7	$2,247	$321

DAMAGE	ACCURACY	FIRE RATE	MAGAZINE	ELEMENTAL
41 (x12)	30.7	0.6	2	-

- ☐ +139% DAMAGE
- ☐ +3 PROJECTILES FIRED
- ☐ 2.2X WEAPON ZOOM

Z1100 XX GENOCIDE MATADOR

	LEVEL	BUY	SELL
	22	$100,590	$14,370

DAMAGE	ACCURACY	FIRE RATE	MAGAZINE	ELEMENTAL
77 (x12)	33.3	1.0	12	-

- ☐ +67% DAMAGE
- ☐ +3 PROJECTILES FIRED
- ☐ 3.6X WEAPON ZOOM

SPR1 ZZ GENOCIDE SHOTGUN

	LEVEL	BUY	SELL
	13	$9,947	$1,421

DAMAGE	ACCURACY	FIRE RATE	MAGAZINE	ELEMENTAL
37 (x9)	72.9	0.4	6	-

- ☐ +34% DAMAGE
- ☐ +150% MELEE DAMAGE
- ☐ 2.9X WEAPON ZOOM

BA 11 COMBAT SHOTGUN

	LEVEL	BUY	SELL
	31	$67,067	$9,581

DAMAGE	ACCURACY	FIRE RATE	MAGAZINE	ELEMENTAL
91 (x9)	45.8	0.4	6	-

- ☐ +38% DAMAGE

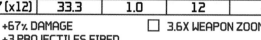
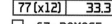

"IF IT TOOK MORE THAN ONE SHOT
THEN YOU WEREN'T USING A JAKOBS."

ZPR15 ZZ GENOCIDE CARNAGE

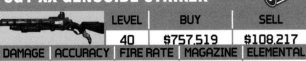

	LEVEL	BUY	SELL
	40	$452,144	$64,592

DAMAGE	ACCURACY	FIRE RATE	MAGAZINE	ELEMENTAL
670	72.9	0.7	2	-

☐ +659% DAMAGE

HOLY CRAP! IT SHOOTS ROCKETS!

SPR1100 GENOCIDE SHOTGUN

	LEVEL	BUY	SELL
	48	$1,927,023	$275,289

DAMAGE	ACCURACY	FIRE RATE	MAGAZINE	ELEMENTAL
165 (x9)	45.8	0.6	12	-

☐ +51% DAMAGE ☐ 2.2X WEAPON ZOOM

LEGENDARY WEAPON
SG1 XX GENOCIDE STRIKER

	LEVEL	BUY	SELL
	40	$757,519	$108,217

DAMAGE	ACCURACY	FIRE RATE	MAGAZINE	ELEMENTAL
114 (x9)	56.7	0.5	6	-

☐ 29% DAMAGE ☐ +30% CRITICAL HIT DAMAGE
☐ +150% MELEE DAMAGE

THE *STRIKER* IS THE MOST ACCURATE SHOTGUN
MONEY CAN BUY. IT PACKS A TIGHT SPREAD AND BIG
CRITICAL HIT BONUS.

SNIPER
RIFLES
ARE FOR
CHUMPS

ZX340 ZZ GENOCIDE SHOTGUN

	LEVEL	BUY	SELL
	48	$2,276,512	$325,216

DAMAGE	ACCURACY	FIRE RATE	MAGAZINE	ELEMENTAL
157 (x9)	53.8	0.6	6	-

☐ +44% DAMAGE ☐ 2.9X WEAPON ZOOM

CLAPTRAP
DANCE OFF

SNIPER RIFLES

Jakobs makes roughly 16,200 varieties of sniper rifles.

DVL550 XX FEARSOME THUNDER

	LEVEL	BUY	SELL
	4	$6,013	$859

DAMAGE	ACCURACY	FIRE RATE	MAGAZINE	ELEMENTAL
118	95.9	0.4	6	-

- ☐ +112% DAMAGE
- ☐ +150% CRITICAL HIT DAMAGE
- ☐ 2.4X WEAPON ZOOM

GGN FEARSOME SNIPER

	LEVEL	BUY	SELL
	13	$12,943	$1,849

DAMAGE	ACCURACY	FIRE RATE	MAGAZINE	ELEMENTAL
185	98.6	0.4	6	-

- ☐ +50% DAMAGE
- ☐ +150% CRITICAL HIT DAMAGE
- ☐ 2.7X WEAPON ZOOM

LEGENDARY WEAPON
VRR29 ZZ FEARSOME SKULLMASHER

	LEVEL	BUY	SELL
	22	$49,931	$7,133

DAMAGE	ACCURACY	FIRE RATE	MAGAZINE	ELEMENTAL
377	98.4	0.5	3	-

- ☐ 84% DAMAGE
- ☐ +300% CRITICAL HIT DAMAGE
- ☐ 1.3X WEAPON ZOOM

MAKES THEIR BRAIN HURT

THE *SKULLMASHER* FIRES MULTIPLE PROJECTILES. THINK OF IT AS A LONG-RANGE SHOTGUN.

KING OF CLAP

DVL ROLLING THUNDER

	LEVEL	BUY	SELL
	31	$73,773	$10,539

DAMAGE	ACCURACY	FIRE RATE	MAGAZINE	ELEMENTAL
443	96.7	0.3	6	-

- ☐ +50% DAMAGE
- ☐ +150% CRITICAL HIT DAMAGE
- ☐ 1.0X WEAPON ZOOM

GGN40 SOLID SNIPER

	LEVEL	BUY	SELL
	40	$248,675	$35,525

DAMAGE	ACCURACY	FIRE RATE	MAGAZINE	ELEMENTAL
574	95.7	0.4	6	-

- ☐ +45% DAMAGE
- ☐ +150% CRITICAL HIT DAMAGE
- ☐ 1.8X WEAPON ZOOM

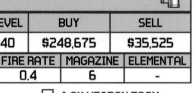

"IF IT TOOK MORE THAN ONE SHOT
THEN YOU WEREN'T USING A JAKOBS."

VRR590 ZZ FEARSOME THUNDER

	LEVEL	BUY	SELL
	40	$992,985	$141,855

DAMAGE	ACCURACY	FIRE RATE	MAGAZINE	ELEMENTAL
650	98.1	0.5	3	-

- ☐ +64% DAMAGE
- ☐ +150% CRITICAL HIT DAMAGE
- ☐ 2.5X WEAPON ZOOM

DVL SOLID THUNDER

	LEVEL	BUY	SELL
	48	$1,195,740	$170,820

DAMAGE	ACCURACY	FIRE RATE	MAGAZINE	ELEMENTAL
847	96.7	0.3	6	-

- ☐ +73% DAMAGE
- ☐ +150% CRITICAL HIT DAMAGE
- ☐ 1.5X WEAPON ZOOM

LEGENDARY WEAPON
GGN20 LONG SKULLMASHER

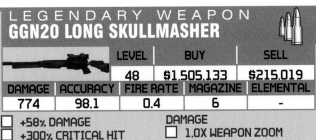

	LEVEL	BUY	SELL
	48	$1,505,133	$215,019

DAMAGE	ACCURACY	FIRE RATE	MAGAZINE	ELEMENTAL
774	98.1	0.4	6	-

- ☐ +58% DAMAGE
- ☐ +300% CRITICAL HIT
- ☐ 1.0X WEAPON ZOOM DAMAGE

MAKES THEIR BRAIN HURT

THE *SKULLMASHER* FIRES MULTIPLE PROJECTILES.
THINK OF IT AS A LONG-RANGE SHOTGUN.

CLAPTRAP
DANCE OFF

HYPERION

THERE ARE MANY WEAPONS IN THIS WORLD, BUT ONLY THE BEST HAVE WHAT IT TAKES TO BEAR THE HYPERION INSIGNIA. EVERY GUN THAT LEAVES OUR FACILITY HAS BEEN TESTED BY MULTIPLE INDEPENDENT INSPECTORS AND IS GUARANTEED TO MEET OUR IMPOSSIBLY HIGH STANDARDS. ALL HYPERION GUNS ARE METICULOUSLY CALIBRATED BY OUR TECHNICIANS AND CERTIFIED TO LEVELS OF ACCURACY NEVER BEFORE SEEN IN THE INDUSTRY. WHETHER YOU'RE A PROFESSIONAL MARKSMAN OR SIMPLY SOMEONE WHO APPRECIATES A FINELY-CRAFTED PIECE OF MACHINERY, YOU CAN'T GO WRONG WITH A HYPERION. FINANCING IS AVAILABLE TO THOSE WHO QUALIFY.

"SUCCESS REQUIRES MAKING EVERY OPPORTUNITY COUNT."

HYPERION'S MODEL LINES

LEVEL	LINE
1 TO 12	SUBSTANDARD
13 TO 21	VALDE
22 TO 30	MELIOR
31 TO 39	ULTRA
40 TO 48	MAGNUS
50	OPTIMUS

REPEATER PISTOLS

Hyperion makes roughly 75,600 varieties of repeater pistols.

HRD.G WICKED LACERATOR

	LEVEL	BUY	SELL
	6	$4,872	$696

DAMAGE	ACCURACY	FIRE RATE	MAGAZINE	ELEMENTAL
24	91.7	2.8	12	-

- ☐ +200% MELEE DAMAGE
- ☐ +14% RECOIL REDUCTION
- ☐ +38% RELOAD SPEED
- ☐ 4.1X WEAPON ZOOM

BLR4 WICKED REPEATER

	LEVEL	BUY	SELL
	42	$9,961	$1,423

DAMAGE	ACCURACY	FIRE RATE	MAGAZINE	ELEMENTAL
42	87.5	3.7	16	-

- ☐ +18% DAMAGE
- ☐ +60% RECOIL REDUCTION
- ☐ +25% ACCURACY
- ☐ 4.7X WEAPON ZOOM

CLAPTRAP DANCE OFF

HYPERION

RF5.W WICKED INVADER

	LEVEL	BUY	SELL
	24	$71,463	$10,209

DAMAGE	ACCURACY	FIRE RATE	MAGAZINE	ELEMENTAL
84	92.9	3.4	18	-

- ☐ +1% FIRE RATE
- ☐ +6% RECOIL REDUCTION
- ☐ 4.7X WEAPON ZOOM

12 BULLETS

INVADE YOUR SKULL

The *invader* is equipped with a fantastic scope. while zoomed, this gun fires a deadly continuous burst.

TK.G WICKED REPEATER

	LEVEL	BUY	SELL
	33	$174,216	$24,888

DAMAGE	ACCURACY	FIRE RATE	MAGAZINE	ELEMENTAL
95 (x2)	87.3	5.5	14	-

- ☐ +19% DAMAGE
- ☐ +36% RECOIL REDUCTION
- ☐ +24% ACCURACY
- ☐ +38% RELOAD SPEED

TK.G CRUEL REPEATER

	LEVEL	BUY	SELL
	48	$910,602	$130,086

DAMAGE	ACCURACY	FIRE RATE	MAGAZINE	ELEMENTAL
123	91.7	4.7	12	-

- ☐ +57% RECOIL REDUCTION
- ☐ +50% ACCURACY
- ☐ +38% RELOAD SPEED
- ☐ 3.1X WEAPON ZOOM

HRD REPEATER

	LEVEL	BUY	SELL
	42	$184,919	$29,417

DAMAGE	ACCURACY	FIRE RATE	MAGAZINE	ELEMENTAL
112	88.2	2.6	12	-

- ☐ +18% RECOIL REDUCTION
- ☐ +29% ACCURACY

HRD4.W WICKED RAPTOR

	LEVEL	BUY	SELL
	48	$1,818,726	$259,818

DAMAGE	ACCURACY	FIRE RATE	MAGAZINE	ELEMENTAL
201	88.5	3.1	16	-

- ☐ +100% MELEE DAMAGE
- ☐ +31% ACCURACY
- ☐ -7% FIRE RATE
- ☐ 4.1X WEAPON ZOOM

BLR5.W WICKED REPEATER

	LEVEL	BUY	SELL
	42	$485,870	$69,410

DAMAGE	ACCURACY	FIRE RATE	MAGAZINE	ELEMENTAL
77	89.2	4.6	18	🔥x1

- ☐ +42% RECOIL REDUCTION
- ☐ +35% ACCURACY

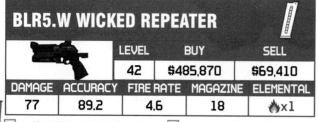

KING OF CLAP

MACHINE PISTOLS

Hyperion makes roughly 75,600 varieties of machine pistols.

TMP2 VILE TORMENT

	LEVEL	BUY	SELL
	6	$2,548	$364

DAMAGE	ACCURACY	FIRE RATE	MAGAZINE	ELEMENTAL
32	92.4	9.0	18	-

- ☐ +82% DAMAGE
- ☐ +55% ACCURACY
- ☐ +61% RECOIL REDUCTION
- ☐ 4.7X WEAPON ZOOM

TMP8 VILE RAGE

	LEVEL	BUY	SELL
	33	$124,481	$17,783

DAMAGE	ACCURACY	FIRE RATE	MAGAZINE	ELEMENTAL
62	88.2	19.7	26	☣x1

- ☐ +29% ACCURACY
- ☐ -10% RECOIL REDUCTION

TMP2 COLD TORMENT

	LEVEL	BUY	SELL
	15	$4,851	$693

DAMAGE	ACCURACY	FIRE RATE	MAGAZINE	ELEMENTAL
50	88.2	8.3	18	-

- ☐ +42% DAMAGE
- ☐ +29% ACCURACY
- ☐ +65% RECOIL REDUCTION
- ☐ +2 MAGAZINE SIZE

TMP2.W GRIM RAGE

	LEVEL	BUY	SELL
	42	$440,811	$62,973

DAMAGE	ACCURACY	FIRE RATE	MAGAZINE	ELEMENTAL
84	91.0	19.2	16	⚡x1

- ☐ +46% ACCURACY
- ☐ -18% RECOIL REDUCTION

TMP2.G VILE TORMENT

	LEVEL	BUY	SELL
	24	$58,023	$8,289

DAMAGE	ACCURACY	FIRE RATE	MAGAZINE	ELEMENTAL
76 (x2)	91.2	7.6	21	-

- ☐ +34% DAMAGE
- ☐ +47% ACCURACY
- ☐ +43% RECOIL REDUCTION
- ☐ +23% RELOAD SPEED

TMP8.G VILE MACHINE PISTOL

	LEVEL	BUY	SELL
	42	$586,880	$83,840

DAMAGE	ACCURACY	FIRE RATE	MAGAZINE	ELEMENTAL
103	89.3	9.0	26	🔥x1

- ☐ +36% ACCURACY
- ☐ 4.1X WEAPON ZOOM

TMP8.W VILE TORMENT

	LEVEL	BUY	SELL
	48	$1,396,192	$199,456

DAMAGE	ACCURACY	FIRE RATE	MAGAZINE	ELEMENTAL
207	92.2	9.9	28	-

- ☐ +100% MELEE DAMAGE
- ☐ +53% ACCURACY
- ☐ -3% RECOIL REDUCTION
- ☐ +69% DAMAGE

CLAPTRAP DANCE OFF

ASSAULT SHOTGUNS

Hyperion makes roughly 30,200 varieties of assault shotguns.

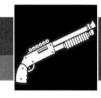

SPR10 LETHAL DEATH

	LEVEL	BUY	SELL
	6	$2,324	$332

DAMAGE	ACCURACY	FIRE RATE	MAGAZINE	ELEMENTAL
14 (x7)	80.6	1.0	5	✳ x2

- ☐ +67% ACCURACY
- ☐ +23% RECOIL REDUCTION
- ☐ -4% DAMAGE

BA 20.G FATAL DEATH

	LEVEL	BUY	SELL
	24	$73,934	$10,562

DAMAGE	ACCURACY	FIRE RATE	MAGAZINE	ELEMENTAL
64 (x7)	70.8	1.0	5	-

- ☐ +50% ACCURACY
- ☐ +32% RECOIL REDUCTION
- ☐ +37% DAMAGE
- ☐ 2.5X WEAPON ZOOM

ZPR630 FATAL SHOTGUN

	LEVEL	BUY	SELL
	33	$374,360	$53,480

DAMAGE	ACCURACY	FIRE RATE	MAGAZINE	ELEMENTAL
98 (x7)	56.1	2.1	7	-

- ☐ +25% ACCURACY
- ☐ +45% RECOIL REDUCTION
- ☐ +48% DAMAGE
- ☐ 3.0X WEAPON ZOOM

SPR330.G FATAL DEATH

	LEVEL	BUY	SELL
	42	$1,990,618	$284,374

DAMAGE	ACCURACY	FIRE RATE	MAGAZINE	ELEMENTAL
102 (x7)	74.6	1.0	7	☣ x2

- ☐ +23% RELOAD SPEED
- ☐ 4.5X WEAPON ZOOM

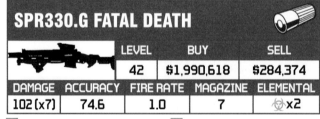

KING
OF CLAP

SG10.W FATAL DEATH

	LEVEL	BUY	SELL
	42	$696,017	$99,431

DAMAGE	ACCURACY	FIRE RATE	MAGAZINE	ELEMENTAL
114 (x7)	75.2	1.6	5	-

- ☐ +57% ACCURACY
- ☐ +18% RECOIL REDUCTION
- ☐ +23% FIRE RATE
- ☐ 4.0X WEAPON ZOOM

ZX10 RAGING SHOTGUN

	LEVEL	BUY	SELL
	48	$869,631	$124,233

DAMAGE	ACCURACY	FIRE RATE	MAGAZINE	ELEMENTAL
87 (x7)	65.7	1.9	5	-

- ☐ +41% ACCURACY
- ☐ +30% RECOIL REDUCTION

LEGENDARY WEAPON
BA 630.W FATAL BUTCHER

	LEVEL	BUY	SELL
	48	$7,034,419	$1,004,917

DAMAGE	ACCURACY	FIRE RATE	MAGAZINE	ELEMENTAL
141 (x3)	62.2	7.0	7	-

- ☐ +25% RECOIL REDUCTION
- ☐ +500% BURST FIRE COUNT
- ☐ 3.0X WEAPON ZOOM

LEGENDARY WEAPON
ZX330.W FATAL BUTCHER

	LEVEL	BUY	SELL
	15	$18,368	$2,624

DAMAGE	ACCURACY	FIRE RATE	MAGAZINE	ELEMENTAL
30 (x3)	62.2	9.5	7	-

- ☐ +50% RECOIL REDUCTION
- ☐ +35% ACCURACY
- ☐ +500% BURST FIRE COUNT

AHHH...

FRESH MEAT!

The *Butcher* fires a devastating five-shot burst.

HYPERION

COMBAT RIFLES

Hyperion makes roughly 31,500 varieties of combat rifles.

CR40.G GENOCIDE COBRA

	LEVEL	BUY	SELL
	15	$16,590	$2,370

DAMAGE	ACCURACY	FIRE RATE	MAGAZINE	ELEMENTAL
60	94.6	10.0	12	-

- [ ] +50% ACCURACY
- [ ] +69% RECOIL REDUCTION
- [ ] +8% RELOAD SPEED
- [ ] 3.2X WEAPON ZOOM

HLK10.W GENOCIDE POUNDER

	LEVEL	BUY	SELL
	33	$202,776	$28,968

DAMAGE	ACCURACY	FIRE RATE	MAGAZINE	ELEMENTAL
244	95.3	3.9	6	-

- [ ] +57% ACCURACY
- [ ] -32% RECOIL REDUCTION
- [ ] +129% DAMAGE
- [ ] -154% FIRE RATE

TCH DEATHLY COBRA

	LEVEL	BUY	SELL
	24	$23,730	$3,390

DAMAGE	ACCURACY	FIRE RATE	MAGAZINE	ELEMENTAL
76	93.6	13.0	12	-

- [ ] +41% ACCURACY
- [ ] +62% RECOIL REDUCTION
- [ ] 1.4X WEAPON ZOOM

AR.G GENOCIDE COBRA

	LEVEL	BUY	SELL
	42	$1,158,318	$165,474

DAMAGE	ACCURACY	FIRE RATE	MAGAZINE	ELEMENTAL
158	96.7	15.0	12	☣ x2

- [ ] +70% ACCURACY
- [ ] +66% RECOIL REDUCTION

TCH400.W GENOCIDE POUNDER

	LEVEL	BUY	SELL
	48	$2,445,842	$349,406

DAMAGE	ACCURACY	FIRE RATE	MAGAZINE	ELEMENTAL
247	94.1	5.3	6	-

- [ ] +46% ACCURACY
- [ ] +64% RECOIL REDUCTION
- [ ] 3.2X WEAPON ZOOM
- [ ] -87% FIRE RATE

HLK50.G GENOCIDE COBRA

	LEVEL	BUY	SELL
	48	$5,380,851	$768,693

DAMAGE	ACCURACY	FIRE RATE	MAGAZINE	ELEMENTAL
282	95.7	7.7	12	-

- [ ] +60% ACCURACY
- [ ] +57% RECOIL REDUCTION
- [ ] +23% RELOAD SPEED
- [ ] 3.6X WEAPON ZOOM

KING
OF CLAP

LEGENDARY WEAPON
AR300.W GENOCIDE DESTROYER

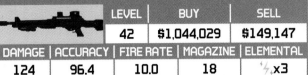

	LEVEL	BUY	SELL
	6	$8,638	$1,234

DAMAGE	ACCURACY	FIRE RATE	MAGAZINE	ELEMENTAL
48	96.6	6.0	6	-

- [ ] +63% RECOIL REDUCTION
- [ ] -67% FIRE RATE
- [ ] 2.4X WEAPON ZOOM

LEGENDARY WEAPON
CR320 GENOCIDE DESTROYER

	LEVEL	BUY	SELL
	42	$1,044,029	$149,147

DAMAGE	ACCURACY	FIRE RATE	MAGAZINE	ELEMENTAL
124	96.4	10.0	18	⚡x3

- [ ] +67% ACCURACY

THE DESTRUCTOR
HAS COME

the *destroyer* offers good accuracy and damage and fires a deadly continuous burst while zoomed.

PATROL SMG

Hyperion makes roughly 170,100 varieties of patrol sub-machine guns.

KKA140 MALEVOLENT BRUISER

	LEVEL	BUY	SELL
	6	$4,361	$623

DAMAGE	ACCURACY	FIRE RATE	MAGAZINE	ELEMENTAL
22 (x2)	85.4	6.9	66	-

- [ ] +13% ACCURACY
- [ ] -21% RECOIL REDUCTION
- [ ] +42% DAMAGE

TEK5.W MALEVOLENT STINGER

	LEVEL	BUY	SELL
	15	$17,395	$2,485

DAMAGE	ACCURACY	FIRE RATE	MAGAZINE	ELEMENTAL
27	94.7	13.3	46	🔥x3

- [ ] +38% FIRE RATE
- [ ] +62% RECOIL REDUCTION

CLAPTRAP DANCE OFF

HYPERION

RF200.G MALEVOLENT BITCH

	LEVEL	BUY	SELL
	24	$105,714	$15,102

DAMAGE	ACCURACY	FIRE RATE	MAGAZINE	ELEMENTAL
114	94.9	2.5	18	-

☐ +128% DAMAGE   ☐ +16% RELOAD SPEED
☐ +44% RECOIL REDUCTION

SMACK 'EM

the *bitch* delivers high accuracy and good damage with a big critical hit bonus!

HX 32.G MALEVOLENT STINGER

	LEVEL	BUY	SELL
	33	$311,962	$44,566

DAMAGE	ACCURACY	FIRE RATE	MAGAZINE	ELEMENTAL
97	91.7	14.2	28	-

☐ +31% RELOAD SPEED   ☐ +41% FIRE RATE
☐ +59% RECOIL REDUCTION   ☐ 2.9X WEAPON ZOOM

TEK550.G MALEVOLENT SMG

	LEVEL	BUY	SELL
	48	$4,663,407	$666,201

DAMAGE	ACCURACY	FIRE RATE	MAGAZINE	ELEMENTAL
108	92.8	10.8	46	⚡x3

☐ +56% RECOIL REDUCTION   ☐ -8% RELOAD SPEED

TD430 MALEVOLENT BRUISER

	LEVEL	BUY	SELL
	42	$772,212	$110,316

DAMAGE	ACCURACY	FIRE RATE	MAGAZINE	ELEMENTAL
123	87.5	8.3	36	-

☐ +25% ACCURACY   ☐ +32% DAMAGE
☐ +59% RECOIL REDUCTION   ☐ 3.9X WEAPON ZOOM

RF100 TWISTED THUMPER

	LEVEL	BUY	SELL
	48	$3,668,763	$524,109

DAMAGE	ACCURACY	FIRE RATE	MAGAZINE	ELEMENTAL
223 (x2)	82.8	2.5	30	-

☐ -3% ACCURACY   ☐ +104% DAMAGE
☐ -12% RECOIL REDUCTION   ☐ +2 MAGAZINE SIZE

KKA540 MALEVOLENT BRUISER

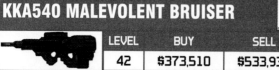

	LEVEL	BUY	SELL
	42	$373,510	$533,930

DAMAGE	ACCURACY	FIRE RATE	MAGAZINE	ELEMENTAL
142	92.9	12.2	55	-

☐ +31% FIRE RATE   ☐ +52% DAMAGE
☐ +72% RECOIL REDUCTION   ☐ 4.3X WEAPON ZOOM

KING OF CLAP

SEMI-AUTO SNIPER RIFLES

Hyperion makes roughly 18,000 varieties of semi-automatic sniper rifles.

LB HARD SNIPER

	LEVEL	BUY	SELL
	15	$9,527	$1,361

DAMAGE	ACCURACY	FIRE RATE	MAGAZINE	ELEMENTAL
205	98.3	1.2	5	-

☐ +67% ACCURACY
☐ +41% RECOIL REDUCTION
☐ +150% CRITICAL HIT DAMAGE
☐ 1.0X WEAPON ZOOM

PPZ370.W FEARSOME SNIPER

	LEVEL	BUY	SELL
	24	$74,109	$10,587

DAMAGE	ACCURACY	FIRE RATE	MAGAZINE	ELEMENTAL
264	97.7	2.9	7	-

☐ +53% ACCURACY
☐ +55% RECOIL REDUCTION
☐ +50% FIRE RATE
☐ 1.5X WEAPON ZOOM

LEGENDARY WEAPON
PPZ1270.G FEARSOME EXECUTIONER

	LEVEL	BUY	SELL
	6	$29,022	$4,146

DAMAGE	ACCURACY	FIRE RATE	MAGAZINE	ELEMENTAL
53	97.8	2.9	15	-

☐ +57% RELOAD SPEED
☐ 2.7X WEAPON ZOOM

LEGENDARY WEAPON
LB1170.G FEARSOME EXECUTIONER

	LEVEL	BUY	SELL
	33	$419,279	$59,897

DAMAGE	ACCURACY	FIRE RATE	MAGAZINE	ELEMENTAL
174	96.8	1.2	15	🔥x3

☐ +33% RELOAD SPEED

BAM BAM

BAM BAM BAM!

The *executioner* contains an extended magazine and fires in a deadly five-shot burst while zoomed.

HYPERION

PPZ50 FEARSOME SNIPER

	LEVEL	BUY	SELL
	42	$748,447	$106,921

DAMAGE	ACCURACY	FIRE RATE	MAGAZINE	ELEMENTAL
531	97.7	2.1	5	-

- ☐ +55% ACCURACY
- ☐ +66% RECOIL REDUCTION
- ☐ +150% CRITICAL HIT DAMAGE
- ☐ 2.4X WEAPON ZOOM

PPZ30.G FEARSOME SNIPER

	LEVEL	BUY	SELL
	48	$3,476,858	$496,694

DAMAGE	ACCURACY	FIRE RATE	MAGAZINE	ELEMENTAL
687	98.6	2.1	5	-

- ☐ +72% ACCURACY
- ☐ +64% RECOIL REDUCTION
- ☐ +23% RELOAD SPEED
- ☐ 1.5X WEAPON ZOOM

LB7.W FEARSOME THUNDER

	LEVEL	BUY	SELL
	42	$1,689,009	$241,287

DAMAGE	ACCURACY	FIRE RATE	MAGAZINE	ELEMENTAL
699	97.7	1.8	7	-

- ☐ +53% ACCURACY
- ☐ +3% RECOIL REDUCTION
- ☐ +21% FIRE RATE
- ☐ 2.7X WEAPON ZOOM

LB570 FEARSOME WRATH

	LEVEL	BUY	SELL
	48	$2,490,313	$355,759

DAMAGE	ACCURACY	FIRE RATE	MAGAZINE	ELEMENTAL
428	96.2	1.4	7	☣x3

- ☐ +44% RECOIL REDUCTION
- ☐ 2.4X WEAPON ZOOM

ROCKET LAUNCHERS

Hyperion makes roughly 44,100 varieties of rocket launchers.

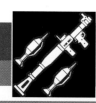

LEGENDARY WEAPON
RPG720.W COLOSSAL NIDHOGG

	LEVEL	BUY	SELL
	33	$494,151	$70,593

DAMAGE	ACCURACY	FIRE RATE	MAGAZINE	ELEMENTAL
1246	98.3	0.9	2	-

- ☐ +82% RECOIL REDUCTION
- ☐ +79% ACCURACY
- ☐ 3.3X WEAPON ZOOM

DEATH RAINS
FROM ABOVE

The *Nidhogg* delivers high damage with a fast reload speed. At a preset range, the rocket explodes and fires several additional rockets downward.

RPG10
EVIL ROCKET LAUNCHER

LEVEL	BUY	SELL
6	$1,785	$255

DAMAGE	ACCURACY	FIRE RATE	MAGAZINE	ELEMENTAL
125	95.1	0.7	2	-

- ☐ +52% RECOIL REDUCTION
- ☐ +41% ACCURACY
- ☐ 1.9X WEAPON ZOOM

RWL51
COLOSSAL ROCKET LAUNCHER

LEVEL	BUY	SELL
24	$55,524	$7,932

DAMAGE	ACCURACY	FIRE RATE	MAGAZINE	ELEMENTAL
482	95.1	5.0	5	-

- ☐ +63% RECOIL REDUCTION
- ☐ +41% ACCURACY
- ☐ +500% BURST FIRE COUNT
- ☐ 2.7X WEAPON ZOOM

SPC20.G
COLOSSAL ROCKET LAUNCHER

LEVEL	BUY	SELL
15	$13,587	$1,941

DAMAGE	ACCURACY	FIRE RATE	MAGAZINE	ELEMENTAL
247 (x3)	95.8	0.9	3	🔥x4

- ☐ +58% RECOIL REDUCTION
- ☐ +29% RELOAD SPEED

RPG50.W
MASSIVE HARPOON

LEVEL	BUY	SELL
48	$1,695,785	$242,255

DAMAGE	ACCURACY	FIRE RATE	MAGAZINE	ELEMENTAL
1231	96.1	0.9	1	⚡x4

- ☐ +60% RECOIL REDUCTION
- ☐ +53% ACCURACY

SPC10
HELIX ROCKET LAUNCHER

LEVEL	BUY	SELL
42	$383,334	$54,762

DAMAGE	ACCURACY	FIRE RATE	MAGAZINE	ELEMENTAL
606 (x3)	95.1	0.9	3	-

- ☐ +58% RECOIL REDUCTION
- ☐ +41% ACCURACY
- ☐ 2.7X WEAPON ZOOM

SPC71.G
COLOSSAL ROCKET LAUNCHER

LEVEL	BUY	SELL
48	$2,731,813	$390,259

DAMAGE	ACCURACY	FIRE RATE	MAGAZINE	ELEMENTAL
1112	87.5	2.9	3	-

- ☐ +68% RECOIL REDUCTION
- ☐ -50% ACCURACY
- ☐ +23% RELOAD SPEED
- ☐ +300% BURST FIRE COUNT

RWL270
COLOSSAL ROCKET LAUNCHER

LEVEL	BUY	SELL
42	$2,038,638	$291,234

DAMAGE	ACCURACY	FIRE RATE	MAGAZINE	ELEMENTAL
1079	95.1	1.0	2	☣x4

- ☐ +55% RECOIL REDUCTION
- ☐ 4.9X WEAPON ZOOM

CLAPTRAP DANCE OFF

HYPERION

ATLAS

IT IS SAID THAT THE GREEK GOD ZEUS FOUGHT FOR 10 LONG YEARS AGAINST THE TITANS, ONLY TO HAVE THE BATTLE END IN A DRAW. WE AT ATLAS LIKE TO BELIEVE ZEUS COULD HAVE WON THE FIGHT IN HALF THE TIME IF ONLY HE HAD ONE OF THE GUNS FROM OUR LEGENDARY LINE OF FIREARMS. ALL ATLAS GUNS OFFER EXCEPTIONAL RATE OF FIRE, DAMAGE, AND AN EPIC LEVEL OF HIGH TECHNOLOGY. REGARDLESS OF YOUR GOD, YOU NEED NOT LOOK TO THE HEAVENS FOR SALVATION FROM ADVERSITY. ATLAS WEAPONRY CAN ANSWER YOUR PRAYERS AND GRANT YOU A POWER FEW MORTALS HAVE EVER EXPERIENCED. PROVE YOURSELF AS A TRUE BELIEVER. JOIN THE SELECT RANKS OF ATLAS OWNERS AND BECOME A GOD AMONG MEN!

REPEATER PISTOLS
Atlas makes roughly 71,200 varieties of repeater pistols.

HRD4 WICKED RAPTOR

	LEVEL	BUY	SELL
	10	$5,467	$781

DAMAGE	ACCURACY	FIRE RATE	MAGAZINE	ELEMENTAL
42	92.8	2.9	18	-

- ☐ +68% DAMAGE
- ☐ +23% RECOIL REDUCTION
- ☐ +6 MAGAZINE SIZE
- ☐ -16% FIRE RATE

BLR5 WICKED REPEATER

	LEVEL	BUY	SELL
	19	$28,350	$4,050

DAMAGE	ACCURACY	FIRE RATE	MAGAZINE	ELEMENTAL
49	80.0	5.4	20	-

- ☐ +10% DAMAGE
- ☐ +6% RECOIL REDUCTION
- ☐ +8 MAGAZINE SIZE
- ☐ +39% FIRE RATE

"FOR WHEN THE WEIGHT OF THE WORLD IS ON YOUR SHOULDERS."

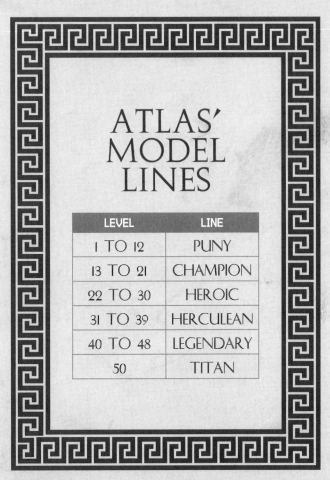

ATLAS' MODEL LINES

LEVEL	LINE
1 TO 12	PUNY
13 TO 21	CHAMPION
22 TO 30	HEROIC
31 TO 39	HERCULEAN
40 TO 48	LEGENDARY
50	TITAN

"IT IS NOT OFTEN THAT MORTALS ARE ALLOWED TO WIELD THE POWER OF THE GODS."

CLAPTRAP DANCE OFF

ATLAS

RF PUNY REPEATER

	LEVEL	BUY	SELL
	28	$13,517	$1,931

DAMAGE	ACCURACY	FIRE RATE	MAGAZINE	ELEMENTAL
69	83.3	3.3	13	-

- ☐ +3% DAMAGE
- ☐ -37% RECOIL REDUCTION
- ☐ +1 MAGAZINE SIZE

TK4 WICKED REPEATER

	LEVEL	BUY	SELL
	37	$260,988	$37,284

DAMAGE	ACCURACY	FIRE RATE	MAGAZINE	ELEMENTAL
81	78.7	5.5	18	⚡,x2

- ☐ -11% DAMAGE
- ☐ 4.7X WEAPON ZOOM

HRD5 BAD REPEATER

	LEVEL	BUY	SELL
	46	$484,708	$69,244

DAMAGE	ACCURACY	FIRE RATE	MAGAZINE	ELEMENTAL
153	83.3	3.1	13	-

- ☐ -58% RECOIL REDUCTION
- ☐ +31% DAMAGE
- ☐ -8% FIRE RATE
- ☐ +1 MAGAZINE SIZE

RF4 WICKED REPEATER

	LEVEL	BUY	SELL
	48	$1,050,700	$150,100

DAMAGE	ACCURACY	FIRE RATE	MAGAZINE	ELEMENTAL
189	92.8	4.5	18	-

- ☐ +54% DAMAGE
- ☐ +6 MAGAZINE SIZE
- ☐ +9% RECOIL REDUCTION
- ☐ +26% FIRE RATE

TK5 WICKED REPEATER

	LEVEL	BUY	SELL
	48	$1,538,922	$219,846

DAMAGE	ACCURACY	FIRE RATE	MAGAZINE	ELEMENTAL
122	80.0	5.2	20	-

- ☐ +100% MELEE DAMAGE
- ☐ +8 MAGAZINE SIZE
- ☐ +26% RECOIL REDUCTION
- ☐ 3.1X WEAPON ZOOM

PAIN HEALS

LEGENDARY WEAPON
BLR WICKED TROLL

	LEVEL	BUY	SELL
	46	$1,439,585	$205,655

DAMAGE	ACCURACY	FIRE RATE	MAGAZINE	ELEMENTAL
188	87.2	3.7	13	-

- ☐ +61% DAMAGE
- ☐ +14% RECOIL REDUCTION
- ☐ +1 MAGAZINE SIZE

THE **TROLL** IS A HIGH STABILITY WEAPON THAT GRANTS ITS WIELDER THE POWER TO REGENERATE HEALTH.

REVOLVER PISTOLS

Atlas makes roughly 90,000 varieties of revolver pistols.

AX10 SAVAGE JUSTICE

	LEVEL	BUY	SELL
	-	$1,330	$190

DAMAGE	ACCURACY	FIRE RATE	MAGAZINE	ELEMENTAL
26	91.7	2.3	6	-

- ☐ +100% MELEE DAMAGE
- ☐ +47% DAMAGE
- ☐ -21% RECOIL REDUCTION
- ☐ +45% FIRE RATE

RV PRIMAL RAZOR

	LEVEL	BUY	SELL
	19	$15,421	$2,203

DAMAGE	ACCURACY	FIRE RATE	MAGAZINE	ELEMENTAL
258	89.3	1.3	6	-

- ☐ +200% MELEE DAMAGE
- ☐ +119% DAMAGE
- ☐ -24% RECOIL REDUCTION
- ☐ -4 MAGAZINE SIZE

DL220 SAVAGE MASHER

	LEVEL	BUY	SELL
	28	$72,688	$10,384

DAMAGE	ACCURACY	FIRE RATE	MAGAZINE	ELEMENTAL
82 (x7)	83.3	1.1	6	-

- ☐ -53% DAMAGE
- ☐ -70% RECOIL REDUCTION
- ☐ -13% FIRE RATE
- ☐ 2.3X WEAPON ZOOM

MAL31 SAVAGE LAW

	LEVEL	BUY	SELL
	37	$434,938	$62,134

DAMAGE	ACCURACY	FIRE RATE	MAGAZINE	ELEMENTAL
253	93.6	1.7	6	☣x3

- ☐ +5% DAMAGE
- ☐ +28% FIRE RATE

KLR13 SAVAGE JUSTICE

	LEVEL	BUY	SELL
	46	$1,503,698	$214,814

DAMAGE	ACCURACY	FIRE RATE	MAGAZINE	ELEMENTAL
490	96.4	1.0	3	-

- ☐ +57% DAMAGE
- ☐ -16% RECOIL REDUCTION
- ☐ -3 MAGAZINE SIZE
- ☐ 3.7X WEAPON ZOOM

RV200 SAVAGE REVOLVER

	LEVEL	BUY	SELL
	48	$1,556,443	$222,349

DAMAGE	ACCURACY	FIRE RATE	MAGAZINE	ELEMENTAL
552	89.3	1.3	2	🔥x2

- ☐ +69% DAMAGE
- ☐ +11% RECOIL REDUCTION

DL320 SAVAGE VIPER

	LEVEL	BUY	SELL
	48	$1,255,527	$179,361

DAMAGE	ACCURACY	FIRE RATE	MAGAZINE	ELEMENTAL
295	94.4	1.1	6	⚡x2

- ☐ -10% DAMAGE
- ☐ -13% FIRE RATE

LEGENDARY WEAPON
AX SAVAGE CHIMERA

	LEVEL	BUY	SELL
	46	$2,842,259	$406,037

DAMAGE	ACCURACY	FIRE RATE	MAGAZINE	ELEMENTAL
441	91.7	2.3	6	✸x3

- ☐ +42% DAMAGE
- ☐ 4.2X WEAPON ZOOM

A BEAST OF MANY FORMS—FIRE, LIGHTNING, AND POISON

THE **CHIMERA** FIRES ELEMENTAL EFFECTS AT RANDOM.

COMBAT SHOTGUNS

Atlas makes roughly 77,700 varieties of combat shotguns.

BA 15 GENOCIDE SHOTGUN

	LEVEL	BUY	SELL
	10	$11,291	$1,613

DAMAGE	ACCURACY	FIRE RATE	MAGAZINE	ELEMENTAL
42 (x9)	63.9	0.6	2	☣x2

- ☐ -93% RECOIL REDUCTION
- ☐ 3.6X WEAPON ZOOM

ZPR1 WAR SHOTGUN

	LEVEL	BUY	SELL
	19	$18,641	$2,663

DAMAGE	ACCURACY	FIRE RATE	MAGAZINE	ELEMENTAL
45 (x9)	45.8	1.5	6	-

- ☐ +14% DAMAGE
- ☐ +16% RECOIL REDUCTION
- ☐ +49% FIRE RATE
- ☐ 1.5X WEAPON ZOOM

CLAPTRAP DANCE OFF

[ATLAS]

FIVE HEADS OF DEATH

LEGENDARY WEAPON
SG1100 GENOCIDE HYDRA

	LEVEL	BUY	SELL
	28	$205,653	$29,379

DAMAGE	ACCURACY	FIRE RATE	MAGAZINE	ELEMENTAL
97 (x12)	83.6	0.8	13	-

- ☐ +4% FIRE RATE
- ☐ +47% RECOIL REDUCTION
- ☐ +7 MAGAZINE SIZE

LEGENDARY WEAPON
SG340 GENOCIDE HYDRA

	LEVEL	BUY	SELL
	48	$6,457,024	$922,432

DAMAGE	ACCURACY	FIRE RATE	MAGAZINE	ELEMENTAL
195 (x12)	76.4	0.8	6	-

- ☐ +4% FIRE RATE
- ☐ -5% RECOIL REDUCTION
- ☐ 4.0X WEAPON ZOOM

THE HYDRA INFLICTS EXTRA DAMAGE AND FIRES IN A SPECIAL SPREAD PATTERN.

SPR340 GENOCIDE CARNAGE

	LEVEL	BUY	SELL
	37	$311,094	$44,442

DAMAGE	ACCURACY	FIRE RATE	MAGAZINE	ELEMENTAL
518	63.9	0.6	6	-

- ☐ +542% DAMAGE
- ☐ -16% FIRE RATE
- ☐ -1% RECOIL REDUCTION

BA 1 GENOCIDE MATADOR

	LEVEL	BUY	SELL
	46	$1,575,301	$225,043

DAMAGE	ACCURACY	FIRE RATE	MAGAZINE	ELEMENTAL
143 (x12)	30.7	1.0	6	-

- ☐ +38% DAMAGE
- ☐ -72% RECOIL REDUCTION
- ☐ +24% FIRE RATE
- ☐ 2.7X WEAPON ZOOM

ZX15 WAR SHOTGUN

	LEVEL	BUY	SELL
	46	$1,050,203	$150,029

DAMAGE	ACCURACY	FIRE RATE	MAGAZINE	ELEMENTAL
193 (x9)	45.8	1.0	2	-

- ☐ +86% DAMAGE
- ☐ +150% MELEE DAMAGE
- ☐ -9% RECOIL REDUCTION
- ☐ -4 MAGAZINE SIZE

ZPR1100 GENOCIDE SHOTGUN

	LEVEL	BUY	SELL
	48	$5,503,148	$786,164

DAMAGE	ACCURACY	FIRE RATE	MAGAZINE	ELEMENTAL
127 (x9)	63.9	1.2	13	, x2

- ☐ +37% RECOIL REDUCTION
- ☐ 3.6X WEAPON ZOOM

SNIPER RIFLES
Atlas makes roughly 32,400 varieties of sniper rifles.

VRR390 FEARSOME SNIPER

	LEVEL	BUY	SELL
	10	$8,477	$1,211

DAMAGE	ACCURACY	FIRE RATE	MAGAZINE	ELEMENTAL
104	98.6	0.8	3	x4

- ☐ +52% RECOIL REDUCTION
- ☐ -3 MAGAZINE SIZE

GGN SIGHTED SNIPER

	LEVEL	BUY	SELL
	28	$42,966	$6,138

DAMAGE	ACCURACY	FIRE RATE	MAGAZINE	ELEMENTAL
304	96.7	0.6	6	-

- ☐ +15% DAMAGE
- ☐ -19% RECOIL REDUCTION
- ☐ +3% FIRE RATE
- ☐ 1.0X WEAPON ZOOM

LEGENDARY WEAPON
DVL25 FEARSOME CYCLOPS

	LEVEL	BUY	SELL
	46	$3,598,966	$514,138

DAMAGE	ACCURACY	FIRE RATE	MAGAZINE	ELEMENTAL
851	97.4	0.6	6	x2

- ☐ -4% FIRE RATE
- ☐ +82% DAMAGE
- ☐ 3.2X WEAPON ZOOM

I HAVE YOU IN MY EYE, SIR

THE CYCLOPS DELIVERS A HIGH DAMAGE AND POWERFUL EXPLOSIVE ATTACK.

VRR9 FEARSOME SNIPER

	LEVEL	BUY	SELL
	37	$358,855	$51,265

DAMAGE	ACCURACY	FIRE RATE	MAGAZINE	ELEMENTAL
499	97.8	0.8	3	-

- ☐ +23% RECOIL REDUCTION
- ☐ +38% DAMAGE
- ☐ -3 MAGAZINE SIZE
- ☐ 2.7X WEAPON ZOOM

VRR490 FEARSOME SNIPER

	LEVEL	BUY	SELL
	48	$1,880,907	$268,701

DAMAGE	ACCURACY	FIRE RATE	MAGAZINE	ELEMENTAL
612	97.2	0.8	3	-

- ☐ +52% RECOIL REDUCTION
- ☐ +25% DAMAGE
- ☐ -3 MAGAZINE SIZE
- ☐ +25% FIRE RATE

GGN30 HARD SNIPER

	LEVEL	BUY	SELL
	46	$1,025,346	$146,478

DAMAGE	ACCURACY	FIRE RATE	MAGAZINE	ELEMENTAL
658	98.6	0.6	6	-

- ☐ +34% RECOIL REDUCTION
- ☐ +41% DAMAGE
- ☐ +3% FIRE RATE
- ☐ 1.0X WEAPON ZOOM

GGN ROLLING SNIPER

	LEVEL	BUY	SELL
	48	$707,539	$101,077

DAMAGE	ACCURACY	FIRE RATE	MAGAZINE	ELEMENTAL
569	95.7	0.6	6	-

- ☐ -21% RECOIL REDUCTION
- ☐ +16% DAMAGE
- ☐ +3% FIRE RATE
- ☐ 1.0X WEAPON ZOOM

DVL450 FEARSOME SNIPER

	LEVEL	BUY	SELL
	19	$55,846	$7,978

DAMAGE	ACCURACY	FIRE RATE	MAGAZINE	ELEMENTAL
187	96.7	0.6	6	x2

- ☐ +16% RECOIL REDUCTION
- ☐ -4% FIRE RATE

CLAPTRAP DANCE OFF

ATLAS

Wasteland WANDERERS

KING OF CLAP

Pandora is a hostile place filled with dozens of nasty critters of unimaginable shapes and lethality. And that's just the indigenous life! The following pages contain all there is to know about each variety of every species that roams, flies, or slithers across the wastelands of this desolate planet. There are several varieties of data presented in this chapter; to completely understand the significance of each statistical category, please read the following:

1 **NAME:** This is the name of the enemy as encountered during the initial playthrough. Many enemy names change during additional playthroughs (see "varieties" below).

2 **THREAT METER:** This is our subjective assessment of how tough each enemy is, assuming you are equal in level with it. As this gauge fills from left to right, the color within gradually changes from blue to red (a short, blue meter denotes a relatively weak enemy; a full red meter indicates an extremely dangerous foe). This gauge is entirely relative to the player-character's level and that of the enemy.

3 **VARIETIES:** Many of the enemies have different names and statistical ratings if you play through the main campaign a second with the same character. It typically requires two playthroughs to reach level 50. The entire game balances to level 50 on the second playthrough or whenever the player reaches the level cap at 50, whichever comes first.

4 **STRATEGY:** This paragraph of tips and background information is designed to give you some practical insight into each enemy, along with solid tactics for killing it! Much of this information came directly from Gearbox Studios, so you know it's good!

5 **DATA:** The rows of data presented for each enemy do not reflect the actual HP rating or any other attribute for the enemy. Instead, every figure representing health, XP, and damage is actually a measure of how that individual enemy compares to all other creatures if their levels were equal. This can be difficult to understand, but all you need to know is that small numbers work in your favor and high numbers, particularly those with damage ratings above 1.00, are bad for your health. We created the Threat Meter to help give you a quick-glance assessment of the relative danger each enemy poses.

6 **CRITICAL SPOTS:** Most enemies have a particular vulnerability—usually the head or some part of their face—that yields a Critical Hit damage bonus when shot. Read the strategy text for tips on getting each enemy to reveal its weakness, and refer to our Hit Regions targeting diagram at the beginning of each species to see exactly where to score the most damage.

7 **RESISTANCES:** Many enemies are elemental by nature and are, therefore, immune to attacks from that same element. This often shows up in the enemy's name, but it's sometimes concealed (particularly in the case of bosses). Consult this column in the tables to determine which elemental attacks to avoid when fighting a given type of enemy.

8 **SHIELDS:** Not every enemy type has a shield, but many do. This column lets you know whether or not the foe has a shield that you must overcome and, if so, how many. Guardians, for example, have numerous shields. Use shock-based weapons to inflict extra damage to a shield.

1 MIDGET SHOTGUNNER

2nd Playthrough: Angry Little Shotgunner
Fuming Stunted Shotgunner

2 THREAT LEVEL

6 HIT REGIONS

3 Variety	**5** Health	XP	Melee Damage	Range Damage	Radius Damage	Leap Damage	Charge Damage	Critical Spots	**7** Resistances	Weapons	**8** Shields
Midget Shotgunner	0.65	0.65	Varies	Varies	X	X	X	Head	-	Shotgun	Yes
Angry Little Shotgunner / Fuming Stunted Shotgunner	1.30	0.78	Varies	Varies	X	X	X	Head	-	Shotgun	Yes

LEGEND ARMORED MODERATELY VULNERABLE CRITICAL HIT

4 These little guys come running up to you out of nowhere, just hoping you start to laugh at them—nothing pleases them more than blasting the smirk right off someone's face. Don't let their diminutive size or low health fool you; their shotgun packs a punch. Take them out as quickly as possible!

CREATURES
SKAGS

Skags make their home in holes on the side of rocks. These dens typically have a group of Skags living in them. It's not uncommon for a single Skag to keep watch outside the den. If trouble occurs the scout Skag alerts its mates to protect the den. After consuming their enemy, Skags will often regurgitate their bones in a pile. Anything that isn't organically digestible can be found among this searchable pile of bones and vomit. Skags tend to surround their prey and charge in one at a time from different angles, leaping with a bite, then running back to the outskirts of the circle in a sort of strafing run. They do this continuously in an effort to confuse and tire the enemy. This also builds confidence, until eventually they are all frenzied. Usually by then, it's lunch time.

The discovery of fire, corrosive, and electrical versions of the Skag species caused immediate excitement as many began to postulate that Skags could be harnessed to generate cheap power. All efforts to research the idea have so far ended up being very bloody. Despite the lack of useful results there continues to be research funding and volunteers available. Although energy generation has thus far had poor results, much progress has been made in the area of Skag pup training, which some hope will one day turn into a profitable pet business or circus act.

SKAG FAMILY

Variety	Threat
Pup Skag	
Skag Whelp	
Spitter Skag	
Adult Skag	
Elder Skag	
Alpha Skag	
Badass Skag	
Badass Shock Alpha	
Badass Corrosive Skag	
Badass Fire Skag	
Badass Shock Skag	
Badass Corrosive Alpha	
Badass Fire Alpha	

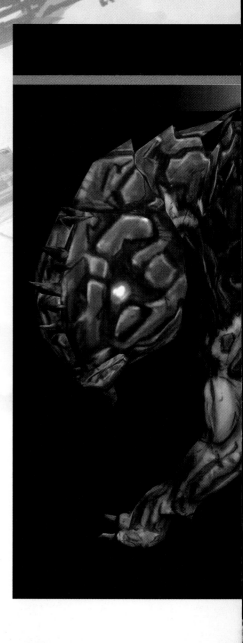

KING OF CLAP

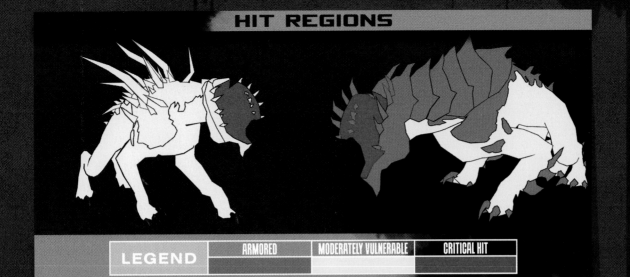

LEGEND	ARMORED	MODERATELY VULNERABLE	CRITICAL HIT

PUP SKAG

2nd Playthrough: Annoyed Pup Skag
Colicky Skag

THREAT LEVEL

Variety	Health	XP	Melee Damage	Range Damage	Radius Damage	Leap Damage	Charge Damage	Critical Spots	Resistances
Pup Skag	0.40	0.40	0.20	X	X	Rare	X	Mouth	-
Annoyed Pup Skag Colicky Skag	0.80	0.48	0.30	X	X	Rare	X	Mouth	-

Pup Skags are harmless one-on-one, but beware of them in packs. They have very low health—and can be easily killed with a melee attack—but should be shot before they get too close. Shooting a Skag in the head causes more damage and also makes them roar, thus exposing their critical hit region inside their mouth.

CLAPTRAP
DANCE OFF

SKAG WHELP

2nd Playthrough: Angry Skag Whelp
Querulous Skag Whelp

THREAT LEVEL

Variety	Health	XP	Melee Damage	Range Damage	Radius Damage	Leap Damage	Charge Damage	Critical Spots	Resistances
Skag Whelp	0.80	0.80	0.30	X	X	0.60	X	Mouth	-
Angry Skag Whelp / Querulous Skag Whelp	1.60	0.96	0.45	X	X	0.90	X	Mouth	-

SPITTER SKAG

2nd Playthrough: Hawking Skag
Sputum Skag

THREAT LEVEL

Variety	Health	XP	Melee Damage	Range Damage	Radius Damage	Leap Damage	Charge Damage	Critical Spots	Resistances
Spitter Skag	1.00	1.00	0.10	0.40	X	X	X	Mouth	☣
Hawking Skag / Sputum Skag	2.00	1.20	0.15	0.60	X	X	X	Mouth	☣

ADULT SKAG

2nd Playthrough: Feral Skag
Bestial Skag

THREAT LEVEL

Adult Skags are the natural evolution of Skag Whelps and have learned to leap and inflict damage through a radius attack. As with other Skags, shooting it in the head causes it to roar, thus exposing its tender soft-spot. Shoot in the mouth for a critical bonus of 5x damage!

ELDER SKAG

2nd Playthrough: Hulking Elder Skag
Stalwart Elder Skag

THREAT LEVEL

Variety	Health	XP	Melee Damage	Range Damage	Radius Damage	Leap Damage	Charge Damage	Critical Spots	Resistances
Elder Skag	2.00	2.00	0.50	0.40	0.25	X	0.60	Mouth	-
Hulking Elder Skag / Stalwart Elder Skag	4.00	2.40	0.75	0.60	0.38	X	0.90	Mouth	-

Skag Whelps are similar to Pup Skags, but slightly larger and a bit tougher to bring down. Most importantly, Skag Whelps are more apt to make a leaping attack at their prey. Shooting a Skag in the head causes more damage and makes them roar, thus exposing their critical hit region inside their mouth. Shooting them in this area of vulnerability does 5x damage!

Spitter Skags try to maintain a safe distance from their prey and attack by spitting globs of corrosive mucous at their target. Corrosive weaponry does very little damage, but shooting them in the mouth is still effective. The best way to handle them is to get in close to avoid their spitting attack and melee them!

Variety	Health	XP	Melee Damage	Range Damage	Radius Damage	Leap Damage	Charge Damage	Critical Spots	Resistances
Adult Skag	1.20	1.20	0.40	X	0.30	0.65	X	Mouth	-
Feral Skag Bestial Skag	2.40	1.44	0.60	X	0.45	0.98	X	Mouth	-

Elder Skags combine the aggressiveness of Adult Skags with the ranged attack of Spitter Skags, but they aren't corrosive. They can also charge you when sufficiently angry. Although they pack a bit more ferocity than other Skags, they are still prone to the standard Skag vulnerability: their mouth. Shooting the Skag in the head forces it to roar. Wait for it to roar, then fire a round down its throat for a critical bonus of 5x damage!

CLAPTRAP
DANCE OFF

ALPHA SKAG

2nd Playthrough: Hardened Alpha Skag
Armored Alpha Skag

THREAT LEVEL

Variety	Health	XP	Melee Damage	Range Damage	Radius Damage	Leap Damage	Charge Damage	Critical Spots	Resistances
Alpha Skag	4.00	6.00	1.00	X	X	Rare	0.50	Mouth	-
Hardened Alpha Skag Armored Alpha Skag	8.00	7.20	1.50	X	X	Rare	0.75	Mouth	-

BADASS SKAG

2nd Playthrough: BadMutha Skag
AssKicking Skag

THREAT LEVEL

Badass Skags are slower than most other types of Skags, but they have a devastating leap attack. Use your speed to avoid attacks, then strafe and jump away from their leap. Shoot the Badass Skag in the head to get it to open its mouth, then fire a shot at its open gob.

BADASS SHOCK ALPHA

2nd Playthrough: BadMutha Shock Alpha
SuperBad Shock Alpha

THREAT LEVEL

Variety	Health	XP	Melee Damage	Range Damage	Radius Damage	Leap Damage	Charge Damage	Critical Spots	Resistances
Badass Shock Alpha	7.00	10.50	0.01	0.50	0.75	X	1.00	Mouth	⚡⚡
BadMutha Shock Alpha SuperBad Shock Alpha	14.00	12.60	0.02	0.75	1.13	X	1.00	Mouth	⚡⚡

BADASS CORROSIVE SKAG

2nd Playthrough: BadMutha Corrosive Skag
SuperBad Corrosive Skag

THREAT LEVEL

Variety	Health	XP	Melee Damage	Range Damage	Radius Damage	Leap Damage	Charge Damage	Critical Spots	Resistances
Badass Corrosive Skag	7.50	7.50	0.80	0.50	1.40	X	X	Mouth	☣
BadMutha Corrosive Skag SuperBad Corrosive Skag	15.00	9.00	1.20	0.75	2.10	X	X	Mouth	☣

KING OF CLAP

Alpha Skags aren't just bigger than the less powerful Skags, but they come equipped with heavy armor that covers much of their head and back. Attack the armor with corrosive weapons to inflict extra damage or pepper their heads with bullets until they open their mouth. Alpha Skags suffer 4x damage when you plug a bullet in their gullet.

Variety	Health	XP	Melee Damage	Range Damage	Radius Damage	Leap Damage	Charge Damage	Critical Spots	Resistances
Badass Skag	6.00	6.00	0.50	X	0.80	1.00	X	Mouth	-
BadMutha Skag AssKicking Skag	12.00	7.20	0.75	X	1.20	1.50	X	Mouth	-

Badass Shock Alpha Skags attack by emitting a ranged electrical attack and tend to stand back from their target like Spitter Skags. Shoot them in their mouth while they perform their electrical attack. Shock weapons do very little damage, so always opt for another kind of gun against this creature.

These Skags attack with a radius attack the spreads corrosive effects far and wide in a radiating pattern. Jump to avoid the radius damage and strafe around the Badass Corrosive Skag to get a shot on it. Try peppering it with bullets to make it roar, then shoot it in its mouth.

CLAPTRAP DANCE OFF

BADASS FIRE SKAG

2nd Playthrough: BadMutha Fire Skag
SuperBad Fire Skag

THREAT LEVEL

Variety	Health	XP	Melee Damage	Range Damage	Radius Damage	Leap Damage	Charge Damage	Critical Spots	Resistances
Badass Fire Skag	9.00	9.00	0.60	0.65	1.50	X	X	Mouth	🔥
BadMutha Fire Skag SuperBad Fire Skag	18.00	10.80	0.90	0.98	2.25	X	X	Mouth	🔥

Badass Fire Skags attack with a radius fire attack that spreads across the floor in a wave of flames. Watch for them to stomp their feet to attack and jump over the blaze. Strafe around the enemy to get a shot on it and avoid attacking with incendiary strikes. Blast it with other elemental attacks and normal bullets to make it roar, then shoot it in the mouth.

BADASS SHOCK SKAG

2nd Playthrough: BadMutha Shock Skag
SuperBad Shock Skag

THREAT LEVEL

Variety	Health	XP	Melee Damage	Range Damage	Radius Damage	Leap Damage	Charge Damage	Critical Spots	Resistances
Badass Shock Skag	11.00	11.00	0.50	0.80	0.80	X	0.50	Mouth	⚡
BadMutha Shock Skag SuperBad Shock Alpha	22.00	13.20	0.75	1.20	1.20	X	0.75	Mouth	⚡

KING OF CLAP

Badass Shock Skags attack with a radius attack, as well as a projectile shock ball. Shoot the projectile out of the air and leap over the radius attack, but beware of the Badass Shock Skag's surprising speed. It's relatively immune to shock-based attacks, so choose a weapon with different properties. Blast it in the head to make it roar, then open fire into its open maw.

BADASS CORROSIVE ALPHA

THREAT LEVEL

Variety	Health	XP	Melee Damage	Range Damage	Radius Damage	Leap Damage	Charge Damage	Critical Spots	Resistances
Badass Corrosive Alpha	12.00	18.00	0.80	0.60	1.10	X	X	Mouth	☣
BadMutha Corrosive Alpha SuperBad Corrosive Alpha	24.00	21.60	1.20	0.90	1.65	X	X	Mouth	☣

This deadly Skag can definitely bring you down if you're not careful. Try to keep some lesser Skags around for a quick-kill in case you're incapacitated and need a Second Wind. Corrosive weapons do little damage against the Badass Corrosive Skag, but its mouth is a major weakness, as with all other Skags.

BADASS FIRE ALPHA

THREAT LEVEL

Variety	Health	XP	Melee Damage	Range Damage	Radius Damage	Leap Damage	Charge Damage	Critical Spots	Resistances
Badass Fire Alpha	15.00	22.50	0.40	0.75	0.50	1.20	X	Mouth	🔥
BadMutha Fire Alpha SuperBad Fire Alpha	30.00	27.00	0.60	1.13	0.75	1.80	X	Mouth	🔥

The Badass Fire Alpha is the deadliest of all non-boss Skags. It not only has a melee and leap attack, but can also breathe flames and emit a fiery radius attack, as well. Run and leap over the spreading fire ring and watch for it to begin spewing fire from its mouth. Dash around it and repeatedly attack with melee attacks while it's breathing fire. Incendiary weapons do very little damage, so use a different elemental attack. Look for it to open its mouth and blast a round down its throat for a critical hit bonus!

CLAPTRAP DANCE OFF

RAKK

The Rakk is a flying horde creature. Fairly weak, they are easy to kill and do little damage, making the threat from individual Rakks low. In greater numbers, however, these creatures become quite dangerous. Rakk use a strafing run style attack. They swarm past an enemy, slashing as they pass, causing small cuts before they loop around and come back for another pass. They continue to swoop upon the same target until it's dead, then land and devour it. Rakk are fast, but not very agile, so their attack runs take up quite a bit of room and there's time between strikes to maneuver or attempt to counterattack. Since Rakk attack in swarms and are rather fast in the air, it's best to use a shotgun when fighting them.

Rakk have been called the Pigeons of Pandora because they're everywhere, they don't taste very good, and any place they stay for a length of time becomes covered in droppings. But unlike Pigeons, Rakk are not afraid of humans and have been known to kill adults and carry off small children. A popular children's movie on Pandora tells the story of a child who is kidnapped by Rakk and raised as their own. In the movie the child eventually returns to human society where he rejects people with all of their ridiculous folly and triumphantly flies off into the sunset with his Rakk friends by his side. Contrary to the story, all of the children carried off by Rakk have been killed and eaten, and none has ever been taught how to fly.

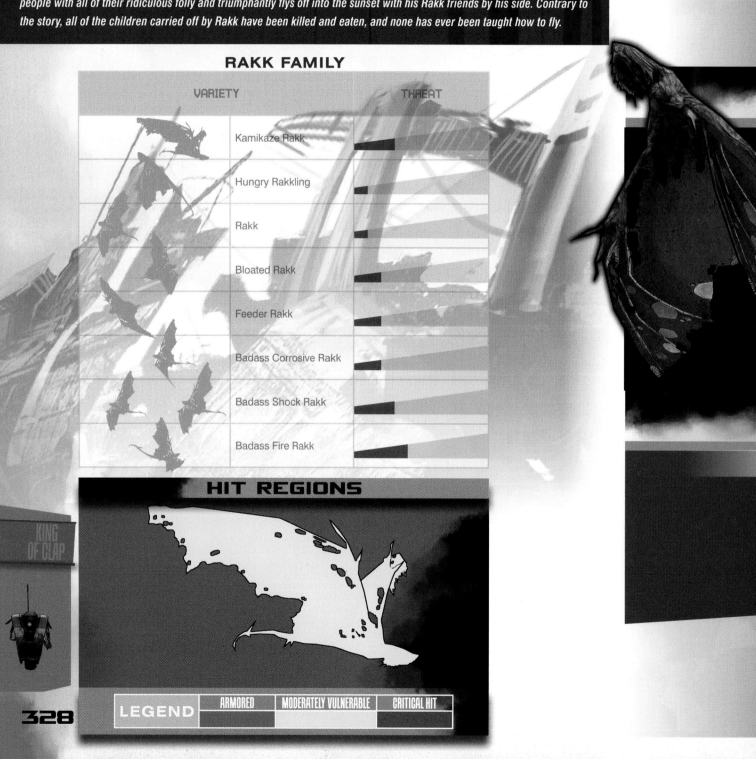

RAKK FAMILY

VARIETY	THREAT
Kamikaze Rakk	
Hungry Rakkling	
Rakk	
Bloated Rakk	
Feeder Rakk	
Badass Corrosive Rakk	
Badass Shock Rakk	
Badass Fire Rakk	

HIT REGIONS

LEGEND	ARMORED	MODERATELY VULNERABLE	CRITICAL HIT

KING
OF CLAP

KAMIKAZE RAKK

2nd Playthrough: Kaiten Rakk
Banzai Rakk

THREAT LEVEL

Variety	Health	XP	Melee Damage	Range Damage	Radius Damage	Leap Damage	Charge Damage	Critical Spots	Resistances
Kamikaze Rakk	0.10	0.40	0.15	X	X	X	X		
Kaiten Rakk Banzai Rakk	0.20	0.48	0.23	X	X	X	X	-	

Kamikaze Rakk explode on contact and are more than willing to sacrifice themselves for the safety of the flock. Blast them out of the sky with a shotgun before they get too close and explode.

HUNGRY RAKKLING

2nd Playthrough: Starving Rakkling
Famished Rakkling

THREAT LEVEL

Variety	Health	XP	Melee Damage	Range Damage	Radius Damage	Leap Damage	Charge Damage	Critical Spots	Resistances
Hungry Rakkling	0.15	0.30	0.05	X	X	X	X	-	-
Starving Rakkling Famished Rakkling	0.30	0.36	0.08	X	X	X	X	-	-

These blue-colored Rakk are easy kills, so get them before they get to you! Equip your shotgun and blast away as they approach, then use melee attacks on the swarm as they get near. Hungry Rakkling are more vulnerable to close-range swats of your gun.

RAKK

2nd Playthrough: Relentless Rakk
Vindictive Rakk

THREAT LEVEL

Variety	Health	XP	Melee Damage	Range Damage	Radius Damage	Leap Damage	Charge Damage	Critical Spots	Resistances
Rakk	0.35	0.70	0.30	X	X	X	X		-
Relentless Rakk Vindictive Rakk	0.70	0.84	0.45	X	X	X	X		-

These basic Rakk attack by swooping down on their prey, then flying high into the sky, circling around, and attacking again. Use the time it takes for them to turn around to reload, take cover, and prepare to fire. Blast away with the shotgun to down multiple Rakk at once.

CLAPTRAP DANCE OFF

BLOATED RAKK

2nd Playthrough: Distended Rakk
Tumescent Rakk

THREAT
LEVEL

Variety	Health	XP	Melee Damage	Range Damage	Radius Damage	Leap Damage	Charge Damage	Critical Spots	Resistances
Bloated Rakk	0.60	1.20	0.30	X	X	X	X	-	-
Distended Rakk Tumescent Rakk	1.20	1.44	0.45	X	X	X	X	-	-

Bloated Rakk sparkle and shimmer against the Pandoran sky and are easier to spot in the distance than others. They are quite a bit larger than lesser Rakk and burst open upon being killed, releasing a pile of undigested weapons for you to sift through… with gloves, hopefully.

FEEDER RAKK

2nd Playthrough: Forager Rakk
Cultivator Rakk

THREAT
LEVEL

Variety	Health	XP	Melee Damage	Range Damage	Radius Damage	Leap Damage	Charge Damage	Critical Spots	Resistances
Feeder Rakk	0.60	1.20	0.30	X	X	X	X	-	-
Forager Rakk Cultivator Rakk	1.20	1.44	0.45	X	X	X	X	-	-

Feeder Rakk are very similar to Bloated Rakk, only they are silver in color instead of yellow. They sparkle in the distance and release undigested weapons when killed. Use your shotgun as they swoop in for the attack, then gather up the goodies they leave behind.

BADASS CORROSIVE RAKK

2nd Playthrough: BadMutha Corrosive Rakk
SuperBad Corrosive Rakk

THREAT
LEVEL

Variety	Health	XP	Melee Damage	Range Damage	Radius Damage	Leap Damage	Charge Damage	Critical Spots	Resistances
Badass Corrosive Rakk	2.50	5.00	X	2.00	X	X	X	-	☣
BadMutha Corrosive Rakk SuperBad Corrosive Rakk	5.00	6.00	X	3.00	X	X	X	-	☣

These toxic green members of the Rakk family don't attack with swooping melee attacks like their cousins do, but rather spit Corrosive projectiles as they swoop past. They won't come as close as the others, so melee attacks are out of the question, but they can be easily shot as they retreat. Jump around and take cover to avoid their corrosive attack, and do not use corrosive weapons against them.

BADASS SHOCK RAKK

2nd Playthrough: BadMutha Shock Rakk
SuperBad Shock Rakk

THREAT LEVEL

Variety	Health	XP	Melee Damage	Range Damage	Radius Damage	Leap Damage	Charge Damage	Critical Spots	Resistances
Badass Shock Rakk	3.50	7.00	X	2.40	X	X	X	-	Shock
BadMutha Shock Rakk SuperBad Shock Rakk	7.00	8.40	X	3.60	X	X	X	-	Shock

Like the Badass Corrosive Rakk, these flying annoyances maintain a safe distance and fire shock balls at their quarry in hopes of neutralizing it from afar. Jump around to avoid the shock balls (or shoot them out of the air), then open fire as they retreat. Shock weapons do little damage against them.

BADASS FIRE RAKK

2nd Playthrough: BadMutha Fire Rakk
SuperBad Fire Rakk

THREAT LEVEL

Variety	Health	XP	Melee Damage	Range Damage	Radius Damage	Leap Damage	Charge Damage	Critical Spots	Resistances
Badass Fire Rakk	4.50	9.00	X	0.80	X	X	X	-	Fire
BadMutha Fire Rakk SuperBad Fire Rakk	9.00	10.80	X	1.20	X	X	X	-	Fire

The Badass Fire Rakk is the *most badass* of all the Badass Rakk. It circles overhead, occasionally swooping in to spit fiery projectiles at its target. Stay on the move (or take cover inside a nearby shack) and jump around to avoid the fireballs, then shoot the Rakk during its retreat.

CLAPTRAP DANCE OFF

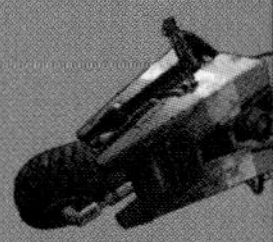

CRABWORMS

Purple is the common color for Crabworms. They spend much of their time underground, waiting to emerge when enticed by food. They also camp out for a few days in their burrows during molting and should not be disturbed during this process. They are extremely territorial and will attack anything that gets close to their home. Males often fight amongst themselves for burrow possession. An adult may measure up to 20 feet long, but on occasion some have been seen to measure over 50 feet. The Crabworm's carapace becomes harder as it matures into an adult. Their claws are strong and powerful, able to cut a man in half. They use their legs and claws to navigate through the ground, usually scavenging for food.

There was a short time where the carapace of Crabworms was believed to be a powerful aphrodesiac. The carapace was usually ground up and drank as part of a tea, although other forms of consumption exist. Adult Crabworm carapaces were so hard that they would often damage the equipment being used to grind them into a fine powder, so the industry preferred using young Crabworms for the process. To avoid damaging the precious carapace, the young Crabworms would be clubbed or stabbed through the eye before their corpses were exported. The fact that there was little to no protest over the cruel treatment of these creatures is probably due to Pandora being on the edge of established space and Crabworms being too hideous for most people to gain any emotional attachment.

CRABWORM FAMILY

VARIETY		THREAT
	Larva Crab Worm	
	Crab Worm	

HIT REGIONS

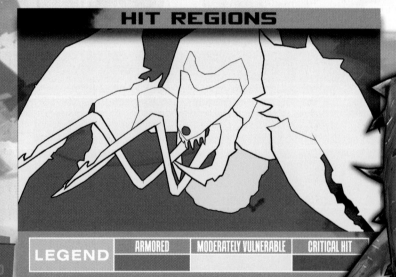

LEGEND	ARMORED	MODERATELY VULNERABLE	CRITICAL HIT

KING OF CLAP

LARVA CRAB WORM

THREAT LEVEL

Variety	Health	XP	Melee Damage	Range Damage	Radius Damage	Leap Damage	Charge Damage	Critical Spots	Resistances
Larva Crab Worm	5.00	5.00	0.50	0.10	X	X	X	Eye	-

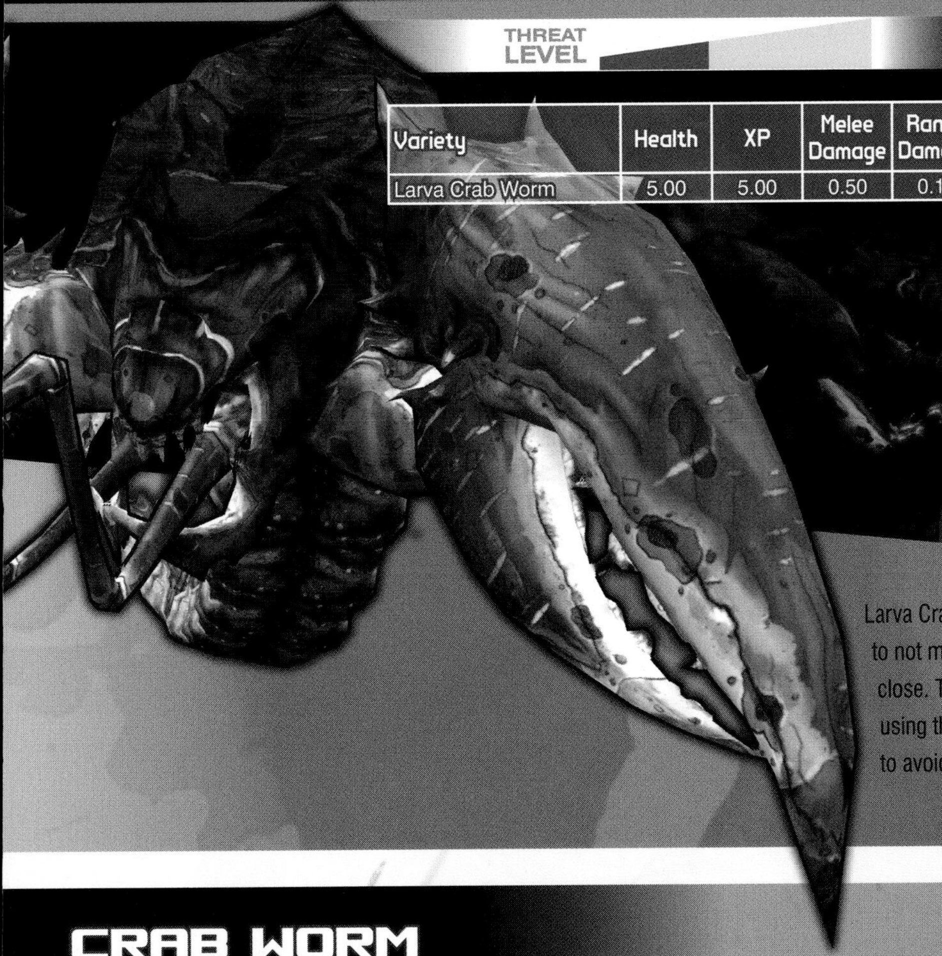

Larva Crab Worms aren't as large as normal Crab Worms and they tend to not make themselves known until their prey mistakenly gets too close. They emerge from the ground and attack by spitting venom and using their powerful claws. Keep your distance, jump around and strafe to avoid the spit attack, then shoot them in the eye.

CRAB WORM

THREAT LEVEL

Variety	Health	XP	Melee Damage	Range Damage	Radius Damage	Leap Damage	Charge Damage	Critical Spots	Resistances
Crab Worm	10.00	20.00	0.80	X	X	X	0.50	Eye	-

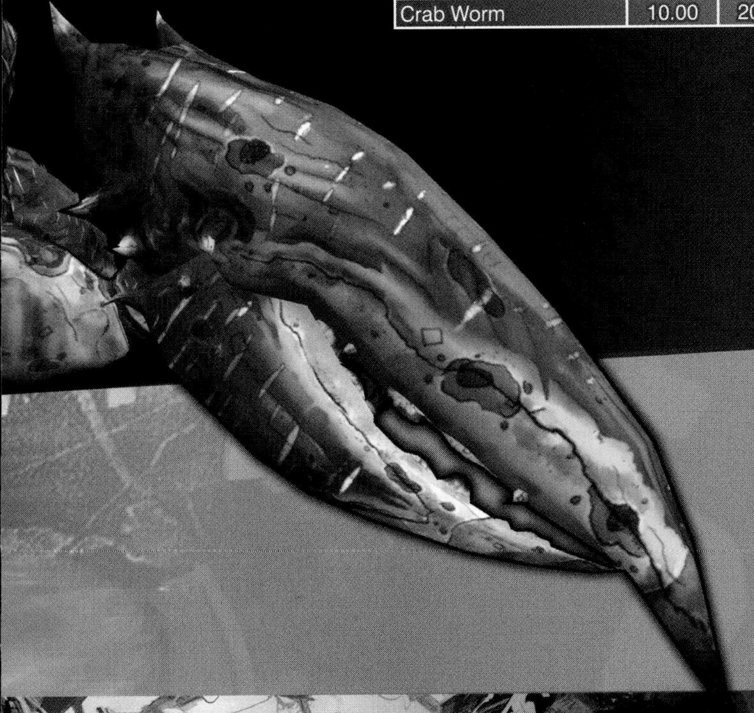

These hulking beasts burrow up from underground, then charge forward to chop their prey in half with powerful claws. Although they don't spit like their smaller companions do, they are capable of causing significant damage by ramming their target. Keep a safe distance away and snipe them in the eye for a critical hit. Shooting them with a powerful enough rifle in this area blows their entire head off!

CLAPTRAP DANCE OFF

SCYTHIDS

The Scythid is similar to a slug, but with insectoid appendages. They vary in size, depending upon the species. The color of Scythids also varies widely, ranging from a dark black-brown to an orange color. Large serrated mandibles give this creature its characteristic appearance. Scythids tend to congregate around moist and polluted areas. They feed on pretty much everything: trash, bone, meat, and vegetation. This nourishment speeds their growth and increases their population. Unlike other creatures on Pandora, Scythids have particularly thin exoskeletons, which makes them very susceptible to damage.

Scythids look like some sort of cross between a slug, a lobster, and a beetle. However, initial genetic tests show that their DNA is more closely related to a horse than any of the previously mentioned creatures. This oddity has gone through rigorous scientific scrutiny and, although findings and research continue to support the finding, it is widely disbelieved and contested. Counter arguments include theories that the species was genetically altered by the Eridians for an unknown purpose and that all of the research in this regard is irrelevant.

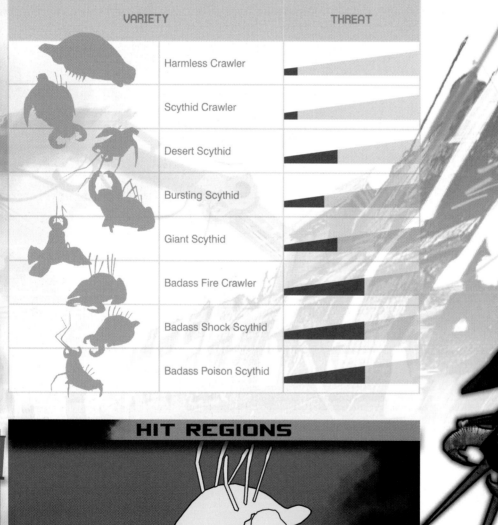

SCYTHID FAMILY

VARIETY	THREAT
Harmless Crawler	
Scythid Crawler	
Desert Scythid	
Bursting Scythid	
Giant Scythid	
Badass Fire Crawler	
Badass Shock Scythid	
Badass Poison Scythid	

HIT REGIONS

LEGEND	ARMORED	MODERATELY VULNERABLE	CRITICAL HIT

KING OF CLAP

HARMLESS CRAWLER

THREAT LEVEL

Variety	Health	XP	Melee Damage	Range Damage	Radius Damage	Leap Damage	Charge Damage	Critical Spots	Resistances
Harmless Crawler	0.05	0.05	0.30	X	X	0.50	X	-	-

These tiny blue Scythids do not attack; rather, they quickly scurry away when an enemy approaches. Shoot them from afar to rack up some easy experience.

SCYTHID CRAWLER

2nd Playthrough: Scythid Slug
Scythid Creep

THREAT LEVEL

Variety	Health	XP	Melee Damage	Range Damage	Radius Damage	Leap Damage	Charge Damage	Critical Spots	Resistances
Scythid Crawler	0.50	0.50	0.05	X	X	0.30	X	-	-
Scythid Slug Scythis Creep	1.00	0.60	0.08	X	X	0.45	X	-	-

Seeking strength in numbers, Scythid Crawlers often appear in large groups. They have very low health, so a single grenade blast can eliminate a pack of them at once. Although weak creatures, they can still pose a threat if they get close enough to leap.

DESERT SCYTHID

2nd Playthrough: Wasteland Scythid
Dune Scythid

THREAT LEVEL

Variety	Health	XP	Melee Damage	Range Damage	Radius Damage	Leap Damage	Charge Damage	Critical Spots	Resistances
Desert Scythid	1.00	1.00	0.10	X	X	Rare	0.50	-	-
Wasteland Scythid Dune Scythid	2.00	1.20	0.15	X	X	Rare	0.75	-	-

Desert Scythids are capable of flying around at low-altitude, and that's when they're at their most dangerous. Stay clear of their aerial bombardments, and either shoot them or use melee attacks (very effective) if they get too close.

CLAPTRAP DANCE OFF

BURSTING SCYTHID

2nd Playthrough: Exploding Scythid
Kablooey Scythid

THREAT LEVEL

Variety	Health	XP	Melee Damage	Range Damage	Radius Damage	Leap Damage	Charge Damage	Critical Spots	Resistances
Bursting Scythid	1.00	2.00	0.30	X	X	0.60	X	-	-
Exploding Scythid Kablooey Scythid	2.00	2.40	0.45	X	X	0.90	X	-	-

GIANT SCYTHID

2nd Playthrough: Mammoth Scythid
Colossal Scythid

THREAT LEVEL

Variety	Health	XP	Melee Damage	Range Damage	Radius Damage	Leap Damage	Charge Damage	Critical Spots	Resistances
Giant Scythid	5.00	5.00	0.75	1.80	X	Rare	X	-	-
Mammoth Scythid Colossal Scythid	10.00	6.00	1.13	2.70	X	Rare	X	-	-

BADASS FIRE CRAWLER

2nd Playthrough: BadMutha Blazing Crawler
SuperBad Scorching Crawler

THREAT LEVEL

Keep your distance from the Badass Fire Crawler; it erupts upon death into a fiery explosion that can incapacitate anyone nearby. Most of this creature's attacks are fire-based, so protect yourself with a fire-resistant shield when you see them coming. Hyperion makes a good one!

BADASS SHOCK SCYTHID

2nd Playthrough: BadMutha Lightning Scythid
SuperBad Galvanizing Scythid

THREAT LEVEL

Variety	Health	XP	Melee Damage	Range Damage	Radius Damage	Leap Damage	Charge Damage	Critical Spots	Resistances
Badass Shock Scythid	9.00	9.00	0.75	0.50	X	X	X	-	⚡⁄₄
BadMutha Lightning Scythid SuperBad Galvanizing Scythid	18.00	10.80	1.13	0.75	X	X	X	-	⚡⁄₄

KING OF CLAP

Bursting Scythids get their name from a proclivity to explode in a powerful detonation upon death, damaging everything around them. Look for their tell-tale color change that indicates when they are low on health, then back away quickly. Obviously, it's best not to melee these little guys!

Giant Scythids may be larger than their brethren, but they're also a lot slower. Take advantage of this sluggishness to out-maneuver their attacks—particularly those of the ranged variety—and move in for a few melee strikes to their backside.

Variety	Health	XP	Melee Damage	Range Damage	Radius Damage	Leap Damage	Charge Damage	Critical Spots	Resistances
Badass Fire Crawler	6.00	6.00	0.60	0.10	X	0.80	X	-	
BadMutha Blazing Crawler SuperBad Scorching Crawler	12.00	7.20	0.90	0.15	X	1.20	X	-	

The Badass Shock Scythid emits a powerful electric blast upon death that can be highly destructive to those within range. Most of this creature's attacks are electric-based, so protect yourself with a shock-resistant shield when facing these foes—Atlas offers a good selection.

CLAPTRAP DANCE OFF

WASTELAND WANDERERS: SCYTHIDS

THREAT LEVEL

Variety	Health	XP	Melee Damage	Range Damage	Radius Damage	Leap Damage	Charge Damage	Critical Spots	Resistances
Badass Poison Scythid	12.00	12.00	0.75	Rare	X	X	0.50	-	☣
BadMutha Venomous Scythid SuperBad Noxious Scythid	24.00	14.40	1.13	Rare	X	X	0.75	-	☣

Like the other Badass Scythids, the Badass Poison Scythid releases a dangerous elemental blast upon death. The poisonous cloud doesn't spread far, but can choke the life out of anyone nearby. Most of this creature's attacks are corrosive, so protect yourself with an appropriate shield from Dahl.

KING OF CLAP

SPIDERANTS

Spiderants are about six feet long. The Workers gather food and build the hive under the ground while the Soldiers and Kings protect the hive. Naturally, the Queen rules them all. She has a larger abdomen and head than the rest of them. The Spiderant's carapace is very thick and able to withstand major punishment. In general, the greatest weakness of these creatures is their unprotected abdomen. The two large front claws are called the "crusher claws," which are used to beat and stab their victims to death. It's said that this bloodied mess is then cocooned in a resin secreted from the abdomen for later consumption. They typically prefer to feast on small Skags, which are abundant in the region and easily slain.

Spiderants are believed to have a highly structured society where each individual Spiderant works for the good of the colony. This is likely why the word "ant" became part of the name for this creature. Although some claim to have found vast underground Spiderant colonies, these individuals have never been able to quite remember specific locations or how they escaped with their lives from such a dangerous place.

SPIDERANT FAMILY

VARIETY	THREAT
Spiderantling	
Spiderant Worker	
Spiderant Soldier	
Spiderant Gyro	
Spiderant King	
Spiderant Queen	
Badass Spiderant Burner	
Badass Spiderant Corrupter	
Badass Spiderant Zapper	

HIT REGIONS

LEGEND	ARMORED	MODERATELY VULNERABLE	CRITICAL HIT

SPIDERANTLING

THREAT LEVEL

Variety	Health	XP	Melee Damage	Range Damage	Radius Damage	Leap Damage	Charge Damage	Critical Spots	Resistances
Spiderantling	0.50	0.50	0.20	X	X	0.40	X	Abdomen	-
Skittish Spiderantling / Agitated Spiderantling	1.00	0.60	0.30	X	X	0.60	X	Abdomen	-

Spiderantlings are the youngest, and weakest, members of the Spiderant species. They may be big enough to leave the nest, but their armor plating has not yet fully developed. Shoot them before they leap because even at this tender age, they can still deal some pain.

SPIDERANT WORKER

THREAT LEVEL

Variety	Health	XP	Melee Damage	Range Damage	Radius Damage	Leap Damage	Charge Damage	Critical Spots	Resistances
Spiderant Worker	0.70	0.70	0.40	X	X	0.60	X	Abdomen	-
Spiderant Toiler / Spiderant Slave	1.40	0.84	0.60	X	X	0.90	X	Abdomen	-

The common Spiderant Workers attack by leaping onto their prey with the hopes of digging in with their claws for a death blow. Although their carapace protects them from head-on attacks, shooting these creatures in the face has a disorienting effect that causes them to reveal their soft underbelly. Melee attacks are particularly effective at wreaking havoc on Spiderant abdomens.

SPIDERANT SOLDIER

THREAT LEVEL

Variety	Health	XP	Melee Damage	Range Damage	Radius Damage	Leap Damage	Charge Damage	Critical Spots	Resistances
Spiderant Soldier	0.80	0.80	0.40	0.15	X	X	0.50	Abdomen	-
Spiderant Warrior / Spiderant Slayer	1.60	0.96	0.60	0.23	X	X	0.75	Abdomen	-

Spiderant Soldiers prefer to charge after their quarry instead of leaping on them. This makes it somewhat easier to predict their movements. They don't expose their abdomen easily and have very thick armor covering most of their body. Lob grenades behind them to blast their bellies apart. Corrosive weapons chew through their armor and cause additional damage.

SPIDERANT GYRO

THREAT LEVEL

Variety	Health	XP	Melee Damage	Range Damage	Radius Damage	Leap Damage	Charge Damage	Critical Spots	Resistances
Spiderant Gyro	1.25	1.25	0.40	X	X	X	1.30	Abdomen	-
Spiderant Beetle / Spiderant Vermin	2.50	1.50	0.60	X	X	X	1.95	Abdomen	-

These tumbling and bumbling Spiderants charge forward in a chaotic roll, eventually coming to a rest with their unprotected abdomen exposed. Quickly shoot this beast in the gut to kill it or charge forward and melee its underside to rupture it at point-blank range.

KING OF CLAP

THREAT LEVEL

Variety	Health	XP	Melee Damage	Range Damage	Radius Damage	Leap Damage	Charge Damage	Critical Spots	Resistances
Spiderant King	2.00	2.00	0.40	0.25	X	1.50	X	Abdomen	-
Spiderant Overlord Spiderant Emperor	4.00	2.40	0.60	0.38	X	2.25	X	Abdomen	-

Spiderant Kings, the evolution of the Spiderant Worker, possess greater health and attacking power. They can strike from afar with a ranged attack, or by leaping onto their prey from considerable distance. Shoot Spiderant Kings in the head to confuse them and force them to spin around, thus revealing their abdomen. This royal variety has heavy armor covering much of its body, so be sure to aim for the belly!

CLAPTRAP DANCE OFF

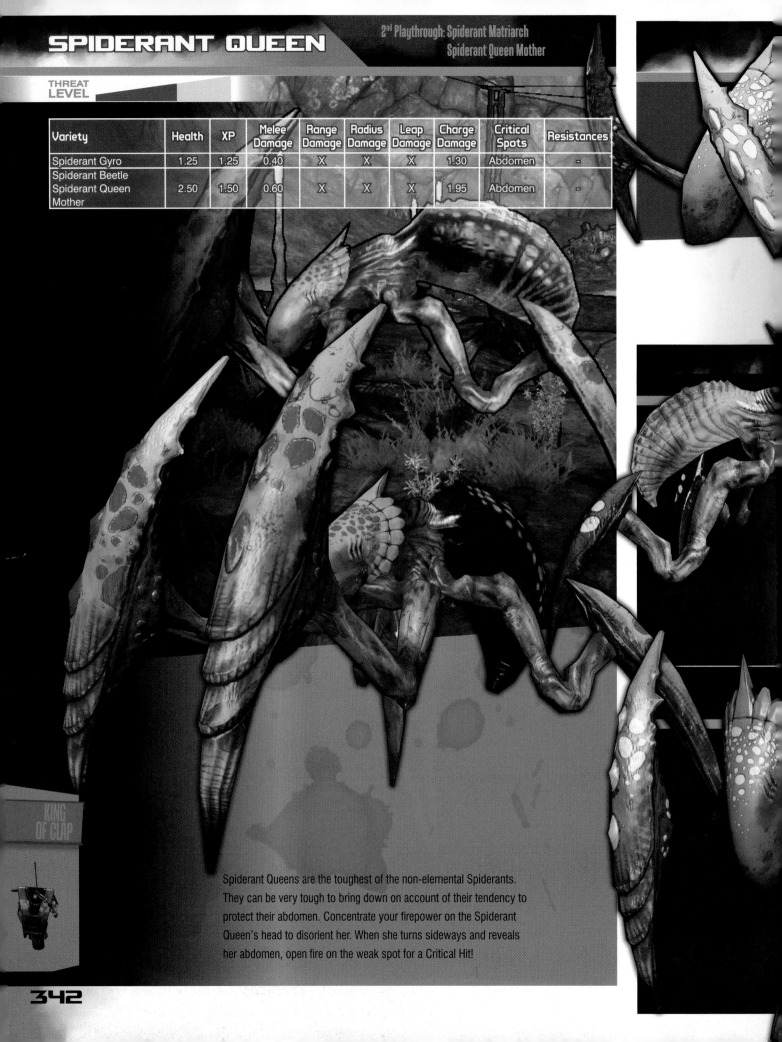

SPIDERANT QUEEN

THREAT LEVEL

Variety	Health	XP	Melee Damage	Range Damage	Radius Damage	Leap Damage	Charge Damage	Critical Spots	Resistances
Spiderant Gyro	1.25	1.25	0.40	X	X	X	1.30	Abdomen	-
Spiderant Beetle									
Spiderant Queen Mother	2.50	1.50	0.60	X	X	X	1.95	Abdomen	-

KING OF CLAP

Spiderant Queens are the toughest of the non-elemental Spiderants. They can be very tough to bring down on account of their tendency to protect their abdomen. Concentrate your firepower on the Spiderant Queen's head to disorient her. When she turns sideways and reveals her abdomen, open fire on the weak spot for a Critical Hit!

BADASS SPIDERANT BURNER

THREAT LEVEL

Variety	Health	XP	Melee Damage	Range Damage	Radius Damage	Leap Damage	Charge Damage	Critical Spots	Resistances
Badass Spiderant Burner	6.00	9.00	0.50	0.40	0.80	0.80	1.50	Abdomen	🔥
BadMutha Spiderant Incinerator SuperBad Spiderant Cremator	12.00	10.80	0.75	0.60	1.20	1.20	2.25	Abdomen	🔥

Badass Spiderant Burners rely on every trick in the book to kill their prey. Their attacks are primarily fire-based and they can attack with their claws, by spitting fireballs, and by leaping and charging. They have tremendously thick armor and are relatively immune to incendiary-based weapons. Use corrosive weaponry to eat through their armor, then aim for abdomens. Avoid getting too close, though; resort to melee attacks only when absolutely necessary.

BADASS SPIDERANT CORRUPTER

THREAT LEVEL

Variety	Health	XP	Melee Damage	Range Damage	Radius Damage	Leap Damage	Charge Damage	Critical Spots	Resistances
Badass Spiderant Corrupter	7.00	10.50	1.00	0.60	1.00	X	X	Abdomen	☣
BadMutha Spiderant Infector SuperBad Spiderant Desecrator	14.00	12.60	1.50	0.90	1.50	X	X	Abdomen	☣

Badass Spiderant Corrupters don't leap or charge like their flaming relatives do, but their toxic spit can inflict some serious damage if you don't dodge it. Focus your firepower on the beast's head to disorient it and force it to turn sideways, then blast away at its abdomen. Corrosive weapons do very little damage against this variety of Spiderant.

BADASS SPIDERANT ZAPPER

THREAT LEVEL

Variety	Health	XP	Melee Damage	Range Damage	Radius Damage	Leap Damage	Charge Damage	Critical Spots	Resistances
Badass Spiderant Zapper	8.00	12.00	0.40	0.40	0.80	X	X	Abdomen	⚡
BadMutha Spiderant Shocker SuperBad Spiderant Fulminator	16.00	14.40	0.60	0.60	1.20	X	X	Abdomen	⚡

CLAPTRAP DANCE OFF

Badass Spiderant Zappers do very little melee damage and don't leap or charge at their prey. However, they more than make up for these deficiencies with a powerful electricity-based radius and projectile attack. Leap away from these attack and quickly counter by shooting at their head, preferably with corrosive weapons to eat through their armor. Watch for them to turn sideways, then blast away at the abdomen. Shock-based weapons are ineffective against Badass Spiderant Zappers.

INDIGENOUS BIRDS

Wings are generally recognized as the flying, feathered friends of Pandora. There are four common types that can be found in almost any region. They tend to fly low over the ground, looking for something to eat. Much of their time is spent perched high atop open areas, scoping out breakfast options. Their diet consists of small mammals and amphibians, but they typically do not bother humans. Wings are sometimes kept as hunting pets by residents of Pandora, but this is very rare.

Pandora's indigenous birds are commonly called "Wings" by the local population. When asked why, responses range from "because that's what they're called" to "because 'Beaks' sounded stupid." Regardless of the name, they are graceful flyers and a beautiful sight to see.

INDIGENOUS BIRD FAMILY

	VARIETY	THREAT
	Northern Common Wing	
	Yellow Crested Wing	
	Red Tailed Wing	
	Trash Feeder	

HIT REGIONS

LEGEND	ARMORED	MODERATELY VULNERABLE	CRITICAL HIT

NORTHERN COMMON WING

THREAT LEVEL

Variety	Health	XP	Melee Damage	Range Damage	Radius Damage	Leap Damage	Charge Damage	Critical Spots	Resistances
Northern Common Wing	0.50	1.00	X	X	X	X	X	-	-

KING OF CLAP

YELLOW CRESTED WING

THREAT LEVEL

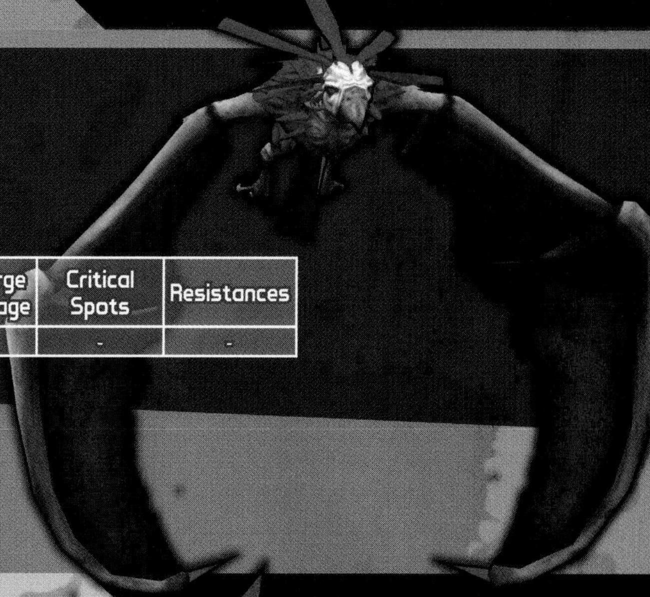

Variety	Health	XP	Melee Damage	Range Damage	Radius Damage	Leap Damage	Charge Damage	Critical Spots	Resistances
Yellow Crested Wing	0.50	1.00	X	X	X	X	X	-	-

RED TAILED WING

THREAT LEVEL

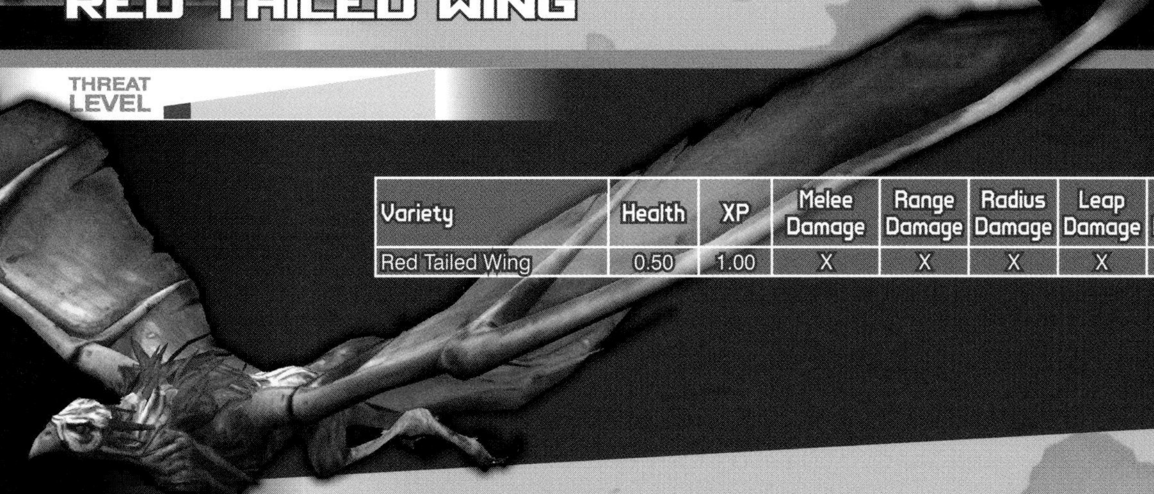

Variety	Health	XP	Melee Damage	Range Damage	Radius Damage	Leap Damage	Charge Damage	Critical Spots	Resistances
Red Tailed Wing	0.50	1.00	X	X	X	X	X	-	-

TRASH FEEDER

THREAT LEVEL

Variety	Health	XP	Melee Damage	Range Damage	Radius Damage	Leap Damage	Charge Damage	Critical Spots	Resistances
Trash Feeder	0.50	1.00	X	X	X	X	X	-	-

WASTELAN   ER   INDIGENOUS BIRDS

HUMANS
BANDITS

"Bandits" is the general term used to refer to the vicious tribes inhabiting Pandora. These criminals from the galaxy's overcrowded penal systems were sent here as mine workers. After numerous years of hard labor, they could earn their freedom and a ticket back to a more civilized planet. The criminals tended to fall into two varieties: those with useful skills (trustees), who were working off their sentences and trusted to keep the machinery and equipment operating; and those with psychotic tendencies (psychos), who had committed violent crimes and came to Pandora for good as an alternative to execution or life in solitary confinement.

One of the prisoners, a brutally violent man named Sledge, ran the largest of the prison gangs. He instigated a mass prison riot and overran the prison, killing most of the remaining guards and escaping from confinement. The surviving settlers, along with some of the less violent trustees, holed up in their settlements as best they could and staunchly defended their territory from the hostile indigenous life, as well as the escaped bands of prisoners. New Haven and Sanctuary are hanging on, but others have gone under. A few other settlers struck out on their own, preferring to take their chances alone rather than joining a larger settlement. The majority of the escaped prisoners grouped living off the land and raiding the remaining settlements or other gangs. They took what they needed to survive and reduce their competition. Many stole the armed runner vehicles used to get around by the guards, and formed roaming packs of bandits.

BANDIT CLAN

VARIETY	THREAT
Bandit Thug	
Midget Shotgunner	
Mutant Midget Psycho	
Psycho	
Burning Psycho	
Bandit Killer	
Bandit Raider	
Bruiser	
Badass Raider	
Badass Psycho	
Badass Bruiser	
Roid Rage Psycho	

There is widespread debate as to how large the bandit population on Pandora is. Many attempts have been made by settlers and mercenaries alike to thin their numbers, but the bandits always seem to come back in full force a short while later. Camps that appeared entirely wiped out only hours before seem to almost magically replenish their numbers. One theory is that the bandits have mastered cloning technology and that as soon as a bandit is killed a signal is sent back to secret cloning labs to build a replacement. While this would explain both their numbers and why so many of them look and sound alike, it is unlikely that a group this uneducated has the mastery of genetics and medical science required for such a feat. Another theory is that the bandits have secret breeding facilities where hunderds of thousands of women are in a constant state of accelerated pregnancy. This theory would explain the absence of females amongst the bandits and has been popular enough to motivate several treasure hunters to search for the so called "Bandit Breeding Grounds," but no one to date has reported any successful findings.

HIT REGIONS

LEGEND	ARMORED	MODERATELY VULNERABLE	CRITICAL HIT

BANDIT THUG

2nd Playthrough: Bandit Goon
Bandit Outlaw

THREAT LEVEL

Variety	Health	XP	Melee Damage	Range Damage	Radius Damage	Leap Damage	Charge Damage	Critical Spots	Resistances	Weapons	Shields
Bandit Thug	0.50	0.70	Varies	Varies	X	X	X	Head	-	Various	Yes
Bandit Goon Bandit Outlaw	1.00	0.84	Varies	Varies	X	X	X	Head	-	Various	Yes

These low-level grunts are fodder for your killing pleasure. Shoot them in the head for a quick kill or move in close for a melee attack—they won't melee back in this situation, so take advantage of their fear by beating them senseless with the stock of your rifle.

CLAPTRAP DANCE OFF

MIDGET SHOTGUNNER

2nd Playthrough: Angry Little Shotgunner
Fuming Stunted Shotgunner

THREAT LEVEL

Variety	Health	XP	Melee Damage	Range Damage	Radius Damage	Leap Damage	Charge Damage	Critical Spots	Resistances	Weapons	Shields
Midget Shotgunner	0.65	0.65	Varies	Varies	X	X	X	Head	-	Shotgun	Yes
Angry Little Shotgunner / Fuming Stunted Shotgunner	1.30	0.78	Varies	Varies	X	X	X	Head	-	Shotgun	Yes

These little guys come running up to you out of nowhere, just hoping you start to laugh at them—nothing pleases them more than blasting the smirk right off someone's face. Don't let their diminutive size or low health fool you; their shotgun packs a punch. Take them out as quickly as possible!

MUTANT MIDGET PSYCHO

2nd Playthrough: Freaky Little Maniac
Apeshit Stunted Lunatic

THREAT LEVEL

Variety	Health	XP	Melee Damage	Range Damage	Radius Damage	Leap Damage	Charge Damage	Critical Spots	Resistances	Weapons	Shields
Mutant Midget Psycho	0.65	0.65	Varies	X	X	X	X	Head	-	Axe	Yes
Freaky Little Maniac / Apeshit Stunted Lunatic	1.30	0.78	Varies	X	X	X	X	Head	-	Axe	Yes

Mutant Midget Psychos can only attack at close arrange with their axe, but they have such puny, little-man muscles they can't exactly swing that hatchet too hard. Consider letting them live until you've defeated the more difficult enemies first, just in case you become incapacitated and need an easy kill for that Second Wind.

PSYCHO

2nd Playthrough: Maniac
Lunatic

THREAT LEVEL

Variety	Health	XP	Melee Damage	Range Damage	Radius Damage	Leap Damage	Charge Damage	Critical Spots	Resistances	Weapons	Shields
Psycho	1.00	1.00	Varies	X	X	X	X	Head	-	Axe	Yes
Maniac / Lunatic	2.00	1.20	Varies	X	X	X	X	Head	-	Axe	Yes

Psychos wield a much larger axe than their Mutant Midget compatriots, and can inflict a good deal more damage if they get close enough to connect. Shoot them before they get in melee range, preferably with a shot right between the eyes for a Critical Hit.

BURNING PSYCHO

2nd Playthrough: Blazing Maniac
Scorching Lunatic

THREAT LEVEL

Variety	Health	XP	Melee Damage	Range Damage	Radius Damage	Leap Damage	Charge Damage	Critical Spots	Resistances	Weapons	Shields
Burning Psycho	1.00	1.00	Varies	X	X	X	X	Head	Fire	Axe	Yes
Blazing Maniac Scorching Lunatic	2.00	1.20	Varies	X	X	X	X	Head	Fire	Axe	Yes

Burning Psychos are statistically identical to normal Psychos, but there is one key difference: Burning Psychos are on fire! See? Told you they were psychotic! Strafe around in a circle to avoid the Burning Psycho's melee attack and respond in kind with anything other than an incendiary-based weapon.

BANDIT KILLER

2nd Playthrough: Bandit Murderer
Bandit Executioner

THREAT LEVEL

Variety	Health	XP	Melee Damage	Range Damage	Radius Damage	Leap Damage	Charge Damage	Critical Spots	Resistances	Weapons	Shields
Bandit Killer	1.00	1.00	Varies	Varies	X	X	X	Head	-	Various	Yes
Bandit Murderer Bandit Executioner	2.00	1.20	Varies	Varies	X	X	X	Head	-	Various	Yes

Bandit Killers possess a variety of weaponry. They try to hang back and shoot you from afar, so pop them in the head for a quick kill or move in close for the melee beatdown! These guys are very similar to Bandit Thugs in that they won't fight back after being struck. Conserve ammo and pistol-whip them into submission.

BANDIT RAIDER

2nd Playthrough: Bandit Ravager
Bandit Desperado

THREAT LEVEL

Variety	Health	XP	Melee Damage	Range Damage	Radius Damage	Leap Damage	Charge Damage	Critical Spots	Resistances	Weapons	Shields
Bandit Raider	2.00	2.00	Varies	Varies	X	X	X	Head	-	Various	Yes
Bandit Ravager Bandit Desperado	4.00	2.40	Varies	Varies	X	X	X	Head	-	Various	Yes

CLAPTRAP DANCE OFF

Bandit Raiders are a bit tougher than standard gun-toting Bandits, so seek cover and lob a grenade or two their way to soften them up first. Of course, if you can spot them from afar and have good aim with the sniper rifle, go ahead and fire away! Shoot them in the head for a Critical Hit.

BRUISER

2nd Playthrough: Brute
Bully

THREAT LEVEL

Variety	Health	XP	Melee Damage	Range Damage	Radius Damage	Leap Damage	Charge Damage	Critical Spots	Resistances	Weapons	Shields
Bruiser	4.00	4.00	Varies	Varies	X	X	X	Head	-	Various	Yes
Brute Bully	8.00	4.80	Varies	Varies	X	X	X	Head	-	Various	Yes

Bruisers may look a few beers short of a six-pack, but they're smart enough to hang back and stay close to cover. They also pack plenty of health and can be quite tricky to bring down if you don't land some headshots on them, or overwhelm them with corrosive or incendiary-based weaponry. Stay behind cover and look for the Bruiser to reload, then shoot him or toss grenades.

BADASS RAIDER

2nd Playthrough: BadMutha Ravager
SuperBad Desperado

THREAT LEVEL

Variety	Health	XP	Melee Damage	Range Damage	Radius Damage	Leap Damage	Charge Damage	Critical Spots	Resistances	Weapons	Shields
Badass Raider	6.00	6.00	Varies	Varies	X	X	X	Head	-	Various	Yes
BadMutha Ravager SuperBad Desperado	12.00	7.20	Varies	Varies	X	X	X	Head	-	Various	Yes

Badass Raiders are among the more aggressive Bandits. Their use of shields, body armor, and high-powered weaponry requires you to take cover whenever they're around. Lob grenades at them from afar or snipe them in the head from high ground.

BADASS PSYCHO

2nd Playthrough: BadMutha Maniac
SuperBad Lunatic

THREAT LEVEL

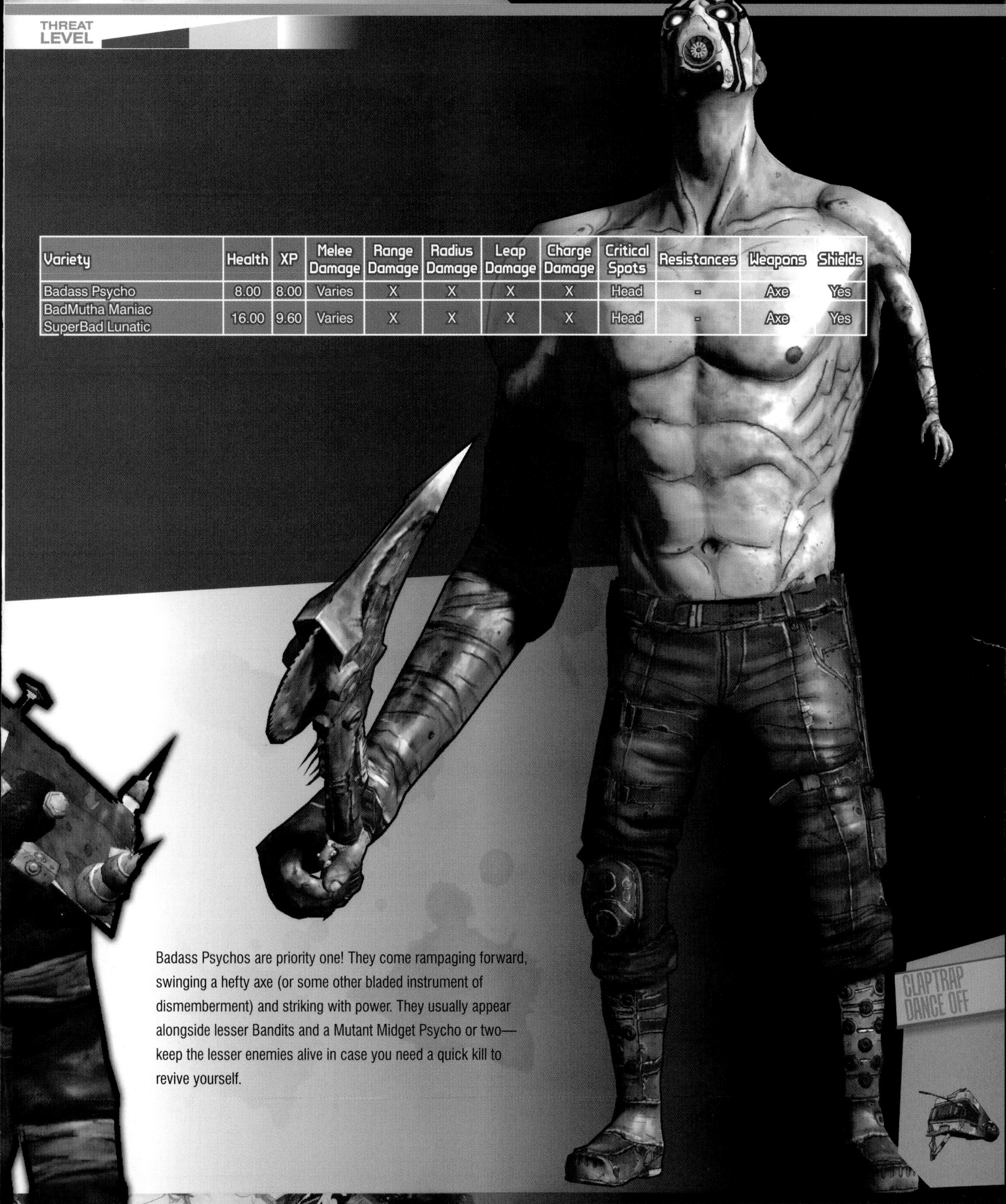

Variety	Health	XP	Melee Damage	Range Damage	Radius Damage	Leap Damage	Charge Damage	Critical Spots	Resistances	Weapons	Shields
Badass Psycho	8.00	8.00	Varies	X	X	X	X	Head	-	Axe	Yes
BadMutha Maniac SuperBad Lunatic	16.00	9.60	Varies	X	X	X	X	Head	-	Axe	Yes

Badass Psychos are priority one! They come rampaging forward, swinging a hefty axe (or some other bladed instrument of dismemberment) and striking with power. They usually appear alongside lesser Bandits and a Mutant Midget Psycho or two—keep the lesser enemies alive in case you need a quick kill to revive yourself.

CLAPTRAP
DANCE OFF

BADASS BRUISER

THREAT LEVEL

Variety	Health	XP	Melee Damage	Range Damage	Radius Damage	Leap Damage	Charge Damage	Critical Spots	Resistances	Weapons	Shields
Badass Bruiser	10.0	10.0	Varies	Varies	X	X	X	Head	-	Various	Yes
BadMutha Brute SuperBad Bully	20.00	12.00	Varies	Varies	X	X	X	Head	-	Various	Yes

If the muscles and the face-paint and spikes aren't enough to make you run for cover, then hopefully these words will: going head to head with this guy is a bad idea! Take cover, lob some Sticky Grenades to set up a trap, and then pick him off with headshots or incendiary-based attacks from afar. It's not uncommon for one of these guys to be packing a rocket launcher, so consider yourself warned!

ROID RAGE PSYCHO

THREAT LEVEL

Variety	Health	XP	Melee Damage	Range Damage	Radius Damage	Leap Damage	Charge Damage	Critical Spots	Resistances	Weapons	Shields
Roid Rage Psycho	14.00	28.00	0.40	X	0.70	X	0.20	Head	-	Fists	-

Roid Rage Psychos pound the ground to attack with a radius blast. They also often charge forward, throwing wild haymakers that you absolutely must avoid to stay on your feet. Strafe left or right as soon as the Roid Rage Psycho begins his charge, then shoot him in the head as he goes by. Make use of your skills and think about using an incendiary-based weapon to burn his flesh.

KING OF CLAP

CRIMSON LANCE

This mercenary army of the Atlas Corporation is extremely well funded and equipped. On Pandora, they view themselves as local law enforcement. The Crimson Lance military/security force is one of the most highly-trained mercenary armies in existence. At the end of the Corporate War, they escaped retribution and restrictions on their business by selling a controlling interest in their company to Dahl Corporation, which now employs the Crimson Lance exclusively as elite security forces.

The Crimson Lance was created by the Atlas Corporation as a way to ensure that they would always have access to elite military and security forces. As the reputation of the effectiveness of the Crimson Lance continued to increase, attacks against the Atlas Corporation quickly decreased, eventually making it difficult to justify the cost of continuing the Crimson Lance. Rather than disbanding them, Atlas decided to contract out the Crimson Lance as mercenaries. Dahl was the first to purchase a contract, and used the Crimson Lance to attack and destroy an Atlas owned supply station. Hours before the attack, Atlas purchased a large insurance policy from Dahl on the station to be attacked. In the end, Dahl paid for both the Crimson Lance contract and the rebuilding of the facility, making it a very profitable venture for Atlas. All current Crimson Lance contracts contain a clause prohibiting them from being directly used against Atlas property and/or interests.

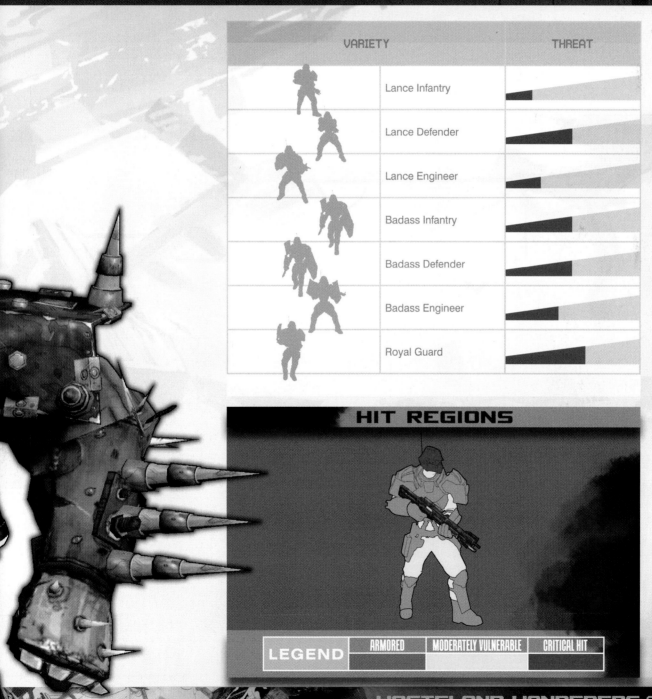

VARIETY	THREAT
Lance Infantry	
Lance Defender	
Lance Engineer	
Badass Infantry	
Badass Defender	
Badass Engineer	
Royal Guard	

HIT REGIONS

LEGEND	ARMORED	MODERATELY VULNERABLE	CRITICAL HIT

CLAPTRAP DANCE OFF

LANCE INFANTRY

THREAT LEVEL

Variety	Health	XP	Melee Damage	Range Damage	Radius Damage	Leap Damage	Charge Damage	Critical Spots	Resistances	Weapons	Shields
Lance Infantry	1.00	1.50	Varies	X	X	X	X	Head	-	Various	Yes
Lance Marine Lance Commando	2.00	1.80	Varies	X	X	X	X	Head	-	Various	Yes

LANCE DEFENDER

THREAT LEVEL

Variety	Health	XP	Melee Damage	Range Damage	Radius Damage	Leap Damage	Charge Damage	Critical Spots	Resistances	Weapons	Shields
Lance Defender	2.00	4.00	Varies	X	X	X	X	Head	-	Various	Yes
Lance Warden Lance Sentinel	4.00	4.80	Varies	X	X	X	X	Head	-	Various	Yes

LANCE ENGINEER

THREAT LEVEL

These well-armed and heavily armored foes can also drop a turret. As with other humans, their weakness is their head and any unarmored parts of their body. Use corrosive weapons to deteriorate their armor and soften them up so you can focus on other tougher enemies. Always leave one or two weakened Crimson Lance around to pick off if you get downed and need a Second Wind.

BADASS INFANTRY

KING OF CLAP

THREAT LEVEL

Variety	Health	XP	Melee Damage	Range Damage	Radius Damage	Leap Damage	Charge Damage	Critical Spots	Resistances	Weapons	Shields
Badass Infantry	4.00	6.00	Varies	X	X	X	X	Head	-	Various	Yes
BadMutha Marine SuperBad Commando	8.00	7.20	Varies	X	X	X	X	Head	-	Various	Yes

Even the lowest level member of the Crimson Lance has a full suit of protective armor. The only areas that aren't protected are the head, insides or their arms, and their inner legs. Use corrosive weaponry to eat through their armor and bring them down.

Lance Defenders not only wear a full suit of protective armor, they also wield a massive riot shield, too. This shield can block all damage and make it very hard to get a clean shot on them. Switch to a corrosive-based weapon and/or grenades to overwhelm them with a force capable of cutting through their armor.

Variety	Health	XP	Melee Damage	Range Damage	Radius Damage	Leap Damage	Charge Damage	Critical Spots	Resistances	Weapons	Shields
Lance Engineer	2.00	3.00	Varies	X	X	X	X	Head	-	Various	Yes
Lance Machinist / Lance Technician	4.00	3.60	Varies	X	X	X	X	Head	-	Various	Yes

Badass Infantry have significantly heavier armor plating than standard Lance Infantry. Avoid shooting the armor, as it greatly reduces the damage your weapons are capable of. Use corrosive-enabled weaponry (or an Artifact and action skill) to chew through the armor and always aim for their head.

CLAPTRAP DANCE OFF

BADASS DEFENDER

THREAT
LEVEL

Variety	Health	XP	Melee Damage	Range Damage	Radius Damage	Leap Damage	Charge Damage	Critical Spots	Resistances	Weapons	Shields
Badass Defender	6.00	9.00	Varies	X	X	X	X	Head	-	Various	Yes
BadMutha Warden SuperBad Sentinel	12.00	10.80	Varies	X	X	X	X	Head	-	Various	Yes

The Badass Defender is a tougher version of the Lance Defender with high health, better armor, and a bit more firepower. Avoid shooting its shield, as it can block all damage. Fire corrosive shots at the Badass Defender's armor or snipe it in the head for a Critical Hit.

BADASS ENGINEER

THREAT
LEVEL

Variety	Health	XP	Melee Damage	Range Damage	Radius Damage	Leap Damage	Charge Damage	Critical Spots	Resistances	Weapons	Shields
Badass Engineer	6.00	6.00	Varies	X	X	X	X	Head	-	Various	Yes
BadMutha Machinist SuperBad Technician	12.00	7.20	Varies	X	X	X	X	Head	-	Various	Yes

KING
OF CLAP

Badass Engineers feature massive armor plates on their shoulder that block all damage. Not only do they pack some heavy firepower of their own, but they also deploy auto turrets, not unlike Roland's Scorpio Turret. Avoid taking fire from their auto turret by dashing behind it—it can only rotate 90 degrees in either direction, but cannot turn all the way around. The auto turret disappears after a while.

THREAT
LEVEL

Variety	Health	XP	Melee Damage	Range Damage	Radius Damage	Leap Damage	Charge Damage	Critical Spots	Resistances	Weapons	Shields
Royal Guard	7.00	14.00	Varies	X	X	X	X	Head	-	Various	Yes

The Royal Guard are not to be taken lightly. These purple armor-clad units are the elite guard of Atlas Corporation's army and must be approached with care. Take cover, utilize choke points, and be sure to equip a corrosive-based weapon. It's worth investing in corrosive grenades just to deal with these aggressive foes.

CLAPTRAP DANCE OFF

GUARDIANS
ALIENS

An ancient alien race, named by humans after the first discovery of alien technology on the planet Eridanus. They are believed to be the constructors of the Vault and other alien structures on Pandora, as well as keepers of The Destroyer. The Guardians chose extinction of their race to prevent The Destroyer from ever breaking free. These robotic, ancient automated soldiers were accidentally reactivated by the Crimson Lance when they acquired the Vault Key.

The theories on the backgrounds of the so called "Guardians" differ radically from one another (even the name "Guardians" is hotly debated, as it implies that they're guarding something, which is not known for certain). One version proposes that they are robotic defenders left behind by the Eridian race to prevent the vault from being found and opened. Another claims that the Eridians placed their brains into these metallic bodies to achieve immortality, and that they simply wish to be left alone. Scooter maintains that they're cyborgs sent back from a dystopian future to impregnate his mother, thus creating an offspring capable of preventing the horrible future they come from, which is why he refuses to call them "Guardians" and insists that you refer to them as "Impregnators." Scooter's theory, though not widely accepted, is included for completeness.

GUARDIAN RACE

VARIETY	THREAT
Sera Guardian	
Guardian Wraith	
Principle Guardian	
Arch Guardian	
Guardian Spectre	
Badass Guardian	

HIT REGIONS

LEGEND	ARMORED	MODERATELY VULNERABLE	CRITICAL HIT

KING OF CLAP

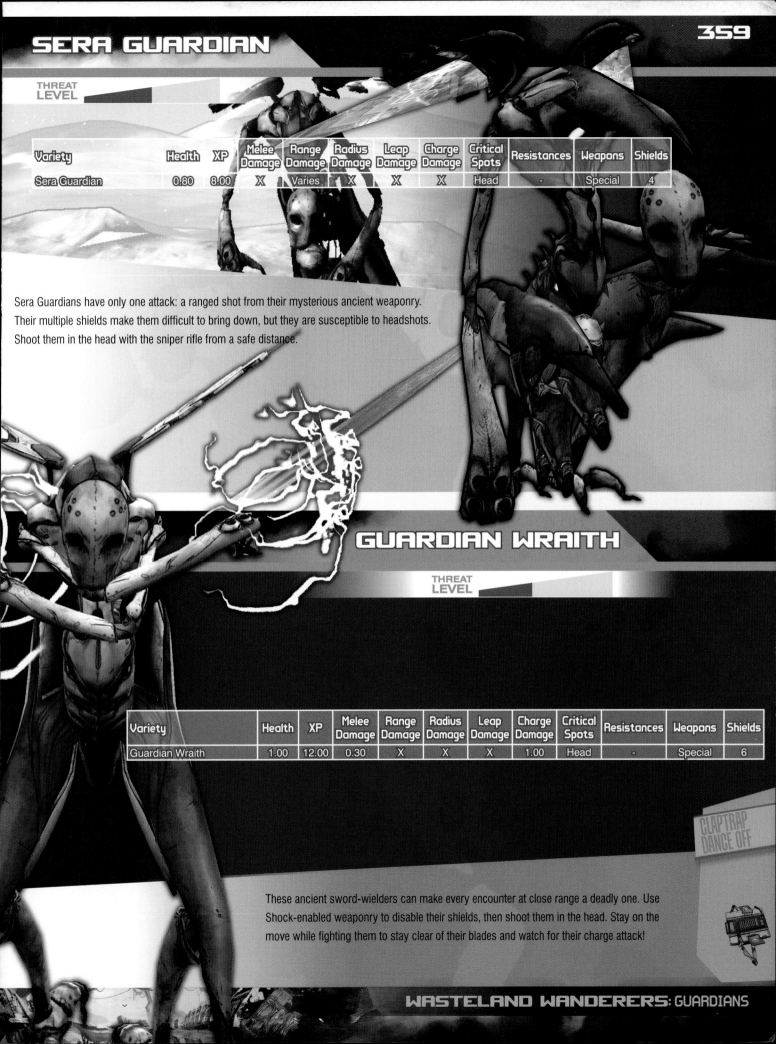

SERA GUARDIAN

THREAT LEVEL

Variety	Health	XP	Melee Damage	Range Damage	Radius Damage	Leap Damage	Charge Damage	Critical Spots	Resistances	Weapons	Shields
Sera Guardian	0.80	8.00	X	Varies	X	X	X	Head	-	Special	4

Sera Guardians have only one attack: a ranged shot from their mysterious ancient weaponry. Their multiple shields make them difficult to bring down, but they are susceptible to headshots. Shoot them in the head with the sniper rifle from a safe distance.

GUARDIAN WRAITH

THREAT LEVEL

Variety	Health	XP	Melee Damage	Range Damage	Radius Damage	Leap Damage	Charge Damage	Critical Spots	Resistances	Weapons	Shields
Guardian Wraith	1.00	12.00	0.30	X	X	X	1.00	Head	-	Special	6

These ancient sword-wielders can make every encounter at close range a deadly one. Use Shock-enabled weaponry to disable their shields, then shoot them in the head. Stay on the move while fighting them to stay clear of their blades and watch for their charge attack!

CLAPTRAP DANCE OFF

PRINCIPLE GUARDIAN

Variety	Health	XP	Melee Damage	Range Damage	Radius Damage	Leap Damage	Charge Damage	Critical Spots	Resistances	Weapons	Shields
Principle Guardian	1.20	12.00	0.30	X	X	X	1.00	Head	-	Special	6

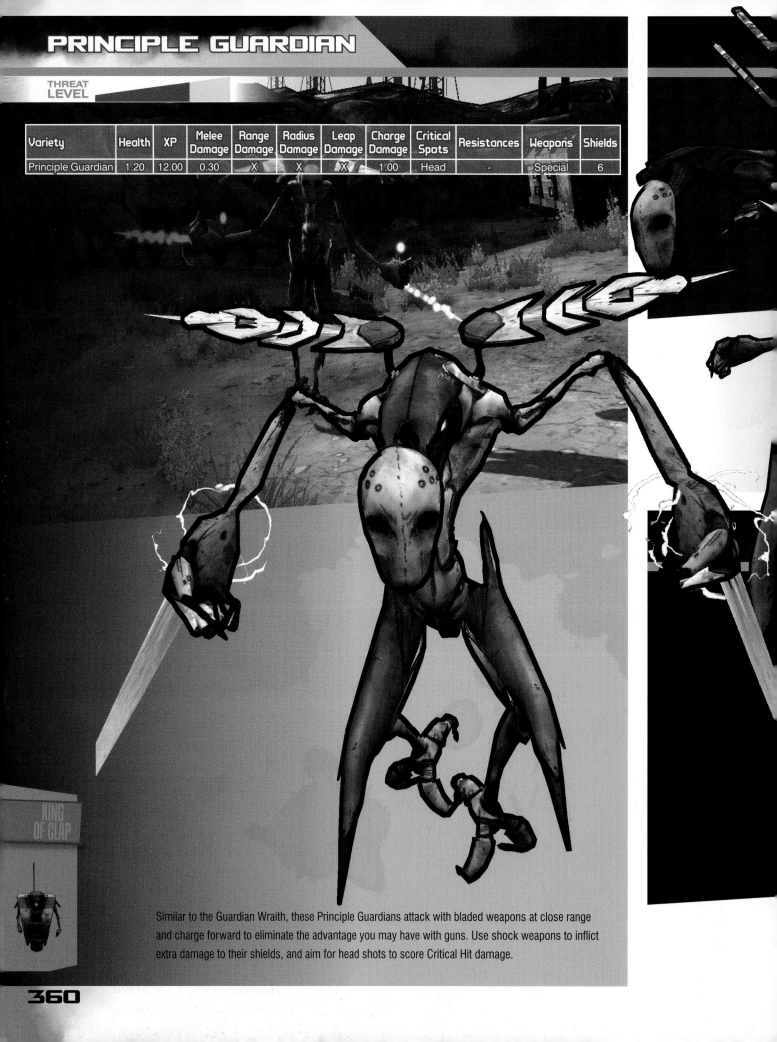

KING
OF CLAP

Similar to the Guardian Wraith, these Principle Guardians attack with bladed weapons at close range and charge forward to eliminate the advantage you may have with guns. Use shock weapons to inflict extra damage to their shields, and aim for head shots to score Critical Hit damage.

ARCH GUARDIAN

THREAT LEVEL

Variety	Health	XP	Melee Damage	Range Damage	Radius Damage	Leap Damage	Charge Damage	Critical Spots	Resistances	Weapons	Shields
Arch Guardian	2.00	24.00	0.30	50.00	1.00	X	X	Head	-	Special	12

Arch Guardians pack a bevy of attacks and should be kept at bay with shock-based weapons and grenades, not to mention frequent bullets to the head. The Arch Guardian can return fire and is quite lethal, but its melee and radius attacks are difficult to avoid. Take cover and shoot at this foe from a safe distance.

GUARDIAN SPECTRE

THREAT LEVEL

Variety	Health	XP	Melee Damage	Range Damage	Radius Damage	Leap Damage	Charge Damage	Critical Spots	Resistances	Weapons	Shields
Guardian Spectre	2.00	40.00	0.30	X	X	X	1.00	Head	-	Special	10

Guardian Spectres pack an amazingly strong set of shields and must be attacked with shock-based weapons if you hope to blast through them. Aim for their heads to inflict additional damage and stay out of range of their sword-like appendages. The further away you are from them, the better off you'll be.

CLAPTRAP DANCE OFF

BADASS GUARDIAN

THREAT LEVEL

Variety	Health	XP	Melee Damage	Range Damage	Radius Damage	Leap Damage	Charge Damage	Critical Spots	Resistances	Weapons	Shields
BadMutha Guardian SuperBad Guardian	8.00	38.40	0.60	X	X	X	2.03	Head	-	Special	32

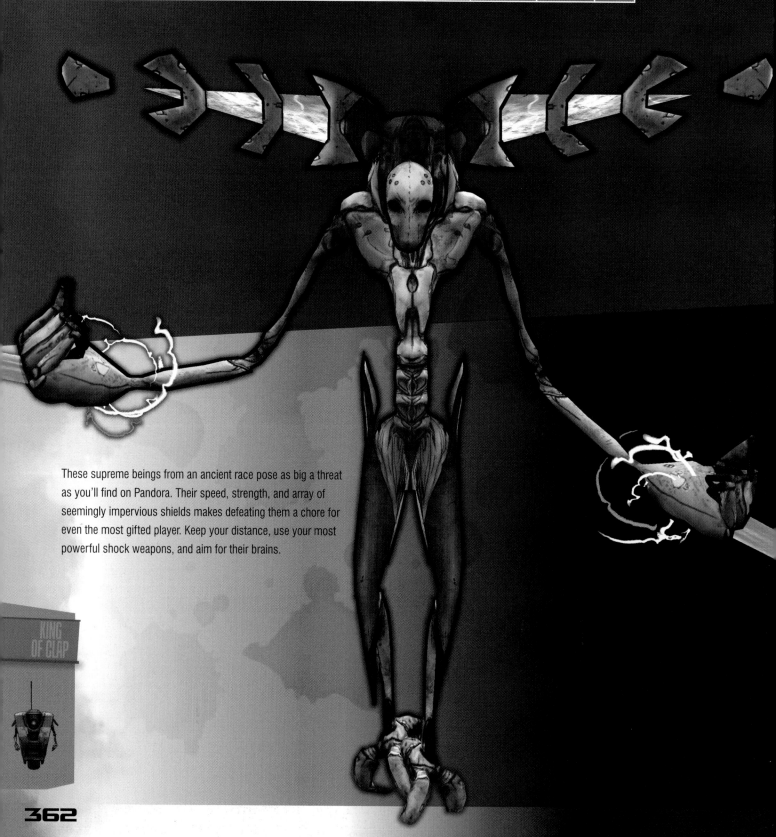

These supreme beings from an ancient race pose as big a threat as you'll find on Pandora. Their speed, strength, and array of seemingly impervious shields makes defeating them a chore for even the most gifted player. Keep your distance, use your most powerful shock weapons, and aim for their brains.

KING OF CLAP

BOSS & NAMED CREATURES

NAMED SKAGS

Several of the more sinister humans who have managed to eek out an existence on Pandora have taken to domesticating their own personal pet Skags. Nobody is quite sure how they manage to keep the Skags from attacking while they sleep, but there's no denying the loyalty these dangerous pets feel to their masters. Not all named Skags are pets, though! Several of them, particularly Moe and Marley, lord over their pack (and their territory) to such a degree that the few settlers who managed to escape an encounter with them decided to give these ferocious beasts a name.

NAMED SKAGS

VARIETY	THREAT
Pinky and Digit	
Scar	
Skrappy	
Moe and Marley	
Skagzilla	

PINKY AND DIGIT

THREAT LEVEL

Variety	Health	XP	Melee Damage	Range Damage	Radius Damage	Leap Damage	Charge Damage	Critical Spots	Resistances
Digit	4.00	6.00	0.40	X	X	Rare	0.40	Mouth	-
Pinky	5.00	7.50	0.40	X	X	Rare	0.40	Mouth	-

Pinky and Digit are Nine-Toes' beloved guard Skags. They aren't exactly tame, but they did allow him to bolt armor plating in their natural, bony armor. Take Digit (brown) out first since he is the weaker of the two. His head is armored, so concentrate fire on his body. Pinky's body is armored, so aim for his head to make him roar, then fire a shot into his open mouth. Corrosive weapons work well against their armor.

Nine-Toes, being a firm believer in the principle of "Safety First," attached artificial armor plating to the natural armor of his two beloved pet Skags, Digit and Pinky. His attempts to armor the fleshy parts of his pets have so far proven unsuccessful.

CLAPTRAP DANCE OFF

SCAR

Variety	Health	XP	Melee Damage	Range Damage	Radius Damage	Leap Damage	Charge Damage	Critical Spots	Resistances
Scar	8.00	16.00	0.50	0.10	0.75	0.60	0.40	Mouth	-

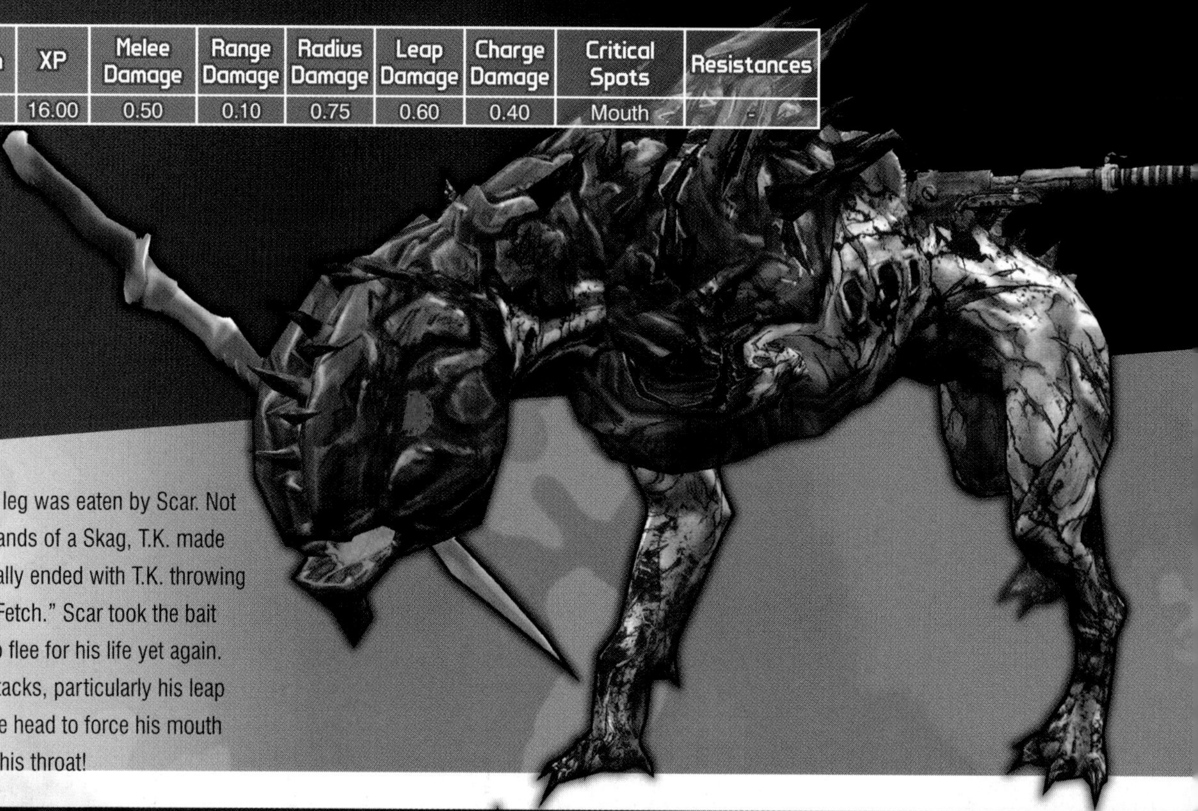

In their first epic battle, T.K. Baha's leg was eaten by Scar. Not being one to accept defeat at the hands of a Skag, T.K. made an attempt at revenge which ironically ended with T.K. throwing his new artificial leg while yelling "Fetch." Scar took the bait allowing T.K. the opening needed to flee for his life yet again. Scar has a number of damaging attacks, particularly his leap and radius attacks. Shoot him in the head to force his mouth open, then fire some rounds down his throat!

SKRAPPY

THREAT LEVEL

Variety	Health	XP	Melee Damage	Range Damage	Radius Damage	Leap Damage	Charge Damage	Critical Spots	Resistances
Young Skrappy	-	-	-	-	-	-	-	-	-
Skrappy "All Grown Up"	12.00	24.00	0.90	0.70	0.55	0.65	0.70	Mouth	-

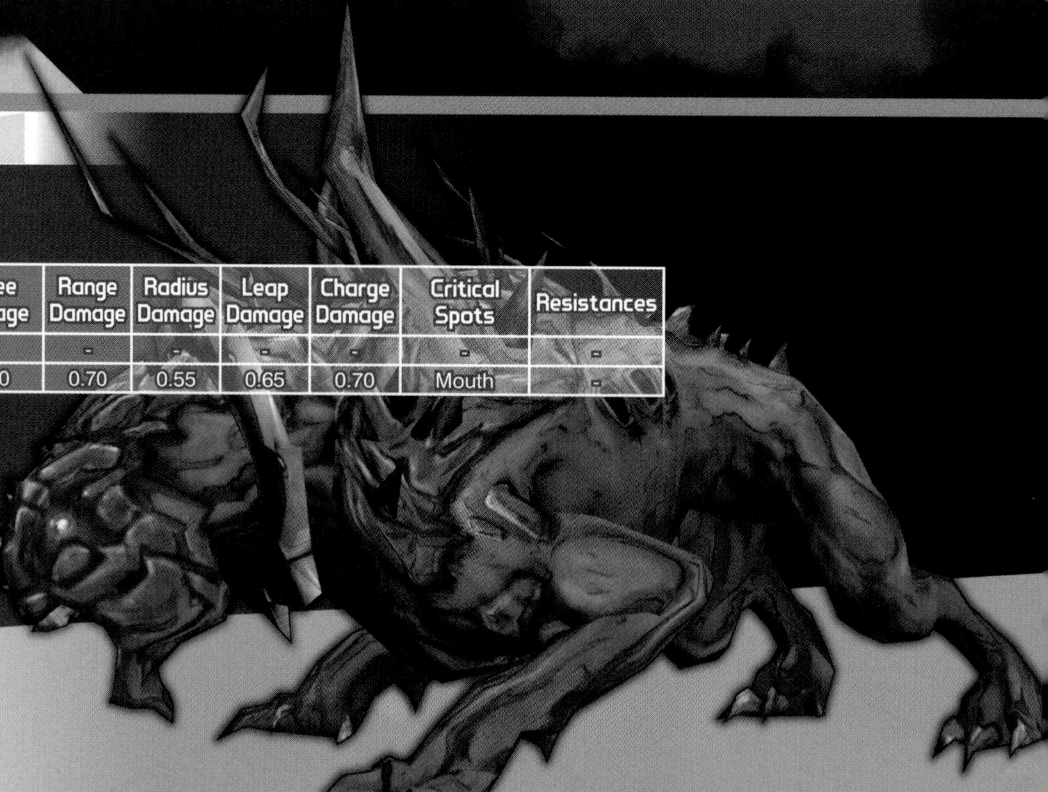

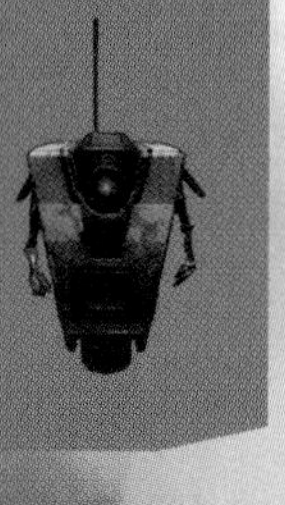

KING OF CLAP

As a young pup, this Skag found its way into Crazy Earl's crusty old heart. Earl somehow survived the experience and has raised Skrappy as a pet. Though Young, Skrappy can't be damaged and does not attack. The adult version is a fierce combatant and requires you to bring a strong shield into combat to protect against Skrappy's melee attacks.

MOE AND MARLEY

Variety	Health	XP	Melee Damage	Range Damage	Radius Damage	Leap Damage	Charge Damage	Critical Spots	Resistances
Moe	10.00	30.00	0.60	X	X	Rare	0.50	Mouth	
Marley	16.00	48.00	0.40	0.80	X	Rare	X	Mouth	

Moe and Marley are both Alpha Skags, ruling over the same pack of Skags. This dynamic duo isn't fully understood, but it's generally believed that Moe is "the bitch." You can shoot Marley's shock balls out of the air while finishing off Moe. Aim for its head to make it roar, then shoot into its wide open chops. Watch out for Moe's fiery radius attack.

SKAGZILLA

Variety	Health	XP	Melee Damage	Range Damage	Radius Damage	Leap Damage	Charge Damage	Critical Spots	Resistances
Skagzilla	30.00	72.00	0.40	0.25	0.50	1.00	0.25	Mouth	

KING OF CLAP

No one knows how large a Skag can grow. The relatively recent human incursion on Pandora may have disrupted the natural life cycle of these creatures. If Skagzilla is any indication, though, a Skag will continue to grow larger and larger until something kills it, or it starves to death. Avoid its leap damage by jumping or backpedaling away. When he rears back to perform his beam attack, use the opportunity to shoot him in the mouth.

NAMED RAKK

Bandits and settlers don't agree on much, but one thing they won't argue over is the sheer horror one feels when spotting either of these legendary creatures of the night. Although some continue to doubt their existence, Mothrakk and Rakkinishu have made believers out of numerous victims over the years. None has ever lived to tell the tale. And then there's the Rakk Hive…

NAMED RAKK

VARIETY		THREAT
	Rakkinishu	
	Mothrakk	

RAKKINISHU

THREAT LEVEL

Variety	Health	XP	Melee Damage	Range Damage	Radius Damage	Leap Damage	Charge Damage	Critical Spots	Resistances
Rakkinishu	6.00	24.00	X	0.12	X	X	X	-	

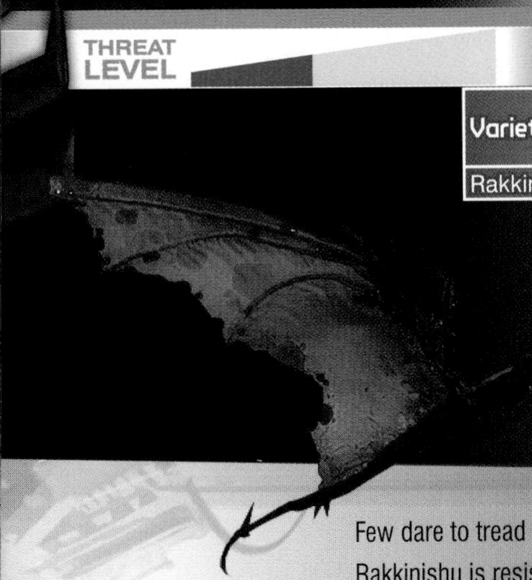

Few dare to tread where this lone Rakk casts its grim shadow over the northern reaches of the Western Rust Commons. Rakkinishu is resistant to all elemental weapons, so use normal or explosive guns to do the most damage. And take cover. Definitely take cover!

MOTHRAKK

THREAT LEVEL

Variety	Health	XP	Melee Damage	Range Damage	Radius Damage	Leap Damage	Charge Damage	Critical Spots	Resistances
Mothrakk	10.00	40.00	X	3.00	X	X	X	-	

This giant horror rules the skies over the Arid Badlands, and is known to carry off people (and the occasional car), mostly at night. You can find cover to avoid damage from the fire ball attacks. Use weapons with long range, like sniper rifles. Just make sure they aren't elemental, since the Mothrakk is resistant to all elementals.

CLAPTRAP DANCE OFF

NAMED SCYTHIDS

It might be hard to imagine the lowly Scythid evolving far enough to achieve cult status, or to become something so grotesque and feared that it's considered unkillable, but that's the reputation that the Slither and Bleeder have gained. Whether the rumors about these mega-Scythids are accurate or not remains to be seen, but they are special. That's for certain.

NAMED SCYTHID

VARIETY	THREAT
Slither	
Bleeder	

SLITHER

THREAT LEVEL

Variety	Health	XP	Melee Damage	Range Damage	Radius Damage	Leap Damage	Charge Damage	Critical Spots	Resistances
Slither	8.00	16.00	0.10	X	X	0.30	X	-	-

Some of the more impressionable bandits formed a cult of worship and sacrifice around this mutant scythed. As a result, Slither became a man-eater, albeit a contented and well fed man-eater. Don't lose sight of him; he's very nimble.

BLEEDER

THREAT LEVEL

Variety	Health	XP	Melee Damage	Range Damage	Radius Damage	Leap Damage	Charge Damage	Critical Spots	Resistances
Bleeder	14.00	56.00	0.70	0.10	X	X	X	-	-

Bleeder is an enigma; a crime against all natural law. How can any living thing bleed for days and not die? Only one way to find out… kill it! Find cover and avoid its ranged attack. Shotguns are effective in doing damage while it's in flight. Try not to let it bleed all over you.

KING OF CLAP

NAMED SPIDERANTS

All Spiderants follow the rules of the hive and obey their individual Queens and Kings, but along the Trash Coast (and beyond) there resides a Queen that rules them all. Queen Tarantella and her mate rule the Spiderant kingdom, and even the most feared Spiderants from elsewhere in Pandora must bow to her majesty's command.

NAMED SPIDERANTS

VARIETY	THREAT
Helob	
Widowmaker	
King Aracobb	
Queen Tarantella	

Her shapely abdomen and long legs have made her the object of affection for many of the Spiderants across Pandora. It is widely believed that if Spiderants had lockers, her picture would dominate the majority of them. No human lockers to date are known to contain pictures of Queen Tarantella.

HELOB

THREAT LEVEL

Variety	Health	XP	Melee Damage	Range Damage	Radius Damage	Leap Damage	Charge Damage	Critical Spots	Resistances
Helob	11.00	22.00	0.50	X	X	0.80	1.30	Abdomen	☣ 🔥 ⚡

One of the deadliest Spiderants, Helob has learned a leap attack that allows him to catch low-flying Rakk and more effectively ambush prey on the ground. You can avoid Helob's leap damage by backpedaling or jumping. Shoot Helob in the head to disorient it, then open fire on its abdomen for maximum damage!

Reports from settlers on the incredible leaping ability of Helob differ radically. They range from "10 feet" to "all the way into outer space." Its actual jumping ability is generally believed to be much closer to the lower end of the reported spectrum, though no scientific data exists to confirm any hypothesis at this time.

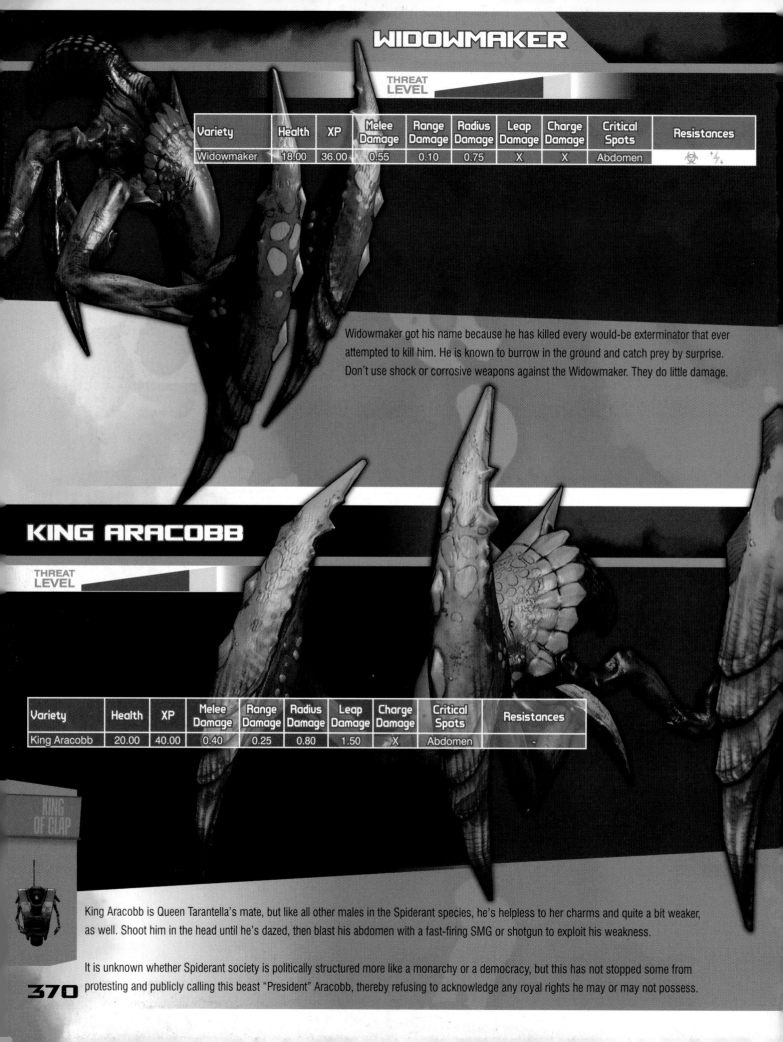

WIDOWMAKER

Variety	Health	XP	Melee Damage	Range Damage	Radius Damage	Leap Damage	Charge Damage	Critical Spots	Resistances
Widowmaker	18.00	36.00	0.55	0.10	0.75	X	X	Abdomen	☣ ⚡

Widowmaker got his name because he has killed every would-be exterminator that ever attempted to kill him. He is known to burrow in the ground and catch prey by surprise. Don't use shock or corrosive weapons against the Widowmaker. They do little damage.

KING ARACOBB

THREAT LEVEL

Variety	Health	XP	Melee Damage	Range Damage	Radius Damage	Leap Damage	Charge Damage	Critical Spots	Resistances
King Aracobb	20.00	40.00	0.40	0.25	0.80	1.50	X	Abdomen	-

KING OF CLAP

King Aracobb is Queen Tarantella's mate, but like all other males in the Spiderant species, he's helpless to her charms and quite a bit weaker, as well. Shoot him in the head until he's dazed, then blast his abdomen with a fast-firing SMG or shotgun to exploit his weakness.

It is unknown whether Spiderant society is politically structured more like a monarchy or a democracy, but this has not stopped some from protesting and publicly calling this beast "President" Aracobb, thereby refusing to acknowledge any royal rights he may or may not possess.

THREAT LEVEL

Variety	Health	XP	Melee Damage	Range Damage	Radius Damage	Leap Damage	Charge Damage	Critical Spots	Resistances
Queen Tarantella	25.00	50.00	0.40	0.50	1.00	X	X	Abdomen	☣ 🔥 ⚡

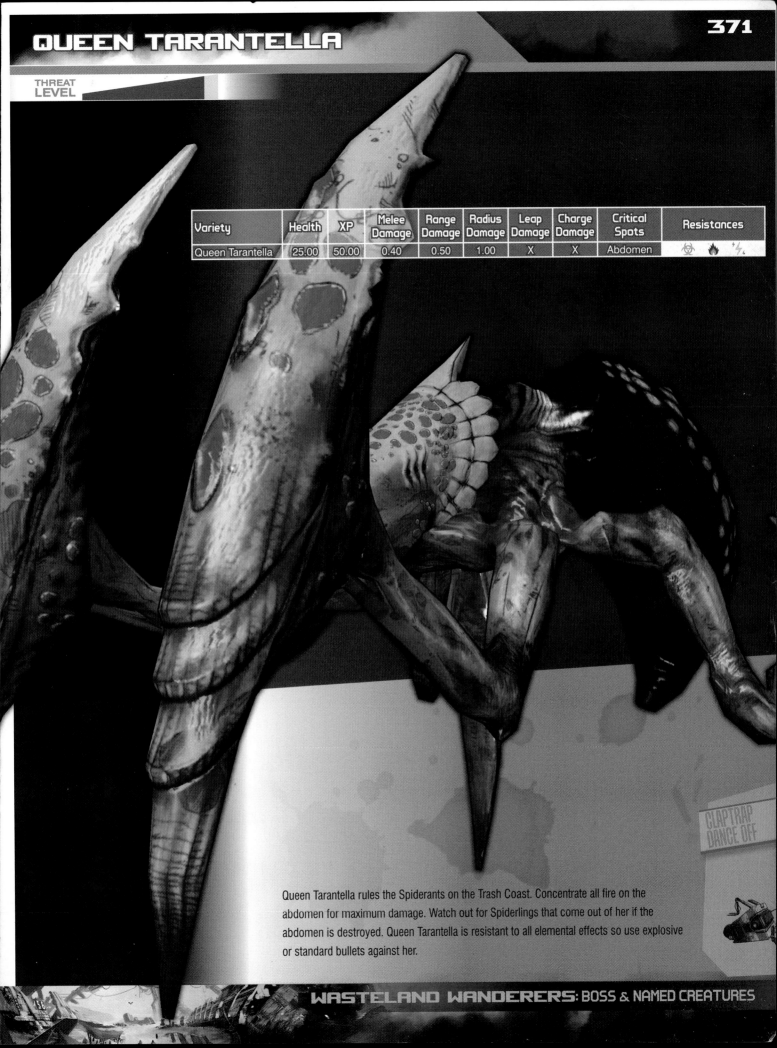

Queen Tarantella rules the Spiderants on the Trash Coast. Concentrate all fire on the abdomen for maximum damage. Watch out for Spiderlings that come out of her if the abdomen is destroyed. Queen Tarantella is resistant to all elemental effects so use explosive or standard bullets against her.

CLAPTRAP DANCE OFF

RAKK HIVE

2nd Playthrough: Awesome Rakk Hive
Ultimate Rakk Hive

THREAT
LEVEL

Variety	Health	XP	Melee Damage	Range Damage	Radius Damage	Leap Damage	Charge Damage	Critical Spots	Resistances
Rakk Hive	80	160	2.00	1.00	1.00	X	X	Eye	–
Awesome Rakk Hive Ultimate Rakk Hive	160	192	3.00	1.50	1.50	X	X	Eye	–

It's uncertain whether the Rakk and Rakk Hive have a symbiotic or parasitic relationship. Either way, it's really, really disgusting. Shoot the Hive in the four glowing eyes located on the face to do critical damage. The Hive falls into fairly predictable attack patterns, so pay attention to find your opening. Do not neglect to kill the Rakk that spawn from it either—they can overwhelm you quickly.

A picture of the Rakk Hive with its mouth censored out appeared on the cover of a xenobiology journal, sparking interplanetary scientific debate over ethics and censorship. The controversy overshadowed the questions being proposed by the journal regarding whether or not the relationship between the Hive and the Rakk is parasitic or symbiotic, which eventually led to unacceptably slow findings and the loss of funding for the scientists.

HIT REGIONS

LEGEND	ARMORED	MODERATELY VULNERABLE	CRITICAL HIT

KING OF CLAP

THE DESTROYER

THREAT LEVEL

Variety	Health	XP	Melee Damage	Range Damage	Radius Damage	Leap Damage	Charge Damage	Critical Spots	Resistances
The Destroyer	1000	?	1.00	1.00	1.00	X	X	Mouth, Eye, Tentacle	-

This powerful being was imprisoned inside the Vault by the Eridians, who sacrificed their entire race to prevent it from consuming our universe. Take cover, then target the spike-throwing tentacles first. You can avoid damage from the tongue by strafing left or right.

HUMAN BOSSES
PANDORA'S WORST

Pandora was always destined to be a place where scoundrels, vagrants, and thugs would be sent to serve out their due punishments, but even amongst all of these low-life degenerates, a few managed to rise up and take control. The turf wars were on! Surviving on Pandora is all about who you know and where you go. Know the right person, and you're in. Go to the wrong side of town, and you're dead. These are the men who draw the lines and make the rules as they go along.

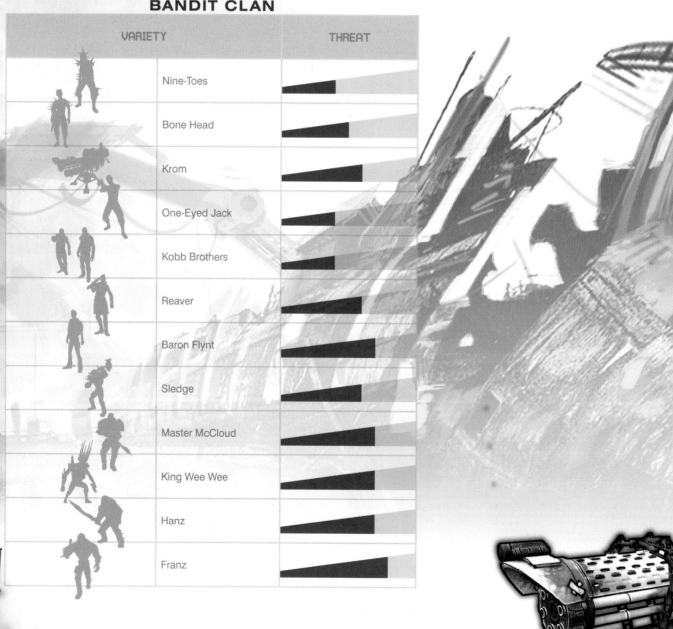

BANDIT CLAN

VARIETY	THREAT
Nine-Toes	
Bone Head	
Krom	
One-Eyed Jack	
Kobb Brothers	
Reaver	
Baron Flynt	
Sledge	
Master McCloud	
King Wee Wee	
Hanz	
Franz	

KING OF CLAP

NINE-TOES

THREAT LEVEL

Variety	Health	XP	Melee Damage	Range Damage	Radius Damage	Leap Damage	Charge Damage	Critical Spots	Resistances	Weapons	Shields
Nine Toes	5.00	10.00	Varies	Varies	X	X	X	Head	-	Special	Yes

Nine-Toes is completely insane, and loves his two pet Skags just a *little* too much. He stages frequent raids on Fyrestone, hoping to curry favor with Sledge. Even Nine-Toes doesn't know how he lost his toe. He suspects that Bone Head took it to use in his voodoo ceremonies. Defeat Nine-Toes before fighting Pinky and Digit. Leaving Nine-Toes alone results in more damage to you in the long run.

BONE HEAD

THREAT LEVEL

Variety	Health	XP	Melee Damage	Range Damage	Radius Damage	Leap Damage	Charge Damage	Critical Spots	Resistances	Weapons	Shields
Krom	5.00	15.00	X	Varies	X	X	X	Head	-	Turret	Yes

One of Sledge's lieutenants, Bone Head had a long-standing rivalry with Nine-Toes. Sledge eventually grew tired of their bickering, and issued a challenge to them: Whoever took over Fyrestone and killed the other would prove themselves worthy to become Sledge's right-hand man. Bone Head is also rumored to practice voodoo. Stay away from his melee rage. And make sure that you're at least level 10 before fighting him.

Bernard Rickenshaw picked up the nickname "Bone Head" at a young age for unknown reasons (he's quite intelligent and his head is absent of any boney protuberance that might warrant the name). Tired of people asking how he got the nickname, he began wearing the skulls of creatures and/or people he had killed over his face so that new acquaintances could extrapolate an answer for themselves, thus saving time.

KROM

THREAT LEVEL

Variety	Health	XP	Melee Damage	Range Damage	Radius Damage	Leap Damage	Charge Damage	Critical Spots	Resistances	Weapons	Shields
Krom	5.00	15.00	X	Varies	X	X	X	Head	-	Turret	Yes

Like Flynt, Krom worked as a prison warden for Dahl until the prisons were abandoned and the convicts set free. His real name is Leslie, which he always hated and changed as soon as Flynt set him up as second in command. If you have a good rocket launcher or sniper rifle, you can do substantial damage to Krom before reaching him.

ONE-EYED JACK

THREAT LEVEL

Variety	Health	XP	Melee Damage	Range Damage	Radius Damage	Leap Damage	Charge Damage	Critical Spots	Resistances	Weapons	Shields
One-Eyed Jack	6.00	12.00	Varies	Varies	X	X	X	Head	-	Special	Yes

Nobody knows where One-Eyed Jack came from. Marcus suspects that he's a black market weapons dealer, and that his bandit persona is simply a front. It's rumored that he lost his eye in a poker game, to an inside straight flush. Keep moving so that Jack never gets a clean shot at you. His revolver (the Mad Jack) does substantial damage. Use your skills to get the upper hand.

KOBB BROTHERS

THREAT LEVEL

Variety	Health	XP	Melee Damage	Range Damage	Radius Damage	Leap Damage	Charge Damage	Critical Spots	Resistances	Weapons	Shields
Jaynis Kobb	6.00	12.00	Varies	Varies	X	X	X	Head	-	Special	Yes
Taylor Kobb	6.00	12.00	Varies	Varies	X	X	X	Head	-	Special	Yes

These two brothers have hated each other since birth. They've never overtly fought one another, opting instead to employ poison, traps, and assassins to do the other in. This has only served to make both stronger and more clever as they outwit or overcome each attempt on their lives. Take care of all the henchmen first. Both brothers are much easier to fight alone. Destroy Taylor's turrets before entering Jaynistown. Beware of the large splash damage radius from his rocket launcher.

REAVER

THREAT LEVEL

KING OF CLAP

Variety	Health	XP	Melee Damage	Range Damage	Radius Damage	Leap Damage	Charge Damage	Critical Spots	Resistances	Weapons	Shields
Reaver	10.00	20.00	Varies	Varies	X	X	X	Head	-	Special	Yes

Jed Stokely lived with his adopted father in New Haven, until the day he decided to murder him and join the bandits, taking the name 'Reaver.' He is notorious, even among the bandits, for having a chip on his shoulder and a daddy issues. Reaver is a sniper, so get in close to put him at a disadvantage.

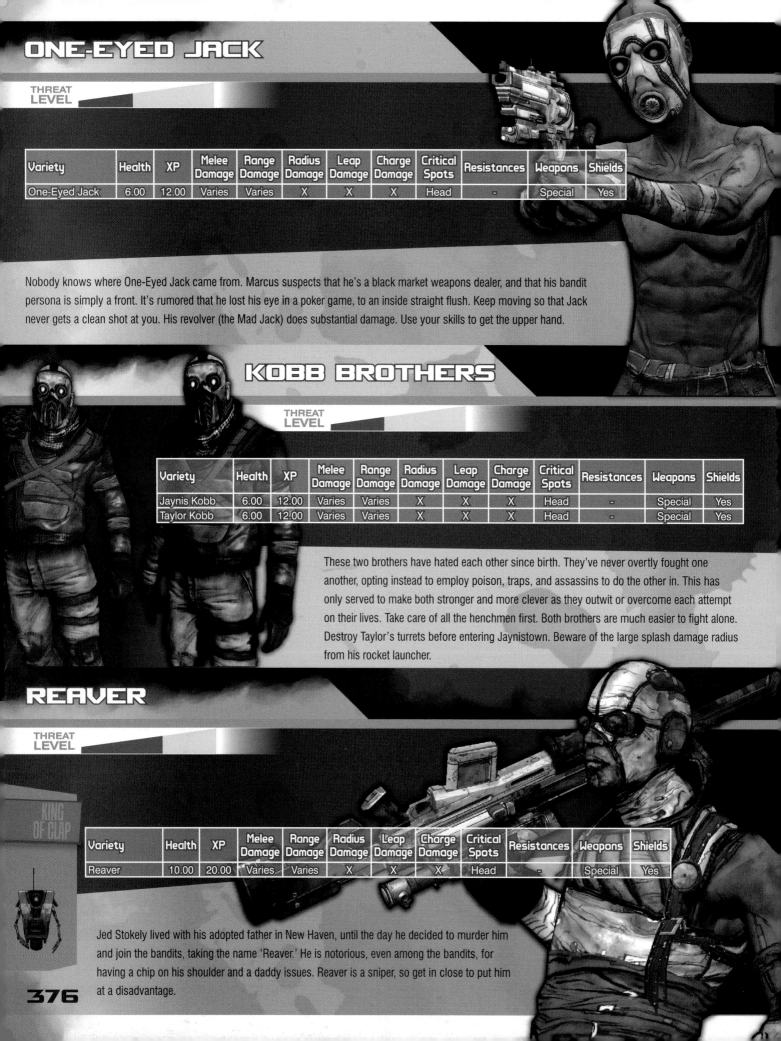

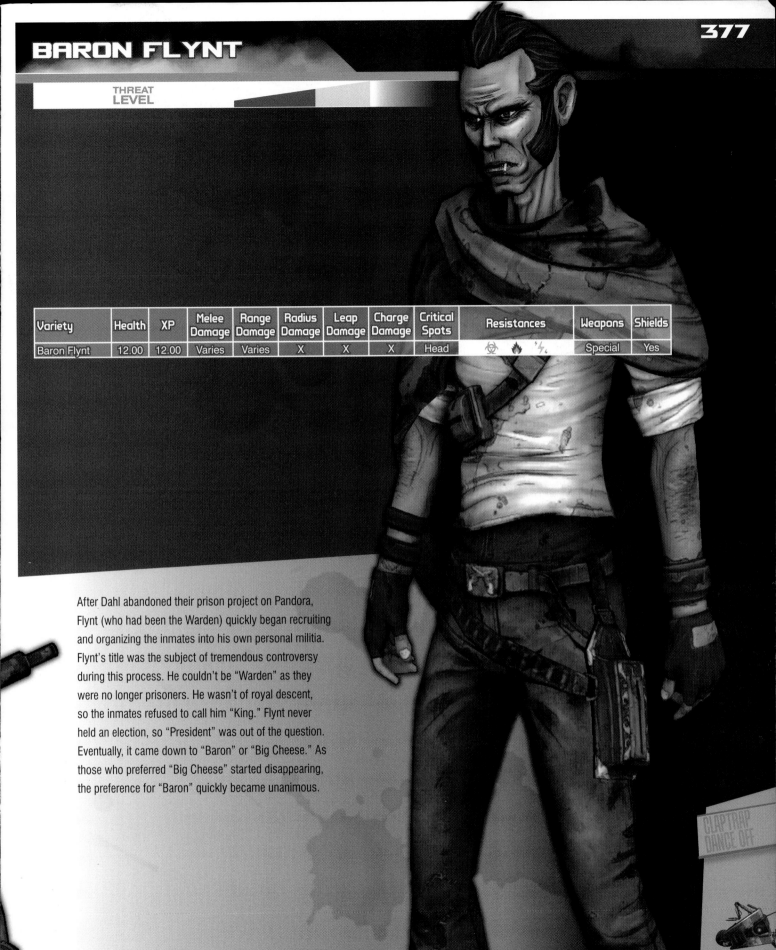

BARON FLYNT

THREAT
LEVEL

Variety	Health	XP	Melee Damage	Range Damage	Radius Damage	Leap Damage	Charge Damage	Critical Spots	Resistances	Weapons	Shields
Baron Flynt	12.00	12.00	Varies	Varies	X	X	X	Head	☣ 🔥 ⚡	Special	Yes

After Dahl abandoned their prison project on Pandora, Flynt (who had been the Warden) quickly began recruiting and organizing the inmates into his own personal militia. Flynt's title was the subject of tremendous controversy during this process. He couldn't be "Warden" as they were no longer prisoners. He wasn't of royal descent, so the inmates refused to call him "King." Flynt never held an election, so "President" was out of the question. Eventually, it came down to "Baron" or "Big Cheese." As those who preferred "Big Cheese" started disappearing, the preference for "Baron" quickly became unanimous.

SLEDGE

THREAT LEVEL

Variety	Health	XP	Melee Damage	Range Damage	Radius Damage	Leap Damage	Charge Damage	Critical Spots	Resistances	Weapons	Shields
Sledge	12.00	24.00	Varies	X	Varies	X	X	Head	☣ 🔥 ⚡	Special	Yes

Leader of a bandit tribe, Sledge is blunt and uncreative, to the extent that when he named his iconic weapon, he simply called it "Hammer." What he lacks in brainpower, however, he makes up for with brute strength and a high pain tolerance. Keep your distance to avoid his Hammer attack. Jump before the Hammer strikes the ground to avoid damage. Clear the room of enemies before turning to Sledge.

MASTER MCCLOUD

THREAT LEVEL

Variety	Health	XP	Melee Damage	Range Damage	Radius Damage	Leap Damage	Charge Damage	Critical Spots	Resistances	Weapons	Shields
Master McCloud	15.00	45.00	Varies	Varies	X	X	X	Head	-	Special	Yes

Master McCloud sees himself as a star-hopping, interplanetary hero. Given half a chance, he will regale anyone with tales of his many exploits. This probably explains why he has been stationed on a remote dustball like Pandora, as far from Atlas HQ as humanly possible. Master McCloud takes extra damage from corrosive weapons, which also lower his overall armor, allowing you to inflict more damage.

KING WEE WEE

THREAT LEVEL

Variety	Health	XP	Melee Damage	Range Damage	Radius Damage	Leap Damage	Charge Damage	Critical Spots	Resistances	Weapons	Shields
King Wee Wee	15.00	30.00	0.20	0.20	0.70	0.40	X	Head	-	Buzz Axe	X

Most of the psychos and midgets among the bandits are the result of a cruel and deliberate regime of torture during pregnancy, and behavioral engineering during childhood. This program was dreamed up and carried out entirely by King Wee Wee, who is the poster child for rage, hatred, and self-loathing.

HANZ

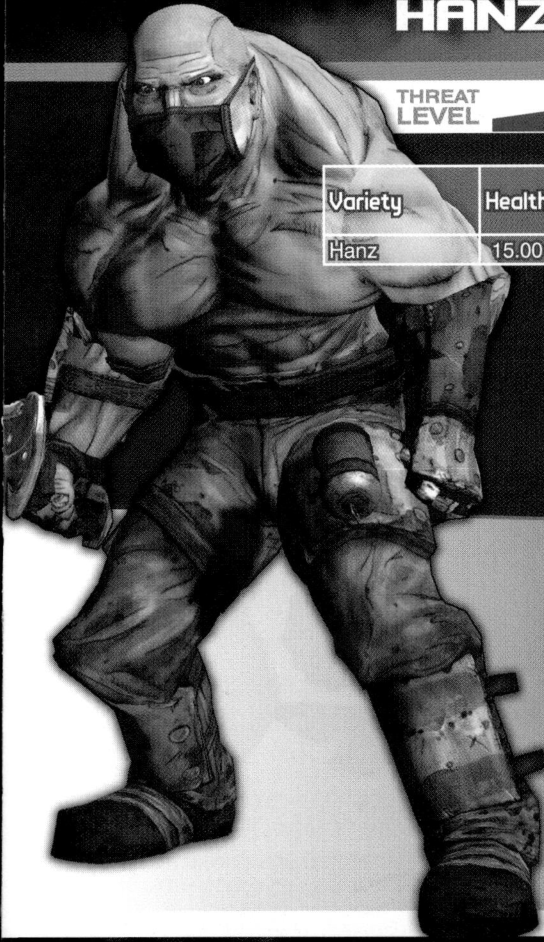

THREAT LEVEL

Variety	Health	XP	Melee Damage	Range Damage	Radius Damage	Leap Damage	Charge Damage	Critical Spots	Resistances	Weapons	Shields
Hanz	15.00	20.00	0.50	X	0.70	X	X	Head	-	Sword	X

Years ago, Hanz was a hardcore LARPer. That is, until he was convicted for decapitating a man pretending to be an elf. He was imprisoned on Pandora, but was later set free by Baron Flynt. He has served as Flynt's bodyguard ever since. No relation to Franz. Keep both Hanz and Franz in view so that you don't get caught between them. Aim for the head for critical damage. Take Hanz out first since his melee attack knocks you back.

FRANZ

THREAT LEVEL

Variety	Health	XP	Melee Damage	Range Damage	Radius Damage	Leap Damage	Charge Damage	Critical Spots	Resistances	Weapons	Shields
Franz	18.00	25.00	Varies	Varies	X	X	X	Head	-	Special	Yes

Franz once ran the best tattoo parlor in New Haven, but was imprisoned after a piercing went horribly wrong and left three dead. Baron Flynt set him free, and he has served as Flynt's bodyguard and enforcer ever since. No relation to Hanz. Keep both Hanz and Franz in view so that you don't get caught between them. Aim for the head for critical damage.

CLAPTRAP DANCE OFF

Achievement GUIDE

Borderlands features 50 Achievements (Xbox 360) and 51 Trophies (PS3) that allow you to show off how far you've gone toward reaching the Vault. The majority of these bonuses can be earned while playing alone, although some do require you to sit down with some friends and play cooperatively either online or in split-screen.

PROGRESSION IN PANDORA

THERE ARE 22 ACHIEVEMENTS/TROPHIES LINKED DIRECTLY TO YOUR PERSONAL PROGRESS THROUGH THE GAME. THE BEST WAY TO GO ABOUT EARNING THESE BONUSES IS TO UNDERTAKE AS MANY MISSIONS AS YOU CAN. PROGRESSION THROUGH THE MAIN STORY ARC—AS WELL AS THE OPTIONAL QUESTS THAT BECOME AVAILABLE—WILL LEAD YOU TO NEW AREAS, REQUIRE YOU TO DEFEAT SPECIFIC BOSS ENEMIES, AND HELP YOU LEVEL UP.

Paid in Fyrestone — GP = 5 — Trophy = Bronze
Complete 5 missions in the Arid Badlands.

Chances are good that you'll complete your first five missions the first time you pop in the disc. Follow Claptrap to Dr. Zed and start running errands for the crazed doctor in Fyrestone. It won't be long before you run into T.K. Baha and, well, who can resist helping a blind man with a shotgun?

Made in Fyrestone — GP = 15 — Trophy = Bronze
Complete all missions in the Arid Badlands.

It's one thing to get paid in Fyrestone, but if you want to get this bonus, you must complete all 44 missions that are available in the Fyrestone area. This includes all missions offered by Dr. Zed, Claptrap, T.K. Baha, Scooter, Shep Sanders, and the Fyrestone Bounty Board. You must also survive the "Circle of Death" and complete Rade Zayben's three arena missions, too.

Paid in New Haven — GP = 10 — Trophy = Bronze
Complete 5 missions in the Rust Commons.

You made it through the Dahl Headland and reached New Haven, but most of your old friends aren't with you. Better meet up with Lucky Zaford and check out the New Haven Bounty Board for missions. You can also find plenty of available missions at the Middle of Nowhere Bounty Board—these count toward your progress in New Haven, as well!

Made in New Haven — GP = 20 — Trophy = Bronze
Complete all missions in the Rust Commons.

If you thought getting made in Fyrestone was tough, you're in for a rude awakening. There are 61 total missions in the New Haven area (including the Middle of Nowhere Bounty Board) and you must meet up with some nasty scoundrels to take them on. The **Mission Checklist** section of this guide has a full listing, but know that you must complete all Claptrap Rescue missions in this region, undertake all Bounty Board quests, and survive three rounds in the Circle of Slaughter. There's much more too, but that ought to be enough to get you started.

Wanted: Sledge — GP = 10 — Trophy = Silver
Kill Sledge.

No spoilers for you here! Follow along in Chapter 1 of our Walkthrough to find out how to go about defeating Sledge.

Wanted: Krom — GP = 20 — Trophy = Silver
Kill Krom.

Not going to tell you about Krom here either. Refer to Chapter 3 of the Walkthrough and follow along with the strategy provided to take him out.

Wanted: Flynt — GP = 30 — Trophy = Silver
Kill Flynt.

So you want to kill Flynt, do you? A lot of people do. Check out Chapter 3 of the Walkthrough for details.

Destroyed the Hive — GP = 40 — Trophy = Silver
Kill the Rakk Hive.

You think you're up to killing the Rakk Hive? If so, flip to Chapter 4 of our Walkthrough for strategy on pulling it off. Here's a tip for your trouble: be sure to bring your big-boy guns!

Destroyed the Destroyer — GP = 50 — Trophy = Gold
Kill the Vault Boss.

Page back to Chapter 4 of the Walkthrough for full details, but only do it if you're actually ready to face this beast.

Discovered Skag Gully — GP = 5 — Trophy = Bronze
Discover Skag Gully.

Skag Gully is located just beyond the far eastern reaches of the Arid Badlands, not far from Dr. Zed and the main Fyrestone encampment. T.K. Baha will help you blast your way in during the "T.K.'s Life and Limb" mission.

Discovered Sledge's Safe House — GP = 5 — Trophy = Bronze
Discover Sledge's Safe House.

Follow Shep Sanders' request and look for the Mine Key at the Zephyr Substation. A note left in its stead will lead you to the Safe House. Venture to the Arid Hills area, west of Fyrestone, and fight your way north to Sledge's Safe House.

KING OF CLAP

Discovered Headstone Mine — GP = 5 — Trophy = Bronze
Discover Headstone Mine.

 You must travel to Headstone Mine while carrying out Shep Sanders' request to kill Sledge. Headstone Mine is located in the south-central edge of the Arid Badlands and requires the Mine Key to enter.

Discovered Trash Coast — GP = 5 — Trophy = Bronze
Discover Trash Coast.

You visit the Trash Coast in search of "Another Piece of the Puzzle." The region is accessible through the Rust Commons East, but a bandit named Taylor Kobb controls all passage in and out.

Discovered the Scrapyard — GP = 10 — Trophy = Bronze
Discover the Scrapyard.

Tannis sends you to meet "Crazy" Earl in the Scrapyard as you explore the Rust Commons West area. The Scrapyard is in the southern end of that area—a long journey from where you first learn of it.

Discovered Krom's Canyon — GP = 10 — Trophy = Bronze
Discover Krom's Canyon.

Krom's Canyon is accessible through Rust Commons East. Follow the river to the northeast, beyond the Catch-a-Ride near the dam, to the entrance in the distance.

Discovered Crimson Lance Enclave — GP = 15 — Trophy = Bronze
Discover Crimson Lance Enclave.

The Crimson Enclave lies southwest of the Salt Flats, although infiltrators will likely want to access it through a hidden cave known as "The Backdoor." You'll first visit the Enclave during the "Get Some Answers" quest.

Discovered Eridian Promontory — GP = 15 — Trophy = Bronze
Discover Eridian Promontory.

The plot mission "Find Steele" will send you on a chase that begins in the Crimson Enclave, continues into the Salt Flats, winds through The Descent, and finally ends at the Eridian Promontory, home of *Borderlands'* ultimate secret.

Ding! Newbie — GP = 5 — Trophy = Bronze
Earn level 5.

 Complete missions and challenges to earn experience and level up to Level 5. You'll likely reach Level 5 right about the time you head off to battle Nine-Toes.

Ding! Novice — GP = 10 — Trophy = Bronze
Earn level 10.

 Level 10 might only be twice as high as Level 5, but it takes quite a bit longer to earn the experience needed to reach it. Continue doing missions in the Fyrestone area and completing challenges to earn experience. With any luck—and if you're good and thorough—you'll pop this bonus right about the time good ol' Scooter gives you an all-access Runner account.

Ding! Expert — GP = 20 — Trophy = Bronze
Earn level 20.

 If you complete all of the missions in Fyrestone and survive your trip through Headstone Mine, there's a good chance you'll be level 20 before leaving the Arid Badlands. If not, you'll likely reach this level shortly after arriving in the Dahl Headland.

Ding! Hardcore — GP = 30 — Trophy = Bronze
Earn level 30.

 With so many dozens of missions available in New Haven and the Rust Commons in general, it's impossible to predict with any degree of certainty exactly when you'll reach level 30, but you will. Spend enough time performing odd-jobs around New Haven to reach level 35 before making your trip to Krom's Canyon.

Ding! Sleepless — GP = 40 — Trophy = Bronze
Earn level 40.

 You may reach level 40 before completing the last of the plot missions, but it will sure make the battle with the Vault Boss a bit easier. Take your time completing the missions in the Dahl Headland and in Rust Commons West and East before heading to the Salt Flats. Complete the missions there and you'll be on your way to reaching Level 40.

Ding! Champion — GP = 50 — Trophy = Bronze
Earn level 50.

WEAPONRY AND GEAR

THE FOLLOWING 10 ACHIEVEMENTS/TROPHIES ALL TEST YOUR SKILL AND VERSATILITY ACROSS A WIDE VARIETY OF GUNS. THEY CAN BE UNLOCKED BY USING VARIOUS ELEMENTAL WEAPONS, COMPLETING ALL CLAPTRAP RESCUE MISSIONS, AND UTILIZING THE VARIOUS OTHER PIECES OF EQUIPMENT IN PANDORA.

Weapon Aficionado — GP = 20 — Trophy = Bronze
Reach proficiency level 10 with any weapon type.

 The more you use a particular type of weapon, the more proficient you become with it. Under normal situations, players will likely become moderately proficient across a number of weapon types, but reaching proficiency level 10 will require you to favor a single weapon type or two. Focus on either the Patrol SMG or Combat Rifle weapon type, but don't worry about this at first. Instead, play the game for a few hours and see what weapon type you naturally use most then focus on that one.

Facemelter — GP = 25 — Trophy = Bronze
Kill 25 enemies with corrosive weapons.

 Equip weapons with the Corrosive elemental effect and defeat 25 enemies with them. The Corrosive effect is most useful against enemies wearing armor, but it can eat the skin off most anything.

1.21 Gigawatts — GP = 25 — Trophy = Bronze
Kill 25 enemies with shock weapons.

 Equip weapons imbued with the Shock elemental ability and defeat 25 enemies with them. Shock is capable of rapidly depleting an enemy's shield, but the high voltage a Shock-enabled weapon yields can kill just about anything.

Pyro GP = 25 Trophy = Bronze
Kill 25 enemies with incendiary weapons.

 Equip weapons blessed with the Incendiary elemental effect and burn 25 enemies into a pile of ash. The Incendiary effect is most potent when melting the skin off Bandits, but fire is an equal-opportunity bringer of pain so feel free to use it against most other enemies, too.

Rootinest, Tootinest, Shootinest GP = 10 Trophy = Bronze
Kill 5 Rakk in under 10 seconds.

 This bonus is easier than it sounds. Simply equip a high-powered shotgun and head to Skag Valley or anywhere else Rakk tend to congregate. Head out into the open and fire at the Rakk to get their attention. Take a few steps back and wait for them to start swooping in for the attack. Open fire with your fastest-firing shotgun or machine gun and watch them drop. This is best done where the species of Rakk are lower in level and more likely to die from a single hit or two, such as in the Arid Badlands area.

There are Some Who Call Me... Tim GP = 25 Trophy = Bronze
Equip a class mod for your character.

 Each character has 4 personal Class Decks and 3 team boost Class Decks that, once equipped, provide a stats boost to multiple skills and weapons abilities. You'll receive your first Class Mod as you complete the final required mission in Fyrestone and prepare to bid farewell to the Arid Wastelands.

You Call This Archaeology GP = 20 Trophy = Bronze
Apply an elemental artifact.

 Artifacts apply an elemental property (Shock, Corrosive, Explosive, or Incendiary) to the character's Action Skill. The first elemental artifact you're likely to come across is a Shock Bolt obtained during the "Shock Crystal Harvest" mission in the Arid Badlands.

12 Days of Pandora GP = 30 Trophy = Bronze
Killed the various inhabitants of Pandora.

 This bonus coincides with the Challenge bearing the same name. Show off your skills with each and every weapon type in the game by racking up the following tallies: 12 assault rifle kills, 11 pistol kills, 10 shotgun kills, 9 SMG kills, 8 sniper rifle kills, 7 melee kills, 6 critical hit kills, 5 Explosive kills, 4 Shock kills, 3 Incendiary kills, 2 Faces melted, and 1 grenade kill. It's the gift of giving, after all!

Fully Loaded GP = 10 Trophy = Bronze
Rescue enough Claptraps to earn 42 inventory slots.

 There are 10 Claptraps scattered across Pandora that need your help. In return for rescuing them, these handy little contraptions increase the inventory space in your Backpack by 3 slots. Although you start out with just 12 slots, you can eventually have 42 by rescuing all 10.

Master Exploder GP = 15 Trophy = Bronze
Kill 25 enemies with explosive weapons.

Equip explosive weapons and look for groups of enemies to blow sky high. Explosive weapons impact everything they hit so don't worry about looking for specific enemy types to harm—shoot everything that moves and watch this bonus pop in no time.

Killed an enemy with the Siren's action skill
Kill an enemy with the Siren's action skill

Killed 15 enemies with the Hunter's action skill GP = 15 Trophy = Bronze
Kill 15 enemies with the Hunter's action skill

Killed 15 enemies with the Berserker's action skill GP = 15 Trophy = Bronze
Kill 15 enemies with the Berserker's action skill

Killed 15 enemies with the Soldier's action skill GP = 15 Trophy = Bronze
Kill 15 enemies with the Soldier's action skill

CLAPTRAP LOCATIONS

NO.	LOCATION
1	Sledge's Safehouse
2	The Lost Cave
3	New Haven
4	Tetanus Warren
5	Earl's Scrapyard
6	Krom's Canyon
7	Old Haven
8	Trash Coast
9	The Salt Flats
10	Crimson Fastness

MISCELLANEOUS MAYHEM

THE FOLLOWING 4 ACHIEVEMENTS/TROPHIES REWARD THE PLAYER FOR EXPLORING PANDORA TO ITS FULLEST AND TAKING ADVANTAGE OF VENDING MACHINES, ARENAS, AND THE CHARACTER'S SIZE 12 BOOTS.

My Brother is an Italian Plumber GP = 15 Trophy = Bronze
Kill an enemy by stomping on its head.

 This is best done with a Skag since they're easy to jump on top of and have a pretty large head. Weaken your foe with a few shots then leap in the air and land on its head. If you have trouble pulling it off, get close to the target and tap the Jump button ever so lightly to hop into the air onto its head.

Pandora-dog Millionaire GP = 50 Trophy = Silver
Earn $1,000,000.

 You don't need to have all million dollars in your possession at once. Rather, just gradually accumulate a total of one million dollars over time by picking up piles of cash on the ground and by completing missions and selling the weapons and other items you find. This might seem impossible at first, but it won't be long before you're finding weapons that can be sold for tens, if not hundreds of thousands of dollars.

Fence GP = 25 Trophy = Bronze
Sell 50 guns to a shop.

 You're bound to unlock this bonus before leaving the Arid Badlands. Just search the Skag Piles, item drops, and every weapon crate you can find. Load up the backpack and head to the nearest vending machine to sell the weapons you've found. It doesn't matter how much they're worth—just sell 50 of them to get this bonus.

You're On a Boat! GP = 15 Trophy = Bronze
I bet you never thought you'd be here.

 You won't find any mermaids waiting for you, but there is indeed a boat in the southeast corner of Treacher's Landing. Explore the area beyond the edge of the map to find a boat. Walk out onto the boat to unlock this secret bonus.

THIS IS HOW WE ROLL

THE FOLLOWING 3 ACHIEVEMENTS/TROPHIES ARE GEARED AT TESTING YOUR ABILITY BEHIND THE WHEEL OF A RUNNER. RUNNERS CAN BE SPAWNED ON COMMAND AT CATCH-A-RIDES ALL AROUND PANDORA. THE LEVEL OF THE RUNNER MATCHES THE LEVEL OF THE CHARACTER SPAWNING THE WEAPON—WHAT YOU DO WITH IT IS UP TO YOU!

Speedy McSpeederton — GP = 10 — Trophy = Bronze
Race around Ludicrous Speedway in under 31 seconds.

Complete the "Death Race Pandora" mission in the Dahl Headland to gain access to the racetrack then hop into a Runner and head on down to race. Even though it's possible to complete a lap in under 31 seconds by playing it clean and mixing well-timed turbo boosts on the straight-aways with smooth steering in the bends, there's also a faster way. Seek the shortcut through the cave to lay down the fastest lap time possible.

Get a Little Blood on the Tires — GP = 20 — Trophy = Bronze
Kill 25 enemies by ramming them with any vehicle.

You gain much less XP for running over enemies instead of hopping out and shooting them with your quiver of weapons, but it's oh-so fun! Grab a Runner near Fyrestone after meeting Scooter and run down the low-level Bandits and Skags in the vicinity.

FRIENDS IN DIGITAL PLACES

BORDERLANDS IS ONE OF THOSE GREAT GAMES THAT CAN BE PLAYED ALONE OR WITH FRIENDS IN A COOPERATIVE MANNER. EVEN BETTER, YOU CAN PERIODICALLY TAKE A BREAK FROM MAKING NICE AND INITIATE A DUEL OR FULL-FLEDGE BATTLE IN AN ARENA!

Duelicious — GP = 15 — Trophy = Bronze
Win a duel against another player.

Players can't harm one another during combat under normal circumstances, but a duel can be initiated with a friendly melee attack. If your friend melees you back, the two characters will be locked in a relatively small area and the fight is on. The duel ends as soon as either player is downed. The victor earns the Achievement/Trophy and the loser gets a Second Wind.

Duelinator — GP = 35 — Trophy = Silver
Win a duel without taking damage.

This bonus ups the ante from the previous one. Now it's not enough to simply win the Duel, but you've got to do it without taking damage. The easiest way to get this is to simply have a friendly agreement before the Duel to help one another win without getting shot. That means telling your friend to not fire his weapon, then you returning the favor in the next round.

Group LF Healer — GP = 25 — Trophy = Bronze
Rescue a groupmate from death in a co-op game.

Teammates can revive one another in multiplayer games by rushing up to their fallen comrade and pressing and holding the Reload button to revive them. The healing player is unable to take any other actions, but the player who was felled will have their full ability to fight. It takes several seconds to fully revive a player so make sure your shield is fully charged before rushing off to play hero.

There's No "I" in "Team" — GP = 30 — Trophy = Bronze
Complete 15 missions in co-op.

All players involved in a co-op team will receive credit for any completed missions so long as that player was at a point in the game where the mission was available to them (they needn't have accepted it yet). Partner up with other players that are essentially at the same point in the game as you (or host a game and invite higher level players to assist you) and complete 15 missions in co-op. The quickest way to do this is to focus on missions posted on the Bounty Boards.

United We Stand — GP = 35 — Trophy = Gold
Defeat the Rakk Hive, the Vault Boss, Sledge, Krom, or Flynt in a co-op game.

Join or host a co-op game and undertake any of the missions that require defeating one of Pandora's most wanted. This bonus will unlock even if you previously defeated the enemy in your own single player campaign or in another co-op game. Either help a newcomer deal a death blow to Sledge or partner with some friends early on and play through as much of the game as possible and let this bonus come naturally over time.

And They'll Tell Two Friends — GP = 10 — Trophy = Silver
Play in a co-op game with either an employee of Gearbox or someone who has this achievement.

There are two ways to go about unlocking this bonus and both require playing with others. The first way is to play with as many different people as you can and hope that you eventually play with one who already has this viral-like Achievement/Trophy. The other way is to head online to your favorite gaming site (or the official Gearbox forums at www.borderlandsthegame.com) and find someone who has it and schedule a play-date.

Can't We Get BEYOND Thunderdome? — GP = 25 — Trophy = Bronze
Win an arena match.

Gather up a party of two or more players and head to one of three arenas in Pandora (Fyrestone Coliseum, The Cesspool, or Devil's Footstool) and arrange your group into teams and begin the fight. Everyone will be transported to the interior of the arena for all-out war between the teams. Players continue to re-spawn until a team scores three wins, then the match is over and everyone is returned to the entrance with the health and ammo they initially entered with. Either play for bragging rights or rig the outcome to help one another unlock this Achievement/Trophy.

PLAYSTATION 3 ONLY

Borderland Defender — Trophy = Platinum
Defeat all bosses and prove to be a powerful force to be reckoned with.

This special Trophy is awarded to those players who manage to earn all 50 other Trophies. Do you have the time, skill, and dedication it takes to go platinum?

BORDERLANDS™
OFFICIAL STRATEGY GUIDE

Written by Casey Loe & Doug Walsh

© 2009 DK/BradyGAMES, a division of Penguin Group (USA) Inc. BradyGAMES® is a registered trademark of Penguin Group (USA) Inc. All rights reserved, including the right of reproduction in whole or in part in any form.

DK/BradyGames, a division of Penguin Group (USA) Inc.
800 East 96th Street, 3rd Floor
Indianapolis, IN 46240

ISBN 10: 0-7440-1020-9
ISBN 13: 9-7807440-1020-6

Printing Code: The rightmost double-digit number is the year of the book's printing; the rightmost single-digit number is the number of the book's printing. For example, 09-1 shows that the first printing of the book occurred in 2009.

12 11 10 09   4 3 2 1

Printed in the USA.

STAFF CREDITS

PUBLISHER
David Waybright

EDITOR-IN-CHIEF
H. Leigh Davis

LICENSING DIRECTOR
Mike Degler

MARKETING DIRECTOR
Debby Neubauer

TRANSLATIONS
Brian Saliba

SENIOR DEVELOPMENT EDITOR
David B. Bartley

SCREENSHOT EDITOR
Michael Owen

BOOK DESIGNER
Doug Wilkins

PRODUCTION TEAM
Wil Cruz
Colin King

AUTHOR ACKNOWLEDGMENTS

CASEY LOE: Thanks to my wife Masayo for all her love and support, Bryan for the co-op sessions, David and the crew at Brady for the great work, and special thanks especially to everyone at Gearbox—both for the help and for making a great game!

DOUG WALSH: What a ride! This was a tremendous project to be a part of and I want to immediately thank my editor David Bartley for getting me on board, and Leigh Davis for having confidence in my ability to balance working on this along with my other projects. We had an excellent team of people assigned to this book and the level of excitement displayed by everyone at BradyGames was invigorating. I want to especially thank my aforementioned editor, David, and "Midwest Doug" Wilkins, for the numerous brainstorming sessions, for the patience and encouragement, and for putting together one hell of a book! I also need to thank my co-author, Casey Loe, who took aim on the walkthrough and managed to avoid spoiling any of the twists & turns for me. It was great working with you, Casey. Snoqualmie Falls Brewery, here we come! Lastly, I want to acknowledge the virtually unprecedented amount of support we received from Gearbox Software. Brian Burleson, Matt Armstrong, Jonathan Hemmingway, and so many others at Gearbox provided a nearly-overwhelming amount of access to the inner-workings of the game and answered every question I could lob their way. Thanks to everyone at Gearbox. I hope your game receives the success it so richly deserves!

gearbox CREDITS

Everyone at BradyGames would like to express our sincere gratitude to the entire Gearbox team. It was a pleasure (and a blast) working with you. Thanks for helping us make an outstanding guide on a truly remarkable game!

PRODUCTION MANAGER
Brian Burleson

WEAPONS STATISTICS
Matthew Armstrong
Jonathan Hemmingway

CREATURE AND CHARACTER STATISTICS
Ruben Cabrera

CLAP TRAP FLIPBOOK RENDERS
Brian Thomas

GENERAL COUNCIL
PJ Putnam

CREATURE AND CHARACTER DESCRIPTIONS AND TIPS
Chris Brock
Ruben Cabrera
Jonathan Hemmingway
Stephanie Puri
Keith Schuler

HIGH RESOLUTION ART RENDERS
Ken Banks
Adam May
Nicholas Wilson

EXPANSION PAGE DESIGN
Mike Neumann

FACT CHECKERS
Matt Charles
Daniel Finnegan
Brian Martel
Mike McVay
Kale Menges
Gabe Simon
Chase Sensky
Keith Schuler
Nicholas Wilson